The Art and Inventions of Max Fleischer

The Art and Inventions of Max Fleischer

American Animation Pioneer

Ray Pointer

Foreword by Jerry Beck

McFarland & Company, Inc., Publishers
Jefferson, North Carolina

LIBRARY OF CONGRESS CATALOGUING-IN-PUBLICATION DATA

Names: Pointer, Ray author.
Title: The art and inventions of Max Fleischer : American animation pioneer / Ray Pointer ; foreword by Jerry Beck.
Description: Jefferson, N.C. : McFarland & Company, Inc., Publishers, 2017. | Includes bibliographical references and index.
Identifiers: LCCN 2016050559 | ISBN 9781476663678 (softcover : acid free paper) ∞
Subjects: LCSH: Fleischer, Max, 1883–1972. | Animators—United States—Biography.
Classification: LCC NC1766.U52 F5836 2017 | DDC 741.58092 [B] —dc23
LC record available at https://lccn.loc.gov/2016050559

BRITISH LIBRARY CATALOGUING DATA ARE AVAILABLE

ISBN (print) 978-1-4766-6367-8
ISBN (ebook) 978-1-4766-2741-0

Front cover illustration by Dick Huemer, digital composite by Shi Briggs

Printed in the United States of America

McFarland & Company, Inc., Publishers
Box 611, Jefferson, North Carolina 28640
www.mcfarlandpub.com

Dedicated to all Fleischer fans
past, present, and future.

Acknowledgments

The following individuals generously shared their time, recollections, and personal affects over the years, without which this book would have been incomplete.

Joe Adamson, Ford Banes, Michael Barrier, Jerry Beck, John Canemaker, Harvey Deneroff, Gene Deitch, Ryan Englade, Beatrice Fleischer-Stone, Bernard Fleischer, Bernie Fleischer, Joe Fleischer, Mark Fleischer, Richard Fleischer, Seymour Fleischer, Campbell Ford, Eric Goldberg, Frank Goldman, Stanley Handman, Jameson Handy, Dr. Richard Huemer, Bob Jaques, J.B. Kaufman, Bob Kennedy, Tom Kneitel, Ruth Kneitel, Stephen Kroninger, Miles Kreuger, Mark Langer, Todd Levine, Eli Levitan, Fraser MacClean, Virginia Kneitel-Mahoney, Leonard Maltin, John McElwee, Russell Merritt, Joseph Neola, Jack Ozark, Jeannie Gayle Poole, Madeline Prager, Mark Punswick, Steve Rivers, Michael Sporn, Tom Sito, Tom Stathes, Beatrice Fleischer-Stone, Dave Tendlar, Jack Theakston, Myron Waldman, Joyce Fleischer-Weinberg, Larry Weinberg, Sandra Weinberg, Berny Wolf, Stephen Worth (Animation Resources), and Don Yowp.

Table of Contents

Foreword by Jerry Beck

"Wanna Be a Member?"

The animated films of Max Fleischer cast a magical spell on all who grew up with them—and that would be almost everyone raised in the 20th century. Max was one of a handful of cartoonists who emerged in the 1910s—inspired by Winsor McCay's *Gerie the Dinosaur*—who could foresee a future in moving drawings, a.k.a. animated cartoons. But he would become more than a cartoonist, pioneering a new art form. He was an innovator, an inventor, as well as an entertainer, who kept his eye as much on the audience as he would on the artists and technicians who brought his ideas to life.

His name and fame would become known far and wide—associated with popular entertainment and animation, rivaled only by Walt Disney. But unlike Disney, the full story of this man and his many accomplishments are really only coming to light now. I grew up, like Ray Pointer did, watching silent *Koko the Clown*, the Jazz Age *Betty Boop*, and action-packed *Popeye* cartoons on television, where their indelible images were forever burned into our young minds.

The Fleischer cartoons were dark. They reflected the harsh realities of their times—particularly the depths of The Depression Era. But they also made us laugh and gave us hope. It was a different point of view from the rosy one Disney and his Hollywood contemporaries were painting in glorious Technicolor.

Even the critics of the day noticed Fleischer was the flipside of Disney. And indeed, the Fleischer universe was populated by individuals straight out of the diverse immigrant culture that surrounded that studio in New York City. Wise-guys and Con Men, obese hippos and "gangsta" gorillas, tattooed sailors and a sexy bitch named Betty (she was originally *a dog*!) These were the denizens of Fleischer's world.

Fleischer's studio simply had no feel for the optimism and blue skies common in other cartoons. Fleischer's take on Disney's *Silly Symphonies* was the *Color Classics*, and they were the stuff of nightmares. Who can forget the miser threatening to burn out the tongues of two innocent urchins in *Little Dutch Mill*, the gigantic phallus-like anteater snout chasing *Ants in the Plants*, and a psychotic *Greedy Humpty Dumpty*? I can't. As kids we loved it. And as adults, we've admired it. Fleischer cartoons were subversive and surreal—*exactly* what cartoons should be. Thanks, Uncle Max!

Inspired by The Fleischer Studio, author Ray Pointer grew up to study animation, and become a professional artist, writer and producer—even leading to meeting Max Fleischer himself. The lessons learned from absorbing these cartoons propelled him into a distinguished animation career. His passion for the Fleischer Studio became a life-long quest to explore the man behind the magic. This book is the result of Ray's decades of research—and no one knows the facts and figures better.

So sit back, relax, turn on some hot jazz and open a large can of spinach. The Fleischer brothers were a true American success story and their work is unforgettable.

Jerry Beck is an animation historian and the author of many books, including The Animated Movie Guide *and* The 50 Greatest Cartoons. *He teaches at Cal Arts in Valencia, California, and blogs at www.cartoonresearch.com*

Prologue

For decades, the history of animation has been dominated by the accomplishments of Walt Disney, leaving the impression that he alone had invented the medium. In reality, the medium of animated cartoons was the result of pioneering inventors, one of the most prominent being Max Fleischer. Fleischer's career as an artist/inventor preceded Disney by a decade, having developed many of the techniques that are still in use in some form today. But as Disney's star shone brighter in the 1930s, Fleischer became overshadowed by many accidents of fate and big business.

Fleischer's role as "Artist-Inventor" served a dual purpose. While his presence provided the basic plot for *Out of the Inkwell* (1919–1927) and *The Inkwell Imps* (1927–1929), his inventions made the cartoons possible. Aside from their novelty, there was a modern sophistication that stressed the anxieties of urban America combined with elements of surrealism and a type of organic progression. As a result, the Fleischer cartoons were rough rather than refined, commercial rather than consciously artistic. But in their unique way, their artistry was expressed through a culmination of the arts and sciences. Fleischer was an avid student of these disciplines, and his vision of animation was an application of technology and cartooning combined with a deliberate violation of natural physics. His philosophy was, "If it can be done in real life, it isn't animation." To fully realize this perspective, one needs to look to the events in Fleischer's life that formed this concept.

Introduction

Max Fleischer and the Fleischer Studio influenced me early in life. I was around four years old when my mother introduced me to the pre–1950 Paramount cartoons being shown early mornings on the Detroit ABC affiliate, WXYZ. I was so fascinated by the magic coming from the pen of the Victorian-looking gentleman that I had a dream about it.

It was the next morning. I'd gotten out of bed and as I entered the living room, *Out of the Inkwell* was on television. In the fashion of *Alice Through the Looking Glass*, I stepped through the screen into a black and white world. There was Max Fleischer, seated in a captain's chair behind a teacher's desk. He stopped what he was doing, swiveled around and picked me up, planting me on his lap like an old uncle. "Uncle Max" said he was pleased to have me come visit him, and proceeded to show me his drawing instruments that included his celluloid triangle, T-Square and crow quill pen. Then pointing to a large ink bottle, he said, "Now Ray, I'm going to bring out the inkwell, and the clown's going to come out!" As Max worked the stopper off the top with a pop, up came Koko, looking around squinting, his eyes adjusting to the light like a mole coming from underground. Then seeing me, he gasped in fright and ducked back into the bottle with a little splash. Wanting to see the clown, I reached forward with my stubby little fingers, and the bottle caught on the desk, causing it to tip over with a huge splash. Max jumped up in reflex, dropping me, and I'd awakened, having fallen out of bed, left leg tangled up in the quilt in the manner of *Little Nemo in Slumberland*. And for several years I harbored a fear/hatred of India Ink in spite of the fact that it smelled like rotten eggs.

This dream came full circle ten years later when I was being interviewed for employment in the Animation Department at The Jam Handy Organization. I was finishing a 30-minute production of *The Wizard of Oz* that I'd been working on for two years. As I was running it in the Camera Room for the department manager, Bob Kennedy, people started drifting in. Soon, I had a full house, with everyone laughing and applauding at all the right places. After the lights had come on, I was introduced to two short, square-shaped elderly men, Frank Goldman, and his best friend, Max Fleischer. Max stepped forward to shake my hand, impressed with what I had to show and paid me some wonderful compliments, predicting many great things in my future. Imagine this coming from such an important figure in the history of animation! It was an experience I will remember the rest of my life. And because of this, it only seemed right that I return the favor of honoring Mr. Fleischer after upsetting his famous inkwell in my innocent youth.

The expansion of the Internet has sparked a rediscovery of the works of Max Fleischer in recent years. Many continue to recognize the magic of his animation and wonder how it was done, how it began, and most of all what brought it to an end? Some of the answers offered to date have been very generalized conclusions due to a lack of access to inside information and a true realization of the medium, the situations, and the parties involved. Seeking the answers has taken decades of detective work; a virtual archeological adventure. And in the process, I have combined interviews, personal insights, and a working knowledge of the industry and film history to piece together as much of the jigsaw picture puzzle as possible. My purpose is to go beyond a clinical career review to look beneath the surface to understand what made this man "tick," and most of all, make him less of a vague enigma.

What you are about to read is a dynamic story, the result of four decades of searching, path crossings, and intimate exchanges with family members who were so gracious and generous with me, treating me as one of their own. Because of this, I was able to delve into the heart of the subject, exploring the influences, motivations, fears, intellect, artistry, and historical events that shaped Max Fleischer and the great studio that bore his name.

1

The Formative Years

Max Fleischer was born July 18, 1883, the second son of Aaron Wolf Fleischer and Malka Palasz-Fleischer. His brother Charles was a year older. Max's actual birth name, according to records of the Rabbinatsamt, was Majer Fleischer. His father, Aaron was a skilled European tailor from Dabrowa, Austria, and Malka was from Krakow. Aaron was an "old world" romantic gentleman with an artistic nature. He had a saying, "Arbeit Macht das Leben zees," which translates as "Work makes life sweet," adding, "But I like to see others work." He had an inclination towards inventing and developed a special sliding marker for accurate hem measurements. Aaron and Malka were known as Wilhelm and Amelia. Amelia was a resourceful, energetic woman with faith, determination, and optimism.

In 1939, due to the escalating war in Europe, Max was required to submit proof of citizenship to Paramount for a security clearance. To simplify matters, his birthplace was given as Vienna, Austria, which had a more artistic and romantic tone. But in fact he was born in Krakow, in the province of Galicia under the Austro-Hungarian Empire. Following World War I, Krakow was absorbed into Poland. And with the Nazi invasion of Poland in 1939, American corporations were cautious about those with ties to besieged countries. So the reference to Vienna was a simpler answer.

The region of Galicia was one of extreme poverty stigmatized as being a Jewish ghetto. Austria under Emperor Charles Franz I embraced the Jewish population, but anti–Semitic sentiments were surfacing by 1887 under the Mayor of Vienna, Karl Lueger. While the threat of persecution seemed the motivation for immigrating to America, the greatest motivation was the pursuit of greater economic opportunities. Wilhelm left Krakow, heading north to the Netherlands en route to the United States.

In his book, *Out of the Inkwell: Max Fleischer and the Animation Revolution,* Richard Fleischer states that Wilhelm left for New York City in early 1887 ahead of his family, and established himself as a high-class tailor. He established his shop in the front of an apartment at 914 6th Avenue, and later at 69 West 46th Street, where his clients included the wives of P.T. Barnum, William Henry Vanderbilt, and Meyer Guggenheim.

Wilhelm had a brother, Leon, two years younger, who was also a tailor. Leon arrived in New York on *The British Queen* in late September 1888. While the prospect of the two brothers forming an enterprise together seems possible, all indications are that they worked separately. Leon lived in New York a short while, then moved to Terre Haute, Indiana, and eventually settled in Dallas, Texas.

One winter day in New York, a city draft horse slipped on the ice and broke its leg. The horse was to be destroyed, but Wilhelm saw an opportunity. He paid $25 for the horse and had it stuffed. He placed it in his shop as a dummy where clients could sit. This com-

Aaron Wolf "William" Fleischer, ca. 1888 (Virginia Kneitel-Mahoney).

bined with a sliding marker of his own invention became the secret to Wilhelm's perfectly draped riding habits since his was the only dress shop in New York where clients could view themselves in a full-length mirror while seated on a stuffed horse. Wilhelm was a quick success and made enough money for his family's passage on the S.S. Rotterdam by late spring.

Fleischer dress label (author's collection).

Upon entering New York harbor, the sight of the Statue of Liberty was impressive on several accounts. To Amelia, it represented a monument to freedom and the inspiration to pursue American ways. Accordingly, Amelia discarded all previous ties to the German language, focusing exclusively on mastering English and becoming completely assimilated into American culture. Accordingly, Wilhelm became Anglicized as "William," as he was known the rest of his life.

Charles and Max were ages six and five respectively, and from their perspective the statue was an amazing blend of art and technology and the beginning of their interests in "modernism" and mechanics, which became the core of their lives. They grew up in the inventive era of Thomas Edison, Henry Ford, and Marconi. They were fortunate to be in the hub of modern developments and business since New York City was converting to electricity at this time. Automobiles were appearing, with radio and motion pictures to follow very soon.

"Charlie" and Max were enrolled in the New York Public School System and were avid students. Since the ages four to six are crucial in language development, they quickly mastered English and lost any trace of their Austrian dialect. Max had displayed a talent for drawing at an

Nancy Fish Barnum (The Barnum Museum, Bridgeport, Connecticut).

Charles Fleischer, standing, Max on bicycle, ca. 1889 (author's collection).

early age. In his brief 1939 biography, he jokingly states that his art career began when he first stood up in his crib and started scrawling on the wallpaper. During these formative years, he was fascinated by trips to Central Park and The Brooklyn Zoo. He was studious, and while in grade school he would be called upon to draw maps for the class, which taught geography better than those in the books.

William became acquainted with members of the New York Police Department and admired their uniforms with brass buttons, which had to be kept brightly polished. But polishing the buttons was a challenge. So William invented a special detachable brass button that could be polished without marring the uniform. As his reputation as a tailor grew, so did his family. All of the Fleischer children displayed artistic and technical aptitudes. William was a self-taught musician and when his children became old enough, he gave them each a musical instrument and taught them to play it, forming a

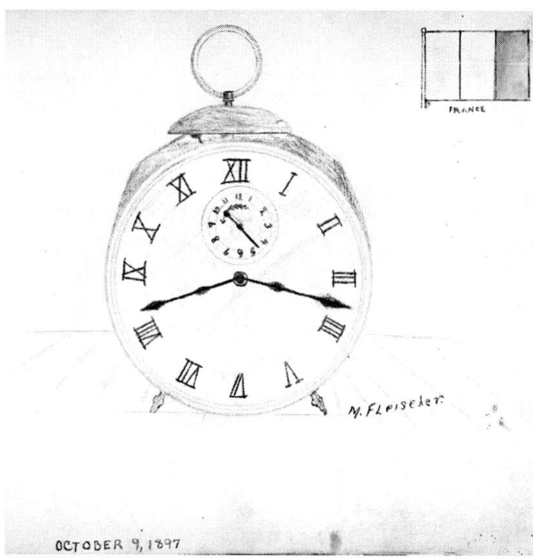

Top, left and above: **Samples from Max Fleischer's early sketchbooks (Virginia Kneitel-Mahoney).**

family orchestra. Lou and Ethel often played duets on the piano. Max favored the guitar and mandolin.

Joseph Fleischer

Joe Fleischer was born in 1889, the first American Fleischer. He had a serious, gentle character with high moral standards. He held a strong sense of loyalty and dedication based on his home values and Austrian roots. He had a natural aptitude for mechanical and electrical matters, much like Charles. He experimented with photography in his teens and had a darkroom in the bathroom—when they had an in-house facility. When he was 23, he built a crystal set radio and heard about the Titanic disaster. His mother could not believe it until it hit the newspapers the next morning.

Louis Fleischer

Born in 1891, Lou was mild-mannered and cerebral, a Jewish version of character actor Barry Fitzgerald, famous for his role as Father Fitzgibbon in the Bing Crosby film, *Going My Way*. With only a year of formal music education under his belt, Lou earned money by playing piano in Chinese restaurants and silent movie theatres. By the time he was in his early teens (1905), he was the primary supporter of the family. In his spare time, he took a course to become a certified Civil Engineer, and worked on the construction of the New York subway system. Lou's keen technical mind combined with his knowledge of music, engineering and mathematics made him a major asset later on.

David Fleischer

Dave followed in 1894 and was a lively contrast to his more docile brothers. He was rowdy, vivacious, and street-wise. He was disinterested in school even though he followed the same paths as his brothers including taking art classes at Cooper Union as Max did. Dave mocked propriety and pretentious manners, finding them a source for jokes. Where Max displayed all of the decorum of Victorian mannerisms and gentlemanly actions, Dave was the complete opposite. The *Popeye* cartoon, *It's the Natural Thing to Do* made decades later was surely a reflection of Dave's attitudes in this regard. A sixth brother, Saul was born in 1900 but died from typhoid fever at the age of two.

Ethel Fleischer

Daughter Ethel was born in 1898. She had a gentle nature and also had a talent for the piano. She later taught piano and was engaged as a concert performer.

The reputation of William Fleischer's tailoring quickly spread along the fashionable 5th Avenue to the extent that he was offered a position with the prestigious B. Altman's

The B. Altman Department Store (Library of Congress).

Department Store around 1892. Once William's clients started coming to the store he was dismissed, having his customers stolen from him. In today's litigious society, William would have had the right to sue. But this thinking was not in his character, and he considered an alternative to re-establish his business.

Mass production at the start of the 20th century threatened custom tailoring. William made one last effort to save his livelihood and went into business with two other partners to manufacture ready-to-wear garments. This business was located at units 9, 11, and 13 East 59th Street. This effort to compete in the established market was short-lived since wholesale buyers would only offer less than their production cost. By 1895 William Fleischer was unemployed, and the family moved to the poor Jewish ghetto section of Brooklyn known as Brownsville; a semi-rural environment of crude, streetwise individuals who became the source of characters and stories decades later. Unable to restore his business,

William became despondent and spent his time in the synagogue, absorbing himself in Orthodox Judaism. It was in this impoverished environment that the Fleischer brothers spent their early years, frequently moving because of difficulties in paying the rent. These experiences set the tone for the cartoons with their gritty urban edge and occasional mockery of Jewish culture that were yet to come. But thanks to the skills of William and the support of Amelia, their only daughter, Ethel, continued to be the best-dressed girl in Brooklyn, in spite of their impoverished state. Amelia made the best of the situation and was resourceful enough to keep food on the table.

In spite of these setbacks, the brothers continued on their paths. Charlie went to Law School, but never took the bar exam after questioning the ethics of the profession. Instead he became an electrical contractor and freelance inventor. Among his inventions was the iconic Claw Digger prize machine found at amusement parks and still in use at the entrances to stores and supermarkets.

Between 1895 and 1897, Max attended Public School 84 at Glenmore and Stone Avenue. Following graduation, he enrolled in The Mechanics and Tradesman's School (1897), entered Evening High School, and also attended The Art Students League, studying under George Bridgeman from 1898 to 1899. Bridgeman was a colorful figure whose classroom smelled of turpentine, charcoal, and perspiration, accented by the tobacco from the cigar he chewed on as he pontificated on the importance of mastering anatomy. While he was a critical taskmaster, he was highly respected. Bridgeman remarked, "Indeed, it is very far from accurate to say that we see with our eyes. The eye is blind, but for the idea behind the eye."[1] This remark made a great impression on Max in this embryonic period and stayed with him the rest of his life. He then attended Cooper Union Institute in 1900, where he began to blossom as an accomplished artist.

Max, 17, while a student at Cooper Union (author's collection).

Now in their teens, Charles and Max hoped to become circus performers. They became skilled with their bicycle, performing

Cooper Union Institute (author's collection).

dare devil acrobatic stunts to the delight and dismay of the neighbors and the Police Department. Lou Fleischer recalled this in great detail:

> When I was about thirteen, living in Brownsville, the family could afford to buy a bicycle. Charlie and Max rode it mostly, doing almost incredible tricks on it. Both rode at the same time. One would stand

upright on the seat holding onto nothing. Then he would crawl through the frame of the bike and change places with the other. One would sit facing backward and peddling, the other steering. They did various other tricks too numerous to mention.[2]

Max's antics, in particular, caught the attention of Ethel "Essie" Goldstein, the assertive daughter of the neighborhood grocer. Essie was boisterous and energetic with an infectious laugh. She was friendly towards the older Fleischer brothers with particular attention towards Max. Max started a long courtship with Essie around 1901. Due to the strictness of their courtship, they learned sign language from a deaf friend, which enabled them to communicate with each other while in the presence of others. The other brothers

Above and below: **Examples of freehand drawing and technical illustration assignments.**

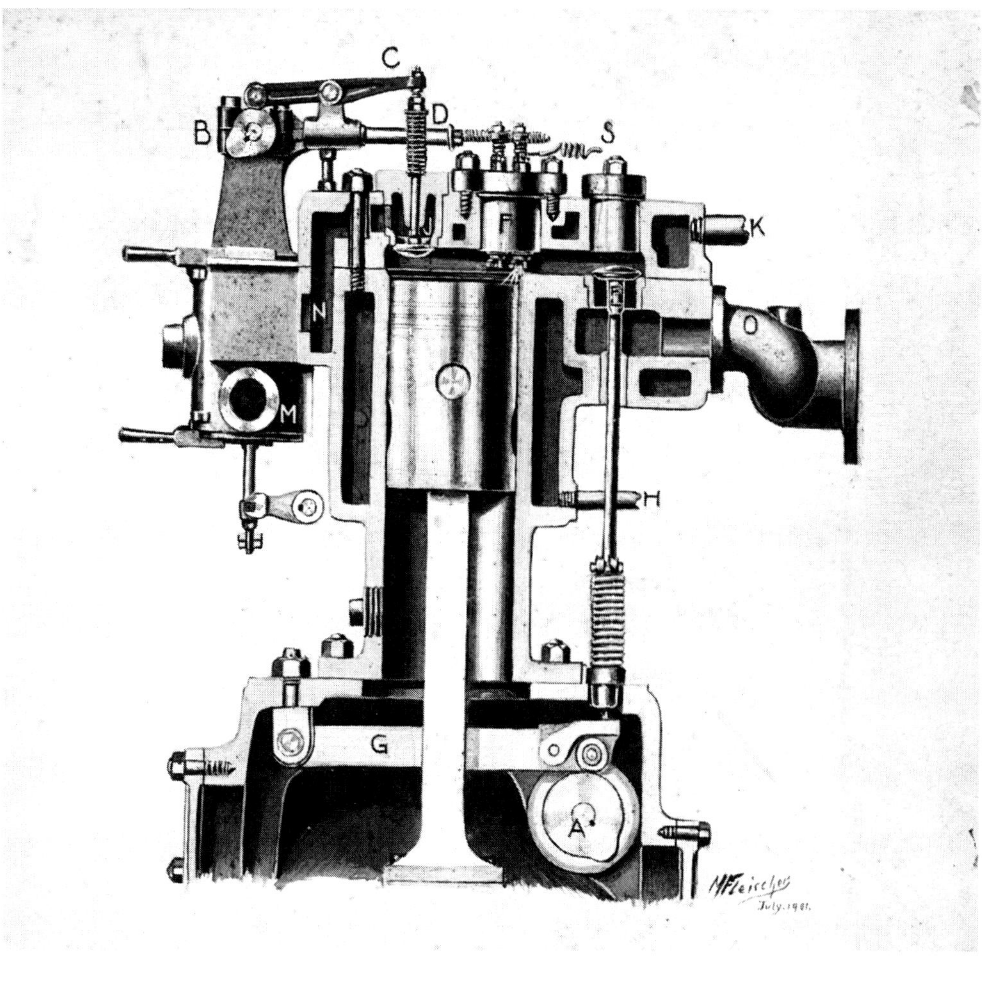

disliked her due to her aggressiveness. Joe called her "Assie."

The early 1900s were the "Gilded Age" of newspaper cartooning led by R.F Outcault, Adolf Dirks, Winsor McCay, George Herriman, and George McManus. By 1900 Max became interested in becoming a cartoonist for *The Brooklyn Daily Eagle*, a major newspaper at the time. He was so eager to learn that he was willing to pay $2 per week just to sit and watch the artists work. Seeing his sincerity, the editor offered him a position as an errand boy at $2 per week.

The experience was invaluable, as he learned photography and photoengraving. He also picked up the habit of smoking, which remained with him the rest of his life. In a year, he was promoted to the Art Department where he drew occasional one-panel fillers using the pen name, "Mack," and by 1902 his work was seen daily. While his one-panel cartoons had a sly or strange social comment, his multi-panel comic strips took on ridiculous physical comedy, made evident in his two continuing comic strips, *Little Algie* and *E.K. Sposher, the Camera Fiend.*

Max at *The Brooklyn Daily Eagle*, ca. 1900 (Virginia Kneitel-Mahoney).

CONTRAST.

Chawles—Aw-an-what do you expect to be when you grow as old as I am?
Kid—A man.

An early single panel cartoon by Max (author's collection).

The *Little Algie* strip was a reflection of life in the impoverished Brownsville while *The Camera Fiend* gave insight to Max's interest in the technology of photography combined with a physical gag at the end. Max was already seeing beyond the restrictions of the multi-panel comic strip, envisioning them one day as moving cartoons. He was still a teenager, making him the youngest cartoonist in the country.

Little Algie comic strip (Mark Langer).

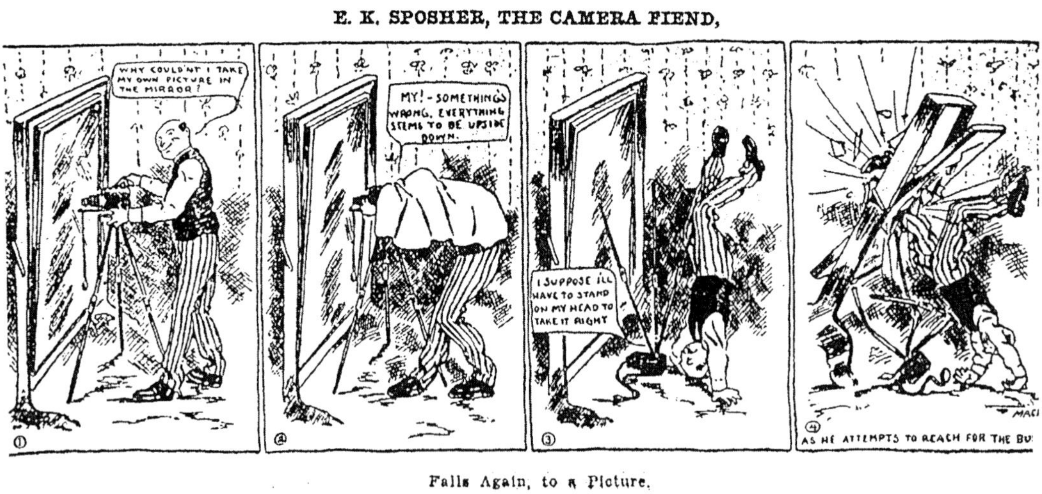

E.K. Sposher comic strip (Mark Langer).

While at *The Eagle*, Max became acquainted with a cartoonist from Adrian, Michigan, John Randolph Bray. Bray had come to New York, having been a cartoonist for *The Detroit Evening News* and had already become an established magazine cartoonist for *Life, Judge,* and *Punch*. Bray was impressed with Max's work, and after learning of a commercial illustration position with The Electro-Light Engraving Company in Boston, he recommended Max for the job. With this prospect, Max married Essie on Christmas Eve, 1905. Their first child, Ruth was born a year later on December 28, 1906.

During his Boston period, Max learned layout and lettering, and mastered airbrushing. He invented his own brand of non-yellowing touch-up paint, his stock in trade. And while

Max and Essie Fleischer's wedding portrait, December 24, 1905 (Virginia Kneitel-Mahoney).

this was a valuable artist's tool, he never patented it. The reasoning here was related more to protecting his trade secrets to ensure his employment, forsaking any pretense of commercial exploitation of his invention. He retained this same thinking throughout his career, using his inventions as an exclusivity to make his product unique among the competition.

Left: **Max, ca. 1910 (Virginia Kneitel-Mahoney).** ***Right:*** **Max's boss, Waldemar Klaempffert (*****Popular Science*** **magazine).**

In 1909, Max and family moved to Syracuse, New York, where he was hired as a catalog illustrator for the Crouse-Hinds Company. He truly loved this position since he was illustrating machinery, which was his obsession. Max's work soon came to the attention of the Editor of *Popular Science* magazine, Waldemar Klaempffert. And in 1910, Max became the Art Editor.

2

The Birth of a Career

The novelty called "movies" was a late 19th century phenomenon resulting from the efforts of several inventors. The earliest known patents for a motion picture camera were by the Englishmen Louis La Prince in 1888 and William Freeze-Green in 1889, followed in 1891 by Thomas A. Edison in the United States. But the most significant of these inventions was a flexible celluloid-based film stock developed by George Eastman, which brought about the modern motion picture and opened the door for an exciting and innovative field with limitless artistic and commercial possibilities.

Edison's Vitagraph Company was the leader in early motion picture production in The United States with the emergence of major directors such as Edwin S. Porter with *The Great Train Robbery* (1903), which featured D. W. Griffith in a small role. It was in this same year that the magic of animation was discovered. *Humorous Phases of Funny Faces* (1903) by J. Stuart Blackton demonstrated the basic concept of stop-motion effects using drawings and cutouts to create the impression of movement. While a novelty, it does not qualify as the first actual animated cartoon in spite of the fact that drawings were used to demonstrate the principle. It was merely a process experimentation film.

The first known cartoon animator is the Frenchman, Emile Cohl. Cohl realized the basic concept of cartoon animation through the production of individual drawings representing every phase of an action. He worked on paper, using simple line drawings to produce fluid animation. According to a rare photograph, it appears that Cohl may have realized the value of using peg registration of his drawings. But he failed to patent it, leaving the concept to be patented in the United States a decade later.

In the United States, the art of cartooning was popularized by *The American* newspaper publisher, William Randolph Hearst. And with the development of motion pictures, the adaptation of cartoons seemed an attractive and logical advancement. The pioneers of animated cartoons came from the established cartooning field with no rules, standards, or procedures to follow. There was no special equipment, process, or knowledge of how things moved. It all had to be invented.

Winsor McCay (1869–1934) was the prominent cartoonist/illustrator known for his comic strips *Dreams of the Rarebit Fiend* and *Little Nemo in Slumberland*. It is unclear as to whether McCay had been exposed to Cohl's work or if Cohl was his motivation for entering the animation field. It is apparent that his interest was to extend his cartooning skills by bringing his characters to life through animation. He wisely chose the characters of his popular *Little Nemo* strip as his first venture, titling it simply, *Little Nemo Moving Comics*. Since McCay took pride in creating all the drawings himself, it took two years to complete his film. *Little Nemo Moving Comics* was first seen publicly in 1911, which would place the start of production in 1909, a year after Cohl's first works. Understanding that the film distribution business was not as immediate as today, it is reasonable to expect that the two men were working on their concepts simultaneously, unaware of what the other was doing. McCay worked primarily from instinct, solving his animation problems through his knowledge of plane geometry and perspective. Once the concept of film timing was worked out, he devised a viewing device similar to the Mutoscope for checking the fluidity of his animation.

Shown as a vaudeville act, *Little Nemo Moving Comics* was seen by artist John R. Bray, who immediately realized the commercial potential for animated cartoons since motion pictures were just starting to grow as a viable industry. In his book, *Winsor McCay: His Life and Art,* John Canemaker makes reference to the recollections of McCay's teenaged assistant John Fitzsimmons, who believed that Bray posed as a reporter under the premise of writing an article about McCay. His ego flattered, McCay freely explained his methods to Bray, never realizing the secrets he was giving away would be used against him. While McCay later billed himself as "The Inventor of Animated Cartoons," he never registered patents on his processes.

One of the laborious aspects of McCay's methods was the meticulous retracing of figure and background. Bray considered methods for simplifying this first through printing the background onto the individual animation drawings, and later through the use of a celluloid overlay. Bray patented both of these methods, and in 1913 he had completed his first animated cartoon, *The Artist's Dream*, also known as *The Dachshund and the Sausage.*

Bray's first animated cartoon was a major achievement in several areas. Not only did it demonstrate the concept of his patent, but it was also skillfully drawn with tone at a time when McCay continued to draw in line only. In addition, this film displays one of the earliest realizations of character animation since the dog's thought process registers on screen as it realizes a way of climbing to the plate of sausages on the kitchen counter. This film also established a format of cutting between a live action artist and his animated drawing, which was to become a commercial convention used in the studio he would soon form.

By the time Winsor McCay's landmark film, *Gertie the Dinosaur* (1914), played in vaudeville, the Bray Studio was releasing commercially produced animation to movie theaters. Bray's dominance in the field was based largely on patents for cel animation production; patents that he controlled along with another cartoonist, Earl Hurd. While Bray's concept used the celluloid overlay as a background for animation inked on paper, Hurd's concept used inked tracings of animation drawings painted on the reverse side for solidity and placed over an illustrated background. "Cel" overlays could also be used to animate parts of characters laid over the stationary balance of the figure, the basic concept applied to Limited Animation produced for television decades later.

The two men merged their concepts under the Bray-Hurd Process Company, which controlled the use of the "Cel Technique" through licensing until the original patents expired in 1931. The Bray-Hurd method greatly reduced the time and labor associated with McCay's films. And while the Bray shorts were not as artistic or accomplished in execution as McCay's, they were commercially successful—beginning with Bray's creation, *Colonel Heeza Liar*, the first original animated cartoon series. The significant difference, however, was that McCay's approach to animation was from a "hobbyist-artist" perspective while Bray's was keenly commercial, forsaking any pretense of artistry with severe limits on quality.

"The Artist's Dream" (The Museum of Modern Art).

One evening in 1914, Waldemar Klaempffert, and his wife attended the movies where one of the Bray cartoons was shown. Seeing the awkward jerkiness, his wife remarked, "Oh, how I hate these things." Bothered by the execution of what they had seen, Klaempffert approached Max the next morning, suggesting that he find a way of improving the execution of animated cartoons by combining mechanics and photography. The solution was Max's first official invention known as the "Rotoscope," which combined a film projector and easel for frame-by-frame references from live action photography. The evolution of this machine was the result of a series of accidents of fate.

Max and his brothers were fascinated by the concept of motion pictures from an outdoor demonstration in 1896. Max was 13, and Charlie was 14. Joe Fleischer, who was seven years old at the time, recalled:

> One night Charles and Max took me by the hand and we walked from our home downtown to West 34th Street where hundreds of people were gathered in the streets looking up at a large white sheet on the top of the (New York) Herald Building.... Across Broadway, on top of another building was Thomas A. Edison's very first projection machine, directing onto the large white sheet across. First were shown some slides of various kinds. Then there was darkness, then a flickering of light, and then lo and behold ... there was (the) Baker's Cocoa Lady actually walking across the white sheet with her cup and saucer of cocoa in motion picture. Records show that these were the very first motion pictures ever shown publicly in the world. And night after night we would walk down to see the very same "walking pictures" as they were then called.[1]

J. R. BRAY.

PROCESS OF AND ARTICLES FOR PRODUCING MOVING PICTURES.

APPLICATION FILED JAN. 9, 1914.

1,107,193. Patented Aug. 11, 1914.

3 SHEETS—SHEET 1.

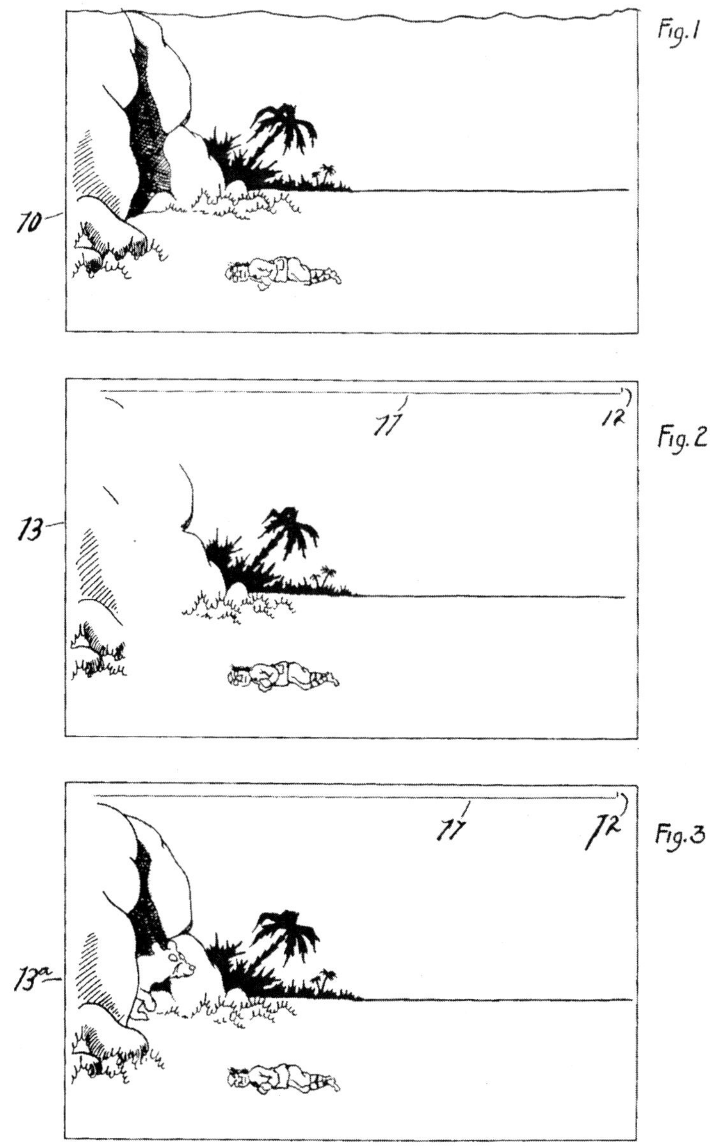

WITNESSES:
E. Coltran
James D. Brown.

INVENTOR
John R Bray
BY
C.W. Fairbank
ATTORNEY

Bray patent application.

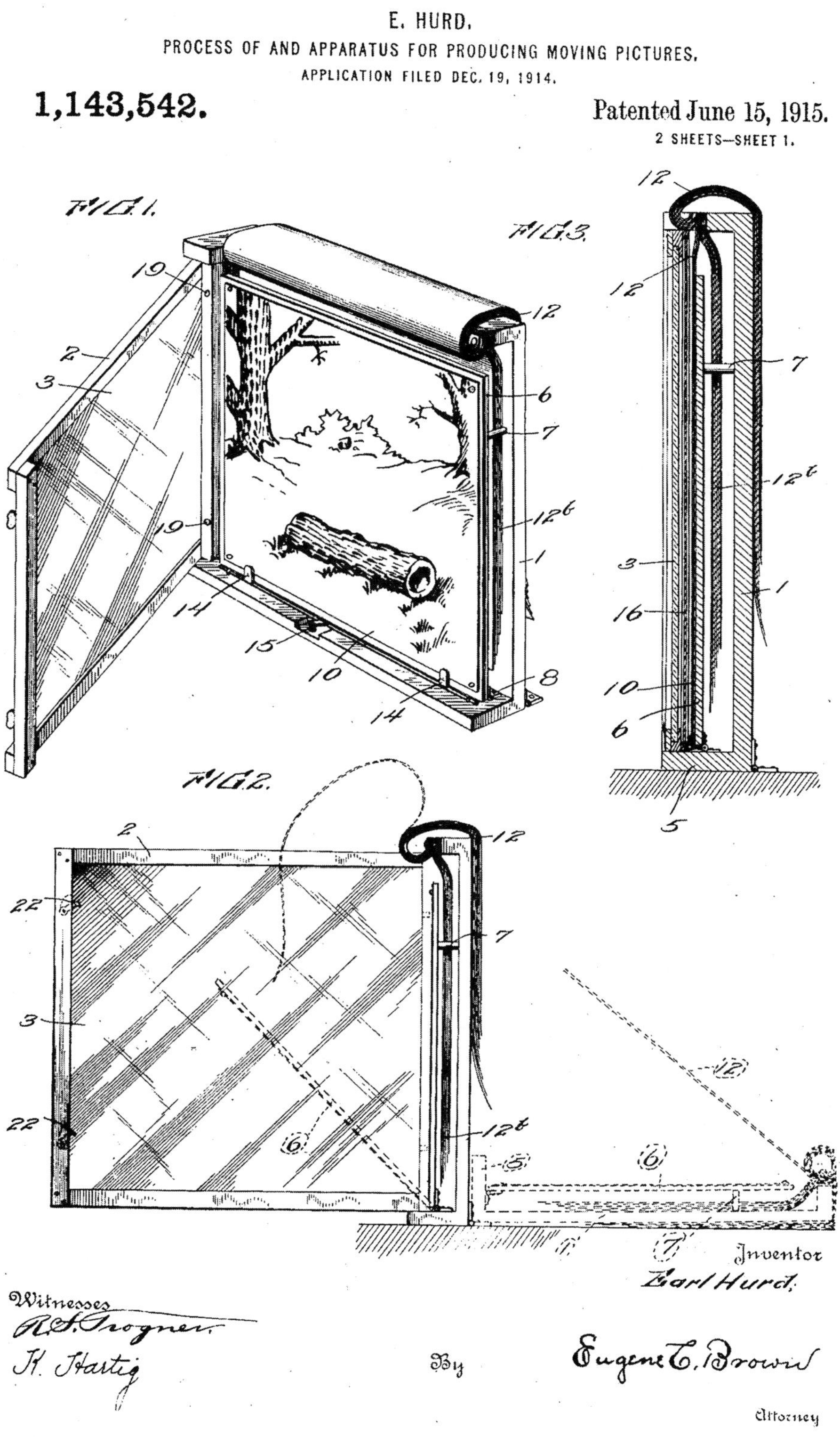

Hurd patent application.

Seeing some of the first publically displayed motion pictures certainly made an impression on the young Fleischer brothers. But it would be 18 years before they would be directly involved with their advancement.

While still living in Brownsville, Charlie and Joe started an outdoor movie theater during the summer of 1914. Since there were no movie theaters in the area, this seemed like a sound idea. But the concept was ill-conceived due to the challenges of rain, humidity, and mosquito infestations. The situation worsened when the Loew's theater chain opened a hard top theater across the street. The Fleischer Brothers' movie enterprise went into receivership and after the assets were settled, including folding chairs and associated equipment, they were awarded the Moy Projector, which was adapted for Max's first Rotoscope device.

Max had a unique talent for constructing working models of his inventions out of cardboard. And while a functioning "model" was sufficient for filing the patent, he needed a full-scale version to complete the process. He had already spent his savings in the initial stages and needed additional funds to build the actual working model. Essie gave him an additional $150 to carry out the Rotoscope to full completion and patent registration. Max explained the Rotoscope concept to his brothers Charlie and Joe, who built the device. Charlie, the electrician, adapted an automobile headlight and car battery for the projection light source, and Joe, the mechanic, adapted the projector, working out the majority of the mechanical functions.

The device itself consisted of a projector mounted on an incline board connected to an easel. The easel had a square opening with an inset glass surface. Paper was placed on the glass with no apparent registration peg system. The patent drawing indicates that registration was achieved by fitting the paper to the corners of the window opening. While the device and process took on the popular name, Rotoscope, this is neither referenced in the patent application, nor was the name Rotoscope registered as a trademark. The patent merely describes "a method of producing moving picture cartoons."

The origins of the name, Rotoscope, can be derived from two sources. One would be a literal translation related to the rotation of the projected film used for tracing and its projection for viewing. The other explanation seems rooted in the Rotogravure, an intaglio printing process of engraving photographs for newspapers used in Max's early career at *The Brooklyn Daily Eagle.*

While most accounts compress the Rotoscope story into the birth of Koko the Clown, this was not the case. There were at least three experiments, which explains the two-year gap between the patent registration and the actual creation of the clown character, generally cited as 1917. Evidence of the first experiment is revealed in the patent drawing, which shows a Boy Scout performing semaphore. Max rented a movie camera, most likely the Universal, which was a hand-cranked model consisting of a rotating disc shutter with a singular opening.

It is reasonable to believe that Max may have shot the footage of the Boy Scout himself. Once the negative was developed and printed, he loaded the short strip of film into the projector and proceeded to trace off the image contours of each frame. Since the few seconds of action consisted of line art only, it is also reasonable to expect that he did this alone, taking four to six weeks working in his spare time.

After the required number of drawings had been finished, Max mounted the camera

Fleischer's Rotoscope patent (U.S. Patent and Trademark Office).

on a kitchen chair aimed at a drawing board placed on another chair, shooting the drawings upright. It is likely that Max enlisted the assistance of Joe and Dave in the shooting of the drawings since Dave indicated a first-hand experience with the early experiments.

> At that time we didn't know how to register the drawings, so we did it with pins. We'd pin them up on a chair and the camera would be on another chair shooting horizontally, and we would change those drawings one at a time, taking the pins out, taking it off the chair, and putting it on the pins again. Then we discovered that it was jumping around on the screen. It was because the camera was on a separate chair, and if the camera moved, the other chair didn't. So there would be a jump. So we put boards across and nailed the two chairs together so that if one moved, the other would move the same way. It kept them nice and steady.[2]

Camera mount (U.S. Patent and Trademark Office).

Once photography was completed, and the film processed, the Moy projector was converted to project onto a screen of four-inch square cardboard. The results were the first life-like animation since McCay's first works, which were originally thought to have been traced from film images in this same manner.

The first experiment revealed inaccuracies in exposures. There was a "flickering" of the image, the result of inconsistent rotation of the disc shutter, open in full position on some exposures and partially open on others. This was part of the cause of "flicker pictures" as early movies were called, due to the hand-cranked cameras and projectors with unregulated speeds. These problems were soon eliminated with the introduction of motorized cameras and projection machines. And in 1916, the industry formed The Society of Motion Picture Engineers to establish a standard of 16 frames or one foot of 35mm film per second, which was essential to defining timing for animation and continued to be the standard of measurement throughout the silent era.

In spite of the inherent technical problems, Max's first experiment proved that the Rotoscope concept worked. For decades, "Fleischer's Secret Process" was considered exclusive, but not enough to sustain a patent unto itself, as a patent is only good for a device that makes a process or concept possible. "Fleischer's Secret Process" was an application of projected images, a phenomenon of nature and the physics of light discovered by Leonardo daVinci. Patents were possible for variations on the projection of images through a machine and a combination of lenses, but the act of projecting them was not something that could be patented. In Fleischer's case the image was projected upward in a rear projection method. Other forms could project from above down onto a surface, or onto a ground glass using lenses and mirrors. While the initial idea was to use film footage as a source for tracing of live action, this process was also valuable as a tool for lining up artwork

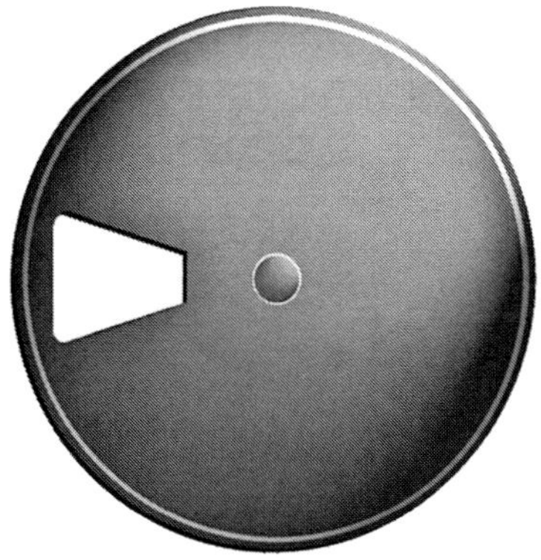

Disc Shutter

The Universal camera (Sam Dodge).

for mattes or combining animation with live action and determining accurate match lines for composited images. Regardless of method or device used, the process itself has taken on the collective name of "Rotoscoping" based on Fleischer's initial invention for which he deserves credit.

Having experienced the initial test of the Rotoscope, Max considered a project better suited towards entertainment. Charlie Chaplin was a rising film comedian and major attraction at the time. According to Joe Fleischer, Max obtained a print of a Chaplin comedy with the idea of making Chaplin cartoons. He selected a section of action running two minutes and 30 seconds, requiring 2,400 images. This time he enlisted his brothers Joe and Dave for assistance on the tracings and blackening in of the figure, using his living room as their first studio.

In the pioneering days of animated cartoons, the concept was still tied to drawings on paper. Most of the earliest characters employed masses of black for a solid form to carry the action. McCay's first works were an exception since his detailed line work filled the screen well enough. Working on paper left the majority of the negative space empty and white, which would be tiring on the eyes after several minutes. The addition of backgrounds served two purposes, to provide a setting and fill in the emptiness of the negative space.

There is no indication that Fleischer's Chaplin experiment consisted of anything more than the moving figure according to the recollections of Joe Fleischer. All effort went into the meticulous tracing and inking of the drawings, which they did at night while working their day jobs. Many times they worked into the early hours of the morning due to the prospect of inventing something new in animated cartoons. Max Fleischer's 1939 autobiography offers the following recollection:

> One evening, we met as usual. We were getting pretty tired around 3:30 a.m. I turned around and my elbow hit a bottle of ink and knocked it off the table and made a great big blot on the edge of the carpet.

> The blot was about as big as five fried eggs, and we couldn't get it out. I knew right there that the experiment was over if the "Missus" ever saw that. So quietly, we tried to blot it up, but it only looked worse. I said, "Where do we go from here?" At 3:30 a.m. the three of us moved all the furniture out of the room, including a darn heavy upright piano into the dining room, turned the rug around so that the spot came under the piano, and we went on with our experiments for six months. Then we moved, and the ink spot was discovered. I got the same "Hell" as though it had just happened![3]

The inkwell accident was prophetic, suggesting the name "Out of the Inkwell," which was to follow in just a few years. And the move to a new apartment that Max referenced followed the birth of his son Richard O. Fleischer on December 8, 1916, one year and two days following the filing date of the Rotoscope.

Once the drawings were completed, Max pondered the flicker from his first experiment. While the details on this are very sketchy, it is easy to assume that Max drew upon his photographic experience for the solution. He would have considered details such as the voltage of the lights, and the problem caused by the camera's disc shutter. It seemed that a consistent exposure could be obtained by disengaging it and closing down the lens F-Stop to the smallest opening. Then using a darkroom timer set at one second, Max removed and replaced the lens cap as he changed the drawings and advanced each frame of film.

After eight months, Max had a finished film running just under three minutes to show, hoping to find a distributor. It is not clear which distributor he went to, or how many. At this time, films were handled through local offices under the States Rights method, which rented films in specific states or groups of states. The major film distributors at the time were the French companies, Gaumont, and Pathé. While Max's recollection does not name either of these companies it does offer an account of one of his meetings.

> I took the film to a distributor and in the blink of an eye it was run off. He said, "That's very nice. What are you going to do with it?" I said, "I don't know. I just thought it was something, that's all." He said, "Could you make one of these every week?" I laughed. "Why no, it's a physical impossibility." "How long did it take you to make this thing?" he asked. "It took about a year," I said. Then he returned, "My dear fellow, go home and make something practical. If you had something we could offer for sale every week, or every month you'd have something. But once a year, NIX!" This was a great disappointment.[4]

According to Joe Fleischer, Max's appointment was with a Frenchman named J.A. Berst, who was the President of Pathé Company of America. He was impressed with the lifelike fluidity but feared being sued by Chaplin for the exploitation of his image. Max was encouraged to come back with something original. While the solution might have been found in Max's early comics, *Little Algy* and *The Photographer Fiend,* his focus was so centered on the technology of creating animation that he failed to look to his past for the solution. In fairness, it would be reasonable to assume that his artistic advancement stood in the way of reaching back to his immature works. He was hard pressed for a new character until his youngest brother Dave provided the solution.

During the years that Max's career was developing, Dave had cultivated a great deal of exposure to entertainment. He worked as an usher at the Palace Theater, where he studied the headline vaudeville performers appearing there. This contributed largely to his sense for gags and comic timing. Among his favorite acts were Webber and Fields' *Pool Room* routine, and comedienne, Bessie McCoy. Bessie McCoy was famous for the song, *The Yamma-Yamma Man*, later imitated by Ginger Rogers in the 1939 biopic, *The Story of Vernon and Irene Castle* (1939).

By now the Fleischer family was living on Coney Island and Dave became interested in being a clown. In his 1968 interview with Joe Adamson, he provided the following recollections:

> My mother gave me money and I went to Steeplechase Park and I saw the clowns there and I wanted to be a clown. So I went and I got some materials from my father ... and I made a clown with three big wide buttons and a pointed hat. And I walked through the streets, and I went into Steeplechase Park and said, "I want to be a clown!" They said, "Oh, give him a job." So they gave me a job.[5]

Bessie McCay as "The Yama Yama Man" (Corbis Archives).

Dave's clown costume was clearly inspired by one worn by Bessie McCoy, with the additions of a black ruffled collar replacing the big white bow, three pom-pom front buttons and a prominent cone-shaped cap also with three pom-poms. The white face with slit eyes was a design common among German circus clowns. The exact year of the creation of the clown and Dave's working at Coney Island is confused. Records from Cooper Union indicate that he was 18 years old and enrolled in a freehand drawing class in 1913 while residing at 1428 Pitkin Avenue, Brooklyn. He was also employed at Pathé as a film cutter. So it is quite likely that his career as a clown preceded this by one to three years. Dave continues:

> I was a kid. I don't remember exactly what age I was. But the suit always fit because it's a big wide loose suit and the neck was wide open. It'd fit anybody. If it fit a little short on you, it'd look just as funny. It didn't make any difference. The clown's nose was black and he had a big wide black mouth. Even in the amusement park I did it in black and white. I never knew that I would use it in a film when I started as a clown. Now that particular suit was the same suit that we used for Koko the Clown.[6]

The story of how the clown was selected for the third experiment varies. It seems likely that Dave suggested filming him in his clown costume and makeup after hearing of Max's initial meeting at Pathé. The concept of a clown seemed ideal on several levels since it represented comedy and was a good pantomime figure, well-suited to silent movies. Charlie and Joe assisted again by building a white backdrop out of a bed sheet and a wooden frame. The backdrop was set up on the roof of Max's apartment building, with Joe operating the hand-cranked camera, Max directing, and Dave performing his clown act. The contrast of the black costume against the white background proved an aid in tracing the figure since it provided a well defined mass to follow. The presence of white on the face, hands, and feet were not extreme enough to disappear since there was enough gray range present especially,

Luna Park, Coney Island, ca. 1913 (History NYC.com).

if the sunlight came from behind. Filming outdoors sometimes had its hazards since one time a gust of wind scooped up the backdrop and sailed off the roof, nearly taking Dave with it.

Once the film was developed, Joe and Dave assisted Max again beginning with the Rotoscope tracings. While Max imagined that the Rotoscope would speed up the process of animation, it proved time-consuming for numerous reasons. Dave Fleischer recalled:

> We animated action the way we feel it's to be animated. But live action if it's traced takes on peculiar forms that you could never image or create. That's why when you use Rotoscope, trace that down and make an animated character out of it, it will have a real, life-like walk. No one that I know could ever make it as real as that because some of he shapes don't even look like a figure. It would look like a cripple. Even a very graceful dance you'll find looks like a leg is bent. You would never draw it like that. It's probably on account of the perspective. It's foreshortened or lengthened, and it looks partially like something else. The only problem in the Rotoscope is that if you move too fast, it blurs, and you've got to guess your line when you trace it.[7]

The tracing took about a month, with an additional four or five months for the inking and photography. Six months later the third experiment was completed, and a meeting was set up to view the finished film. Since Dave was already working at Pathé he was able to secure an appointment. The clown animation was a sensation. While Dave thought that the interest came from the founder, Charles Pathé, it was actually Berst who made the commitment with the brothers.

***Left:* Dave Fleischer as "The Clown" (author's collection). *Right:* Theodore Roosevelt (Library of Congress).**

Berst set the brothers up with a studio in Fort Lee, New Jersey, and built three Rotoscope setups. Joe Fleischer recounts that Berst was in a quandary about how this animated novelty would fit with their line of newsreels, comedies, and serials. Max was impressed with the hunting expeditions of Theodore Roosevelt and thought a cartoon parody about Roosevelt would be a good idea. This idea seemed to agree with Berst's thinking as well since Roosevelt was a popular political figure.

The concept for their first commissioned cartoon was based on *Chanticleer and the Fox*, from *The Canterbury Tales* by Geoffrey Chaucer (1343–1400). Chanticleer was the proud rooster who believed that the sun rose and set based on his crowing. Dave thought this concept was too cerebral and reminded Max that they had the clown, which was liked. But Max held to the political satire believing it to be the better idea because Berst was expecting it. It is an interesting coincidence that the "rooster" was the Pathé mascot, which may have also influenced Max's thinking, hoping to flatter Charles Pathé.

They rented a large rooster costume for Dave while Joe played Roosevelt. Max operated the camera and directed. It is likely that the sight of the company's mascot being lassoed and shot was offensive to Charles Pathé, and after several months' work, the brothers were fired. While on the ferry back home to Brooklyn, the deflated brothers sat apart, the lone

John Randolph Bray (author's collection).

Bray-Paramount Pictograph trade ad (Tom Stathes).

passengers on the boat. Suddenly Joe broke the silence, "That would happen to us!" Joe and Dave laughed it off. But Max took this failure seriously, contemplating his next move. He was back where he started with the sample of the clown animation, making the rounds again.

The American film production/ distribution/ exhibition industry was just starting. In 1912, W.W. Hodkinson merged 11 states rights film offices to form Paramount as the first national distributor. In that same year, he merged with the Famous Players Company founded by Jessie Lasky, Samuel Goldwyn, and Adolph Zukor. Paramount had acquired 500 theaters by 1920 and continued growing through the 1920s. In the process, Paramount established a packaged film program known as "Block Booking," that included a newsreel, feature, and cartoon.

Max secured an appointment with Adolph Zukor at Paramount, and while waiting in an outer office, he saw John Bray, who told him that he had just signed an exclusive contract to produce *The Bray-Paramount Pictograph*, a film magazine consisting of a newsreel, fashion feature, science segments, and cartoon. Bray invited Max to his studio to view the sample reel. Impressed, he hired Max as Production Manager based on their past relationship at *The Brooklyn Daily Eagle* and his regard for Max's abilities as a technical illustrator. While Max's primary value was as an artist, he was first put to work as an animator on Bray's *Colonel Heeza Liar* cartoons.

The Bray Factory

Early animation studios were far from glamorous and were crudely fashioned in ordinary office buildings. The equipment consisted of second-hand desks, kitchen tables, chairs, and homemade shelves. Camera stands were also makeshift adaptations of conventional motion picture

An early animation studio (author's collection).

cameras mounted on 2" × 4" frames. Everything had to be made from scratch in these pioneering days, with the Bray Studio being the major hub of activity.

Bray set up a system of four production units on overlapping schedules that allowed for the steady output of product. The staff of directors and animators included J.D. Leventhal, F. Lyle Goldman, Vernon "George" Stallings, C.T. Anderson, L.M. Glackens, Leighton Budd, Leslie Elton, Wallace A. Carlson, Milton Gross, Frank Moser, Ashley Miller, Clarence Rigby, E. Dean Parmaelee, Jean Gic, Burt Gillett, Grim Natwick, Bill Nolan, J.A. Norling, Walter Lantz, Vincent Colby, C. Allen Gilbert, H.C. Greening, A.D. Reed, Hugh M. Shields, Raoul Barré, Pat Sullivan, Johnny B. Gruelle, Jack King, Isadore Klein, Leon Searl, Bert Green, Ben Sharpsteen, and Will Powers. In addition to Earl Hurd and his *Bobby Bumps* series, Bray employed Wallace Carlson producing *Dreamy Dud*, and Paul Terry with his *Farmer Alfalfa* series. Many of these cartoons caught the attention of the young Walt Disney while he was working for the United Film Ad Company in Kansas City, Missouri. Eager to learn animation, he would go through the cartoon reels as they passed through the company and clip samples from the cartoons from which he copied the actions to learn animation. Even his boy and girl characters in the *Laugh-O-Grams* series bear a striking resemblance to Carlson's Dudley and Mamie.

Mechanics and Science Films (1918–1921)

Thanks to his understanding of science and technical subjects, one of Max's first assignments was *The Electric Bell*, an educational film about the workings of an electric doorbell. The test films from the Rotoscope were considered as source material for a series, but

plans were interrupted by the outbreak of World War I. In light of America's entering the war, J.R. Bray realized the value of film as an educational tool. He sent Max Fleischer and Jack Leventhal, head of the Bray Technical Division, to Fort Sill, Oklahoma where they supervised the production of the first Army training films. The subjects included *How to Operate a Stokes Mortar*, *How to Fire the Lewis Machine Gun*, *Submarine Mine Laying*, and *Contour Map Reading*. These films were effective training tools, leading to a huge demand for educational and advertising films

Left: **Max Fleischer supervising the filming of a model for *How to Read a Contour Map* (Virginia Kneitel-Mahoney). *Below:* Charlie Schettler, Max, and Dave, ca. 1916 (Virginia Kneitel-Mahoney). Note: Dave was serving as a film cutter for the Army Medical Corps.**

after the Armistice. As a result, the Bray Studio became the leader in instructional films, with many production contracts for the Army and Navy that lasted for seven decades.

Films such as Leventhal and Fleischer's *The Submarine Mine Layer* (1917) catered to popular interest in the European war. While many subjects like this were included in the Goldwyn-Bray *Pictograph* newsreel as "Popular Science" segments, they had additional value in the new educational film market. Following the Armistice, Max supervised films on science, engineering, mechanics, and most notably, space exploration with titles such as *All Aboard for the Moon*, *If We Lived on the Moon*, and *Hello, Mars*.

Post-war prosperity gave birth to a new era. A modern age was ushered in with the automobile and electrical appliances that allowed for more leisure time. Baseball was the number one pastime, with the movies becoming a close second. The film industry was growing rapidly with a demand for more innovative films.

Out of the Inkwell (1918–1921)

Following the war, Bray negotiated a new contract with the newly formed Goldwyn Company. It was during this period beginning in 1918 that Fleischer's animation became regular entries in the monthly *Pictograph* reel. Dave Fleischer came to Bray once *Out of the Inkwell* was official. At first he did menial jobs as he learned the production process. Besides performing as the clown for Rotoscoping, he acted in two of the films. In *The Circus* (1920), he appeared as "Jim," the Projectionist and as the Mailman in *The Clown's Little Brother* (1920). He also gained experience directing Max on camera and developing storylines. Directing for silent films consisted of calling out the actions to the performer and determining the pacing as the camera was running. His experience as a film editor also substantiated him as a director since he had an understanding of filmic timing and pacing. But his role as a director at this time was only when needed for filming the live action sequences for *Out of the Inkwell*.

The first animator Max hired was Roland D. Crandall. Crandall was a commercial illustrator originally from New Canaan, Connecticut. He had previously worked for the Hearst International Studio in 1916, where he animated on *Foxy Grandpa* and *The Katzenjammer Kids*. During the war, he animated a 13-reel animated history of war. Max addressed him by the nickname, "Doc," which makes him possibly the first in animation to utter, "What's up, Doc?"

The first three *Out of the Inkwell* shorts were copyrighted as *Pictograph* elements on June 4, 1918; March 24, 1919; and April 23, 1919, respectively. Initially released only under the "Inkwell" series title, they were later reissued with the episode titles *Experiment No. 1*, *Experiment No. 2*, and *Experiment No. 3*. These would most likely have been the Boy Scout, Chanticleer, and Clown experiments. While these experiments were listed on the Bray inventory of films well into the 1950s, no known prints have survived.

The challenge that Fleischer faced with his four animation experiments was the consumption of the time to produce them. The stipulation that Bray's units each produce one film per month necessitated a method to reduce the footage required for animation. Fleischer picked up on a method already realized by his Bray associate, Earl Hurd, who had

OUT OF THE INKWELL

In some of the past Bray Pictographs, we did a little experimenting with a brand new super-animated cartoon.

We wanted to see how the public liked it. We wanted to see if they liked it as well as we did.

They did.

Already "Out of the Ink-well" by Max Fleischer, is the classic of animated cartoons. For humor, surprises, delicacy and accuracy of action, nothing has ever approached this feature.

The little clown who grows right before your eyes out of the pen point and then shrivels up and flows back—just drops of ink, is known from Coast to Coast.

He is going on with many new tricks, inspired by the genius of his creator and aided and abetted by the staff of Bray idea men

He is frequently in the new and greater

Goldwyn BRAY Pictograph

Beginning September 7th, as you have already been informed, the Bray Pictograph is distributed through Goldwyn, and by merely notifying your closest Goldwyn Exchange, your service may be continued. You understand that your service of the Bray Pictograph need not in any way be interfered with or interrupted because of the change in distribution.

If you have not yet realized the unusual features of this greater short-reeler, think of all that is being given in concentrated, crystallized form, weekly.

In addition to the animated cartoon, *comes shortly, the world's first colored cartoon.* (Bray is always the first in every improvement of short-reelers.)

Also Popular Science Adventure; and Romance; Pictures of the Invisible; Cartoons of the leading comics and many other features.

Produced by the BRAY Pictures Corporation

Released through

GOLDWYN

Out of the Inkwell trade ad, September 6, 1919 (Tom Stathes).

applied a combination of animation and live action footage in some of his "Bobby Bumps" cartoons. This concept combined the on-screen cartoonist, and the cartoon star—a format originating in Bray's first animation, *The Artist's Dream*. This format consisted of 75 percent live action and 25 percent animation, which shortened animation production time. And the intercutting of live action and animation gave relief to the eye since much of the animation was still inked on white paper. The novelty that was anticipated in *Out of the Inkwell* was the crossing of the fourth wall by the clown and his interaction with reality, which was also a relief to the eye.

While the concept of a hand appearing to draw on screen was already a Bray convention, Fleischer's innovative combination of Rotoscoped action, conventional animation, stop motion, and live action scenes made his series stand out among the other Bray short subjects. Fleischer also had the Bray processes at his disposal, including the use of cels. To combine "The Clown" with live action footage, cel animation was laid over 8" × 10" still photographs made from a live action 35mm film negative. Dave Fleischer substantiated this:

> You know that over the background you put transparent celluloid and then you draw the action on that celluloid and then photograph them in succession for the action, but the background is still. I thought, "Why can't I take a photograph and then photograph the cartoon through the cel over the live photograph and I will have live action and cartoon combined?" So I got down on the floor and I took a picture of the leg of the desk, and I intended to have the clown climb down that leg. So when I was doing it, one of the top directors in Bray's studio came in and said, "What are you doin,' kid?".... I said, "I'm gonna make the clown climb up this leg here." He said, "It won't work!" And as he walked away, I watched his walk. I wanted to know what a stupid man looks like when he walks.[8]

In some early *Inkwell* films, including *The Clown's Pup* and *The Tantalizing Fly*, one can see a cut directly from "straight" live action footage to the inserted animation using still photographs as backgrounds. While the live action appears to freeze with a slight shift in density and image size, the effect was convincing enough for audiences at the time. The overlay process was an easy method for combining animation with the impression of a live action environment. This worked well enough for a still background but was more complicated if live action was included. The process of making the stills and registering them was expensive and time consuming, requiring precise registration of each photograph. Because of this, Fleischer used the effect sparingly in *The Clown's Little Brother*, where "The Clown" rides a cat bareback and appears to box with the cat in another scene.

Out of the Inkwell was released bi-monthly between 1919 and 1921. During that period, 16 films were produced. The initial series was based on theme concepts developed by Max, evidenced in the titles: *Experiment No. 1*; *Experiment No. 2*; *Experiment No. 3*; *The Clown's Pup*; *The Tantalizing Fly*; *Slides*; *The Boxing Kangaroo*; *The Chinaman*; *The Circus*; *The Ouija Board*; *The Clown's Little Brother*; *Perpetual Motion*; *Poker*; *Restaurant*; *Cartoonland*; *The Automobile Ride*.

The Pictograph was planned around specific subject matter, which dictated the themes for the *Out of the Inkwell* series at this time. Regrettably, only half of the Bray *Inkwell* films survive. *Experiments No. 1, No. 2, and No. 3, Slides, Poker, Restaurant*, and *Cartoonland* are presumed lost, and *The Boxing Kangaroo* exists only as a short excerpt. The loss of *Cartoonland* is particularly great since it featured appearances of all of the major Hearst comic strip characters. The rarity of this film may be linked to a limited licensing agreement and the Hearst policy of destroying any film adaptations of their properties after ten years. This policy became a major issue with future screen adaptations in live action and animation decades later, and a major issue for Fleischer decades later.

It should be noted that at this time, the clown had no name. All references within the films are to "Clown." This is substantiated by the titles *The Clown's Pup* and *The Clown's Little Brother*. While the character was nameless at this time, his personality was established from the start. He has an awareness of being a creation of ink on paper. He is protective of his position and his "space," and is jealous of other figures invading that space. His is defiant of Max, his "creator," motivated for revenge due to some torment imposed upon him. When this happens, he crosses the "fourth wall" to create havoc in "reality."

It is difficult to determine the first film to cross the fourth wall due to the missing installments. The earliest surviving entry, *The Clown's Pup* (1919) shows a drawing contest between Max and the Clown with the Clown confined to the paper, then returning to the inkwell in the end. The crossing of the fourth wall to cause mischief in reality does not seem to appear until *The Chinaman* (1920), which is interesting on several levels. It shows Max as the production manager at Bray interviewing an eccentric artist. Max reviews several of the artist's works that include a dog, a "Gibson Girl" type piece, a cartoon Native American, and a Chinese Laundryman—all ink drawings likely done by Max. He selects the Chinese drawing and sets it upright on his desk. They discuss salary, and the Artist wants $150 per week. Max offers $15, and the Artist accepts. The Artist then says his specialty is portraits and offers to draw Max. As they exit for the modeling area, the stopper on the ink bottle pops off and the Clown steps out. This appears to be the earliest example of the Clown emerging from the inkwell on his own.

The Clown sees the "Chinaman" drawing on the desk and becomes jealous. The Clown attacks the Chinaman, pulling his long braid (considered a great insult in Chinese culture), which snaps back like a rubber band. In stereotypical fashion, a flat iron falls out of the Chinaman's shirt. The two wrestle in a cartoon tumble, with hats exchanged. They tumble again and the Chinaman grabs the Clown by the head, wrings out his neck, then grabs the Clown like a bed sheet, shaking him out, then using his braid as a clothesline, hangs the Clown up to dry while producing a clothespin from his mouth. The Clown works the clothespin off, stabbing the Chinaman in the nose with it, causing the Chinaman to throw the Clown off the paper with a spin. The Clown lands on the desk below, and reaching into the inkwell, he disguises his face to look Chinese. The original title card here reads, "This 'Chink' makeup will fool him!" He returns to the page pretending to be another Chinaman, grabs him by the braid and swings him around, throwing him to the ground. The Chinaman hallucinates about being back in China smoking an opium pipe.

Out of the dream, the Clown picks up the Chinaman like a beach ball and tugs him apart, causing him to "pop" like a balloon, which causes the Artist to turn around and see the Clown on the illustration board previously occupied by his Chinaman drawing. Max has gone to sleep, bored from sitting for his portrait and unaware of what is happening. The Artist tries to block the Clown with his hand, but the Clown gets out from under and jumps to the floor. He pulls himself up to the easel, where he alters the portrait of Max to a large, unflattering nose. The wacky Artist sees the Clown on the easel and tries to grab at him, but the Clown slips inside of the Artist's sleeve, through his clothes, and starts tickling him. The Artist goes into a laughing fit, causing Max to wake up. Max then notices the unflattering portrait, concludes that this is what the Artist is laughing about, and an argument begins. The Clown quietly slips down the Artist's pant leg as the argument escalates into a fight resulting in Max throwing the crazy Artist out of his office. Max re-enters slightly disheveled and sees the Clown laughing at him, perched atop the frame of a picture of a Spanish style house. The Clown bounces up the walk and enters the house, going upstairs, turning on the light with his silhouette in the window. Max goes to his desk drawer and picks up an eyedropper, extracting the Clown from the picture, and returns him to the inkwell.

From the surviving evidence, this was the first use of the interacting between the cartoon figure and "reality," which would continue to be the key element forming the denouement of each cartoon in the series. This story would be reworked as *Big Chief Ko-Ko* (1925), substituting the eccentric Artist with a Native American. While Fleischer's *Out of the Inkwell* was a welcomed installment in the Bray-Goldwyn Pictograph reels, the restrictive production budgets at Bray hindered technical advancements. Additional problems resulted from Bray's deal with Goldwyn, obliging Bray to produce more films than his units could easily deliver. By 1921, Bray was facing legal difficulties due to contractual breaches for non-performance and lack of delivery.

3

The Inkwell Studio

It was 1921 when Bray's major talents departed the studio, with Max Fleischer among them. While Fleischer felt loyalty towards John Bray and held company stock, it was apparent that continued artistic and technical innovation would not be possible under the conservative, litigious atmosphere at Bray. It was at this time that Dave Fleischer won $50,000 on a horse race bet and offered an $800 match to Max's investment in the startup of a new studio, Out of the Inkwell Films, Inc. With their own studio, the Fleischer Brothers had complete creative freedom to explore innovations that would not have been possible at Bray. They opened their studio in a dingy basement apartment at 129 East 45th Street, where a brothel allegedly operated on the upper floors. Max brought in his Bray associate, "Doc" Crandall, and Dave brought in a photographer friend, Charles Schettler. Joe Fleischer also joined the organization as the Chief Mechanic. Charlie came in when electrical jobs were needed, but essentially remained an independent contractor outside of the organization. This structure remained for the next 21 years.

The first release under the new partnership was *Modeling,* which features "Doc" Crandall as the sculptor whose client has a large, ugly nose. The film opens with Max dipping his pen into the inkwell with some slow-moving amoebae-like shapes oozing out, squeezing back into the tip, and then bursting forward to form the Clown, who complains that Max needs to get some fresh ink. Crandall calls for Max's input on the sculpture, to which he replies, "As soon as I get some energy into this clown." He sketches a frozen lake and adds ice skates to the Clown's feet. As Max exits, the Clown slips and slides all over the ice, and once he gains his footing, he cleverly traces out an image of

Crandall's sculpture. The patron comes into the studio and seeing the clay sculpture says, "It's no good. It looks exactly like me!"

Modeling is significant with the addition of Claymation techniques, something quite new to movie audiences. It was also significant for the first application of Max's next invention, the Rotograph, which was an improvement in combining cartoons with moving live action footage. While this appears to be the first application of this technique, the patent was not filed until 1925.

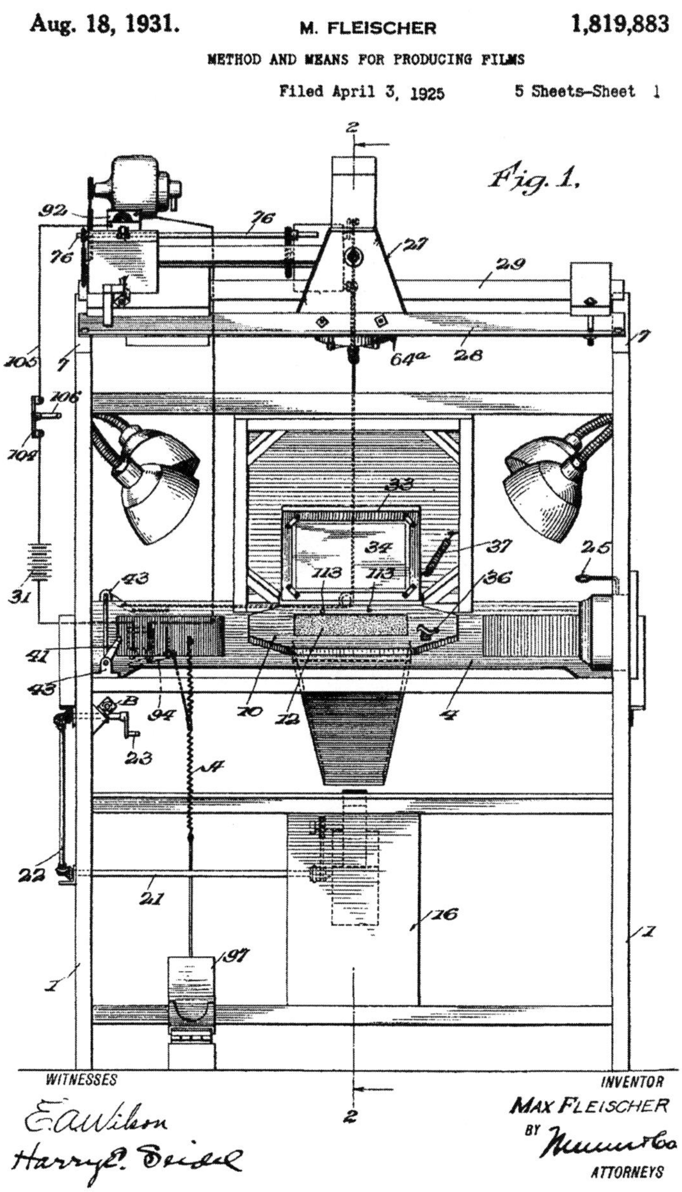

The Rotograph patent (U.S. Patent and Trademark Office).

Instead of making still photographs from the 35mm film, the Rotograph offered a means of re-photographing the live action footage frame-by-frame with the animation cel in front of it. This was a form of rear-projection where the filmed footage was projected onto a glass opening in the camera's compound surface. The image of the projected film provided a backlit source, and when the cel was placed over it, a silhouette was produced. The scene would be photographed progressively, changing the cels and advancing the film for the required footage length. The film in the camera would be reversed to the first frame,

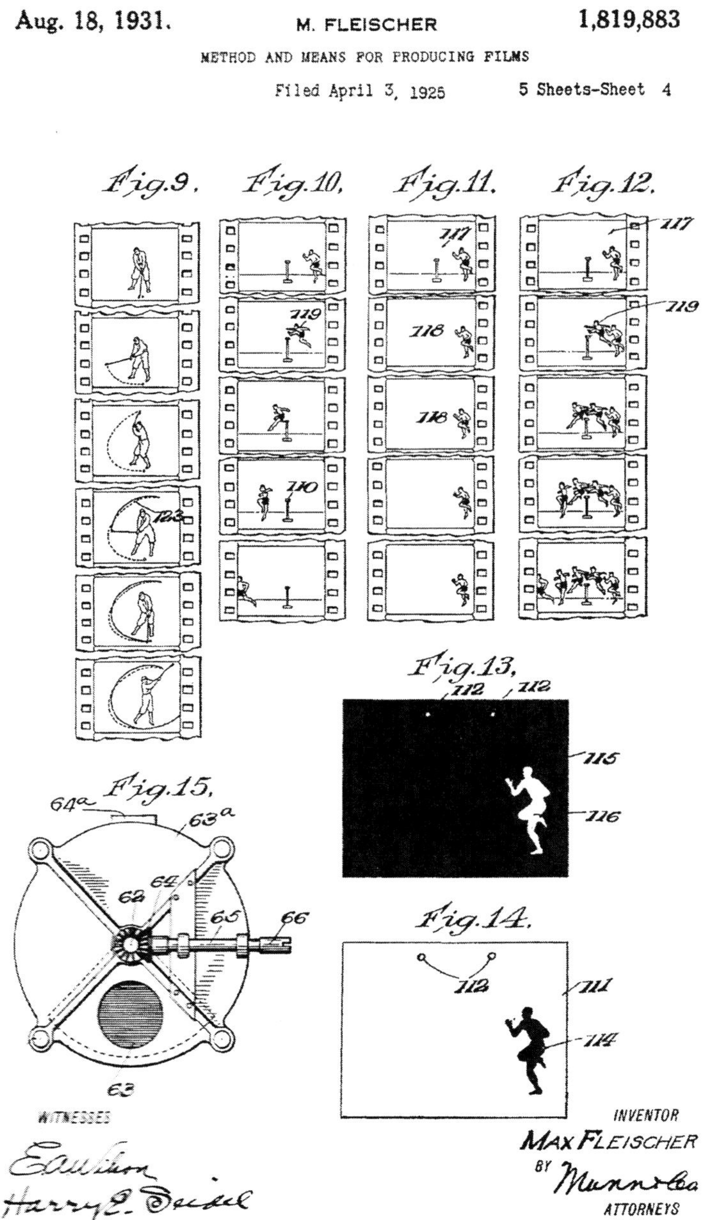

The Rotograph patent (U.S. Patent and Trademark Office).

and the animation would be re-shot top lit using a black card as a background. This was a simple matte process that was later to become commonly known as "aerial image photography," which was widely adapted by the industry for producing titles and various types of process scenes combining art elements with motion picture footage.

At first, *Out of the Inkwell* was distributed through the states rights method, and then picked up by Warner Brothers. In 1922, Margaret J. Winkler assumed distribution when the Warner's dropped short subject cartoons. Miss Winkler had been the executive secretary to Harry Warner, and because of her good business sense, he gave her the *Felix the Cat* and *Out of the Inkwell* contracts. As a result, "Peggy" Winkler started out on top with two of

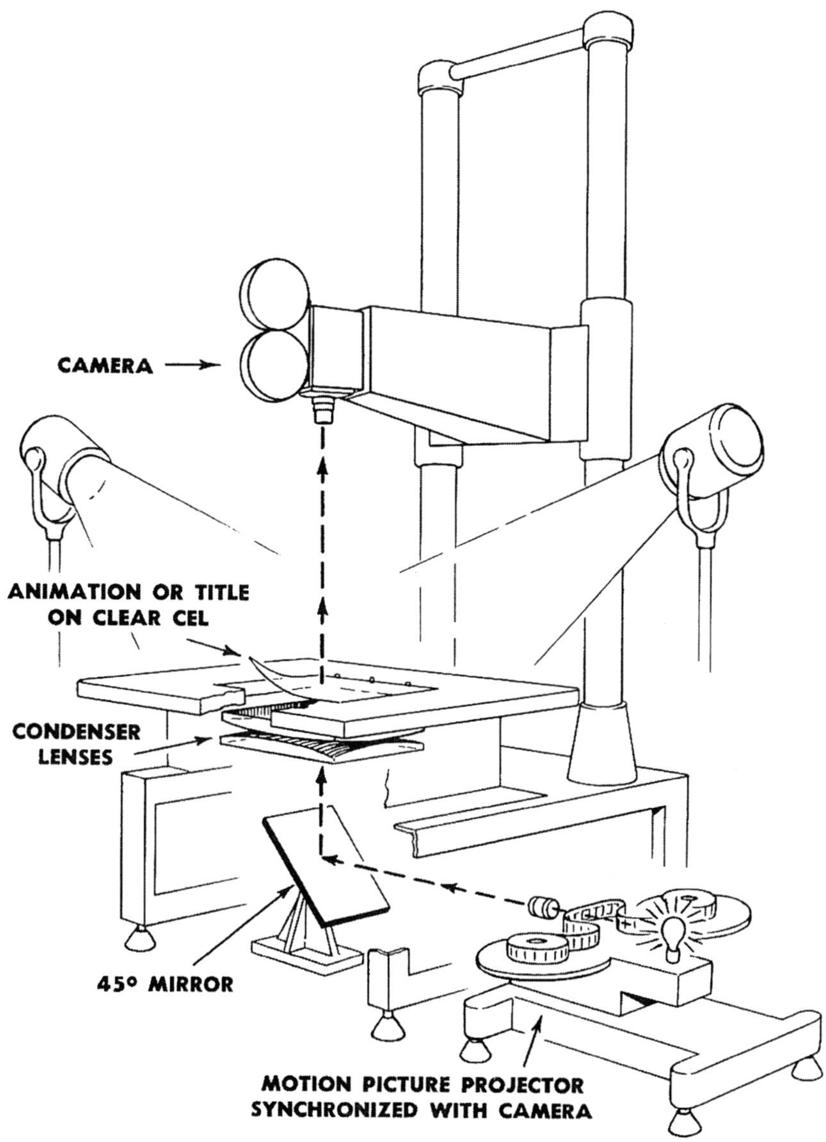

The Aerial Image Process (Oxberry-Berkey Technical).

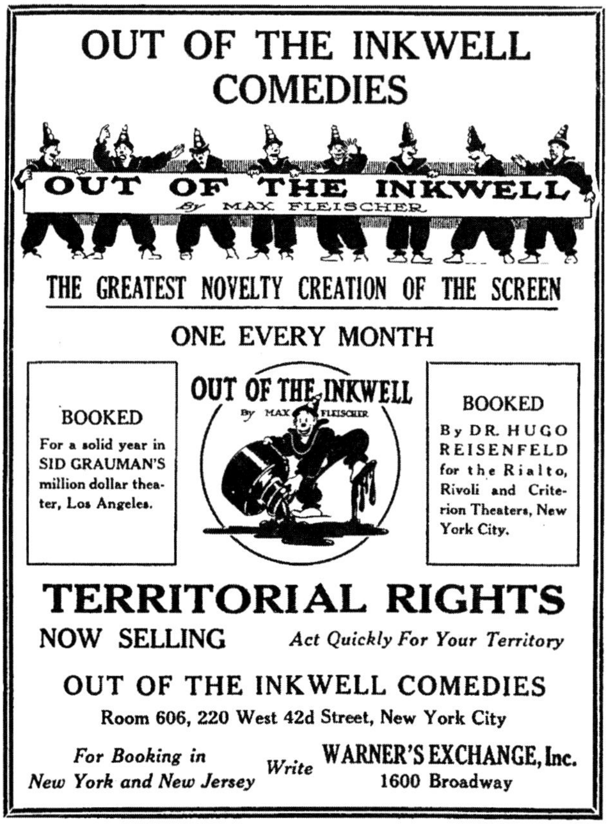

***Out of the Inkwell* trade ad (author's collection).**

the most important animated short subjects of the silent era, becoming the first female film producer/distributor. The following year, Fleischer went with Rodner Productions.

Always interested in education, Max filed a patent on an extended protractor device with a sliding ruler and a pencil point hole at the end. The patent application indicates that this device could be used for teaching drawing through radio broadcast or classroom instruction. Because of Max's reputation from *Popular Science* and the Bray Educational films, the Inkwell Studio was approached to produce scientific films on *Evolution* and *Relativity*.

Evolution is an interesting combination of special effects, live action, stop motion, and animated diagrams. It has been reported that Willis O'Brien, who pioneered stop motion animation in 1917, animated the dinosaur sequence. The creation of the Earth, done with photographic effects, was quite innovative in 1923 and seems to have influenced the opening of *The Right of Spring* sequence in Walt Disney's *Fantasia* (1940). While *Evolution* was produced merely to illustrate the theory, it became a subject of controversy in the Bible Belt when it was shown during the famous Scopes trial involving William Jennings Bryan and Defense attorney, Clarence Darrow.

Relativity was produced under the supervision of Einstein's associate, Dr. Garret P. Serviss and is the more interesting of the two science films. Its full use of animation and photographic techniques clearly illustrate the nebulous concept of the theory, which was not then widely understood.

Nineteen twenty-three was a major turning point for the Inkwell Studio when Dick Huemer arrived and assumed the role as Animation Director. Huemer, originally from the Bronx, attended art school and was hired initially by Raoule Barré on the *Mutt and Jeff* cartoons in 1916. Having learned animation under Barré, Huemer's arrival brought many valuable contributions. First, he redesigned the Clown, naming him "Ko-Ko." Huemer's *Mutt and Jeff* influence suggested the addition of a small comedic companion in the form of a dog character, "Fitz." Fitz became more of the driver of anarchy in the stories, with Ko-Ko becoming more benevolent until convinced by Fitz that a "payback" was in order due to some injustice imposed upon them by "reality."

Huemer's model sheet for Ko-Ko the Clown (author's collection).

Ko-Ko's "Kanine Kompanion," Fitz (author's collection).

Dick Huemer had the unique talent of drawing directly in ink. It was his use of the Gillette #290 pen that resulted in the attractive thick and thin line work that defined the style for *Out of the Inkwell* from this point on. Because Max valued Huemer's skills, he had him make the key animation drawings, leaving the "fill-in work" to be completed by an assistant. To do this, Max assigned Art Davis as Huemer's assistant, creating the position of "Inbetweener." This procedure allowed Huemer to plan out animation with a more efficient production process, allowing for increased output. Many prominent animators got their start as inbetweeners at the Inkwell Studio, and as the staff enlarged, there was a need for supervision and organization of production. One of the first women hired as an inbetweener was Edith Vernick, who became the Inbetween Supervisor. Veteran animators Dave Tendlar, Shamus Culhane, and Berny Wolf had been Inkers on *Krazy Kat* and were all hired at the Inkwell Studio as inbetweeners. Wolf recalled, "Max Fleischer hired me and I went to work as an inbetweener. I didn't know anything about inbetweening, but that was my next step up from *Krazy Kat*."[1]

Dick Huemer (left) "clowns" with friend (unidentified) (Dr. Richard Huemer).

Krazy Kat "Krew" *(left to right) Front row:* Al Windley (cameraman), Al Gould (painter), Al Rose (animator), Manny Gould (animator/director), Ben Harrison (animator/director), Art Davis (animator), Unknown Office Boy. *Back row:* Mike Balukas (inker), Ira Gould (painter), Berny Wolf (inker), Harry Love (assistant animator), Sid Marcus (animator), Jimmy "Shamus" Culhane (inker/assistant animator), Unknown painter, Dave Tendlar (inker/assistant animator) (author's collection).

As co-owner of Out of the Inkwell Films, Inc., Dave Fleischer was trying to find his place in the organization, and the presence of Huemer helped. The collaboration of Dave and Huemer resulted in greater comedy with many alliterative gag titles based on variations of the Ko-Ko name such as *Ko-Ko's Kane*, *Ko-Ko the Kop*, and *Ko-Ko's Kink*. Berny Wolf continued:

> There wasn't much charm between Dave and the creative guys. He was a bit "brusque," didn't understand artists, animators. Max was the ultimate gentleman. Fine, fine person. He had all the credentials. So the animators always turned to Max.... Everything we did for Max was fine, and he accepted it.[2]

Where Max reflected a scholarly personality, Dave seemed rather unschooled and vulgar, which made an impression. "Unlike Max, who had an excellent vocabulary, Dave's speech was full of grammatical errors and malapropisms, delivered in a strong New York accent."[3]

His talent and contribution to the studio was viewed differently, as well: "Dave was no artist. He was a gag writer of sorts. From his speech, I judge that he had very little schooling."[4]

But not all the staff had the benefit of close contact with Max. Dick Huemer's interaction with him was minimal and it was Dave who he'd consult with on the animation.

Max and Dave went off by themselves and thought up the stories.... They would also go off by themselves and shoot the live action. Once it was shot, Max was no longer involved. Dave Fleischer, on the other hand would come sit next to an animator and they would talk.... Not writing anything down, just talk—a private gag meeting. That was the only preparation for the animation.[5]

Among those caricatured: Max, Dave, Lillian Bleecker (Secretary), Burt Gillett, Art Davis, Dick Huemer, Ben Harrison, "Doc" Crandall, Joe Fleischer, Mannie Gould, Al Kaplan (?), Izzy Sparber, Edith Vernick, Sidney Friedman(?), and Sam Stimson (author's collection).

Fleischer staff, ca. 1923 *Seated:* Ben Harrison (1), Lillian Bleecker (2), Frank Paiker (3), Edith Vernick (4), Sid Wallick (5). *Standing:* Izzy Sparber (6), Max Fleischer (7), Sam Stimson (8), Jack Rubin (9), Joe Fleischer (10). *Back row, standing:* "Doc" Crandall (11), Dick Huemer (12) (author's collection).

The Inkwell staff grew to include Ben Sharpsteen, Izzy Klein, Manny Davis, and Burt Gillette, who had animated *Felix the Cat* for Pat Sullivan. The studio outgrew its quarters and on November 30, 1923, moved to the sixth floor of the prestigious Studebaker Building at 1600 Broadway. Built in 1902, the Studebaker Building was originally an automobile showroom, now converted into an office building where many of the film distribution companies held offices. It was also conveniently located one block north of the Paramount Building seated on the triangular block where Broadway and 7th Avenue converged in Times Square. While the Inkwell Studio had become a major force in animation, a contender was waiting in the wings, soon to take center stage.

While all published accounts indicate that Disney was largely influenced by Paul Terry's *Aesop's Fables*, there is no question that he was also influenced by Max Fleischer. From the start, Disney started out with great ambition, packing each of his cartoons with more story and visual attraction by using animation cels and toned backgrounds at a time when most cartoon producers, including Pat Sullivan and the Fleischers, continued to ink on white paper. Disney managed to raise $15,000 to produce six films through a local investor and officially established his first studio on May 23, 1922. His small staff included Ub Iwerks, Friz Freleng, Hugh Harman, Rudy Ising, Lorey Tague, Otto Walliman, Carman "Max" Maxwell, and cameraman "Red Lyon."

While Disney was confident that his product could challenge the competition, it failed to attract a major distributor, which forced him to accept a modest non-theatrical deal with Pictorial Clubs of America. Although the contract called for $11,000 for four more films, Disney received only a $100 advance on each, with the remaining balance due a year later. Although Pictorial Clubs owed Disney a balance on the delivered films, it was never paid. Pictorial Clubs went into receivership and Disney had to sue to recover. To save his company, Disney took on several live action productions. One was a dental hygiene film *Tommy Tucker's Tooth*, made at a cost of $500. With the proceeds, he produced a pilot film, *Alice's Wonderland.*

It is apparent that Walt was aware of Fleischer's *Out of the Inkwell* technique and set out to not only match it, but surpass it. *Alice's Wonderland* successfully emulated the combination of cartoon animation with live action footage with the added feature of combining live action footage of a young girl with an animated environment. Where Fleischer's concept was quickly, simply, and inexpensively produced, Disney's approach was more technically challenging and more complicated. The animation was clearly an improvement over the *Laugh-O-Grams*, and much had been learned based on many of Fleischer's techniques.

In 1924, distributor Edwin Miles Fadiman, and Hugo Riesenfeld formed the Red Seal Pictures Corporation. Riesenfeld was the Theatrical Manager of the Strand, Rivoli, and Rialto theaters on Broadway. Because the *Out of the Inkwell* films were a major part of the program in Riesenfeld's theaters, the Fleischers were invited

Hugo Riesenfeld (George Eastman House).

to become partners. The Red Seal Company committed to an ambitious release schedule of 26 films with The Inkwell Studio as the primary supplier. The following year, Red Seal released 141 films that included documentaries, short comedy subjects, and live-action serials. *Carrie of the Chorus,* also known as *Backstage Comedies*, was one of the Red Seal series that featured Max's daughter, Ruth, in a supporting role. Ray Bolger made his screen debut in this series and dated Ruth for a short time.

Red Seal released cartoon novelty series such as *The Animated Hair Cartoons* by Cartoonist "Marcus," and *Inklings. The Animated Hair* series resembled the on-screen hand drawing gimmick established in *Out of the Inkwell.* In this case, "Marcus" produced high-quality ink line portraits of celebrities and political figures. Then through stop motion animation techniques, the lines and forms would break away to entertainingly re-form the

Ruth Fleischer and Ray Bolger in *Berth Marks* from the *Carrie of the Chorus* series (author's collection).

Charlie Schettler working an image transition for the *Inklings* series (Todd Levine).

portrait into another. *Inklings* was similar in concept to the *Animated Hair* films, but was more of a visual puzzle novelty using a variety of progressive scratch-off/reveal techniques and rearranged animated cutouts to change the images.

Ko-Ko Song Car-Tunes

"Follow the Bouncing Ball!" (author's illustration).

It was during this time that Dr. Lee de Forest started filming his early Phonofilms experiments featuring several of the major Broadway headliners. The Red Seal company began acquiring more theaters outside of New York and equipped them with deForest sound equipment, displaying "talkies" three years before the sound revolution began. Because of Max's interest in technology, Riesenfeld introduced him to deForest. And it was through this partnership that Max produced a number of the *Ko-Ko Song Car-Tunes* as sound releases. Of the 36 song films produced between 1924 and 1927, 12 were produced as sound films beginning in 1926 with standard silent versions as well. The first sound release was *Mother Pin a Rose on Me.* Other sound releases included *Darling Nellie Gray, Has Anybody Here Seen Kelly?, When the Midnight Choo-Choo Leaves for Alabam', Coming Through the Rye, My Wife's Gone to the Country, Margie, Oh, How I Hate to Get Up in the Morning, Sweet Adeline, Old Black Joe, Come Take a Trip in My Airship,* and *By the Light of the Silvery Moon.*

The origin of the song films has varying accounts. Dave Fleischer recalled that in early 1924:

> Charles K. Harris, the famous songwriter, came to the studio and asked Max if we could get an audience to sing to a cartoon. My brother came in and asked if I could do it, and I said, "Yes!"[6]

Another version states that songwriter and vaudevillian, Gus Edwards, famous for *School Days* approached Max in a similar manner. In either case, Max agreed without having any idea of how to go about it and turned to his brothers for the answer. Lou Fleischer's son, Bernie, remarked on the foundation of the concept:

> Nobody will say who thought of (it), but the idea of the "sing-alongs" came from my dad who did it in silent movie houses. It was a very big hit. While the projectionist was changing reels, they would actually put a slide up and sing along with it. And my dad always thought, "Gee it would be great to have some sort of pointer to hit the lyrics." And I'm pretty sure that it was Max who thought of a ball bouncing on it.[7]

Richard Fleischer explained further:

> In order to help the audience stay in tempo with the song's words that were projected on the movie screen, he invented the famous "Bouncing Ball," which would bound from word-to-word in time with the music.[8]

The pairing of Max Fleischer with Charles K. Harris was a major business announcement in *Film Daily* followed by a favorable reaction to their collaboration.

Film Daily January 20, 1924

Song Cartoons Planned by Harris and Fleischer

Red Seal—State Rights Distribution—To Be in One Reel

Chas. K. Harris and Max Fleischer of Out-of-the-Inkwell Films arranged with Red Seal Pictures to produce a series of old-time animated song cartoons. A perfect synchronization of popular song music with animated cartoons is promised. The first release is now in work and will be finished in the next few weeks. Strict secrecy is being maintained as to just how the effects are going to be produced, but it is known that some rather unusual machinery has just been devised and installed in the Out-of-the-Inkwell studios, to handle this novelty properly. The series will be distributed by Red Seal through state right exchanges.

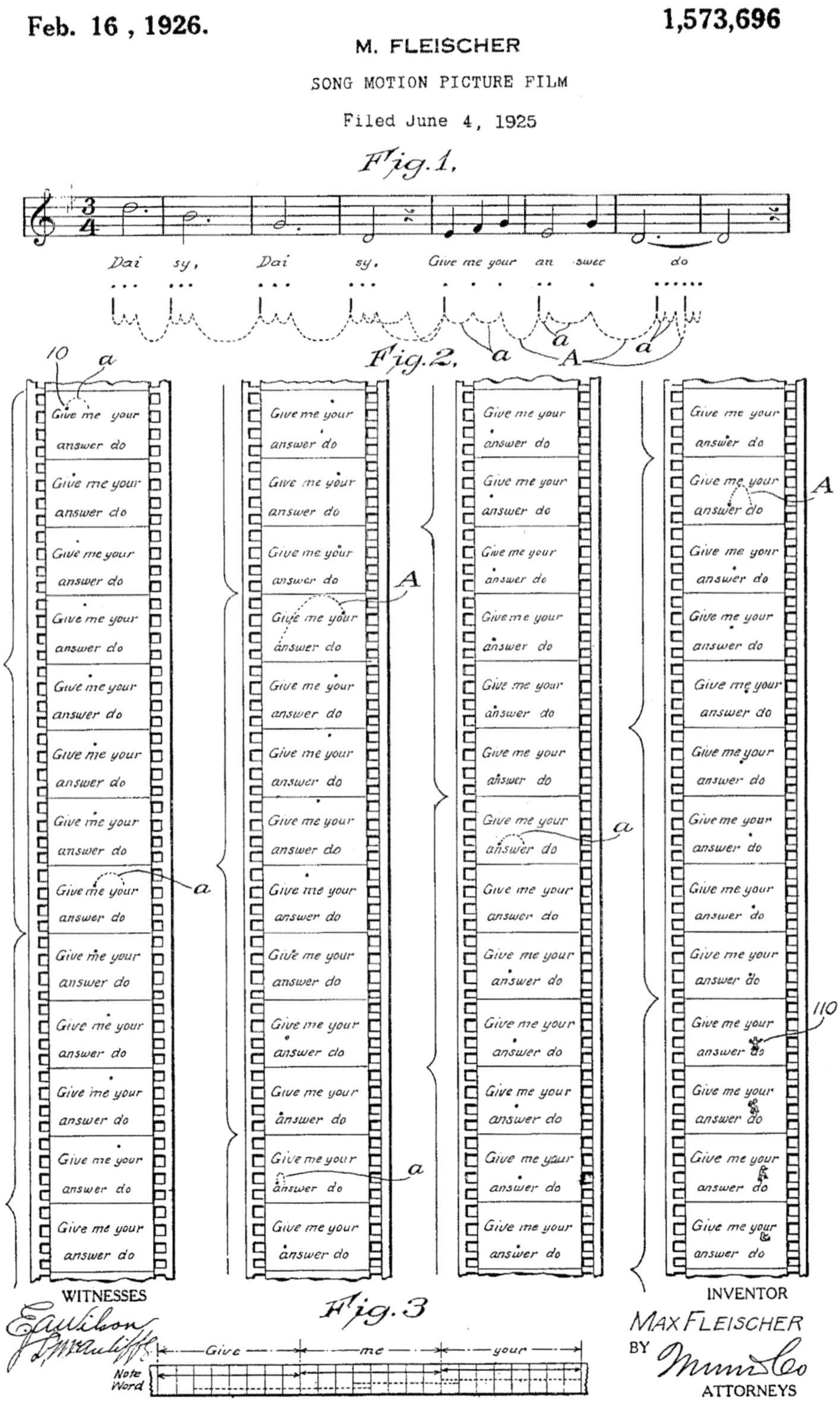

The Bouncing Ball patent (U.S. Patent and Trademark Office).

Film Daily, March 9, 1924

"Song Cartoons"—Charles K. Harris and Max Fleischer

Well Handled Novelty

Type of production: 1 reel novelty

Here's a new idea in song reels, presented by Charles K. Harris, the music publisher who is responsible for the songs and Max Fleischer whose animated cartoons skip nimbly from word to word of the song and lend much charm and some laughs. There is no picturization of the action described in the song—simply the words which run along the screen in large single-line type that moves slowly from right to left in time to the music and on which the tiny cartoon figures dance. The songs included are *Mother, Mother, Mother, Pin a Rose on Me*, *Come Take a Trip in My Airship* and *Goodbye, My Lady Love*.

In early *Song Car-Tunes* such as *Margie* and *When the Midnight Choo-Choo Leaves for Alabam'* the ball is animated, looking like a beach ball clumsily hitting the words without precise timing. This awkwardness was eliminated when Lou suggested filming the ball live. Bernie Fleischer continues:

> Dad actually became "The Bouncing Ball." They worked out a situation where they put the lyrics on a drum, which Joe would turn. And my dad had a baton that was all black, except it had a white ball on the end. And he wore a black glove and they had a black sleeve that he would put over it, and he would actually bounce the ball. And the drum would turn to the next set of lyrics, and they would have the music playing, and he would bounce the ball on each lyric as it came by.[9]

Charles K. Harris (author's collection).

These recollections seem to make reference to the sound versions since many of the silent song films such as *In the Good Old Summertime* seem to have the ball bouncing randomly at too slow of a tempo. In general, it was due to Lou Fleischer's musical background that the "Bouncing Ball" tempo became accurate, delighting audiences with its live presence that helped establish them as the first audience participation films. The *Song Car-Tunes* usually displayed white lyrics on a black background. This use of high contrast made the lyrics legible when the House Lights would be raised, signaling the audience to join in—a theatrical tradition going back to vaudeville.

When Red Seal started buying films from outside sources, their fortunes started dwindling. Their increase from 26 titles in 1924 to 141 the following year was the main source of their overhead

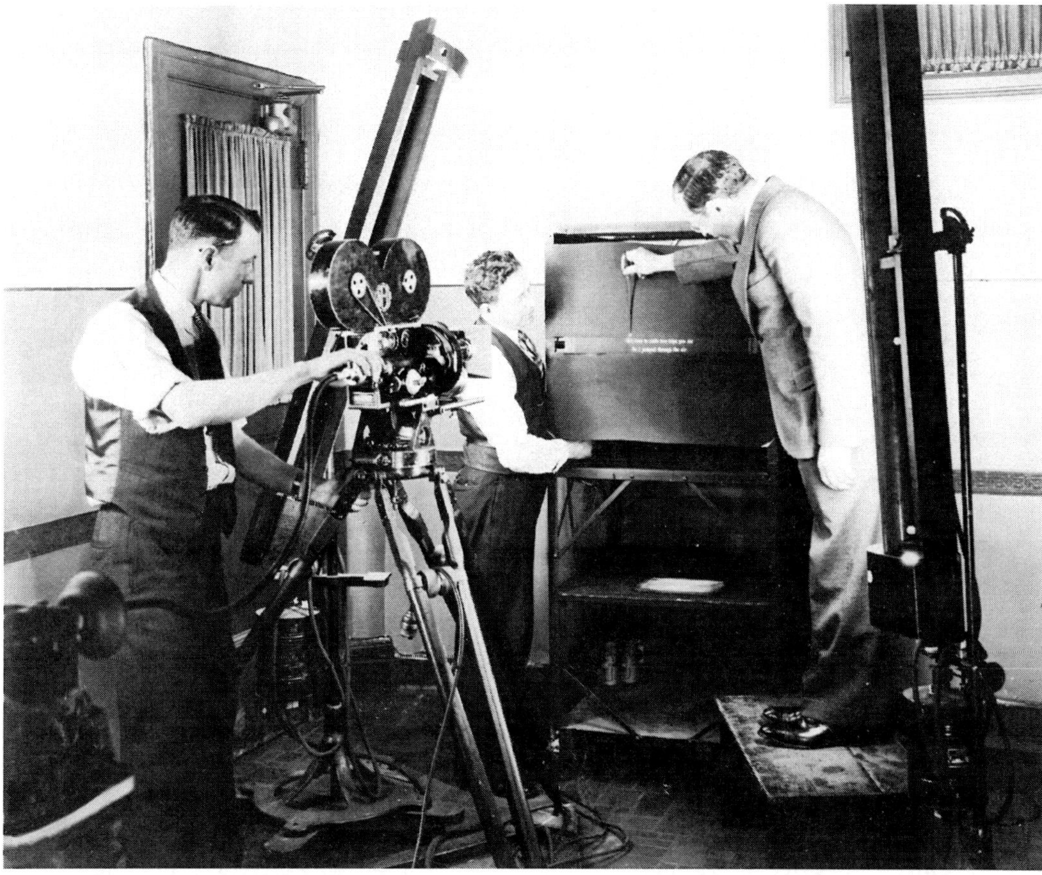

Charlie Schettler on camera, Joe Fleischer operating drum, and Lou Fleischer "bouncing" the ball, ca. 1930 (author's collection).

expenses. This led to major conflicts with Fadiman, resulting in his quick exit from the company. Max Fleischer had renewed his contract for three more years when the company fell into financial problems affecting not only the Fleischers but deForest and his sound films. Red Seal owned 56 theaters, extending as far west as Cleveland, Ohio. But after only two years of operation, Red Seal was broke. The film lab held their negatives due to unpaid bills totaling $218,000. Max sought an appointment of receiver in bankruptcy in October 1926. Just as the situation looked hopeless, Alfred Weiss appeared from the horizon with a Paramount contact.

No one seems to know where Alfred Weiss came from, but in November 1926, shortly after Max started bankruptcy procedures, Weiss crawled out of the woodwork and offered to take over Red Seal and Inkwell, pay their bills, and put them back in business. He seemed heaven-sent. He wasn't. He was, however, the only wheel in town, and Max felt that he had to go for it. Weiss became the President of both Red Seal and Inkwell. Max was hired on as Vice-President and Dave as Art Director at salaries of two hundred dollars a week each with scheduled increases up to three hundred dollars per week.[10]

Adolph Zukor and Sam Katz were looking for a steady supply of short subjects for their growing Publix Theater chain. They had already contracted with Charles Mintz for the production of Krazy Kat and were looking for more cartoons. Alfred J. Weiss had entered into a production relationship through his Artcraft Company to provide Paramount with low-budget short subjects.

> On the basis of Max's name and reputation, Weiss wangled a distribution contract out of Paramount Pictures. The Red Seal Company was abandoned. Weiss ... took the grand screen credit, "PRESENTED BY" for himself. Finally, he changed the well-established *Out of the Inkwell* series name to *Inkwell Imps* (and) started releasing through Paramount.[11]

The Paramount deal provided financing and distribution. Max Fleischer signed the Weiss deal in January 1927 and in the process Weiss gained ownership of the films previously held by the lab. Due to certain legal issues connected to the dissolution of the old company and its holdings, the title to the *Out of the Inkwell* series was changed for the Paramount contract to *The Inkwell Imps,* and the hyphen was dropped in the name, "Ko-Ko" during the first season of releases. A formal announcement in *Film Daily* established Paramount's new commitment to short subjects.

Film Daily, April 12, 1927

208 SHORT SUBJECTS ON FAMOUS PROGRAM

With 208 releases already assured, Paramount is completing its short subject line-up for 1927–28. In addition to the 104 issues of Paramount News, there will be 26 *Krazy Kat* cartoons produced by Winkler Pictures, Inc., and 26 *Out-of-the-Inkwell* (original title) cartoons produced by Out-of-the-Inkwell Films, Inc. The Winkler Company also will produce five novelties and five short comedies and comedy/dramas.

The fall of 1927 was significant for the premier of the landmark, *The Jazz Singer.* During this time, Max hosted a birthday dinner honoring Winsor McCay, recognizing him as the "inventor of animation." Some 30 animators gathered at Roth's Restaurant, including Paul Terry, Dave Fleischer, Pat Sullivan, Otto Messmer, Richard Huemer, Shamus Culhane, I. Klein, and Walter Lantz—all owing their careers to McCay. Legend has it that the famous animated stag film, *Eveready Harton in Buried Treasure*, was shown for the amusement of McCay and the guests.

> The first porno cartoon was made in New York. It was called, *Eveready Harton* and was made in the late 20s, silent of course—by three studios. Each one did a section of it without telling the other studios what they were doing. Studio A finished the first part and gave the last drawing to Studio B, etc. Involved were Max Fleischer, Paul Terry, and the Mutt and Jeff Studio. They didn't see the finished product 'till the night of the big show. A couple of guys who were there tell me the laugher almost blew the top off the hotel where they were screening it.[12]

All attending seemed amused except for the guest of honor. Richard Huemer said McCay rambled on about his "split system," which the studio animators "had figured out long ago." Sensing he was losing his audience, McCay quickly got to the point. "He wound up with a statement," said Klein, "which has remained in my mind. 'Animation should be an art. That is how I conceived it. But as I see what you fellows have done with it, is making it into a trade. Not an art, but a trade. Bad Luck!'" He sat down to scattered applause.[13] Everyone was obviously stunned by McCay's bitter perspective as he watched an industry pass him by, leaving his name in the animation field to obscurity by the 1920s, an event due to repeat itself for Max Fleischer a decade later.

For the year 1927, it was business as usual with no anticipation of the revolution that was on the horizon. The tidal wave caused by the demand for sound films closed some studios and gave new life to others. Max made it his business to know about the latest technologies and already had experienced working with sound. Paramount hurried to wire its theaters and convert its studios for the production of sound films. Many early "talkies" of late 1927 to 1928 were hybrid silent/sound films since some had begun as silent but quickly converted for sound. And while early sound films struggled with the restrictions of the microphone, sound cartoons were free of these technical limitations and able to display greater imagination in the use of sound.

This period is particularly puzzling in the Fleischer history with regards to their relationship with Weiss. Their "Angel Investor" soon proved to be "The Devil in Disguise." Dave Fleischer recalled:

> This man was a sort of militaristic German Jew. When he talked, he would stand up, click his heels and say, "David, do this, and do that!"... One day he came in to me and said, "David, have you got your contract? We can't find ours, and there's something I want to see in it." So I went to my lawyer and asked, "What do you think he wants?" He said, "Make a Photostat copy, and let him have your contract." I got a hold of a fellow from Paramount, who was an accountant. I knew that Weiss needed an accountant, so I had him apply for the job. One day my man called me and said, "Dave, we got him! They tore out page so-and-so and put another in, and you're licked according to the new contract and he's probably going to throw you out and Max!'"[14]

Consequently, Max and Dave quit. The absence of the Fleischers is evident in the last six *Inkwell Imps* films, which substitute an actor for Max as the studio artist. Beginning with *Ko-Ko's Conquest,* Max is absent in name and presence with his credit "Produced by Max Fleischer" missing from the opening titles. And following their resignations, Weiss disappeared, leaving the company hanging in uncertainty, which was confirmed in a letter from Walt Disney to his brother, Roy, on February 9, 1929. While on a business trip to New York Walt wrote:

> ... the Inkwell outfit has broken up—Both the Fleischers are out and the place is practically deserted—I was over there today and found that they only have a few assistant animators working, finishing up the few remaining pictures on the year's schedule and are not planning on any next year—they are going to release a few song cartoons—but I think they are old ones they are digging out and synchronizing [with sound].[15]

My Old Kentucky Home was one of the silent reissues with added animation for a sound re-release. While assumed for decades to have been animated in 1926, it has been discovered that the animation of the dog speaking "Follow the Ball and join in, everybody" was done in 1929 after the Fleischers had left. *Tramp, Tramp, Tramp; The Boys Are Marching* was also re-issued with new animation added for sound.

"Follow the ball, and join in, everybody!" (author's collection).

The Weiss sound reissues of *Song Car-Tunes* and *Out of the Inkwell* were recorded by Metropolitan Studios in Ft. Lee, New Jersey, with music and synchronization supervised by Joseph S. Deutsch.

Ko-Ko's name remained in new main titles, but the names of Max and Dave Fleischer were removed. Weiss must have found some value in the older films to reissue them to exploit Fleischer's reputation without his involvement. This was repeated when Weiss acquired several of the *Alice Comedies* from Charles Mintz and re-released them through low-budget Westerns distributor, Raytone Pictures to exploit the name of Walt Disney. Judging by the quality of the soundtracks, they were weak competition. And in Disney's case, it was not the quality of the technology, but the concepts of the cartoons that were noticed most.

Paramount had two major cartoon series, *The Inkwell Imps*, produced by The Inkwell Studio, and *Krazy Kat* produced by Charles Mintz. *Krazy Kat* was extremely popular, supported by a saturation ad campaign in the trade papers. It was an act of fate that Mintz went to Columbia, clearing the way for Max as the exclusive provider of cartoons for Paramount. Had it gone the other way, Max would have been out of business because Ko-Ko was imprisoned by the bankruptcy of the Inkwell Studio, leaving Fleischer without a star character.

The hugely popular *Mutt and Jeff* series had ceased production in 1926, and the prospect of a sound series seemed a perfect choice. Paul Terry had approached creator Bud Fisher about animating *Mutt and Jeff* ten years earlier but found him too difficult to work with. So, the next likely studio would have been Fleischer's. While a Fleischer collaboration would have been very successful, Fisher's reputation continued to be a barrier. Ironically, the Van Beuren Studio would soon create a poorer imitation of "the original animated odd couple" named "Tom and Jerry," not to be confused with the famous MGM cat and mouse duo that would surface in the 1940s. When *Mutt and Jeff* was offered in sound versions, they were sloppily produced remakes of a selection of mid–20s cartoons with annoying kazoo voice substitutes, released in the two-emulsion Cinecolor process termed Kromocolor. It's a shame that *Mutt and Jeff* did not benefit from the Fleischer treatment.

> Max and Dave were well and truly in deep trouble. They had barely enough money to hire one or two animators, but not enough to rent studio space. Things were what can best be described as bleak—until, one night my father came home looking somehow strange. I suppose I'd never seen him with an expression of shock on his face. He came into the kitchen and said to my mother, 'Essie, sit down. I've got something to tell you.' She sat down looking puzzled and a little scared. My father seemed to be fighting back some inner emotion. Then quietly, he told her the news. A dear friend of his, Frank Goldman, one of the owners of Carpenter-Goldman, a film-processing laboratory based in Long Island City, had heard of the fix Max was in and had offered him space in his company's quarters for free—and for as long as he wanted it.
>
> My mother sat there dumbfounded for a moment, then slowly put her hand to her mouth and started to cry. My father stood there, his lower lip trembling, his eyes blinking as they filled with tears. She got up and embraced him. He was now laughing and crying at the same time, and so was she. It was a tableau that has never faded from my mind. I was thirteen at the time and old enough to recognize that my father's reaction was not simply one of relief but one of being tremendously touched by the friendship of Frank Goldman."[16]

Frank Goldman is an obscure pioneer who was still active at The Jam Handy Organization in the late 1960s. He developed the early color process, Synthechrome, and also patented the three-hole animation punch. Its purpose was to relieve wear and stress on cels being placed and removed from the registration pegs. The subsequent wear affected accuracy in registration, a crucial issue for animation photography. Goldman's invention also addressed the problem of the crescent-shaped reflections known as "Newton Rings" caused by cel buckling with the two-peg system.

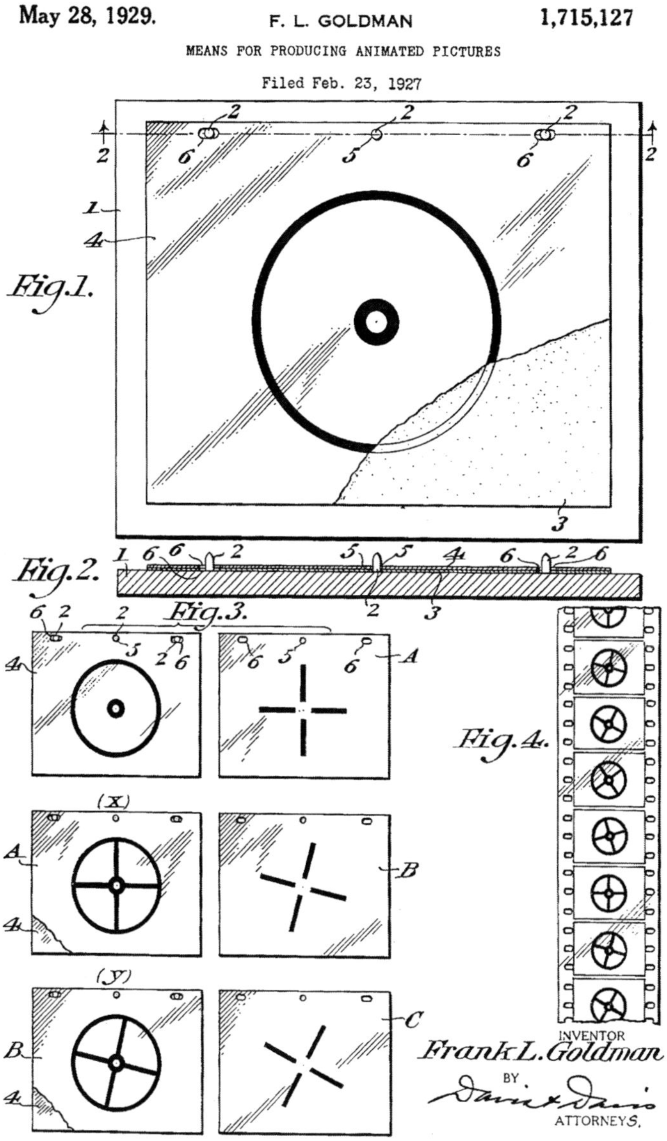

The Three-Hole Registration patent (U.S. Patent and Trademark Office).

Goldman's concept used three pegs, the center hole fitting the peg tightly to anchor the cel. The two outer pegs were rectangular, with the holes punched slightly wider than the pegs. With the platen coming down onto the cels, they would flatten evenly from the center out. This three-hole method was the foundation of the Acme and Oxberry cel punch and peg registration systems used throughout the animation industry years later. So it was through the generosity of Max's best friend, Frank Goldman, that the Fleischer enterprise was rescued once again and set back on its feet.

4

Fleischer Studios, Inc.

Max re-invented his enterprise as Fleischer Studio, Inc., in March 1929, with himself as president, and Dave as vice-president. With Weiss out of the picture, Max was able to secure a new contract with Paramount to produce a revival of the song films titled, *Screen Songs* for sound release. The new company operated with a small staff, working out of Carpenter-Goldman Laboratories at 161 Harris Avenue, Long Island starting in April 1929, remaining for the next seven months.

In addition to theatrical cartoons for Paramount, Fleischer Studios returned to the

Fleischer Studio staff 1929: Sidney Wallick (1), Edith Vernick (2), George Cannata (3), Al Eugster (4), Seymour Kneitel (5), Max Fleischer (6), Charles Schettler (7), Sid Marcus (8), Abner Kneitel (9), George Ruffle (10), head of Bill Nolan (11), Fred Lewis (12), Rudy Zamora (13), Joe Fleischer (14), William Henning (15) (author's collection).

production of industrial films. One of the most significant was *Finding His Voice*, a demonstration film written by Charles W. Barrell (credited as W.E. Erpi—a.k.a. Western Electric-Electrical Research Products, Inc.) explaining the Western Electric sound-on-film recording and reproduction process. The recording process was based on photographing the sound waves of a frequency modulation signal, which became the dominant process used by the industry until 1956.

Finding His Voice opens with the iconic *Out of the Inkwell* beginning of a hand holding a pen, drawing two parallel lines that become a strip of motion picture film. The strip of film coils itself into a roll and morphs into a character spouting a singing scale, "Mi, mi, ah, ah, ah," with the notes floating from his mouth, settling and forming a xylophone. The character named Talkie plays a section of the famous Rossini *Anvil Chorus.* Just as Talkie is basking in the spotlight, another film roll named Mutie jumps in from above and kicks the xylophone, which rolls off-screen.

Mutie has a handkerchief gag over his mouth. The only sounds he can make are muffled kazoo buzzes, while his talking appears on screen in the form of dialogue balloons as in the earliest silent animated cartoons. Talkie says, "Hey Mute, what's the idea busting up my act?" Mutie replies in dialogue balloon style, "Hello, Talkie! Sorry to bust in, but where in the world did you get your voice?" Talkie explains, "Why, Mutie I'm a new man. Haven't you heard about the wonderful things that Dr. Western did for me? He pepped up my pulse, gave me a set of vocal chords. You ought to see him. Take it from me. You'll never land a job the way you are." To this, Mutie responds again in screen type, "Lead me to him, Talkie. I've been out of work so long I'll take a chance on anything!"

With that, the two magically "whisk" themselves to the outer door of the laboratory of Dr. Western. Talkie knocks several times on the door. After no response he smashes the window, and the two whisk through the opened window panel to find Dr. Western focused on his sound equipment. Dr. Western then recognizes Talkie and asks, "What's on your mind now?" Talkie then asks the doctor to put " Mutie through the works." The film continues with references to silent and sound film technology, specifically the difference between the old silent speed of 60 feet per minute and the new sound speed of 90 feet per minute.

The various details about the recording and reproduction of sound are explained largely through animated diagrams with some early attempts at animated mouth action. The most convincing is the singing of *Just a Poem at Twilight,* which was broken down by musical phrases. Once converted, Mutie is an over-active film roll, and both Talkie and Mutie end the presentation with *Good Night Ladies.* They mime the rowing of a boat, which then appears as they continue singing, only to be swallowed by a whale, who then dives showing his tail signifying "The End."

This pioneering sound cartoon is a curiosity in that it struggles with synchronizing spoken dialogue, yet synchronizes the singing perfectly. Since the songs were musically structured, the animation of the lyrics was determined by metonymical phrasing. It would be another year until more precise animated dialogue would be realized. The voices for *Finding His Voice* were Carlyle Ellis as "Dr. Western," Walter Scanlan as "Mutie," and Billy Murray as "Talkie." Murray was an established recording artist famous for the song, *In My Merry Oldsmobile* recorded in 1909. He was the first full-time cartoon voice artist for Fleischer Studios. His nasal tenor voice is heard in the early Fleischer sound cartoons, becoming the voice of Bimbo during his various incarnations. Bruce "Cookie" Bowers was a boyhood friend of Max Fleischer and nightclub performer who did funny animal sounds and dialects. While it is unclear which characters or cartoons he performed for, he was active during the period of 1931–1932.

Industrial films were familiar territory since Max Fleischer's initial entry into animation was with industrial and educational films such as *The Electric Bell (1918)*, *How the Telephone Talks (1920)*, *That Little Big Fellow*, and *Now You're Talking (1927)*. Fleischer continued producing industrial films into the early 1930s including *Suited to a T* for the East India Tea Company, *In My Merry Oldsmobile* for General Motors, *A Jolt for General Germ* for Lysol, *Tex in 1999*, and *Step on It* for Texaco. *Film Daily* offered reviews of a few of these lost films:

Film Daily, November 16, 1930

"A Jolt for General Germ"
(Publix Commercial Ad Film)
Paramount Time, 6 mins.

This is a Max Fleischer cartoon designed to advertise Lysol, and it entertains very satisfactorily while it advertises. A story is in back of the cartoon work, the plot dealing with an army of germs descending upon a country with old Gen. Germ acting as the villain after the heroine, where upon a courier is dispatched to a drug store for a bottle of Lysol, and a sprinkling of this liquid immediately wipes out the germ army, general included. Sound effects are employed to enhance the action. The cartoon work is excellent.

Film Daily, January 18, 1931

"Step on It"
(Publix Commercial Ad Film)
Paramount Time, 7 mins.
Swell Cartoon

Except for one spoken line, "Why don't you give me the right kind of oil?" followed by a 24-sheet display of a Texaco (Texas Oil Co.) sign, this cartoon short made by the Fletcher [*sic*] studios has no earmarks of anything but a slick little piece of entertainment. It shows the Fire Department being called out on a job. The Chief's car has a hard time trying to make its way along the streets. Finally it breaks down completely, at the same time gasping out that it's the fault of the poor oil put in at the "Junkey Motor Oil Station." After the car has been fed with Texaco stuff it becomes rejuvenated and dances merrily to the scene of the fire, getting there just in time to ride up the side of the building and save the pretty heroine, then continuing up to the moon. A very diverting subject any way you look at it.

While sponsored films were lucrative, they did not equal the security of theatrical production contracts. With his track record of successful and popular *Koko the Clown* cartoons and his unique knowledge of working with sound-on-film, Max was able to exploit his relationship with Paramount. He concluded a new pact with the company to finance and distribute all Fleischer Studios productions. Desperate times dictate desperate measures, and Max desperately needed Paramount to get him back in business.[1]

The sound revolution was a crucial period in filmmaking. Paramount developed its newsreel division to compete with the Fox Movietone Newsreel, which had existed since 1927. Along with this new division, Paramount built its film processing laboratory and sound recording facility on West 43rd Street where the soundtracks for the Fleischer cartoons were recorded starting in early fall, 1928. Paul Terry had recorded sound for his *Aesop's Fables* cartoon, *Dinnertime* in August. While *Dinnertime* did not go into general release until the end of the year, *Film Daily* ran a detailed account of New York screenings revealing that it had been shown on Broadway two weeks before Disney had arrived in New York to record the soundtrack for *Steamboat Willie*.

Film Daily, August 22, 1928

First Cartoon in Sound

Playing at Mark Strand "Dinner Time," the Pathé Aesop's Film Fable which claims the distinction of being the world's first animated cartoon subject in sound, is currently being seen and heard at the Mark Strand, New York. The cartoon was made with the (RCA) Photophone process, and is being shown at the Mark Strand on Western Electric equipment.

By early September, Disney had arrived in New York looking for a company to record his soundtrack. He visited the major film recording entities, Western Electric and RCA with his planned synchronized score. He watched a demonstration of Terry's *Dinnertime* and was unimpressed with what he saw. He remarked in a telegram to Roy, "It was the rottenest *Fables* I've ever seen. Just a lot of racket and nothing else."[2]

In October Disney saw a sound cartoon he liked, *The Sidewalks of New York*, which was showing at the Rivoli on a program with a Paramount feature, Eric Von Stroheim's *The Wedding March*. It was a Fleischer song cartoon of the kind they had been making since 1924. "Most of it was just synchronized with (the) orchestra playing the tune,"[3] Walt Disney wrote to Roy Disney and Ub Iwerks. The bouncing ball on the screen would have made synchronization relatively easy, but he singled out for praise the last part of the film, where, "they had the letters and characters doing all kinds of funny things in time to the music that got lots of laughs."[4]

What had been added was metamorphosis animation of a kind that had become a Fleischer specialty, one that Disney rarely if ever used. He noted that the Fleischer cartoon "is an entirely different sort of thing than ours." "What the Fleischers were doing," he wrote, "was more along the lines of the novelties that Carl Stallings had proposed."[5]

The Sidewalks of New York was the first of the new *Screen Songs* series. What is puzzling is exactly how the Fleischer contract was re-negotiated since *Sidewalks* was in production and exhibited during the period prior of the break with Weiss. The *Film Daily* review from Sunday, October 21, 1928, references it as released by Paramount-Inkwell. The general release and copyright date came nearly four months later, on February 5, 1929.

The second entry, *Old Black Joe*, did not play on Broadway until March 10, 1929, going into national release April 5, 1929. *Film Daily* reviews from this point reference Max Fleischer, not Paramount-Inkwell, reflecting a direct relationship with Paramount. On the surface, it appears that the general releases were already in place during the time Max was establishing Fleischer Studios, which suggests no interruption in production. It also suggests that a deal with Paramount may have been in the works four months earlier. But this does not explain the worry that Max experienced following his exit from Weiss and starting over at Carpenter-Goldman. The only conclusion to be made here is based on the backlog of completed films that were held for release as theaters were being equipped for sound, which took nearly a year to a year and a half or more. This was just another accident of fate where time was on Max's side—this time.

Fleischer Studios quickly became solvent just before the infamous October 29 stock market crash. By late November 1929, the studio moved back to its home at 1600 Broadway and quickly expanded to a staff of 90.

> Max Fleischer, President of Fleischer Studios, Inc., issued a statement yesterday concerning the bankruptcy petition filed on Monday (January 12, 1930) by Out of the Inkwell Films, Inc. in which he said that he had withdrawn as Vice President and Director of the company last January (1929), and no longer has any association with it.[6]

The *Talkartoons* replaced the silent *Inkwell Imps,* deriving its name from the obvious novelty of "talking pictures." The *Talkartoons* pioneered several techniques in mastering synchronization and the intricacies of animated dialogue. The first, released on August 25, 1929, was *Noah's Lark.* This cartoon is an interesting combination of ink and painted cel animation with the inked paper method used in the *Out of the Inkwell* series. This loosely constructed cartoon is largely a demonstration of animation synchronized to music with a few attempts at animated dialogue set to musical rhythms. While the dialogue is rather loose and rubbery, more precise mouth action would be mastered a few months later.

The addition of sound brought about an added expense that called for more precise planning than in the silent days. Before sound, cartoons were loosely based on a single theme or idea, and each animator would add onto what the other animator had done until a story emerged. But now a more precise timing and conforming to set footage lengths was required.

Before sound, there was no use of exposure sheets— records showing how many exposures each drawing required, or which order the drawings were to follow. Roland "Doc" Crandall recalled that this was worked out under the camera. All of this changed due to the presence of sound, which was dominated by music. Lou Fleischer developed the studio's "Bar Sheets" based on Music Composition Sheets, with measures representing one third of a second, or eight frames. The supervising animator used these to determine animation timing, and these directions would then be transferred to the vertical exposure sheets with corresponding eight frame divisions. Interestingly, all composers for cartoons arrived at the same solution for cartoon timing based on a musical foundation, which was the standard for decades.

Hot Dog, the fourth *Talkartoon* introduced the new star of the series, Bimbo, who was inspired by Richard Fleischer's pet Belgian Griffon. *Hot Dog* is the point where Lou Fleischer became head of the new Music Department. Lou's first assignment was to transcribe the rhythm of a 78rpm record of Eddie Peabody playing *St. Louis Blues* on a banjo. Lou came in the late afternoon, and on the way home, while standing holding the strap on the swaying crowded subway, the record under his arm accidentally broke in half. Panic-stricken, he got off at the next stop and bought a replacement at a nearby record shop. Once home he proceeded to work as late as he could, fearing that the neighbors would be disturbed because his phonograph had no volume control, playing loudly. When Lou returned the next morning, he apologized to Dave that he had not been able to finish the entire transcription. But Dave was happy, saying it was enough to keep an animator busy for a week. This was the initiation of Lou Fleischer into the fold of Fleischer Studios, where he acted as the Music Producer, completing the quintet of the Fleischer Brothers team. But Lou's role went beyond the supervision of the music. He brought about technical perfection in synchronization, placing him in great demand. Lou recalled:

> My brother Joe was a general machinist and electrician, and he had installed one of the first office intercom systems. I was there a short time and all you heard all day long was, "Calling Lou Fleischer, Lou! Calling Lou Fleischer, Lou" I think I was the busiest of all of the brothers from all of the calls.[7]

The first "Bimbo" (author's collection).

Animated dialogue in early Fleischer cartoons tended to be over-exaggerated and rubbery, timed to a metronome. This resulted in an unnatural and stilted delivery. All of this was improved under Lou's guidance. He took pride in saying that he developed the smaller fluid lip movements that became a standard element in Fleischer animation.

The process of bringing post-synchronized sound to animated cartoons was an exact science. For the first Fleischer sound cartoons, Max H. Manne was hired as Musical Director due to his experience with the first major synchronized cartoon, *Dinner Time*. Manny Baer replaced Manne the following year. There was an immediate need to establish constant tempos to remain in sync with the film's inherent rhythm. Various methods were tried from ink marks to punched holes on the projected Work Print. One of the most interesting methods was the "bouncing ball" baton, commonly referred to as "The Beater." A patent was filed on January 3, 1930, by Animator George Rufle for a mechanical indicator device consisting of a white disc attached to a white strip. The beater was recessed into a channel on the left side of the animation field, visible to the full camera aperture area.

Popular entertainer Eddie Peabody (Todd Levine).

With the introduction of the optical soundtrack, early sound films were shot in a nearly square aspect ratio of 1.22:1 as opposed to the silent proportion of 1.33:1. This loss of image width was necessary to allow room for the soundtrack and was referred to as movietone aperature. All Fleischer sound cartoons were shot in this format until 1933.

The beater advanced and repeated in an auto-

Caricature of Lou Fleischer.

matic cycle due to cams connected to the opening and closing of the platen. As the animation was shot, the platen was lifted, the cel or art changed, and as the platen was lowered, the cam advanced the beater to the next position. The tempo was regulated by the use of various cams, which would advance the beater in wide increments for a fast tempo, or smaller increments for a slower tempo. The image of the mechanical beater was photographed in the space that would be occupied by the soundtrack and visible on work prints

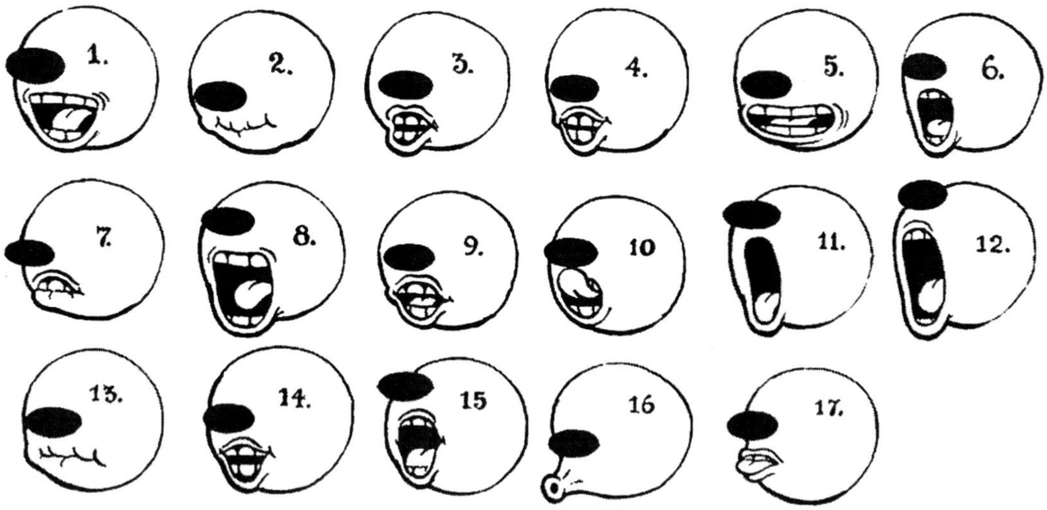

Early Mouth Chart (author's collection).

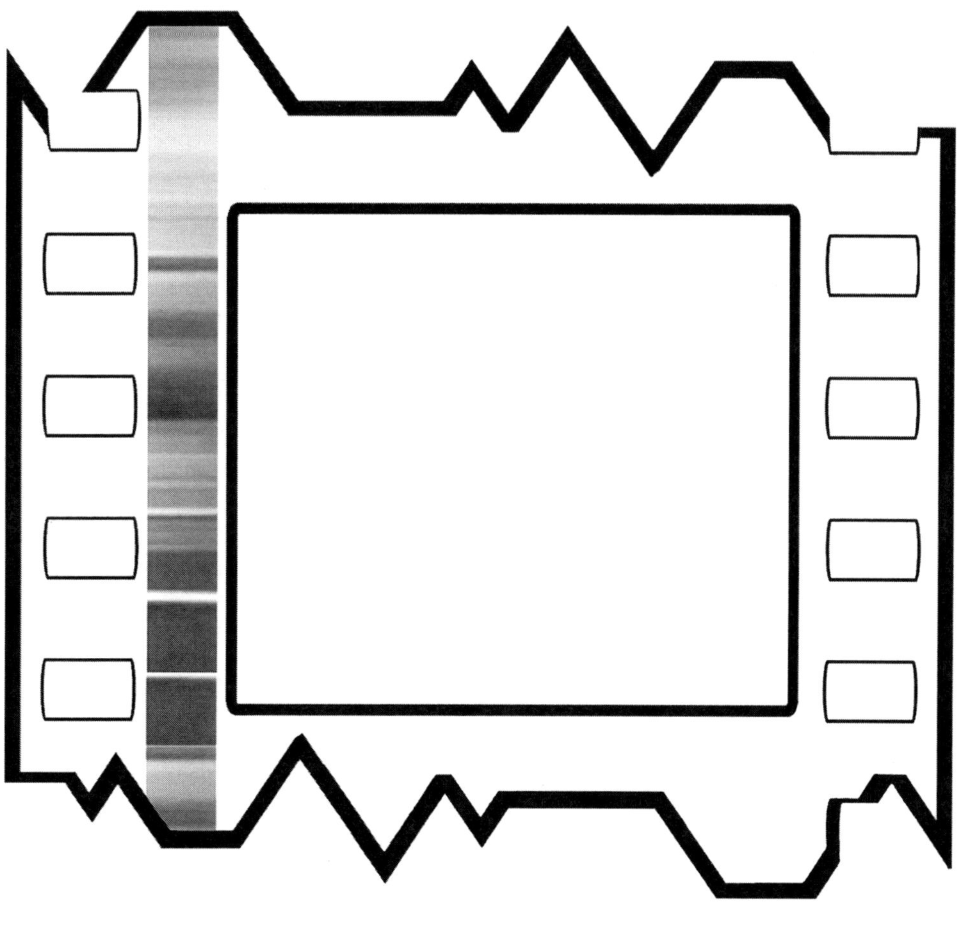

Movietone aspect ratio (author's illustration).

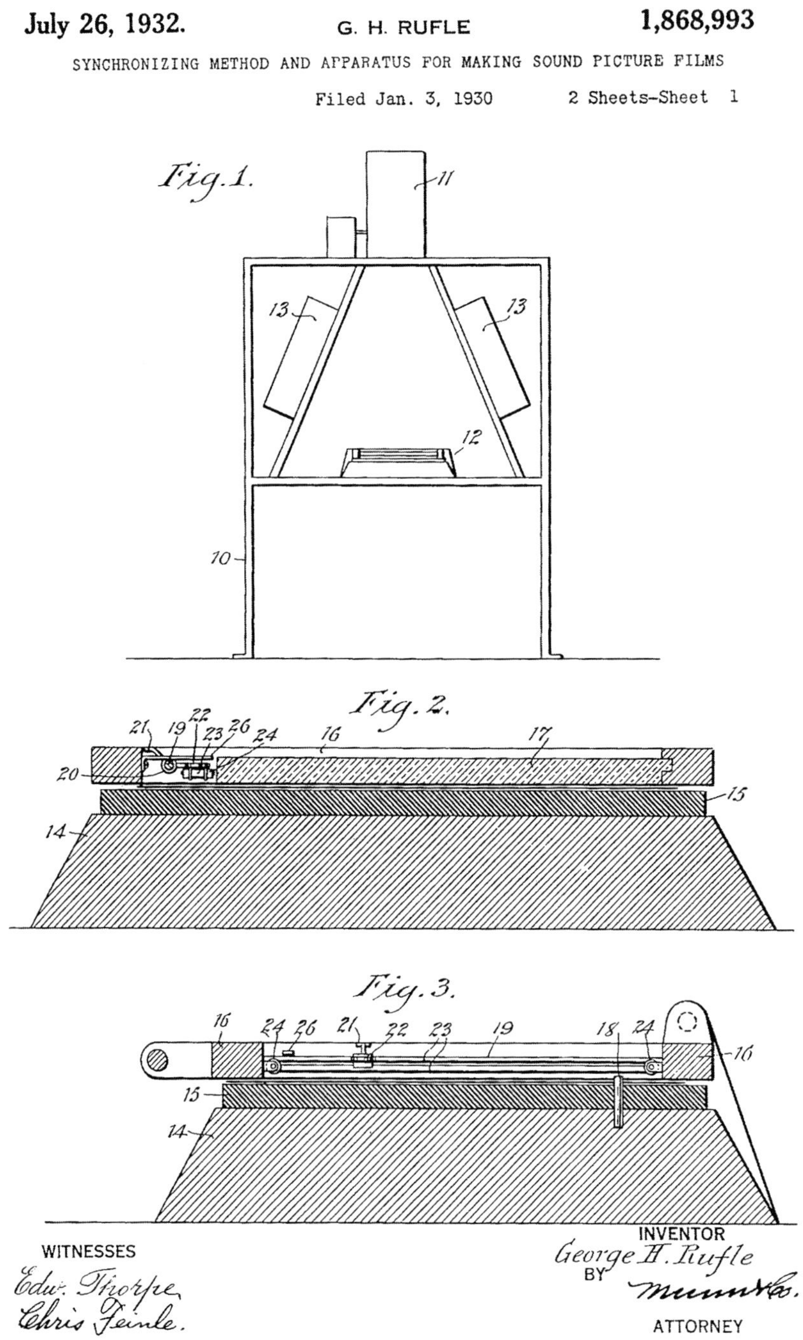

Rufle patent (U.S. Patent and Trademark Office).

projected at full aperture opening. The baton image in the soundtrack area on the negative would be masked when making Release Prints, allowing for the exposure of the soundtrack. And when projected, the soundtrack area would also be masked off, showing a nearly square picture.

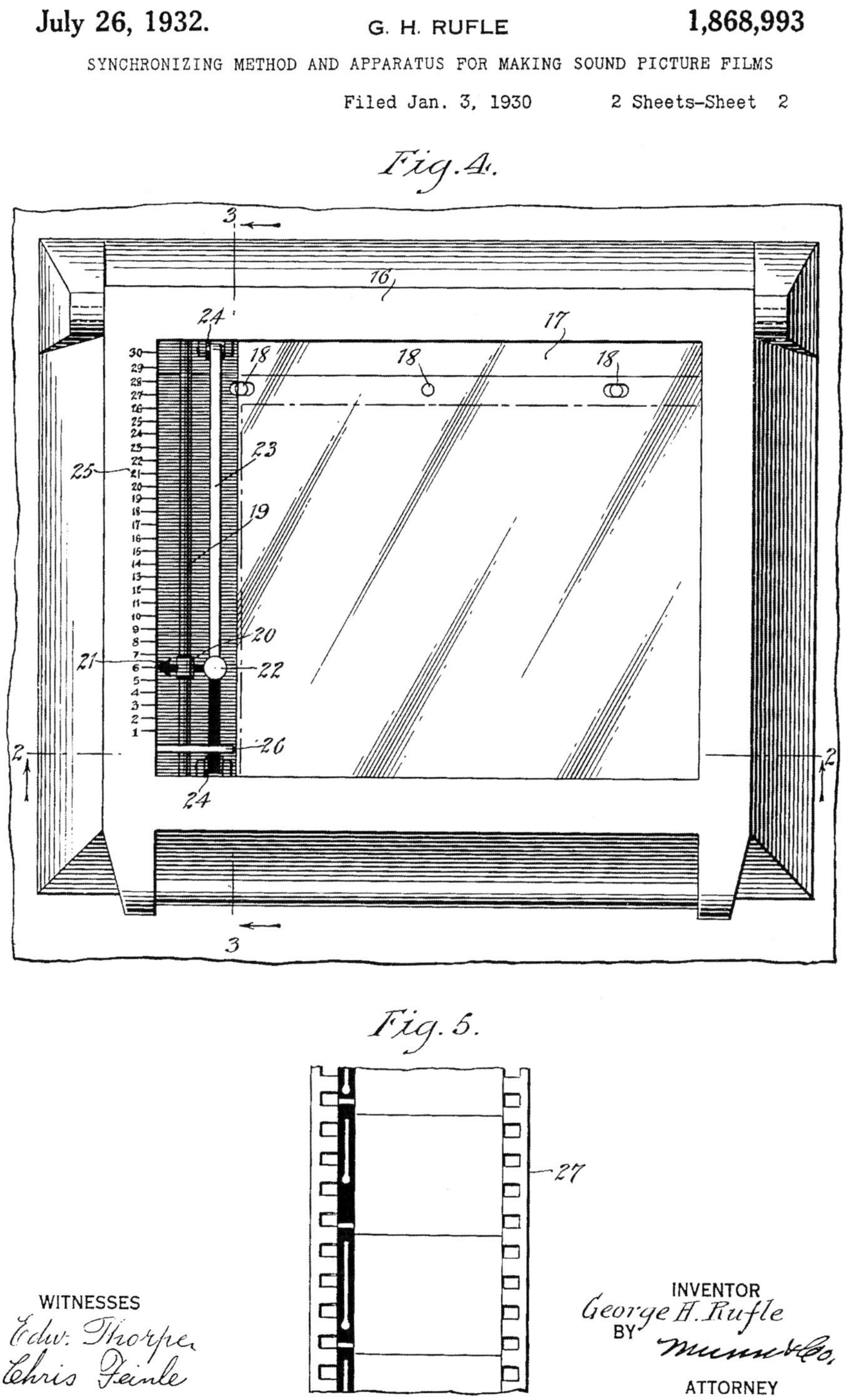

Rufle patent, page 2 (U.S. Patent and Trademark Office).

The patent drawing shows that this was a framed enclosure that could be attached to the compound table of the animation camera stand when needed. Other applications of the beater used a recessed channel cut into the table surface. While the beater worked with animation in a still or fixed field, it could not be used for trucking (zoom) shots because the baton channel would move off frame as the camera moved in close or come into frame as the camera pulled back to full position. The beater could not be used with pans since the artwork tended to be two to three feet long, which would cover the "beater channel." In these cases, the beater would have to be shot separately and printed into the track area—an awkward procedure and an added expense. Alternative methods for marking the tempo on Work Prints seemed more logical as indicated in Max's patent applications filed in 1931.

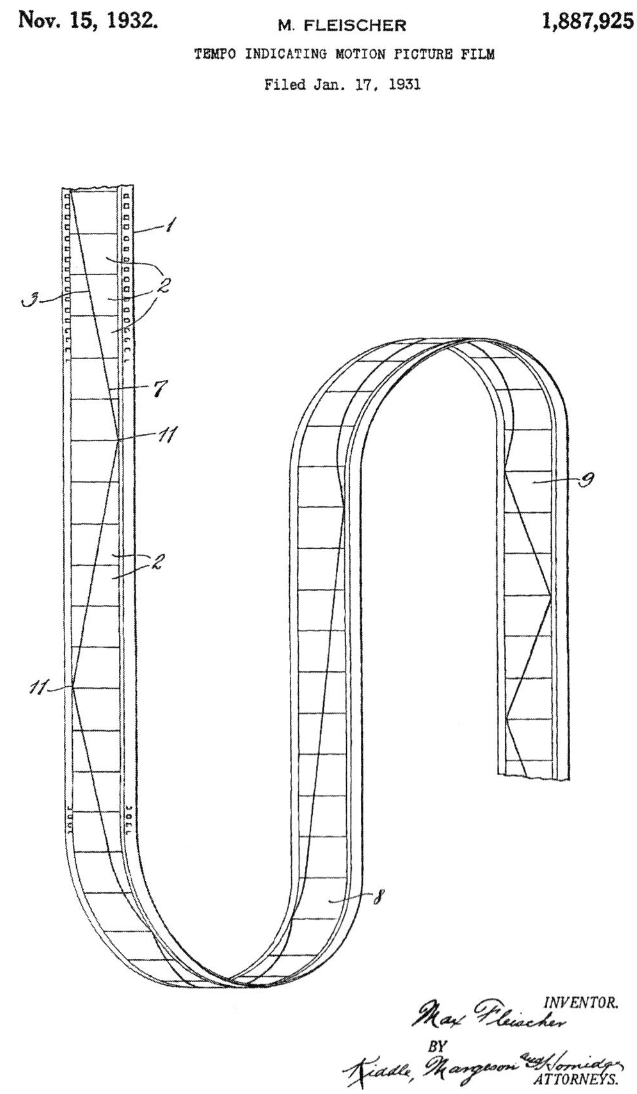

Tempo Indication patent (U.S. Patent and Trademark Office).

He wrote:

> To synchronize the sound selected to accompany the pictures, and which may consist of music, instrumental or vocal, or of dialogue, et etcetera, according to present practices, a motion picture print of the picture is projected before the performers who are to furnish the sound, so that the action may be noted, and the tempo of the sound accordingly regulated. After several views of the projected print, assuming that orchestral music is to be employed, the orchestra performs under the guidance of its conductor who watches the action of the projected pictures and times the music accordingly as best he may. This music is recorded, and the record is later printed on the soundtrack of the prints, which carry the pictures. This method requires many rehearsals, and at best, indifferent synchronization is secured.

The patent application continues:

> While these baton representations serve to improve synchronization, they involve the necessity of photographing the baton or other indication device in association with the photographing of drawings. Furthermore, none of these methods give any warning or signal of an approaching change in tempo whereby the conductor of the orchestra may be appraised of an approaching change to which he can accommodate the tempo of his music immediately.

The patent describes the process of physically marking a film print with a pencil or etching tool, making zig-zagging lines to lead the conductor to the points of tempo change. This is merely a procedure and not a device making the procedure possible. And since film editors marked work prints for various cues, this concept alone was not entirely unique to merit a patent. It was, however, the foundation for a device that followed.

While an extension of the earlier tempo-indication concept, this patent displays a specific device for marking the tempo applied to pre-recorded sound. This device marked a paper tape with a mounted grease pencil to show the frames where musical beats occurred. To economize, the length of the paper roll was one-third of the length of the motion picture film. With film speed at 90 feet per minute, this device operated at one-third of film speed, or 30 feet per minute. With 1,440 frames in one minute of film, the same number of frames were indicated on the tape. The operator listening to the playback would tap the grease pencil holder (36) in response to the musical beats, making a mark covering the number of frames for each beat as illustrated in Figures 3 and 4.

An alternative method allowed for a side to side marking as in Figure 5. Once the playback was completed, the tape roll would be wound back to the head, and a frame counter meter (Figure 2, item 29) would be used to count the frames as they corresponded to the markings on the tape. If the beat hit every six frames, the meter would show each beat frame progressively from frame one to frame 1,440 of each minute, and changes in tempo or pauses within that minute would be marked accordingly. The director would then take the readings from the tape and mark the beat locations on his exposure sheets. If a beat came every eight frames, the exposure sheet would be marked accordingly with a circled "X" in red. This gave the animators a specific reference to the rhythms they were to work to, animating walks, dance steps, runs, or any other action in a scene that needed to conform to a rhythm.

Both the beater and the zigzag marker processes pertained to post-production recording, but a method of analyzing pre-recorded dialogue and singing had to be realized. This was the concept of the Cue Meter, which was a frame counter used to determine the exact number of frames of each syllable to obtain accurate lip movement. Page 1 illustrates the soundtrack on 35mm motion picture film with an indication of recorded dialogue.

Jan. 2, 1934. M. FLEISCHER 1,941,980

MAKING OF SOUND SYNCHRONIZED MOTION PICTURES

Filed Jan. 17, 1931

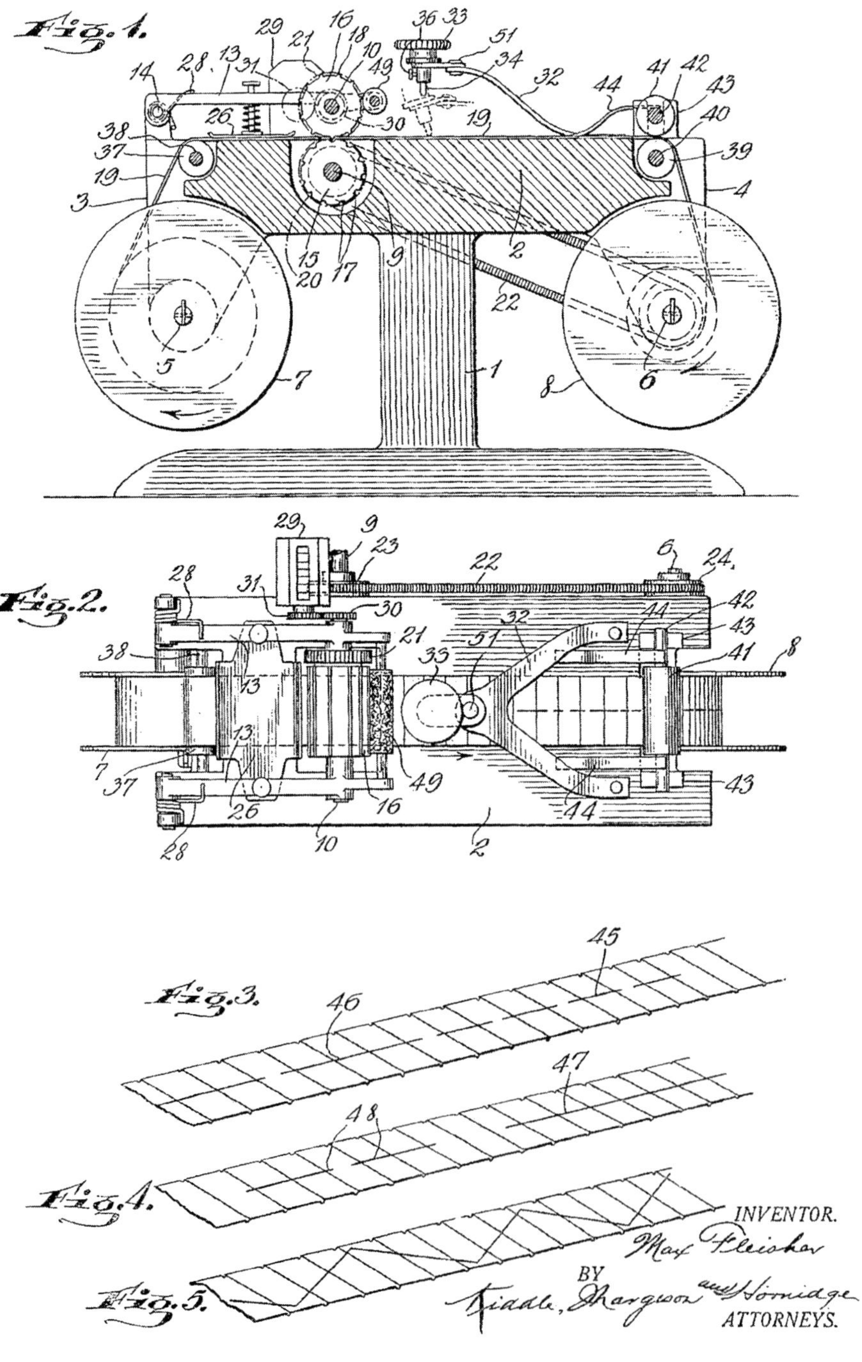

Synchronization Marker patent (U.S. Patent and Trademark Office).

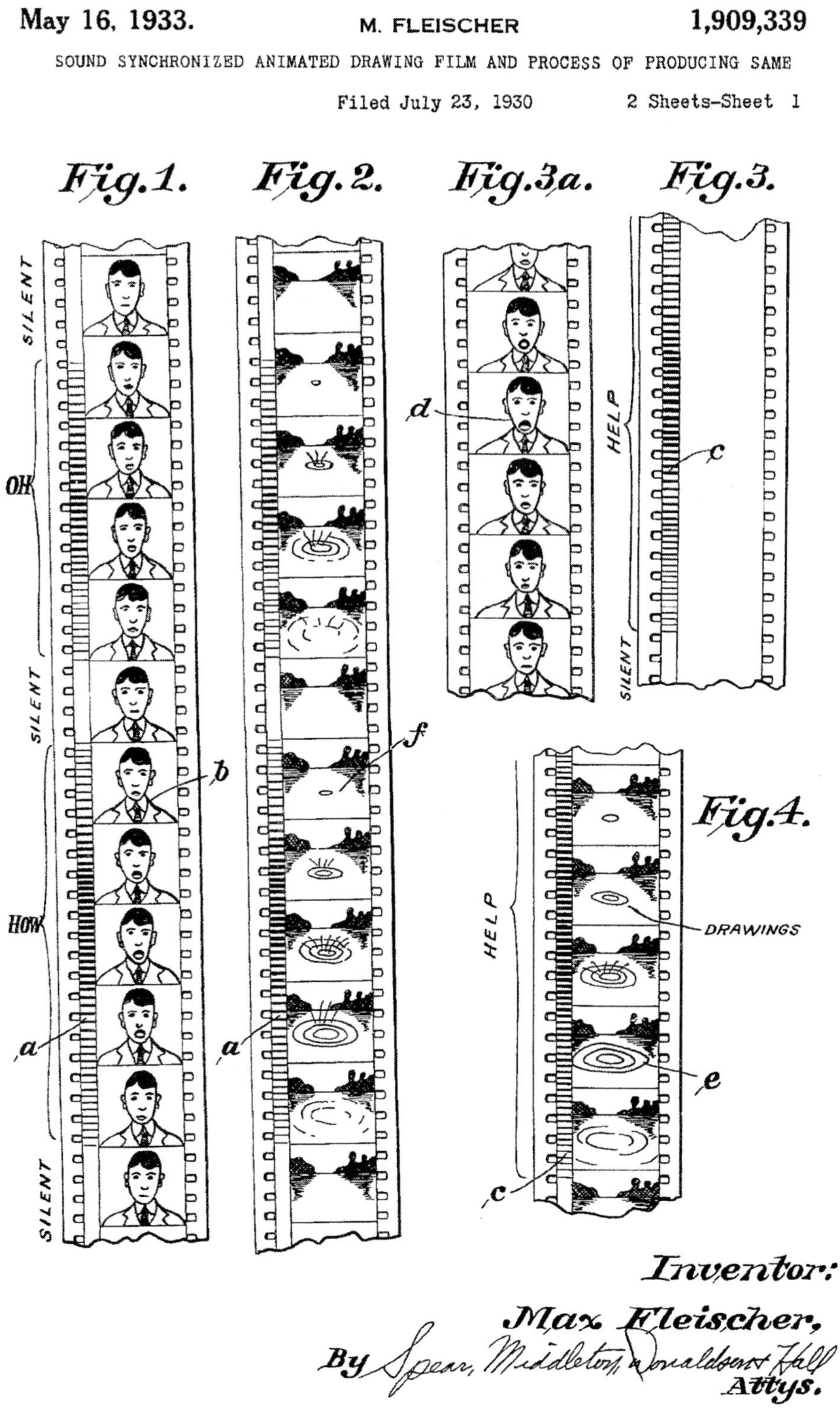

Cue Meter patent (U.S. Patent and Trademark Office).

May 16, 1933. M. FLEISCHER 1,909,339

SOUND SYNCHRONIZED ANIMATED DRAWING FILM AND PROCESS OF PRODUCING SAME

Filed July 23, 1930 2 Sheets-Sheet 2

Fig. 5.

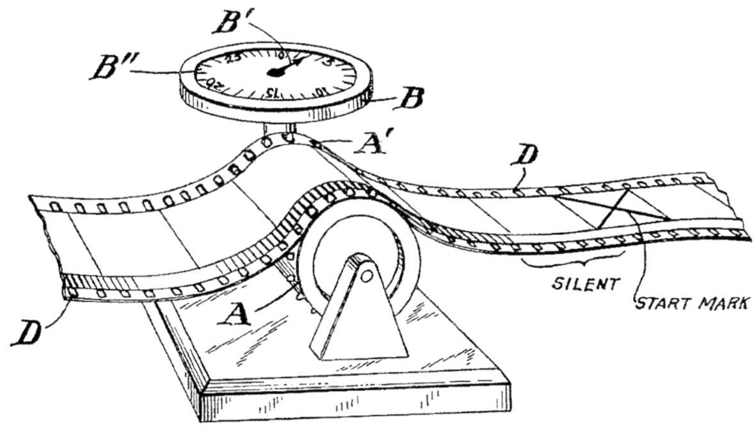

Fig. 6.

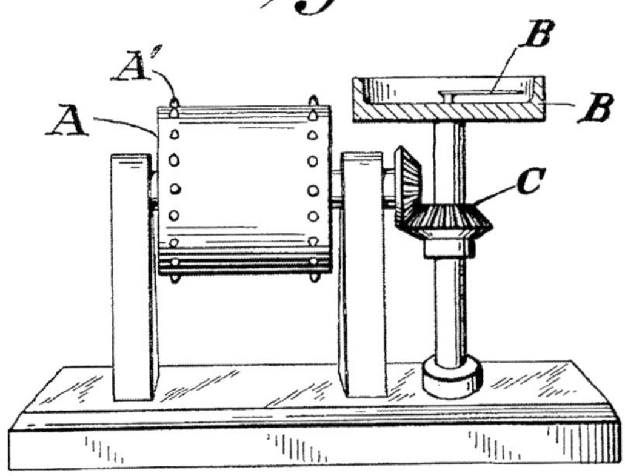

Inventor:
Max Fleischer,
By Spear, Middleton, Donaldson & Hall
Attys.

Cue Meter patent, page 2.

Page 2 illustrates the Meter for measuring the impulses of syllables for obtaining accurate analysis of soundtracks. This was a vast improvement over the earlier metronome-based approach to animating dialogue. With the cue meter, animators knew in advance how many frames were needed for each word and syllable with greater accuracy.

Dave Fleischer developed his own concepts for sound and tempo indication. His first patent filed on November 21, 1929, called for an improvement in methods of making sounds and sound effects drawn by hand. The concept attempts to duplicate the principle of the variable density photographic soundtrack with its varying horizontal bars.

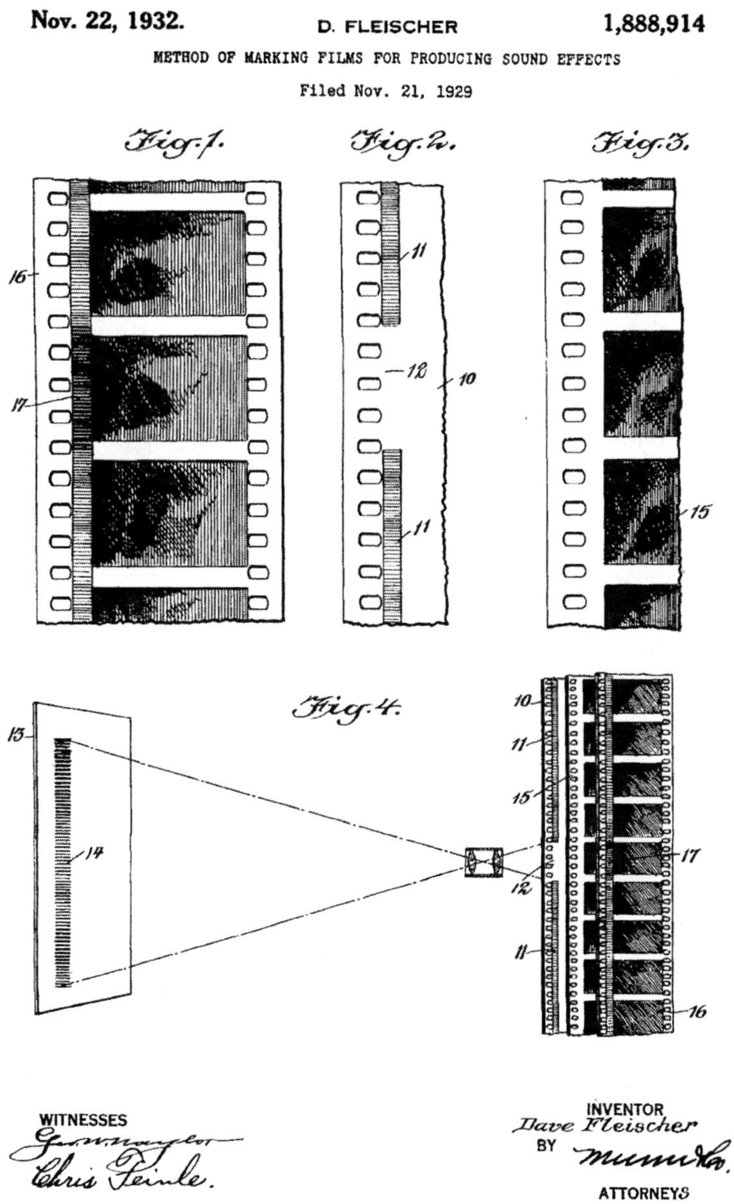

Hand-drawn Sound Effects patent (U.S. Patent and Trademark Office).

Although the application consistently refers to producing soundtracks that are "manually delineated," it does not specify whether the lines are drawn in ink, pencil or any other drawing medium. Since the principle of the photographically-recorded soundtrack is based on exposing an active sound wave, the image is soft compared to the hard edge of ink or pencil lines. Therefore, it is not clear as to exactly how such handmade tracks could duplicate mechanical/photographic soundtracks since it is virtually impossible to determine the degree of spaces and gradations or their frequency of spaces corresponding to sounds without reference. Such a process could only produce a series of oddball sound effects such as flutters, bumps, and buzzes because the hand-drawn lines are too hard-edged and opaque. Because of this, Dave's patent was limited, having no apparent practical use, and there is no indication that it was ever used in the production of the cartoons.

Dave's second patent was a tempo indicator filed simultaneously with Max's two patents. Instead of marking the work print, Dave's invention called for a series of punched holes appearing in the center of the frame decreasing from three to one. Interestingly, the majority of the description on page 1 is identical to page 1 of Max's application and serves the same purpose.

Lou Fleischer punched holes in the soundtrack area at designated frames. When run over the optical soundhead, an audible "pop" would be heard, creating what was referred to as a "click track." The punched film strip would then be spliced together, end to end forming a "loop" that would run continuously on the playback soundhead. The sound of the "click" would be fed through headphones worn by the conductor. This was another mechanical method for tempo indication. Lou Fleischer did not take out a patent since he did not invent a specific device for punching the holes. Anyone could punch film or mark it in a similar fashion to produce the same effect. As a result, the click track was discovered by several others and applied at other studios around the same time.

While these methods perfected the process, offering precision in synchronization, the ideas themselves were not exclusive to Fleischer Studios. The only patent of value was the cue meter. But there is no indication that it was licensed for use by the competition. This would have been motivated by a need to retain "secret processes" to sustain uniqueness among the competition. Capitalizing on patents is what made corporations like RCA and Western Electric contenders in the communications field. Yet because of their generalized nature, these patents were not sufficient enough to generate ancillary income for Fleischer Studios. This is the dilemma of the intellectual process.

The Fleischer Sound

One of the features of Fleischer sound cartoons of the 1930s is the live quality of the soundtracks, thanks to performances arranged like a radio broadcast with live microphone mixes feeding directly onto the recorded soundtrack. Dave Fleischer described the arrangement at the Paramount News Lab recording studio:

> We had everything in that little studio, with mikes all over the room and there was no way that we could separate them. We had to do them all together at one time, and when you start off, you just hear a lot of jumble and noise because all the mikes are hitting into each other. We had to weed them out very carefully. It took hours. If the mixers tried to do that today, they'd go crazy. If we had one mistake,

May 9, 1933. **D. FLEISCHER** **1,907,774**

TEMPO INDICATING MOTION PICTURE FILM

Filed Jan. 17, 1931

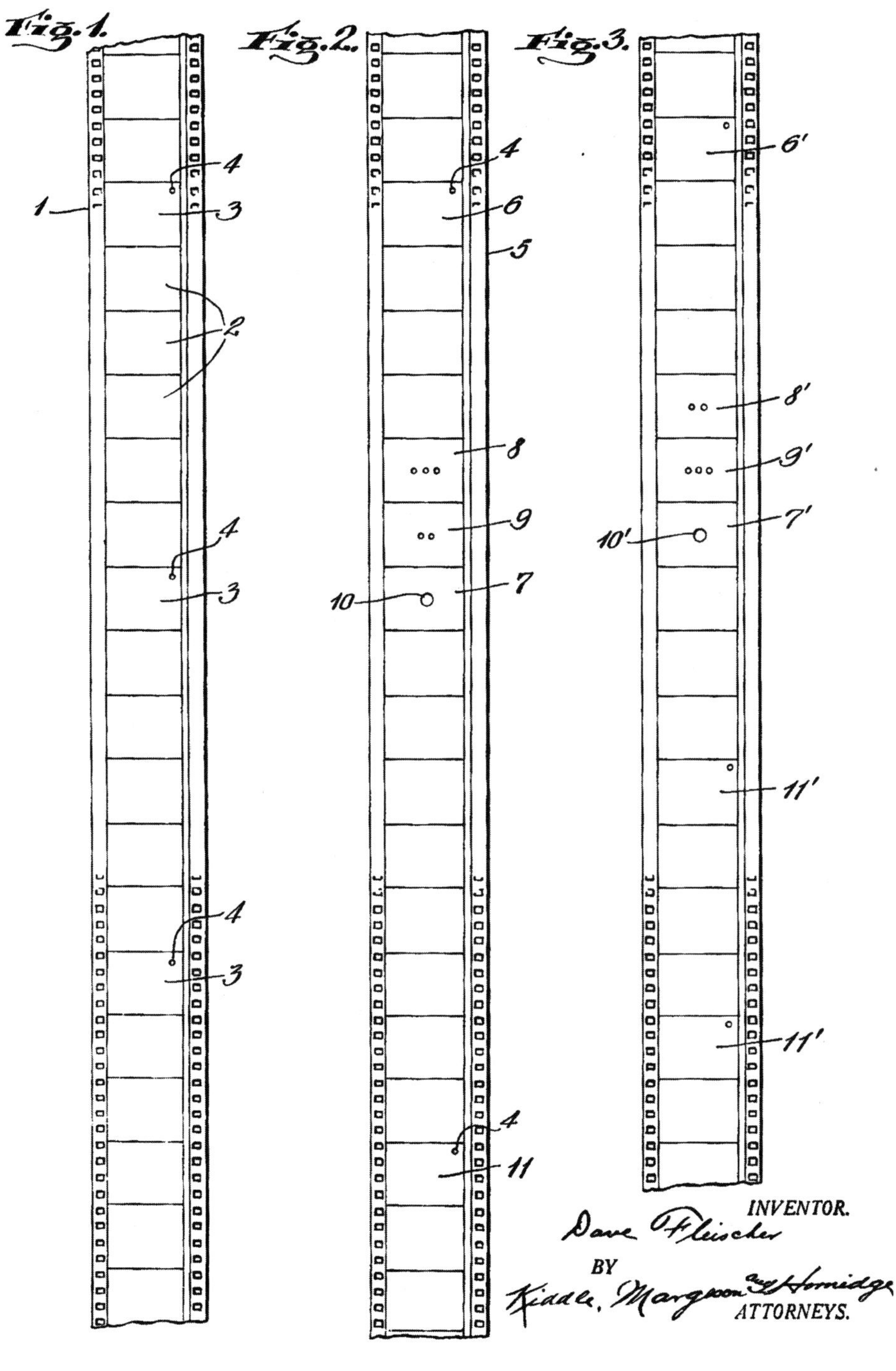

Tempo Indication patent (U.S. Patent and Trademark Office).

> we had to shoot (record) all over again. We were doing *Noah's Lark* and at the very end of the picture, with all the music going, the drummer had to finish by blowing a whistle and hitting the drum with a stick. But he was so nervous, and had so much to do that instead he hit the drum with the whistle and blew on the stick, and we had to shoot (record) that whole thing over again.[8]

As film recording techniques improved, the use of mix-downs from multiple tracks became the standard. But Fleischer Studios continued using the post-sync method until 1938, retaining that live, spontaneous quality. Dave Fleischer continued:

> The way we made sound in those days, I don't believe anybody today could do it. Today they dub a picture. They make it, then they put the music on a track, and the dialogue on a track, the narrator on another track, and the sound effects on still another track. Then they go into a mixer room, run it on nine heads and blend them all.[9]

A recording session for *Shine On, Harvest Moon* at the Paramount News Lab. (Todd Levine).

Fleischer Studios gained fiscal strength between 1930 and 1931. While 1931 has been cited as the "Depths of The Depression," it was not reflected by the prolific activity documented by *Film Daily*.

Film Daily, January 26, 1930

"Afraid to Come Home in the Dark"(Screen Song)
Paramount Time, 7 mins.
Amusing Song Cartoon

A Max Fleischer song cartoon based on the popular song of some two decades ago. Has been given the usual ingenious treatment and will provide several minutes of pleasant amusement for any class of folks.

Film Daily, September 21, 1930

"The Glow Worm" (Screen Song)
Paramount time, 5 mins.
English-German song cartoon

A novelty in song cartoons in that it is bi-lingual, opening in German and closing in English. Subject matter concerns glow worms, caterpillars, and such, cavorting in harmony with off-stage singing, with a change of characterizations for the English and German. Each version is preceded by an announcement in German telling what is about to take place. Then the words are flashed on the screen in both German and English. Rates fair and probably more suitable for the foreign country than here.

Film Daily, October 5, 1930

"Swing, You Sinners"(Talkartoon)
Paramount Time, 8 mins.
Clever Cartoon

Something out of the ordinary in cartoon subjects. With "Sing, You Sinners" for its musical background, the caricatures carry out the idea of a ghostly nightmare haunting a would-be chicken thief. The idea in its entirety, from adapted lyrics to cartoon work, is clever and ought to be a treat for audiences anywhere.

Film Daily, February 22, 1931

"Alexander's Ragtime Band" (Screen Song)
Paramount Time, 6 mins.
Swell Song Cartoon

One of the best Fleischer song cartoons to date. With the catchingly tuneful Irving Berlin song hit as its basis, a batch of comical antics is presented through a medium of an old dog of a music teacher giving lessons to a comical little pupil. Works up to a nice punch finale. A hit filler for any bill.

Film Daily, March 29, 1931

"Ace of Spades" (Talkartoon)
Paramount Time, 6 mins.
Good Cartoon

Right up to the high standard of the Fleischer cartoon product. Bombo [*sic*] playing the part of a card sharp, enacts his comicalities at a card game. Some songs are in a Negro Spiritual vein. Whole job is well handled, and the subject should click anywhere.

Film Daily, April 19, 1931

"Betty Co-Ed" (Screen Song)
Paramount One Reel

This Max Fleischer cartoon packs much entertainment. Rudy Vallee and his band play through the piece and the crooner himself appears a few moments to sing part of "Co-Ed." Verses of the song are flashed on the screen with the bouncing ball marking time. The cartoon antics of Betty and the collegiates are amusing.

Film Daily, September 27, 1931

"Little Annie Rooney"(Screen Song)
Paramount Time, 6 mins.
Neat

Among the best of the Fleischer song novelties based on popular old tunes with the audiences invited to join in the choruses. Good artwork and synchronization, along with the comedy make it a neat filler.

Film Daily, November 8, 1931

"Jack and the Beanstalk" (Talkartoon)
Paramount Time, 6 mins.
Fair Cartoon

Nothing specially out of the ordinary in this animated. The title just about explains what it's about, the hero of the action utilizing the beanstalk to ascend up into the clouds and rescue the girl from the menacing clutches of the giant. Art work and score are okay.

Film Daily, December 6, 1931

"Kitty from Kansas City" (Screen Song) **Paramount** 8 mins.
Novelty Cartoon

A Max Fleischer cartoon with Rudy Vallee during a song as part of the animated plot. It is a clever combination of the cartoon characters, with Rudy worked into the developments as he waits for the animated heroine at the railroad station. His song is all about the dumb sweetie from Kansas City, and Rudy appears disguised as an old timer with a mustache and brown derby.

The large profits from the Screen Songs now made Fleischer Studios solvent to the tune of $14,000 per quarter. Max was most concerned with staying in business and keeping his staff employed, seeing Paramount as his safety net. Emanuel Cohen approached Max with an investment proposition based on the newfound successes of Fleischer Studios. Max recalled in a letter to his attorney, Stan Handman:

> I attended a Paramount convention in California about 1932 or 1933. At that time, Emanuel Cohen was Vice-President of Paramount. He called me aside in one of the meeting rooms at the convention hotel (The Ambassador, I believe) and told me that he and the high-ups in Paramount were very much surprised at the way the *Screen Songs* were selling. He said they had no idea they would be such a tremendous success.

The letter goes on:

> This situation, Cohen said, reflected upon him because my contract would mean a great deal of money to me (Fleischer Studios), but would mean very little to Paramount. In Cohen's words, "They're all shouting about the Screen Songs, and you, Max will be the only one to benefit." Then he said, "Max, you can say 'NO' to my request, if you like, to revise our contract in order that Paramount get a fairer share of the deal." Naturally, I said that I did not like to feel we had a one-sided contract.[10]

According to an announcement in *Film Daily*, the convention was in 1931.

Film Daily, April 19, 1931

Paramount Convention Sidelights

A highlight of an evening session was the showing of a Max Fleischer cartoon, "Paramount on Parade to Zukor's Farm," which wowed the conventioneers. It does some powerful kidding with various Paramount execs depicted.

"Paramount on Parade to Zukor's Farm," is considered another lost Fleischer cartoon since no known print or negative is known to exist. Max continued:

> Shortly after Vice-President Emanuel Cohen was dismissed from Paramount, Cohen invited me to his home and made me the following offer. He intended going into business for himself and asked me to refuse renewal of my contract with Paramount and go with him. I refused saying that I believed we would eventually make money, even thought it seemed difficult at the time. Mr. Cohen offered to deposit a half million dollars in any bank of my choice, the money to be used for production. He wanted no stock. All he wanted was distribution of the product. He said he wanted no red tape to hinder me. Accordingly, the entire deposit would be subject to withdrawal for production on my signature alone. I did wonder why a product that apparently lost money for Paramount seemed to be so attractive to Emanuel Cohen. I turned Cohen's proposal down with, "Sorry Mannie, but my lot is cast with Paramount. I still believe I'll come out all right." Mannie said, "If you don't know how Paramount is doing you, you'll find out when it's too late."[11]

Cohen was certainly in the position to know the value of the Fleischer cartoons. And it is ironic that when Max was made to realize the full power of his Paramount contract that he did not exercise that power when it came time to renew. He fell victim to his own philosophy: "Strive for as much power and authority as you can possibly get, and the more you get, the less you use." His sense of fairness interfered with his business sense. Accordingly he renegotiated giving Paramount more of a share, ignoring Cohen's offer and warnings. And what seems like a missed opportunity should be balanced with Max surviving two bad experiences with outside partners. Now that the Depression was on, the risk seemed too great to break away from what seemed to be the "cash cow."

The surface appearance of a large theatrical organization such as Paramount would have appeared financially solid. But in 1930, the company faced a deficit of $15 million. The original Paramount-Famous Lasky Corporation filed for bankruptcy and reorganized as Paramount-Publix, then cashed in the full value of its 2,000 theaters, reorganizing as Paramount Productions in 1933, reorganized again as Paramount Pictures, incorporated in 1936, and finally as Paramount Pictures Corporation. And during all of the reorganizations, Max remained loyal, continuing to have faith in Paramount.

While the *Screen Song* series started out employing standard songs such as *Yankee Doodle Boy*, *My Pony Boy*, and *Yes! We Have No Bananas*, the series soon integrated live action appearances of celebrities of Broadway, radio, and recordings. Many of these *Screen Songs* were planned as promotions for live theatrical appearances. This was part of a new marketing plan launched by Paramount for the 1930–1931 season. A *Film Daily* publicity statement released November 29, 1931, mentioned a number of innovative concepts using big names and novelties in their short subject package, including the introduction of well-known personalities as a master of ceremonies including the original Mr. Shean of "Gallagher and Shean" fame, Cab Calloway of the Cotton Club, and Rudy Vallee and this Connecticut Yankees.

Rudy Vallee was the first on-screen celebrity, appearing in *Betty Co-Ed* (1931), and returned in *Kitty from Kansas City* (1931). He also appeared in a cameo in *Rudy Valle Melodies* (1932). Other celebrities included Arthur Tracy in *Russian Lullaby* (1931) and *Romantic Melodies* (1932), Ethel Merman in *Let Me Call You Sweetheart* (1932), *You Try Somebody Else* (1932), *Time on My Hands* (1932), and *Song Shopping* (1933). The Mills Brothers appeared in three *Screen Songs*: *I Ain't Got Nobody* (1932), *Dinah* (1933), and *When Yuba Plays the Rumba on the Tuba* (1933). Lillian Roth appeared in *Down Among the Sugar Cane* (1932) and *Ain't She Sweet* (1933).

Rose Marie, famous from television's *Dick Van Dyke Show*, was an established child singer in the late 1920s and made a number of early Vitaphone shorts for Warner Brothers billed as "Baby Rose Marie." She appeared in the *Screen Song*, *Sing Babies, Sing* (1933). Radio comedians, Stoopnagle and Bud, appeared in the zany *Stoopnocracy* that also featured 12-year-old Harold Nicholas of the famous Nicholas Brothers Dance Team as a baby Cab Calloway.

By 1935, the *Screen Songs* series capitalized on the new Swing era and featured appearances by a number of the big band orchestras. By this time the series had essentially been given exclusively to "Doc" Crandall as Chief Animator, and the series settled into newsreel parodies with blackout gags. This series of films was even more commercially oriented with the films being booked a week in advance of the appearances of each orchestra. From 1935 to 1938, the *Screen Songs* featured the orchestras of Abe Lyman, Richard Huber, Hal Kemp, Vincent Lopez, Joe Reichman, Dick Stable, Nat Brandywine, Hal King, Shep Fields, Gus Arnheim, Jay Freeman, Jerry Baline, Bert Block, Frank Dailey, and Jimmy Dorsey. Although a popular attraction, the *Screen Songs* series was retired after nine years.

The Story Department

Just as sound demanded precise control over film footage, it also called for more formal story structure with the formation of The Story Department under Animator Ted Sears,

***Above:* (*left to right*) Tom Johnson, Jack Ward, Joe Stultz, and two unknowns (Todd Levine). *Right:* Dave Fleischer (La Cinémathèque Québecoise).**

who left to work for Walt Disney in 1931. He was replaced by Bill Turner, who was promoted from the Camera Department and teamed with Jack Ward and Joe Stultz. Many of the head animators contributed to the development of stories, which were "written" in the form of a collection of story sketches pinned up on a corkboard for presentation. This practice commonly referred to as "Storyboarding" went into common practice throughout the industry by this time, most famously at the Disney studio.

Recent books on Disney show the use of story sketches drawn on typewritten scenarios or multiple panels on a single sheet of paper. This might suggest that the formal Storyboard process of pinning up story sketches for rearranging and editing may not have been put into practice by Disney until the arrival of Sears. So it is quite likely that the actual concept of the formal push pin assembled storyboard originated with Fleischer Studios. Max was active in the story concepts and would review the storyboards on Friday evenings in an open forum with the entire studio. And it was in the Story Department that Ruth Fleischer met her future husband, Seymour Kneitel.

> Dave spent his whole day working in the Story Department and going from one animator to the next, feeding them gags. Dave looked like a large teddy bear—rotund rather than fat—with an endearing habit of holding his half-clenched hands against his chest like a puppy begging for a biscuit. I never saw a man who enjoyed himself more. All day he walked around with a pleased smile on his face, almost euphoric.[12]

5

The Queen of the Animated Screen

Betty Boop

Just as the coordination of animation and sound was evolving, so was the character, Bimbo. His design originated in some cartoons as a reincarnation of Fitz, or some form of him with the circular head and black bulb nose. He began as a white dog character with a big black clown's nose and floppy ears. In others, he was a round-headed black dog with short ears and a small body. Some versions of Bimbo looked like Toby the Pup, a character created by Dick Huemer, who left Fleischer Studios to work for Charles Mintz in Los Angeles.

Left: **Original animation drawing from Betty Boop's May Party (Todd Levine).** ***Above, left to right:*** **Jack Carr, Sid Marcus and Dick Huemer with their character, Toby the Pup, 1930 (Dr. Richard Huemer).**

Bimbo as he appeared in *Dizzy Dishes* (author's collection).

In other cartoons he was a tall black dog with a small derby, but still sporting the large black clown's nose. It was this later version of Bimbo that was used in the landmark cartoon *Dizzy Dishes*, which introduced a "Rubenesque" poodle character modeled after the popular singer, Helen Kane. The true origin of the Kane caricature is unknown, but a cover recording was made before the cartoon was put into production since the soundtrack obviously was pre-recorded for the breakdown of the lyrics and syllables. For the voice, Margie Hines (1909–2011) was hired to record a cover of Helen Kane's recording of *Lovin'*. The assignment of designing the character was given to veteran animator, "Grim" Natwick, whose talent for drawing women was admired within the industry.

Grim Natwick (1890–1990)

Myron "Grim" Natwick was born in Wisconsin Rapids, Wisconsin on August 16, 1890, and studied at the Art Institute of Chicago, the very school that was recommended to Winsor McCay. Natwick studied art in Vienna for three years and gained skill in drawing the female figure, beginning his commercial art career as a sheet music illustrator. In 1916, he went to work for the Hearst International Studio as an animator on the *Happy Hooligan*, *Bringing Up Father*, and *Judge Rummy* series. He replaced Dick Huemer at Fleischer Studios when he left to work for Charles Mintz in 1930.

According to Natwick, Dave Fleischer gave him a Helen Kane sheet music cover as a facial model with directions to create a female dog character to work with Bimbo. His first concept was a literal poodle on all four legs with a pelvic-shaped human head combined with long floppy ears and a black button nose. It was not appreciated by Dave, who directed him to add a female human body in no uncertain terms. Natwick's revision placed the head onto the body of a rather stout female human figure. This was the beginning of what was to develop as Fleischer Studios' biggest star, Betty Boop.

Above: **Betty concept sketches by Grim Natwick.** ***Below:*** **Natwick's formal prototype for "Betty" (both photographs from Animation Resources.org).**

Helen Kane (Todd Levine).

Rough character concepts for Barnacle Bill by Grim Natwick (Todd Levine).

Helen Kane (1904–1966)

Helen Kane was born Helen Clare Schroeder in 1904, the youngest child of Louis Schroeder and Ellen Dixon-Schroeder. Miss Kane grew up in the Bronx attending St. Anselm's Parochial School where she began performing in school plays. By age 15, she was on the professional stage where she toured the Orpheum Theater circuit, performing with the Marx Brothers in *On the Balcony*. In November 1924, Helen Schroeder married department store buyer Joseph Kane and continued to use her married name professionally for the rest of her career.

Miss Kane's biggest career break came in 1927 in the musical, *A Night in Spain*. It was at the Paramount Theater that her career took off when she sang *That's My Weakness Now* with her additions of scat lyrics, "boop-boopy-doop." She was then cast in Oscar Hammerstein's *Good Boy*, where she introduced her signature song, *I Wanna Be Loved by You*, in 1928.

Helen Kane resonated with the "flapper culture," and was signed to a Victor recording contract. Her popularity was so great that she inspired many imitation contests, some of which led to cover versions of songs by rival record companies out to exploit the novelty of Miss Kane's style of singing. Columbia Records released two discs of a Helen Kane impersonator credited as "Anonymous." Two of the songs were *I'm Fallin'* and *I'd Do Anything for You*. Record historians have identified the mystery girl as Kathryn (Kate) Wright.

Paramount signed Miss Kane to make a series of musical films beginning in mid–1929 that included *Nothing but the Truth, Sweeties, Pointed Keels, Paramount on Parade, Dangerous Nan McGrew*, and *Heads Up*. Her last film appearance was in the musical short, *A Lesson in Love* (1931). While it was thought that her representation of the 20s flapper was finished with Depression Era audiences, the integration of her personality in animated cartoons proved to be a renaissance that blossomed without her. Part of this explanation might be found in the medium itself.

The cartoon world of animation, especially as practiced by the Fleischer Studio was capable of enhancing a personality suggested by Helen Kane, and going beyond that personality. While Miss Kane's song and film material had a saucy tone to it, animation was capable of going further with visual symbolism, hyperbole, and anthropomorphism—a quality not possible in live action. These elements combined with the identifiable caricature were the source of the humor and popularity of the cartoons. But the most logical action on Paramount's part was clearly economical. Considering that Miss Kane was reportedly paid $100,000 per picture, the economics of a cartoon incarnation at a cost of $5,000 was most apparent-especially when Paramount faced the first of a series of bankruptcies starting in 1930. As a means of business survival, Paramount dropped a number of its musical stars, and Helen Kane was one of them. So as Helen Kane's star fell, Betty Boop's was on the rise.

While the cabaret singer in *Dizzy Dishes* was intended as an incidental character, she clicked with audiences immediately, and Paramount urged the Fleischers to use her again, continuing her development. The character informally referred to as "Betty" made her second appearance in *Barnacle Bill*, where she was named "Jenny Lee." What is most notable is the review date by *Film Daily*, which precedes the release date of August 9 for *Dizzy Dishes* by six days.

Film Daily, August 3, 1930

"Barnacle Bill"

Max Fleischer **Time, 12 mins.**

Good Cartoon

One of those silly but funny animal animateds, with Barnacle Bill, the tough sailor, calling on his girl and making violent love to her. All the neighborhood tries to horn in, and meanwhile the musical accompaniments and funny cartoon effects make this one extremely laughable. Winds up with the girl's old man coming back and bouncing Bill out on his ear. It will please the grown-ups as well as the kids, for it is very cleverly handled.

This is another indication that films opened in New York ahead of their general release or copyright dates. *Barnacle Bill* was officially released on August 31, 28 days later and would back-date the New York screening of *Dizzy Dishes* to early July 1930. The space of one month gave the studio time to respond with another vehicle for Betty after the enthusiastic response to Betty's first appearance. Margie Hines was called in again to record the voice and singing. For some unknown reason Miss Hines was not called back for the next cartoons and recorded for rival studio Van Beuren during the period 1930 to 1931, using the same Helen Kane voice. Hines returned nearly a year later starting with *The Herring Murder Case.*

Paramount executives continued to urge Fleischer Studios to develop Betty with the Helen Kane personality. Grim Natwick gave Betty further definition in his designs for *Mysterious Mose* and *The Bum Bandit.* While the look was evolving, the voice in both cartoons for some reason was not the Helen Kane impersonation. Radio personality Harriet Lee has been identified as the tough, Nan McGrew in *The Bum Bandit.* And while the voice in *Mysterious Mose* is rumored be that of Ann Rothschild, this cannot be confirmed, leaving it a mystery. The new voice did not enhance Betty in spite of her makeover. While the review of *The Bum Bandit* criticizes it for too much dialogue, it may not have been a matter of quantity, but "quality."

Concept Sketch for *The Bum Bandit* (Todd Levine).

Film Daily, May 10, 1931

"The Bum Bandit" (Talkartoon)

Paramount, Time, 6 mins.

Okay

Quite a bit of talk in this animated cartoon short subject showing Bimbo pulling off a train robbery only to discovery that his wife, Dangerous Nan McGrew is one of the passengers. A conflict follows, and she comes out victor. The idea, art work and synchronization are excellent. However, inclusion of considerable dialogue, with a corresponding decrease in action, detracts somewhat from the effectiveness of this type of short.

Harriet Lee (Fleischer Studios).

Mae Questel (Todd Levine).

Whether the return to the Helen Kane impersonation came directly from Paramount or not, it was clear that the voice had to be recast. And after Max Fleischer saw the 23-year-old Mae Questel in a Helen Kane imitation contest, she was soon put before the microphone, beginning with *Bimbo's Silly Scandals* (1931).

Mae Questel (1908–2011)

Mae Questel was born September 13, 1908, in New York City and raised in the Bronx. Her parents were Simon Kwestel and Frieda Glauberman. At an early age, Mae displayed a talent as a mimic and dialect comic and performed for amateur shows and charitable functions. While she attended dramatic school for a brief period, her Orthodox Jewish parents urged her to pursue a career in teaching. But her love of performance drew her to the stage. She was working in vaudeville by age 17, beginning at the RKO Fordham Theater after winning a talent contest for her impersonation of Helen Kane. By 1930 she was playing the famous Palace Theater on Broadway, billed as a "Personality Singer of Personality Songs," where she imitated celebrities such as Fanny Brice, Marlene Dietrich, Ruth Etting, and Maurice Chevalier. And it was seeing this act that motivated Max Fleischer to hire her.

Miss Questel proved to be a versatile performer and became the third voice artist for Fleischer Studios. But she was not used again for several months. She continued to appear in several Paramount short subjects, on radio and stage. Miss Questel returned to the role of Betty a year later for the classic, *Minnie the Moocher* (1932), and continued to record for the last *Talkartoons*, becoming the primary voice of Betty Boop due to her talents for improvisation and ad-libs.

First Betty Boop model sheet (author's collection).

Bonnie Poe (1912–1993)

Bonnie Poe was the third Helen Kane imitator and was heard largely in the cartoons made in 1933 and 1934. In addition to the voice of Betty Boop, she was the original "oafish" voice of Olive Oyl in the first eight *Popeye* cartoons until Mae Questel assumed the role for the balance of the series until 1938. Miss Poe did voices for children and incidental characters, including the Mae West imitation in the Popeye cartoon, *Never Kick a Woman*. She remained active until 1938, when Fleischer Studios moved to Miami, and she seems to have left the business from that point.

Within a year, Betty made the transition from an incidental human-canine breed to a totally human female character. While much credit has been given to Grim Natwick for her creation, her transformation into the cute cartoon girl was due to the work of Berny Wolf, Seymour Kneitel, "Doc" Crandall, Willard Bowsky, and James "Shamus" Culhane who continued working with her after Natwick left in early February 1931 to direct for Ub Iwerks on the west coast. Culhane recalled:

> With Grim Natwick's talent for animation and his sound knowledge of the female figure, Betty Boop became an alluring little sexpot. Al Eugster, Berny Wolf, and I were able to make reasonable facsimiles of his conception, but the other animators were not up to the problems of moving her around freely. While the four of us could draw profiles, the rest of the crew stuck grimly to full faces, or at best, three-

Above: **Second Betty Boop model sheet (author's collection).** ***Below:*** **"Ugly Betty" (Animation Resources).**

quarter views. Very often she would dance and sing with her head in one position, looking very stiff-necked. Foreshortened arms and legs were avoided as well because of a lack of drawing ability.[1]

The canine hybrid was an awkward design from the start with a black nose and floppy ears on a human head. During her next appearances, the black nose was change to a human button nose. In *The Bum Bandit*, Betty starts out with the human nose and ends up with the black dog's nose for the last time. The droopy ears continued being an animation design problem for what was essentially a cartoon human female. Betty finally became the all-girl character we know in *Mask-A-Raid* where the dog ears changed to her signature hoop earrings. Earlier publicity art showing the dog ears was altered with concentric curves to look like earrings, even though the earrings were drawn as circles on all subsequent model sheets. The high wire walking scenes in *Boop-Oop-A-Doop* reveal a last minute alteration of the dog ears, an indication that this cartoon was begun before the model change.

Within a year, Betty Boop had risen from being a featured incidental character to the star of the *Talkartoons*, meriting her own series starting mid–1932. The growing popularity of Betty Boop clearly made her "The Queen of the Animated Screen" and she was becoming the most important property of Fleischer Studios. Interestingly, Betty continued to evolve, appearing older with each year. Between 1931 and 1932 she appears to be age 16. In some cartoons, such as *The Dancing Fool* and *A Hunting We Will Go*, a smaller and younger Betty is seen based on the animators who drew her.

The Jazz Baby

Betty's Jazz Baby image took audiences back to the carefree days of the flapper, and Depression audiences instantly took her to their hearts. This persona was enhanced by Lou Fleischer's interest in jazz. He frequented The Cotton Club in Harlem and envisioned teaming Betty with some of the major performers of the day. The first was *Minnie the Moocher*, her first of three cartoons made with the talents of Cab Calloway. Betty teamed with other jazz greats including Louis Armstrong in *I'll Be Glad When You're Dead You Rascal You* (1932), and Don Redman in *I Heard* (1933).

Publicity still of Max Fleischer and his star (author's collection).

Betty not only attracted the public's attention but also that of The National Legion of Decency. The Motion Picture Association of America enforced specific restrictions on films starting in 1933. Just as issues of language and implied sexual content were targeted in live action films, Betty's cartoons came under particular scrutiny. Her appearance and actions were viewed as obscene. Her neckline was too low, her dress too short, the garter on her leg and even her walk were too suggestive and inciting of sexual arousal. But to the public, Betty Boop was an ersatz sex symbol, and Max clearly had a big star on his hands.

Political satire was featured in *Betty Boop's Ups and Downs* (1932), which comments on the Great Depression. Betty is forced to leave her home due to foreclosure. Bimbo comes by with a horse and wagon to move her few belongings. As we pull back, we see the entire neighborhood is for sale. We continue further and we see a For Sale sign on the continental United States and finally, the Earth.

All of the planets gather around while the Moon acts as auctioneer. The opening bid of "50" comes from Mars. The next bid of "40" comes from Venus. Finally, Saturn in the image of a derby-wearing Hassidic Jew bids, "20" and wins. He rubs his hands and says, "I gott 'em! I gott deh whole Woyelt, I got!" As he reaches beneath his beard for the moneybag, he mutters under his breath, "Hear, hear you Gunnuf, you." He pulls up the For Sale sign attached to a rope connected to "The Earth's Magnet." He tosses the sign aside, pulls up on the rope saying in a singing tone, "I'll pull out gravity from de Oyth and see vuht happin!" Suddenly everything is pulled upward. Trees and houses rise into the air, rain reverses and falls upward.

Betty and Bimbo in the horse-drawn wagon are headed uphill and rise into the air. The contents of the wagon drift away, and Betty gets out of the wagon to retrieve them as they float in the air. In the process, her skirt is pulled upward due to reversed gravity. This was another opportunity to show Betty's panties for a laugh at her expense.

After several more anti-gravity gags including two gossiping Jewish cat housewives, we dissolve to Saturn racing around Earth with the magnet clinging to his hat exclaiming, "I knew I got stuck." He throws the magnet back to Earth, and with a big flash of lightning, everything starts to be pulled back. Among the objects falling back to Earth is an elephant, which lands in the middle of the Atlantic and Pacific Oceans, morphing into the Continental United States, a symbol of the then current Republican Administration, cited as the cause of the Depression.

Back on Earth, we return to Betty's neighborhood and former lot. A pillow lands, she lands on the pillow, and a house comes down on her followed by an apartment building falling on top, followed by a hotel building on top of that. Betty rides the elevator to the top, bursting through the roof and completes her song, "Any old place upon this earth is home sweet home to me."

Another political satire is *Betty Boop for President* (1932). This cartoon was ahead of its time with Betty as both the first female and movie star to run for President. The highlights of the campaign feature her morphing into caricatures of Herbert Hoover and Al Smith as she sings her campaign song, *When I'm the President*. There is a curious, unnatural skip in the succession of Betty's political caricatures following the Hoover incarnation, which suggests that another politician was portrayed, possibly Franklin D. Roosevelt, and was removed from the negative later. Why this happened is unknown considering he won the election.

The biggest laugh occurs during the imaginary sequence of President Boop in the Capital as she proposes social programs for the nation. The Republicans and the Democrats are represented by their mascots, elephants and donkeys, seated in rows on opposite sides. The banter goes as follows:

PRESIDENT BOOP: What this country is in need of is a lot of "Hi-Dee-Ho," "Boop-A-Doop" and chocolate ice cream.
DEMOCRATS: We say yes!
REPUBLICANS: And we say no!

PRESIDENT BOOP: Now we will get things for nothing, movies, cabarets, and jazz.
DEMOCRATS: We accept it.
REPUBLICANS: We reject it.
DEMOCRATS: You're an elephant!
REPUBLICANS: You're an ass!

As Betty Boop ascended as the "Animation Queen," her right to the crown was to be challenged in the real world. On May 4, 1932, Helen Kane launched a $250,000 lawsuit against Paramount-Publix Corporation, Fleischer Studios, Incorporated, and Max Fleischer, claiming that the Betty Boop character was a deliberate caricature of her and the subsequent cartoons had destroyed her career. A 1931 *Film Daily* ad substantiates that Betty Boop was an intentional likeness of Helen Kane. Paramount took the position that they held priority to her film image, justifying the production of cartoons based on her personality. The case finally went to court on April 18, 1934.

Paramount provided the legendary attorney, Louis Nizer, paired with Lou Phillips for their defense. For three weeks, Max Fleischer and members of his staff testified before the New York Supreme Court to determine the origin of Betty's "singing style." Max Fleischer was named as a defendant in the case and took full credit for the creation of Betty Boop. It is to be understood that Max's testimony was not entirely false since according to corporate laws he was solely responsible for the product of his studio regardless of the individuals who did the actual work while employed by him. And by doing so the actual artists, including Grim Natwick, Berny Wolf, Seymour Kneitel, and Willard Bowsky among the many others were protected from inclusion in the suit.

Asked if he had ever seen Miss Kane perform before he began drawing Betty Boop cartoons in 1930, Fleischer recalled an entertainment at which she sang in 1928. Her numbers were rewarded by "great applause," he added. "Aren't you influenced," Miss Kane's lawyer asked, "by the people you meet in life when you create a cartoon character?," "Not exactly," replied Fleischer.

"Is the hairstyle of Betty Boop one of the figments of your imagination?" "Yes," said the artist. The attorney previously had observed that Betty Boop and Miss Kane affected similar coiffures. "When you saw Miss Kane in 1928," he pursued, "did you look at her nonchalantly or studiously?" Defense counsel objected, and Justice McGoldrick told Fleischer he need not answer. In creating Betty Boop, the cartoonist said his principal contributions had been the rolling eyes and mature figure. Miss Kane, who says she has been "booping" since 1920, listened closely to Fleischer's testimony. She wore a flaming red hat with a long brown feather that had a habit of tickling her attorney's ear when he bent over to confer with her.[2]

While Miss Kane and her attorney made the claim that the hairstyle of Betty Boop was similar, it is clear that Betty's hair was short and close to the head, her face framed by eight spit curls balanced by six more curls on the back of her head. Miss Kane wore a "feathered" hairstyle without spit curls.

After reviewing Miss Kane's films and a selection of Betty's cartoons, the court was baffled over the true origin of the Betty Boop persona. The only question was whether Fleischer Studios had exploited Miss Kane's name or picture for commercial purposes. In *Stopping the Show* (1932), the first official cartoon of the Betty Boop series, Betty is shown on a vaudeville stage doing impersonations. This sequence was a reprise of Mae Questel's vaudeville act, and the animation appears to have been made from Rotoscoped footage of Miss Questel filmed at the Paramount News Lab during the recording session.

In this cartoon, each of the impressions is set up with a photograph on an easel and the voice, or "impression" of the personality requests an imitation from Betty. As a convenience, the easel grows an arm and hand holding up a megaphone with animated lips seen inside the megaphone's cone. In the case of the speaking voice for Fanny Brice, Mae Questel does an impersonation while the real Chevalier is heard on the soundtrack. Recent prints contain an unnatural cut that implies that something was deleted from the original negative that may have proved Miss Kane's case.

The first impersonation sequence begins with Betty singing *That's My Weakness Now*, a song originated by Helen Kane. While there is no "talking" photograph of Miss Kane requesting the impression, there is evidence that this footage existed since the faint image of her is seen in the background as it pans across the audience. The omission of references to Miss Kane in this cartoon was obviously a cover up to protect Paramount and Fleischer. Miles Krueger, Curator of The Museum of the American Musical Theater, remarked, "There was no question whatsoever that she (Helen Kane) was the role model for Betty Boop. Betty Boop looks like her, sings like her, says 'boop-boop-a-doop' all the time—after all her name is 'Betty Boop' and quite obviously is a copy of Helen Kane."

Next, the court narrowed the case down to the origin of the singing style. Stage comediennes such as Fanny Brice and Irene Franklin had used "baby talk" delivery for years as a standard type of character. But it was Helen Kane's application as a voluptuous woman that was different.

While Miss Kane claimed to have used "boop-boop-a-doop" as early as 1920, this was false based on her history. She first used it when she introduced *I Wanna Be Loved by You* in the Broadway Show, *Good Boy* in 1928. Another Kane hit, *That's My Weakness Now*, also from 1928, used scat syllables such as "bah-bah-be-bah," and "whutten-dutten-duh," belying her exclusivity to "boop-boop-a-doop."

Each of the actresses hired as the voice of Betty Boop were called to testify and demonstrate their versions of the singing style. When Ann Rothschild was called to the stand, she testified that she had been singing in a similar style as a form of "scat singing" in Greenwich Village nightclubs in the 1920s. Bonnie Poe and Margie Hines were called to demonstrate their talents and interpretations. Miss Hines was questioned on the meaning of the "boop-boop-a-doop" sounds. She replied, "Well, I call them 'licks.'" When Mae Questel testified, she told of how she was discovered in a Helen Kane imitation contest and was declared the winner by Miss Kane. She then produced evidence in favor of the defense, showing an autographed picture signed, "To Mae Questel, the only 'other' Helen Kane." This endorsement clearly defeated the image claim made by Miss Kane.

The next question was whether any of Helen Kane's recordings had been used in the cartoons. When songs originated by Miss Kane had been used, they were "covered" by one of the imitators. The attorneys spent the next several days dissecting each actress' use of the syllables, discerning the difference between "boop-oop-a-doop," "boop-boop-a-doop," "boop-oopy-doop," "boo-boo-be-do," "poo-poopy-do," and even "poop-poopy-do-do." This silly semantics argument became a source of uproarious laughter for the courtroom, with attorneys arguing the differences between a "boop-oopy-doop" and a "poop-poopy-doop," as well as the difference between "boop-poop" and "poo-poop." Members of the court, including the stenographer, were confused. After this exhaustive review of the "boop-oop-a-doopery" history, the stenographer threw up his hands in despair and the testimony of meaningless sounds was retracted.

Miss Kane's claim was challenged further by testimony from Alfred Evans, an associate of Rudy Vallee's who stated that Edith Griffin had used the same syllables, "boop-a-doop" in Nebraska as early as 1927. Miss Griffin had been using this technique when she recorded for Victor Records in 1928, the same year that Helen Kane was discovered.

On May 2, new evidence was introduced that proved that syllables similar to Helen Kane's were used before. Lou Walton (a.k.a. Lou Bolton), theatrical manager for a black entertainer, Esther Jones known by her stage name, "Baby Esther," testified that his client had used baby-talk words like "boo-boo-boo," and "doo-doo-doo" in songs at a New York cabaret as early as 1925. Walton continued, stating that Miss Kane and her manager had seen his client's performance in April 1928, and just a few weeks later was seen using the "boop" interpretations at a New York theater. The testimony of "Baby Esther" would have been crucial at this point. But for some unknown reason, she was unavailable, either deceased or untraceable. Adding to the mystery is the lack of any confirmed photographs of Miss Jones. Recently an image has surfaced on the Internet claiming to be Esther Jones. This has been traced to the collection of photographs by James Van Der Zee housed by The Art Institute of Chicago, identified only by the title, "Do Tell." This cannot substantiate the woman as Esther Jones since the model is not identified.

Paramount and Max Fleischer were very worried about losing the case until an early sound-on-disc test film of "Baby Esther" was discovered. This seemed to be the key element for the defense until it reached the crucial point of the controversial syllables. The film had broken from past use and had been spliced back together in several places. Because the sound was on a separate medium from the film, the relative position of image to sound impulse was lost by fractions of a second due to each splice, throwing the synchronization off at that one important spot. Max approached Lou with the problem, which had to be solved by the next morning. An optical film soundtrack was transferred from the disc and Lou went to work. He viewed the print on the Movieola and determined at which points the synchronization was lost. He worked through the night with their Film Cutter, Kitty Pfister, splicing in black film slugs to replace the right number of lost frames to reposition the film frames and restore the synchronization.

Paramount kept a cab waiting all through the night until they were finished. The corrected print was rushed to the Paramount News Lab for a new composite print for a demonstration in court that morning. The film proved that "Baby Esther" was the true originator of the singing style, uttering the syllables, "Boop-oop-a-doo." Justice Edward McGoldrick ruled in favor of Paramount and Fleischer based on this evidence stating, "The plaintiff has failed to sustain either cause or action by proof of sufficient probative force." In his opinion, "the singing technique did not originate with Miss Kane."[3]

It was fortunate that the attorneys were not privy to the technical aspects of film because Miss Kane's attorney could have objected on the grounds that the film had been "faked" because of the alterations made to restore the synchronization even though it was an authentic filmed performance. In spite of this, the "Baby Esther" film was the crucial evidence that brought the case to a close.

With her claims to the singing style defeated, Helen Kane maintained that Betty Boop was a deliberate caricature of her. But it could also be said that Miss Kane and Betty were influenced by the look of Clara Bow, Paramount's "It Girl" of the 1920s. Miss Bow never made issues of being copied by Miss Kane since she apparently lived by the adage, "Imitation is the sincerest form of flattery."

While the Helen Kane case was a major victory for Paramount and Fleischer Studios, the legal issues over Betty Boop were not over. Following the trial, Max Fleischer issued a public statement.

Beginning in 1932, authorized wooden Betty Boop dolls were marketed, designed by Joseph Kallus. Additional authorized merchandising included the Betty Boop Pocket Watch, manufactured by the E. Ingraham Company. It was featured in the Montgomery Ward Mail Order catalog marketed to boys, and was the only character merchandise of the day that featured a female character.

Clara Bow, the "It Girl" (author's collection).

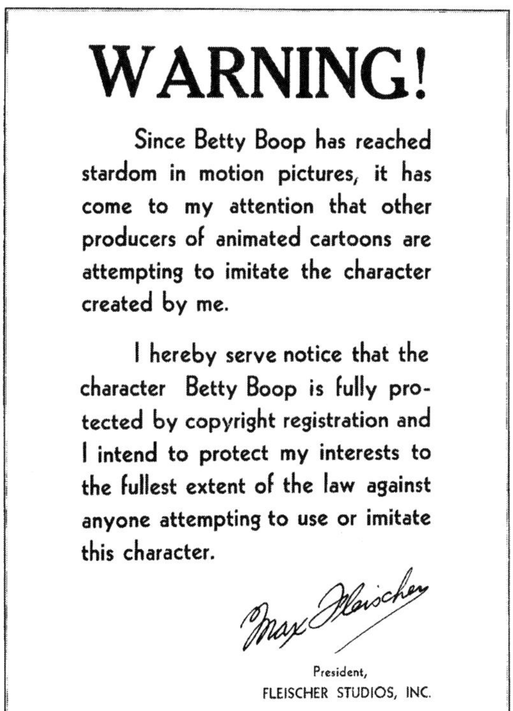

WARNING!

Since Betty Boop has reached stardom in motion pictures, it has come to my attention that other producers of animated cartoons are attempting to imitate the character created by me.

I hereby serve notice that the character Betty Boop is fully protected by copyright registration and I intend to protect my interests to the fullest extent of the law against anyone attempting to use or imitate this character.

Max Fleischer

President,
FLEISCHER STUDIOS, INC.

Left: Trade announcement (author's collection). _Right:_ Betty Boop Doll patent (U.S. Patent and Trademark Office).

"Betty Boop's Trial" (author's collection).

Because of the popularity of the "Queen of the Animated Screen," others were out to exploit her image. In November 1934, Fleischer Studios sued the Freundlich Doll Company for copyright violation in the manufacture of a line of Betty Boop dolls. Freundlich attempted to act on the omission of "Inc." in the copyright notice due to the fact that the doll image was issued through the "Fleischer Art Services." In spite of the technicality, the court ruled: "failure to add 'Inc.' to the name Fleischer Studios was not fatal to the notice or the proprietor of the copyright. The omission in no way disguised the identity of the party who had registered the copyright."[5] Once again, Betty's "boop-oop-a-doop" could not be taken away.

6

Betty Boop on the Couch

A Character Analysis

In the world of the cartoon vamp, Betty Boop was a paradoxical combination of child-like innocence and realized sexuality—a sexy tease finding herself in near compromises of her virtue. In her early films, Betty is the subject of ogling and lust from lascivious males. *Boop-Oop-A-Doop* (1932) is quite frank and advanced in addressing the subject of sexual harassment. The circus Ringmaster clearly lusts after her, following her into her tent, rubbing her leg and whispering in her ear, "Do you like your job?" (Betty nods out of fear.) "Well if I were you, I'd…" Betty slaps him after he makes the indecent proposition, which leads into her song *Don't Take My Boop-Oop-A-Doop Away*. Ko-Ko the Clown overhears her cries for help and fights off the villain, saving the heroine in true melodramatic form.

In *Chess Nuts* (1932), two elderly men in live action are playing a game of chess. The chess board transforms into animated characters with Ko-Ko as the White Pawn, Bimbo as the White King, Betty as the Black Queen, and an old curmudgeon as the Black King. A series of gags reflecting certain "fantasies" of bondage and voyeurism follow. As the chess pieces play an improvised game of football, Betty is standing on the window ledge of the castle and giving a cheerleader's chant while a tiny long-eared dog-like character looks up her short skirt.

The Black King lassoes her by the ankles and pulls the lasso upward as a means of lifting Betty's skirt to reveal her frilly panties. The lasso stops at her breasts and she promptly pushes the lasso back down and lowers her skirt. While Betty attempts to fight him off, he picks her up, carrying her in his arms, saying, "I'll take care of you right now." The King then proceeds to bind Betty to a column, saying, "Don't you see the love light in my eyes?" The lit candles are phallic symbols that go limp when Betty blows them out. The King carries Betty into the bedroom, muttering again, "Nothing can save you now, me proud beauty!" to which we hear Betty crying out "Let me alone you big brute, you!" followed by some curious off screen squeals as the bed gallops out, wiping its "feet" and exiting the scene. When the scene cuts, we see Betty wiggling her arms and legs still in the arms of the King as Bimbo enters to rescue Betty.

The two kings battle and Betty tries her hand at "crowning" the nasty King by throwing dishes. She throws a vase and her skirt curls up only to have the table chivalrously pull it back down to which she says "Oh, thank you!" Then she throws another vase, breaking a hole in the wall. We see two mice in bed. One, presumably the male, wakes up and the camera pans right to him returning to his "proper" bed with a quick glance to the audience.

James "Shamus" Culhane was one of the animators on *Chess Nuts* who was frustrated with his assignments on Betty Boop:

> ... the story department was never sophisticated enough to take full advantage of Betty. Sex was usually depicted as endless attempts on her virginity. She was never given a male counterpart, again because of the flawed concept that action was more important than character motivation. Instead, the scripts were like vaudeville skits, sometimes veering dangerously towards burlesque..."[1]

Why did Fleischer's storymen never succeed in writing more romantically about Betty Boop?

> When women were thought of in terms like "quiff," "snatch," and "gash," a la Studs Lonigan, there was no possibility of a story being written where Betty Boop used her charms in a light, flirtatious manner. Betty was a "good" girl with a hymen like a boilerplate, and her sex life would never be more than a series of attacks on her virginity by unpleasant characters with heavy hands. But heavy-handed or not, at least these plots had a certain lusty humor.[2]

Culhane's sentiments offer great insight to the atmosphere that was dominated by men with their fantasy concepts about women that entered into the character, Betty Boop. Considering their cultural and educational level, creating material for Betty would surely be limited in scope since men would not directly relate to the sensitivities of a female character such as this. As a result, the formats were fashioned using Betty as a "prop" for stories.

The first format was the musical revue vaudeville sketch as in *Dizzy Dishes* (1930), *Barnacle Bill* (1930), *Bimbo's Silly Scandals* (1931), and *Stopping the Show* (1932). The second format was the mystery parody format that lent itself to surrealism in such cartoons as *The Herring Murder Case* (1931) and *Bimbo's Initiation* (1931). The third format was the fairy tale parody as in *Jack and the Beanstalk* (1931), *Dizzy Red Riding Hood* (1931), *Snow White* (1933), and *Poor Cinderella* (1934). The fourth was the jazz cartoon format that included three with Cab Calloway: *Minnie the Moocher* (1932), *Snow White* (1933) and *The Old Man of the Mountain* (1933); *I'll Be Glad When You're Dead, You Rascal You* with Louis Armstrong; and *I Heard* with Don Redman.

To understand the concepts and content associated with Betty Boop, one needs to consider the backgrounds of the artists and animators. While some of the Fleischer animators such as Culhane and Myron Waldman attended art college and had more refined tastes, the others did not. Most of them were young men in their late teens and early twenties with nothing more than a high school education at the most. Some had not even finished high school. Many had attended Cooper Union or the Art Student's League, as had Max. They could draw, and that qualified them for employment. Like the Fleischers, they came from rough New York environments, having personalities similar to Dave Fleischer's. Theirs was an atmosphere of wild living, speakeasies, and gambling. In fact, Dave's office was the local betting parlor. Several of the young Fleischer animators lived a wild lifestyle of consuming bootleg liquor and weekend Bridge-playing with prostitutes. This explains the one-dimensional sexuality and chauvinistic humor displayed in these cartoons.

The *Talkartoon, Bimbo's Express* (1931), contains an example of the type of burlesque humor that Culhane cites. Bimbo is a moving man, and arrives at Betty's front door. Betty is seen inside in the foreground still in her nightgown, clipping her toenails with a pair of scissors. Bimbo knocks several times and identifies himself as the moving man. The dialogue in true burlesque format runs as follows:

(Knocks on door three times)
BETTY: "Yes?"
BIMBO: "Does Miss Betty live here?"
BETTY: "Yes!"
BIMBO: "This is the Moving Man."
BETTY: "Yes!" "Do you want to come in?"
BIMBO: "Yes!"
BETTY: "I can't open the door now, I'm in my 'nightie'!"
BIMBO: "Alright, I'll wait 'til ya take it off!"

In spite of it all, audiences in general found delight in Betty's romps with the risqué, which got her into trouble from time to time. Ironically, it was the risqué content of Mae West's films that saved Paramount from bankruptcy and prompted a stricter enforcement of the Production Code in 1934, which placed specific limitations on the content of films. While nothing indecent was displayed, double entendres were enough for concern. West's debut film *Night After Night* contained this famous line of dialogue:

HAT CHECK GIRL: "Goodness, what beautiful diamonds!"
MAE WEST: "Goodness had nothing to do with it, dearie!"

Miss West's film *She Done Him Wrong* contains the famous line, "When I'm good, I'm very good. When I'm bad, I'm better!" The New York stage abounded with plays containing innuendo and profanity for the sake of drama and realism. Such shows played well in New York, but concerns were raised about how the movies would be influenced once sound was introduced with particular concern about the impressions made on children. While still a bit conservative by comparison, movies were becoming quite bold in their content, which was a subject of concern in Middle America.

The Production Code

In order to stay in business, the film industry realized the need to "clean up" its image. The solution was found in the creation of a standards organization for the industry. Will H. Hays, an Elder in the Presbyterian Church, former Postmaster General under President Warren G. Harding, and the former head of the Republican National Committee, was selected to reform Hollywood's image. In 1922, Hays founded the Motion Picture Producers and Distributors of America (MPPDA) serving as its president for 25 years with a handsome salary of $100,000 a year. While Hays presented a list of suggested guidelines, they were generally disregarded. It was evident that films with racy and violent content generated ticket sales, and the conditions of the 1930s Depression forced studios to garner income in every way possible. But by 1931, the industry agreed to abide by the Hays Code, which consisted of two parts. The first part was concerned with morality. It was assumed that certain "adult-leveled" material would self-censor with regards to "impressionable" viewers and their supervision by adults. This assumption was thought to apply to many of the Fleischer cartoons, and particularly Betty Boop. Accordingly, the Hays Code was more of a joke than a reality. But conditions were to take a serious change.

The Breen Era

She Done Him Wrong was a major Mae West moneymaker for Paramount. But it was West's song, *I Like a Man That Takes His Time*, that demanded censoring in several states, causing Paramount to recall all release prints and cut the controversial middle stanzas. This ushered in a new and stricter policy under Joseph Breen. The Production Code was amended on June 13, 1934, and all films released after July 1, 1934, were directed to conform to its standards, which remained in place for thirty years. While it seemed like a compromise in free speech, this form of self-regulation was followed to stave off government censorship. Paramount cooperated with the new guidelines especially with the election of Barney Balaban as President of Paramount in 1936. Under Balaban, Paramount took a more responsible position in "explaining America, its customs, and its people to the world." This new content policy was in emulation of the more general audience films produced by MGM, but at lower cost. Just as Paramount looked to the "Tiffany" of live-action studios, they hoped to have Fleischer emulate the "Tiffany" of animation and definition of wholesome entertainment, Walt Disney.

The Fleischer's solely owned character, Betty Boop, was the subject of censorship and criticism under the new Production Code. Her bathing suit/negligée costume was too skimpy with its low neckline and short skirt that displayed her signature garter. Even though Betty was nothing more than an optical illusion, she was treated as if she were a real threat to morality with her appearance and actions. Her final tease with the audience was in *Betty Boop's Trial* (1934). This was the introduction of Betty Boop's first and only human "love interest," "Freddy" as a motorcycle cop who chases after Betty and hauls her into the court. Fortunately, Betty quickly becomes a "friend of the court" and the jury declares her "not guilty!" Expressing her joy, she leaps into the air, landing with a graceful slow motion pirouette. Costumed in a cute winter outfit, she still had a short skirt and the signature garter. While Betty's panties had been seen before, this was the only time that the audience viewed them in full turn around. It would be their last look.

Betty continued to be paired with Freddy for a year, placing her in silly "damsel in distress" situations. The first of these was *Betty Boop's Lifeguard* (1934). Next came a series of old time melodrama parodies, *She Wronged Him Right* (1934), *Betty Boop's Prize Show* (1934), *No, No, a Thousand Times, No!* (1935), and *Honest Love and True* (1938). This mini-series introduced Phillip the Fiend as the villain. It seems this format was inspired by the Fanny Zilch series produced by Paul Terry. This series lampooned the silent movie Pearl White serials, featuring the love triangle of Fanny—the Banker's Daughter, Oil Can Harry—the Villain, and Stongheart—the "fae" Hero in a far more successful manner in spite of the crude drawing and awkward animation. Warner Brothers released *Those Were the Days*, a *Merry Melodies* cartoon with a damsel in distress sequence involving a villain kidnapping the heroine and escaping in a balloon, only to have the hero arrive on the scene, fight with the villain atop the balloon, and save the heroine. This same situation was repeated a year later with Betty Boop in *No, No, a Thousand Times No*.

Perhaps the best of the Betty/Freddy parings was *There's Something About a Soldier* just for concept and cartoony content. Whether intentional or not, Freddy bears a resemblance to popular tenor Arthur Jarrett, which could have taken the series in a musical romantic sitcom direction much like the Popeye cartoons. But this was never realized by

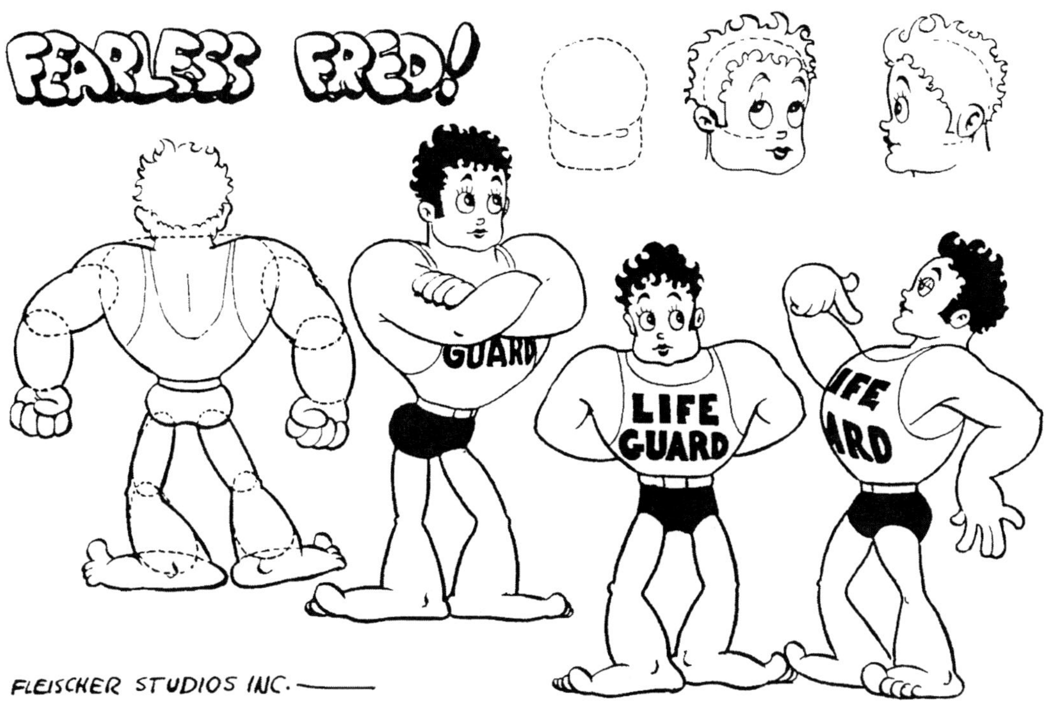

Freddy model for Betty Boop's Lifeguard (author's collection).

the writers, and Freddy was dropped after six cartoons. By this point it seemed that the Story Department was going through the motions of finding cute formulas just to get the cartoon made. In spite of the slick production values and consistent animation, the value of the Betty Boop series was slipping, relying on "cuteness" to get by. Oddly, Paramount continued ordering the series and Fleischer obliged.

Pudgy

Pudgy was a cute puppy character designed by Myron Waldman, seemingly inspired by Terrytoons' Puddy the Pup, who had a more interesting and appealing personality. Pudgy was introduced in *Little Pal,* which was the final appearance of Betty in her infamous costume. While obviously intended as "cute," Pudgy was one-dimensional and old-fashioned in his doughy design, looking more like a companion to Dick Huemer's *Scrappy* style from 1930. Most of the stories in this Betty Boop sub-series placed Pudgy in cloying childhood situations with Betty acting as a coddling and sometimes scolding mother figure. But two entries broke away from this formula, returning to the Fleischer element of surrealism, *Riding the Rails* and *Pudgy Picks a Fight.*

In *Riding the Rails,* Pudgy tries to follow Betty to work. While she sends him home, he continues following her and gets lost in the subway, being chased by the subway cars with their fronts morphing into the faces of threatening monsters, sending him home in the tradition of the runaway child. *Pudgy Picks a Fight* has a more intriguing premise built

Pudgy model sheet by Myron Waldman (Ryan Englade).

around Betty luxuriating over her new fox fur featuring the clasping jaw. This was a send-up to Paramount chief, Adolph Zukor, who began as a furrier and invented the self-clasping fox fur. Pudgy thinks the fur is alive and becomes jealous of it, grabbing it in his mouth and beating it on the floor. When it appears lifeless, a ghost image of Pudgy rises from the fur and a series of surrealistic scenes follow, playing on Pudgy's imagined guilt. The shadows from the blinds falling across Pudgy's chest look like prison stripes. The shadow of the cuckoo looks like the pointing finger of guilt with the clock striking eight "coo-coos" simulating "guilty-guilty-guilty-guilty." He trips over a vacuum cleaner, accidentally turning it on, and it sounds as if it is laughing maniacally while sucking him towards it. The shadow from a floor lamp looks like a hangman's noose. Drapes blown in the wind look like the "long arms of the law" reaching for him. The radio announces, "The mask knows you're guilty!" Betty then shows Pudgy that the fur is not alive, and he destroys it in anger after this anguish.

Pudgy remained as Betty's puppy companion until the end, making his last appearance in *The Scared Crows* (1939).

Grampy

For most of the period 1936 to 1938, Betty's cartoons were built around song gimmicks with rather routine, serviceable plots that did not reach any further in their comedic content, characterization, and imagination. One of the better concepts came with the introduction of Grampy in 1935. The character design with the dome-shaped head and black nose suggests a curious link to Koko the Clown, as if to suggest that Grampy was merely Ko-Ko in retirement. Everett Clark, who had done incidental voices such as Freddy and various elderly characters, was the voice of Grampy. Clark was also the voice of Olive Oyl's Grandmother in *Let's Celebrake* (1938).

Everette Clark (author's collection).

Grampy shared an interesting connection to Max's fondness for contraptions. The purpose of Grampy was to solve some problem through his ability to throw together mechanical devices out of existing objects. The set-up for the problems originated with incidents where Betty was a victim of an out of control situation, leaving her to call on Grampy for help. Grampy's inventions were pure cartoon material in the tradition of Rube Goldberg, proving to be both clever and amusing while also seeming plausible. It was unfortunate that the story format had reduced Betty to a weak and helpless "female" as an excuse to bring in Grampy to "save the day" in the second half of the cartoon—a format to be repeated in the 1940s with *Superman* and copied in the Paul Terry parody, *Mighty Mouse.* Grampy could have starred in his own series as a replacement for Betty Boop, and his debut in *Betty Boop and Grampy* hints at a series pilot but this was never realized. He was given one starring vehicle in the *Color Classic, Christmas Comes but Once a Year* (1936).

The Grampy entries continued until 1937, concluding with *Zula Hula.* Betty and

Grampy are in his airplane, caught in a thunderstorm. The plane crash lands on a desert island, and Grampy fashions living quarters and appliances out of the available resources including a bamboo hut with automatic fans operated by two pelicans tugging on a fish. While visually amusing, the cartoon is marred by the Black stereotyped cannibals.

Wiffle Piffle

Another attempt at creating a new comical character came in the unappealing Wiffle Piffle with his balloon-like head, bulbous nose, crossed eyes, side-ways shuffle-walk, and high-pitched nasal voice by Jack Mercer. He was introduced as a sometime recurring character in the later *Screen Songs* series, beginning with *I Wished on the Moon* (1935), continuing with *Talking Through My Heart*, and ending with *Never Should Have Told You* (1937). A form of this same character appeared in *Magic on Broadway*. He also appeared in two Betty Boop cartoons from 1937, *Whoops, I'm a Cowboy*, and *The Hot Air Salesman* before being retired from use. Obviously his one-joke gimmicky walk was not enough to sustain great interest.

Altering Betty Boop to fit the Production Code took its toll. While she should have

Wiffle Piffle (Todd Levine).

been retired in 1934, Betty coasted through to 1938. Then Graham Place redesigned her in 1939 and destroyed what was left of her appeal. While Betty Boop started out as a carefree icon of the Jazz Age, she was warped into a helpless, judgmental spinster, and finally a dumb brunette clothes horse with a beach ball–like head stuck on a naturally proportioned body.

Her final appearance was *Rhythm on the Reservation* (1939). While *Yip-Yip-Yippy* appears at the end of the Betty Boop series, it is a forgettable one-shot about a "Drug Store" mail order cowboy "wannabe" without Betty. Imagine if they had reprised Betty in the Dangerous Nan McGrew role. Instead, *Yip-Yip-Yippy* is a very ordinary and forgettable cartoon featuring a bland Soda Jerk designed to fill the release schedule and comply with the contract. Too bad.

The Graham Place version of Betty Boop, 1939.

7

The Fleischer Factory

The Fleischer Look

By 1929, all animation studios were committed to the full use of sound and animation cels. This brought on the creation of the Ink and Opaque Department with Ruth Fleischer as the first supervisor at Fleischer Studios. While Ruth displayed artistic abilities, Max remarked that his reason for putting his daughter in charge was "to keep an eye on her and keep her out of the Yiddish Theater." Shortly after this she met Seymour Kneitel, and they began their courtship, eventually marrying on December 24, 1931, the 26th anniversary of Max and Essie.

The Fleischer Studios inking and opaquing department (Michael Barrier).

Max's 26th anniversary, 1931. (*Front, left to right*): Essie (1) and Max Fleischer (2), Ruth Fleischer (3) and Seymour Kneitel (4). *Second row:* Richard Flesicher (5), Ethel Fleischer-Phillips (6). *Lower right, counterclockwise:* Amelia Fleischer (7), Lou (8) and Libby Fleischer (9), Molly (10) and Joe Fleischer (11), William Fleischer (12) (author's collection).

On December 10, 1929, Max Fleischer signed a licensing agreement for the Bray cel techniques at the cost of 10 cents per finished negative foot. The full use of animation cels brought greater tone and atmosphere to cartoons, making them more attractive and easier on the eye. And the Fleischer black and white cartoons are considered to be the most beautiful, due largely to the leadership of Eric Schenk, who used a sepia ink wash technique. The cels featured characters painted in grays, and when placed under the platen for photography, this combination enhanced the contrast for black and white film. Many unemployed illustrators, architects, and theatrical scene painters found work at Fleischer Studios. Among them were Robert Little, Anton Loeb, and Shane Miller.

Several of the early Fleischer backgrounds resemble a stylization depicted in German Expressionism films such as *The Cabinet of Dr. Caligari* (1920) and *Nosferatu* (1922). *The Cabinet of Dr. Caligari* was a particular favorite of Max. Richard Fleischer recalled:

> The first movie I remember was a film that my father particularly wanted me to see. I was probably seven, and he told me that it was something I had to see. He took me alone during the day, to an "art-house theater." I never forgot the experience. The film was *The Cabinet of Dr. Caligari.* I still carry an image from it around in my head—a tall, pale-faced thin man in a long black coat, his eyes circled in black, standing in a narrow hallway, its walls askew. I remember not so much being frightened as somehow being hypnotized by the image.
>
> I've never really figured out why my father wanted me to see that surrealistic masterpiece. By no stretch of the imagination was it a film for children. Perhaps, with this film, he was initiating me into the world in which he lived. His animated cartoons always relied heavily on surrealism for their effect. Perhaps it was his way of stretching my imagination, of making me aware that there was more than one way of looking at reality.[1]

Left: From _Bimbo's Silly Scandals,_ 1931 (Todd Levine). _Right: Let's Get Movin',_ 1936 (Todd Levine).

***Betty Boop's Halloween Party*, 1933 (Todd Levine).**

A second painting technique used was the opaque gouache method, popular with illustrations for magazines as well as commercial and industrial design presentations. Oddly, some *Popeye* cartoons such as *The Jeep* (1938) switch between both background techniques within the same cartoon.

But overall, it is the sepia wash technique that defined the Fleischer look that is most appreciated.

Top: Still from _Dr. Caligari,_ 1920 (author's collection). _Bottom:_ Still from _Dr. Caligari,_ 1920.

Left: **Combination gouache and wash technique by Eric Schenk for the Betty Boop cartoon, *Red Hot Mama*, 1934 (Todd Levine). *Right:* Overlay cutout of entrance to Hell (Todd Levine).**

These are examples of background transitions using the wash technique. A background cutout was matched and registered to the main background with the transitions made through in-camera dissolves.

Middle: **Composited overlay and main background (Todd Levine). *Above, left:* Background "A" (Todd Levine). *Above, right:* Matching background "B" for "Hell freezing over" transition (Todd Levine).**

Additional Examples of "Black and White" Fleischer Backgrounds

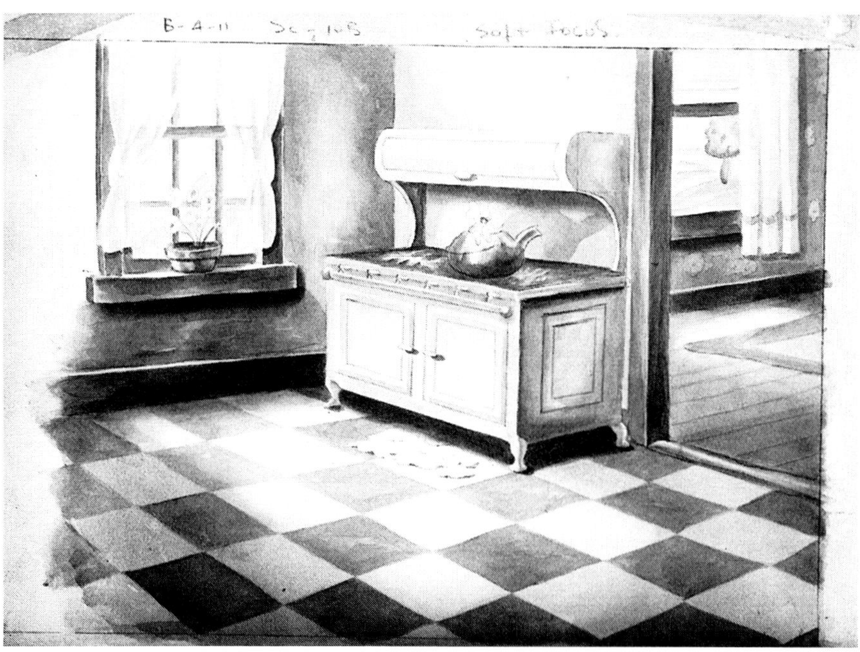

Top: Let's You and Him Fight, **1933 (Todd Levine).** ***Bottom: Little Soap and Water,*** **1935 (Todd Levine).**

***The Hyp-Nut-Tist*, 1935 (Todd Levine).**

Color

The 1930s brought about great technological advancements in motion pictures, first with sound, followed by color. While color processes had existed in the silent era, they were not widely used due to the instability of some, but largely due the limitations and expense of the processes. Since there was no color negative film at the time, animation was photographed as filtered impressions on black and white film. The earliest known color cartoon was *The Debut of Thomas Cat* (1920), produced by the Bray Studio in the Brewster Color Process. Other color systems such as Synthechrome, developed by Carpenter-Goldman Laboratories, and two-color Technicolor continued in limited use throughout the 1920s.

Technicolor was developed in 1916 by MIT graduates Herbert Kalmus, Daniel Frank Comstock, and W. Burton Wescott. Throughout the 20s, they refined the two-color process which used red and blue-green. While interesting to see, the two color method offered a limited and distorted reproduction of color since light comprises equal amounts of red, green, and blue. The studios made an investment in early Technicolor musicals between 1929 and 1931, then abandoned them due to the effects of the Depression.

In 1932, Kalmus introduced the three-color Technicolor Process, which offered full spectrum color reproduction. Kalmus approached the studios hoping to gain interest, but his timing was bad, especially when he approached Paramount. Paramount was reorganizing following a bankruptcy, unwilling to take on the added expense of color production. And since Fleischer Studios was financed by Paramount, the chance for acquiring the new Technicolor process was lost to Walt Disney, who shrewdly signed a four-year exclusivity ending in September 1935, prohibiting competing producers from releasing in three-color Technicolor until 1936. In 1932, The Motion Picture Academy of Arts and Sciences created the Short Subject Cartoon category and awarded it to Walt Disney's *Flowers and Trees* for being the first use of the three-color Technicolor Process.

With this award and its significance, Disney created a market for color cartoons, and Max continued to petition Paramount about producing in color. Then in 1934, Paramount approved the production of the *Color Classics* series as an answer to Disney's *Silly Symphonies*. The drawback was that Fleischer was limited to the two-color processes for two years. The first entry in the series was *Poor Cinderella*, produced in the red and cyan Cinecolor Process developed by William T. Crispinel and Alan M. Gundelfinge. To understand the process and its limitations, one needs to consider the composition of film.

Film consists of two sides, a base side and an emulsion side. The emulsion is the light sensitive, photochemical side of the film that captures the image, and it is the emulsion side that is focused on when projected. Records indicate the existence of separate red and "blue" negatives, with prints made using a dye application to a special double emulsion film, one for red, and the other for cyan (blue-green). With two emulsion layers, it was impossible to have complete focus, leaving one color slightly blurred. This was the limitation of the first *Color Classic* release, *Poor Cinderella*.

Cinecolor was a "bipack," process where two negatives were run through the camera simultaneously to photograph two separate spectra of light. This complicated system used a red dyed orthochromatic negative, sensitive to cool colors (blue, green, and blue-green). The ortho negative was dyed red to act as a filter when placed in contact with the second negative, a Panchromatic film, which was sensitive to all colors, and acted as the red record. Art directors generally avoided purple, lavender, or pink because they did not reproduce faithfully in printing. While Cinecolor produced brilliant reds, oranges, blues, browns and flesh tones, bright greens and violet were distorted and muted.

Poor Cinderella was an extra-long cartoon featuring Fleischer Studios' star character, Betty Boop, sporting auburn hair. For decades, *Poor Cinderella* had been seen in black and white prints made from the "blue" negative, which made Betty look like a platinum blonde. Then in early 1980, the original negatives were deposited at UCLA, and a reconstructed color answer print was made on modern 35mm film stock bringing both colors into full focus, which is viewable today.

For the first year, all of the subsequent *Color Classics* were produced in two-color (red and blue-green) Technicolor starting with *Little Dutch Mill* (1934). The color schemes were tailored to the limited color response of two-color Tech, which explains the turquoise skies. Reds, browns, and grays reproduced accurately, but the compromise of blue-green diminished yellow to a cream-like hue.

In the two-color Technicolor Process, two exposures were made representing each "frame" of animation, resulting in a "red" exposure followed by a "blue-green" exposure. The impression on the corresponding color frames would be run through a dye application to produce the composite color print. Since the color dyes were applied to a single emulsion, the two-color Technicolor image was much sharper than Cinecolor.

To compensate for the limited spectrum of the two-color processes, Max Fleischer developed a three-dimensional background effect. This method promoted as the "Stereoptical Process" consisted of model set backgrounds referred to in short as "setbacks," constructed on a large turntable moved in small increments between each exposure. The adapted Bell and Howell camera was positioned on a lathe bed and could be moved toward or away from the set as indicated in Figures 4 through 6. Fleischer animation art of the 1930s measured 6" × 8", related to the 1:1.33 film aspect ratio. While this was generally referred to as "8 Field," the cels were shot closer to a 5" × 7" area to avoid photographing the edges of the cels. This was the "standard" position for the setback, with "4 Field" being the closest position. In the beginning there was a risk in the background sometimes jerking to a stop due to the graduations of the worm gear threads. This was eventually perfected with the addition of .001 inch threads. In either case, the effect was still stunning.

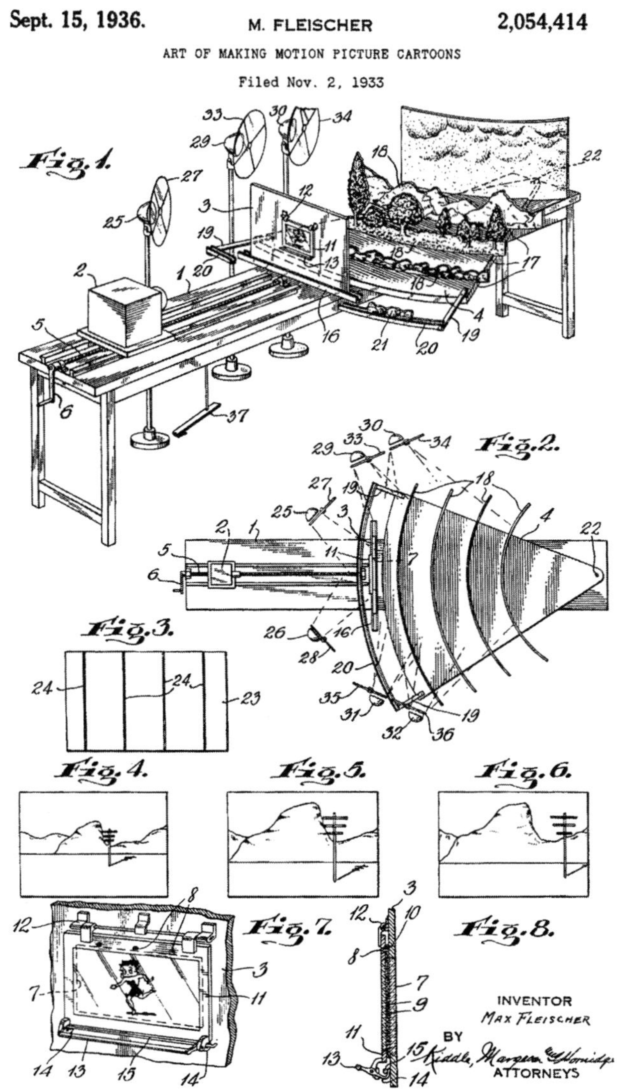

"Stereoptical" patent (U.S. Patent and Trademark Office).

Note that the patent application refers to merely the "art of making motion picture cartoons," and makes no reference to the name "Stereoptical Process."

The first patent application filed November 2, 1933, illustrates the concept, but does not go into great detail about the actual workings of the mechanism itself. The second patent filed December 5, 1936, is very specific, illustrating in five pages the mechanical workings of the apparatus.

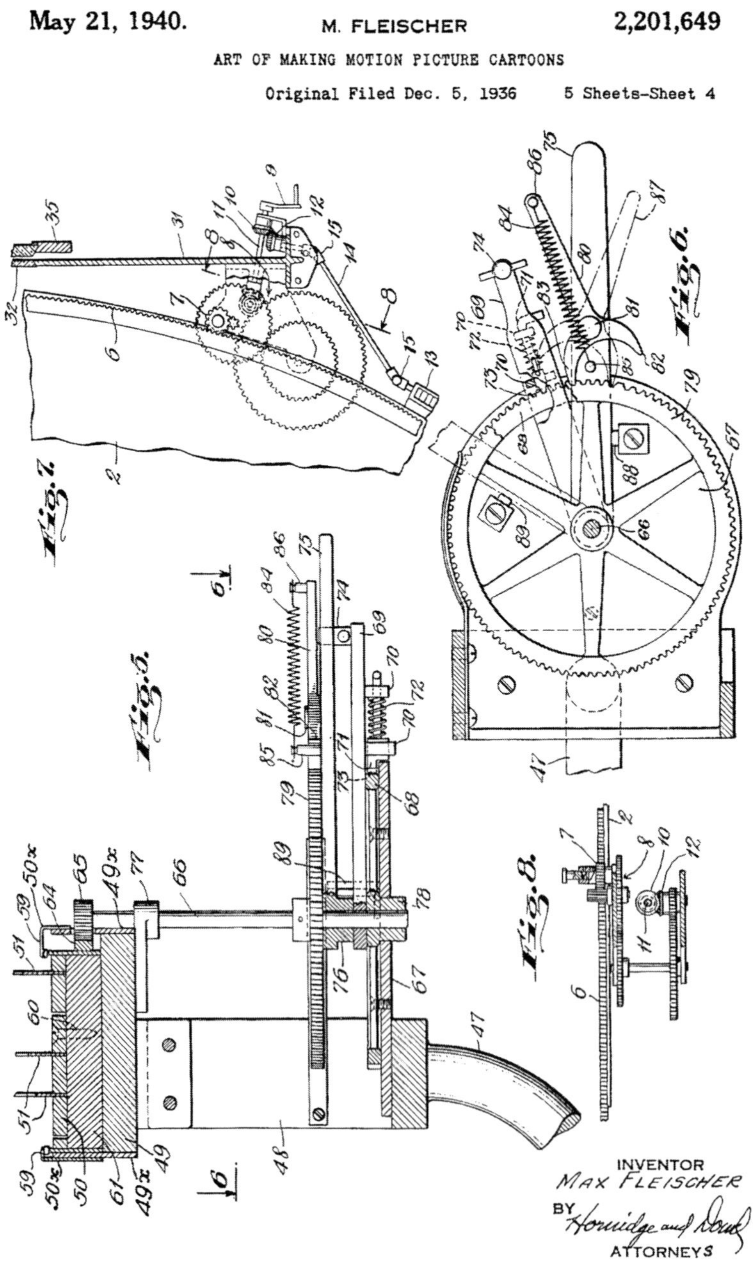

Stereoptical mechanism details, page 4.

While the patent is in Max Fleischer's name, the device was actually developed by Johnny Burks of the Camera Department. Whenever the layout supervisors and head animators needed match lines and references to the model sets, they would refer to Burks. After about an hour or two, Burks would provide the necessary registration lines on a cel for the director/layout supervisor to follow.

The model sets were constructed of papier-mâché, balsa wood, clay, and cardboard. In the beginning, there was a glaring inconsistency going from the flat painted backgrounds to the model sets. Eventually, a stylistic consistency was achieved by having the set elements painted by the Background Department. The Stereoptical Process continued to be used to a lesser degree after 1938 due to many issues associated with the time and the expense in its use. The last notable use was in the short *Ants in the Plants* (1940), and the opening title sequence in Fleischer's second feature, *Mr. Bug Goes to Town* (1941).

Railroad roundhouse setback under construction for *Play Safe*, 1936 (author's collection).

EISCHER
TUDIOS
N.Y.

The Color Classics

On the surface, the Max Fleischer *Color Classics* seemed like an imitation of Disney's *Silly Symphony* series. But they were unique, and can be divided into three categories: miniature musicals such as *Poor Cinderella*, moralistic stories such as *Little Dutch Mill* and *Greedy Humpty Dumpty*, and "charm stories," like *Time for Love, Musical Memories,* and *Always Kickin'*. Some entries contained elements of horror. Where the Disney versions of fairy tales tended to neutralize their original horror elements, the Fleischer team relished in them. The old Miser in *Little Dutch Mill* threatens to burn the tongues out of the two children, Hans and Gretel, true to the original fairy tale scare tactics of the Brothers Grimm. *The Cobweb Hotel* has a mood right out of Frankenstein with the addition of color. *Greedy Humpty Dumpty* has a great fall in a moral tale about the dangers of greed in this combination of *Mother Goose*, *King Midas*, and Greek Mythology, with a touch of the Tower of Babel from the Old Testament. And *Play Safe* takes a little boy fascinated by trains along a nightmarish runaway train ride full of Fleischer surrealism.

Max Fleischer's Stereoptical Process was a major feature in the first two years of the series. The name "Stereoptical" was derived from the Stereopticon viewer, popular during the Victorian era. This was a device that produced a three-dimensional illusion using cards with binocular photographs representing the positions of the left and right eye. While the Stereoptical Process did not use a viewer or glasses, the illusion of third dimension was due to the use of the setbacks as described earlier. The most extensive use of the process was in *Musical Memories* (1935). This cartoon is built as a showcase for the Stereoptical Process since the story is about an elderly couple reminiscing about their lives as they view a number of Stereopticon photos. With each photo, the camera assumes the point of view and the audience is taken into the 3D impression. *Musical Memories* contains the most extensive use of the Stereoptical Process with a total of 10 dimensional scenes. This is notable since the process was normally reserved for fewer scenes due to the time consumption in shooting them. In this case, the story called for it, and the device served the story—a philosophy that was practiced by Walt Disney.

While the *Color Classics* were intended as one-shot cartoons, they spawned sequels and sub-series. *Educated Fish* (1937), the second Fleischer cartoon nominated for the Academy Award, saw its characters reprised two years later in *Small Fry* (1939). The third Oscar nomination, *Hunky and Spunky* (1938), featured a team of father and son donkeys that lead to seven additional cartoons produced over the next three years, ending with *Vitamin Hay* (1941), the last of the *Color Classics* series—a total of 36 produced over a six year period.

Fleischer Animation

Another important element of the look of Max Fleischer cartoons was the fluidity and grace of the animation, which his studio was built upon. This was based on standards set by the Timing and Checking Department, which included Nellie Sanborn, Alice Morgan,

Opposite, top: **Zoo setback for *Little Swee' Pea* (1936) (author's collection).** ***Bottom:*** **Charlie Schettler operating one of the smaller Stereoptical units (author's collection).**

and Bill Turner. They checked the animator's exposure sheets and drawings and established the rule that drawings should overlap the preceding to maintain fluidity. But what may be seen as fluid animation in many cases has been criticized as being formulaic and lethargic:

> The Fleischer animators of the early thirties appear to have drawn extremes that progressed from one to the next in a predictable pattern, with in-betweens of the same kind...
>
> Animating in that metronomic fashion probably gave birth to most of the slow, mechanical timing that was so prevalent in the early thirties (and that Walt Disney was trying to get rid of when he encouraged his animators to vary the spacing of their in-betweens.) It was, however, only at the Fleischer Studios, thanks to the Timing Department, that so sterile a method became in effect the officially sanctioned way to animate.[2]

While Fleischer Studios had timers and checkers, there was still a need to review the quality of the animation prior to commitment. Disney addressed this issue through the introduction of pencil tests for analyzing the action in terms of acting, continuity, and perfecting of timing. Pencil tests were an unheard of concept at Fleischer Studios. And the attitude was that any animator worth his salt already knew how things would move without tests. This lead to a formulaic approach developed by each animator, and because of this, the work of certain animators is identifiable due to a sameness of approach.

Production settled into a routine pattern to meet the demands of the commercial atmosphere at Fleischer Studios. While this brought about efficiency in production, it pre-

An animator at work on a Betty Boop cartoon, ca. 1932 (author's collection).

vented any opportunity for experimentation and artistic growth; a matter that concerned many of the young animators who eventually left for the west coast. Shamus Culhane articulated the issue with frankness:

> As I thought about it, I began to realize the potential of animation for all kinds of artists, not only cartoonists. Some day, fine art would have its place in this medium. The only person I confided in about these theories was Berny Wolf. He agreed with me that the Fleischer Studio was not the place to air such views. Now that Natwick and Sears had gone, there was nobody in the studio who could teach us anything. I was unhappily aware that much of the animation around me was very poor.[3]

Max was certainly aware of the progress that Walt Disney was making, but continued to dismiss him, believing he was taking animation in the wrong direction. Although many of the loyal Fleischer animators admitted that Disney animation was "different," they failed to see how and why it was better. Culhane tried to approach Max about the artistic merits of animation and later received a letter with a justification of his position:

> During the span of years from 1914, I have made efforts to retain the "cartoony" effect. That is, I did not welcome the trend of the industry to go "arty." It was, and still is, my opinion that a cartoon should represent, in simple form, the cartoonist's mental expression. In other words the "animated oil painting" has taken the place of the flashiness and delightfulness of the simple cartoon. In my opinion, the industry must pull back, pull away from the tendencies toward realism. It must stay in its own backyard of "The Cartoonist's Cartoon." The cartoon must be a portrayal of the expression of the true cartoonist, in simple, unhampered cartoon style. The true cartoon is a great art in its own right. It does not need the assistance or support of "Artiness." In fact, it is actually hampered by it.[4]

This justification seems a paradox in light of the artistry displayed in the background art that gave the Fleischer cartoons definition among the competition. And the value of pencil tests as Disney was doing was dismissed. On June 29, 1932, Max patented a drum-like device with a rotating shutter operated by a hand crank for testing animation.

The illustrations indicate that the concept was based on the old arcade Mutoscope, with the addition of a rotating shutter to cover the changing images similar to a film projector. While its primary purpose was for lectures and demonstrations, Animator Jack Ozark spoke of seeing Max using it in his office to review and correct animation. The illustrations indicate that the drum could hold from 12 to 16 drawings, limiting it to a foot of animation. For Max, the concern was strictly fluid action for its own sake. Walt Disney was more focused on the context of the action, and the stories of his *Sweat Box Pencil Test* sessions have become legendary. Fleischer Animator Berny Wolf told of the famous 13 corrections he made for a scene of the Jimmy Durante pelican characters in *Elmer the Elephant* (1936).

> Walt looked at it and said, "Who did that?" I slumped down in the chair and said in a little voice, "I did." Walt looked back with one eyebrow up, he said, "You know better than that!" So I took my stuff out of the reel and went back to my desk with it. And for the next week I handed in my corrections. And I didn't know what the Hell was wrong with them. I made 13 corrections on the one scene. I had it back in Sweat Box at least six times. The bulk of the time Walt wouldn't even pay any attention to it. Jackson directed it. So I said what's wrong with it? And he said (whispering), "Berny, I don't know what's wrong with it." He'd say "Why don't you ask 'so-and-so'"? I asked "so-and-so" and he wouldn't know. I'm going crazy. The next time in the Sweat Box, Walt says, "When are you going to correct that?" I get back to my desk and take the whole reel out down to my room to see if I can figure what the Hell it was. And I looked at everybody else's work as well as mine, and I finally caught it. It was ever so subtle. The action flow went (left to right). My Durante went (left to right). So I flopped my drawings, re-shot it (with) bottom lights. (Now) he went (right to left). I get it in the reel and Walt says, "Finally! Finally!"[5]

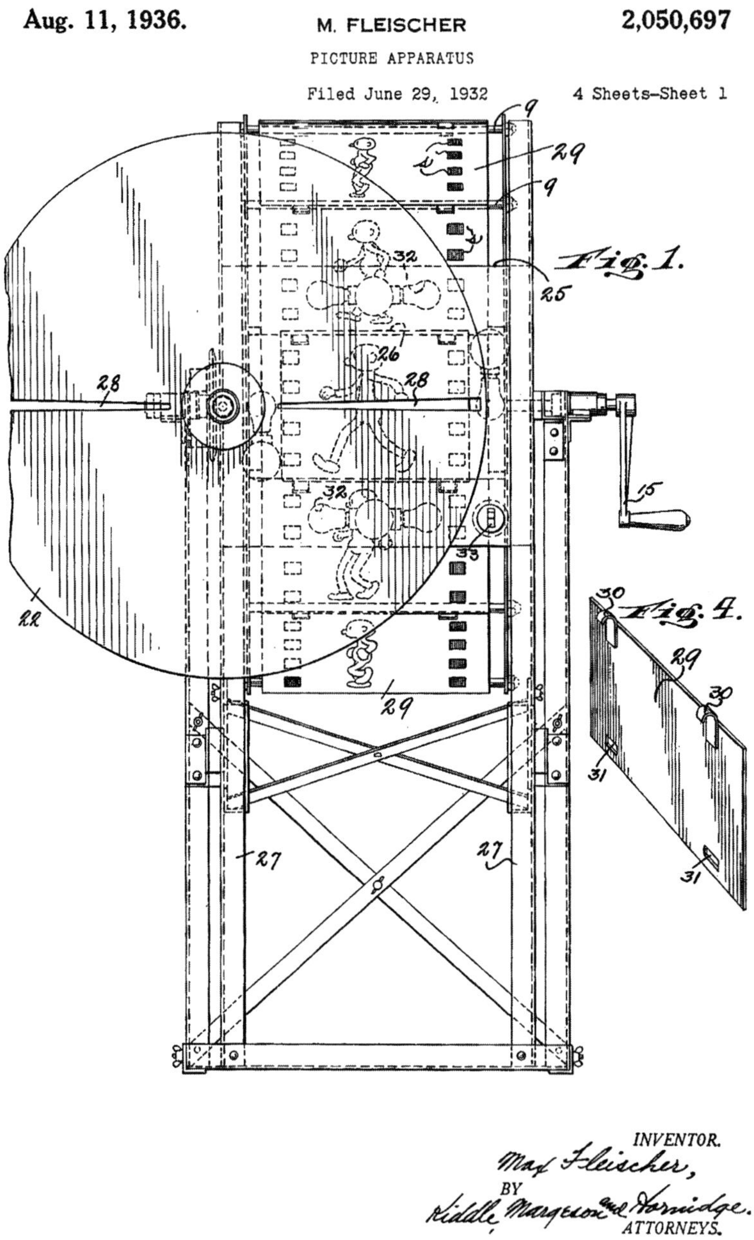

Picture Apparatus patent, page 1 (U.S. Patent and Trademark Office).

The Fleischer Camera Department

The role of the Camera Department cannot be overlooked since this was the last stop in the production process, the photography and finishing on film. The department was headed by Charles Schettler, a photographer friend of Dave Fleischer's, who had been with the studio since its inception. Schettler was assisted by Leonard McCormick and John

Aug. 11, 1936. M. FLEISCHER **2,050,697**

PICTURE APPARATUS

Filed June 29, 1932 4 Sheets-Sheet 4

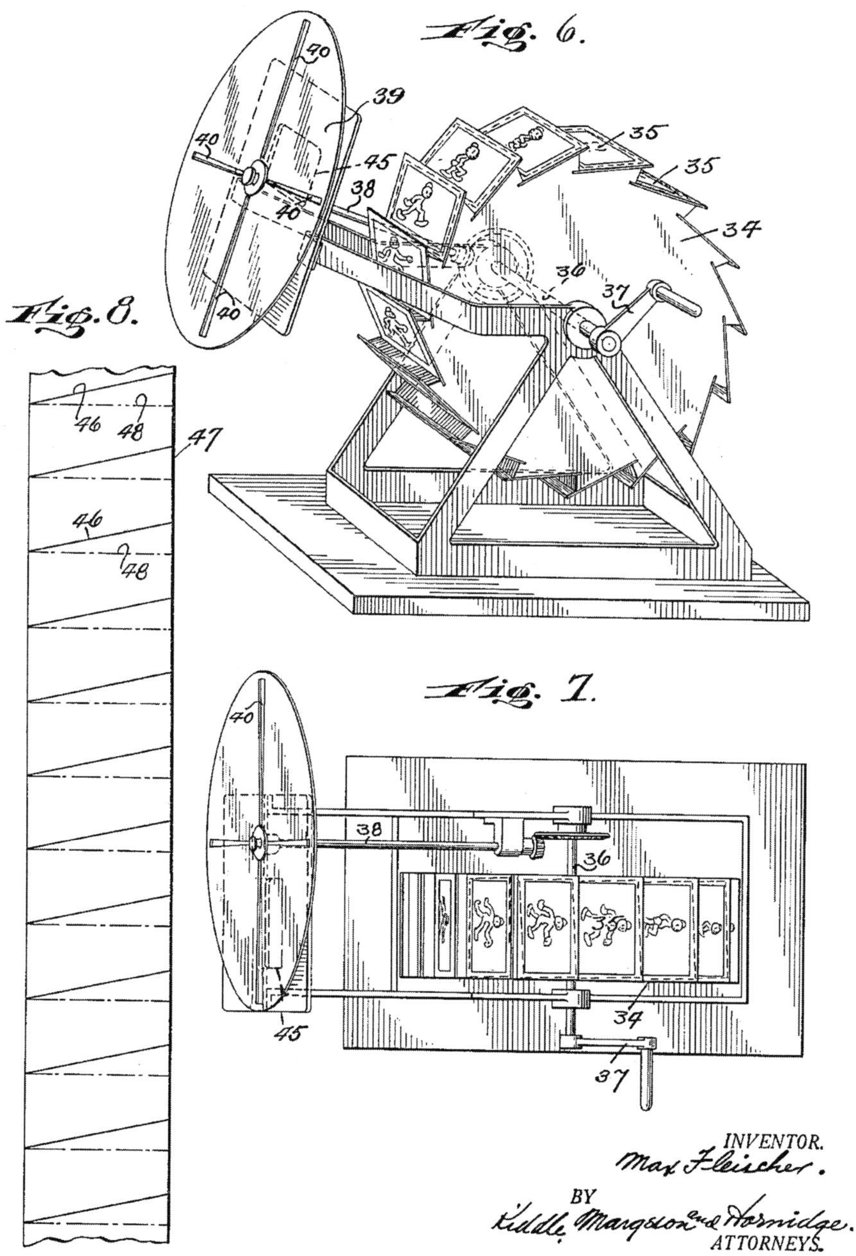

Picture Apparatus patent, page 2 (U.S. Patent and Trademark Office).

Fleischer Studios camera room, 1931. *Left to right:* Izzy Sparber, Leonard McCormick, Charlie Schettler, Kitty Pfister, possibly Johnny Burks—partially hidden (Todd Levine).

Burks, with other operators added as production demands increased. But the work of Schettler, McCormick, and Burks contributed largely to the output of clean photography and smooth camera moves in light of the challenges associated with the equipment.

In these pioneering days, each studio manufactured its own animation cameras and compounds based on two foundations, horizontal lathe beds and vertical frames. While the Bowles (Acme) Animation Camera was coming into use on the west coast, eastern studios such as Fleischer's continued using their own "homemade" equipment, adapting standard motion picture cameras with varying degrees of efficiency. The horizontal upright model was based on copy camera designs used in printing and commercial photography. The camera mount traveled on a lathe bed rail allowing the camera to be moved towards or away from the art in precise increments.

Operating the horizontal model was awkward and took up floor space. But most of all, it required the operator to stand and make more physical moves to place and replace cels and artwork for photography. It was cumbersome for shooting multiple cel levels and more problematic with foreground overlays (OL) in scenes. Since there was only one peg bar in use, the OL had to be removed and replaced with each cel change. There was a risk of accidentally omitting the OL on an exposure, causing it to disappear on an exposure. The other risk was wear on the cel registration perforations due to the constant removal

Standard camera setup made from a lathe bed (Todd Levine).

and replacing on the pegs. This would result in a "wiggle" due to lost registration of what was supposed to be a solid element in the setting. This flaw can be seen in the underground pan in the Superman cartoon, *Mechnical Monsters* (1941) where the foreground level "bumps" up and down during the pan. The solution was later found in the use of top and bottom pegs, registering overlays on top pegs with the active animation level on bottom pegs. By this method, the active cel level could be slid behind the overlay without removing it from the pegs. The addition of top and bottom pegs was found in the design of the animation stands that were coming into use. But at Fleischer Studios, all animation art was punched for top peg use. This configuration was practical for such upright configurations since the top pegs were used to "hang" the cels. This was particularly useful for the Setback camera, which generally used one cel level of animation with the camera aimed at a model background.

The Fleischer Studios Production Manual reveals that there were four types of camera setups for shooting animation with flat backgrounds: a Standard Field Camera; a Standard Field Sliding Peg Camera; an Approach Camera, and a Sliding Peg Approach Camera. Originally, the Standard Field was 6" × 8". Later the Standard Field was increased to 12 Field (12" × 9" art area) with a "Large Field," or 16 Field (16" × 12") for their feature work. Both Standard Field Cameras could shoot vertical, horizontal, or diagonal pans, but could not approach or recede on scenes. This was the purpose of the Sliding Peg Approach Camera. All of the individual features of these cameras were soon incorporated as standard options on all animation camera stands that followed.

What is most important to realize is that the continued advances in animation production brought about a need for mechanical applications to the photographic process made more complicated with the introduction of color photography due to its strict technical specifications on exposures. Seeing the end results, it is easy to take it for granted because it all worked. But knowing how it was obtained establishes the important role of science and engineering in the continued growth of the animation medium. And while Fleischer Studios was certainly focused on advancing animation through technology, it is ironic that it did not develop the efficient camera compounds that were coming into use by this time. Had they done it, this would have been a major exploitable Patent that would have generated ancillary income.

The Fleischer Sound

The aural atmosphere of the Fleischer cartoons can be attributed to the music and quality of musicianship on the soundtracks during the New York period. And because of the proximity to Broadway, a large talent pool of professional musicians was readily available. Many times big names such as Tommy and Jimmy Dorsey would sit in on recording sessions just for the fun of it. Much of this fun was due to the music provided by the staff of talented composers and arrangers. In-house, Lou Fleischer had Art Turkisher and Lloyd von Hayden as assistants in scoring and arranging. At the same time, several prominent composers and songwriters contributed to the Fleischer "sound" as well.

George Steiner (1900–1967)

George Steiner was born in Budapest, Hungary in 1900 and began a career of composing and conducting at the age of 18. He was associated with Paramount Studios in New York as a staff composer of background and mood music and is credited on music cue sheets for Fleischer Studios between 1929 and 1936.

Sammy Timberg (1903–1992)

Sammy Timberg had a long association with Fleischer Studios, with the many songs he composed for their classic cartoons. A relative of Seymour Kneitel, Timberg was a Tin Pan Alley song writer from Scranton, Pennsylvania. He began his career in his teens, studying under Rubin Goldmark, whose previous pupils had been George Gershwin and Aaron Copeland. When his father died, he joined his brother, Herman in Vaudeville at age 16, where he played straight man and wrote specialty songs for the duo of Timberg and Timberg. Timberg soon became involved in the early career of the Marx Brothers, writing material and serving as musical director. He wrote music for several Broadway shows produced by Busby Berkley, including *The Street Singer* and *The Duchess of Chicago,* before settling into a staff position with Paramount, where his long association with Fleischer and Famous Studios began. He was first teamed up with Sammy Lerner for the live-action short subject, *Musical Justice (1931)*, which starred Rudy Valle with an on-screen appearance of Mae Questel as Betty Boop where she introduced Lerner and Timberg's song, *Don't Take My Boop-Oop-A-Doop Away.*

Timberg was responsible for the largest share of songs that formed the foundation of many of the *Popeye* and *Betty Boop* cartoons including *We Aim to Please*, *I'm King of the Mardi Gras*, and specifically, *Brotherly Love*, with lyrics by Dave Fleischer. Timberg composed songs for the *Color Classics* series for which he received screen credit. He also co-wrote *It's a Hap-Hap-Happy Day* and the *Superman March* with Winston Sharples. Timberg remained with Fleischer Studios' successor, Famous Studios, until 1943. From 1943 until 1947, he wrote scores for Columbia Pictures' Screen Gems cartoon studio. Timberg then went onto a third career preparing specialty material for performers such as Jackie Gleason, Don Adams, and Eddie Gormet well into the 1960s until his retirement.

Winston Sharples (1909–1978)

Winston Sharples was born in Fall River, Massachusetts, earning his B.A. at Harvard and his M.F.A. in Drama at Carnegie Institute, with additional studies at the Yale School of Drama. He began playing piano on the radio in Connecticut in 1930 and later performed with The Vincent Lopez Orchestra. Sharples became Musical Director of Van Beuren Animation Studios after the untimely death of Gene Rodemich, acting as composer and arranger from 1934 until 1936. When Van Beuren closed, Sharples joined the Fleischer Studios as a freelance arranger for the next six years, and became sole music director and arranger for Famous Studios when Sammy Timberg left in 1943. Sharples' arrangements seem apparent in cartoons such as *Pudgy and the Lost Kitten* and *Always Kickin'*. But his signature of triumphant brass did not surface until his arrangement for the first *Superman* cartoon in 1941.

Sharples managed to retain the rights to many of his music cues from the 1950s Paramount cartoons, and entered a partnership with Hal Seeger to form Scroll Productions, which licensed the reuse of these cues by independent animation studios. Many were used in Joe Oriolo's *Felix the Cat* television series, and Paramount's television productions of *Popeye, Beetle Bailey,* and *Barney Google*. These cues were also used by Total Television Productions for *King Leonardo, Tennessee Tuxedo*, and Seeger's own productions of *Out of the Inkwell* and *Milton the Monster*. Sharples was a serviceable musician who adapted to new musical styles and was retained by Paramount Cartoon Studios until its closing in 1967.

Additional songwriters and lyricists contributed to the Fleischer sound.

Bob Rothberg (1901–1938)

Bob Rothberg was a native of New York and another of the Tin Pan Alley songwriters who in his short 37 years created memorable songs for *the Color Classics*, *Popeye*, and *Betty Boop* cartoons. Among them were *Why Am I So Beautiful?* from the *Popeye* cartoon, *Morning, Noon, and Nightclub* (1937).

Tot Seymour (1889–1966) and Vee Lawnhurst (1905–1992)

Tot Seymour was born Grace Mann in New York City and attended the famous Miss Ely's School of Music. She became one of the first female lyricists on Tin Pan Alley and was in great demand in the 1920s. While staff lyricist for Irving Berlin's publishing company, she wrote special material for Fannie Brice, Mae West, and Sophie Tucker.

Vee Lawnhurst was born Laura Lowenhurtz in New York City and became a skilled pianist at an early age, cutting piano rolls and making records. Teamed with Tot Seymour, she was the composing half of the team, which their publisher, Famous Music, promoted as "the first successful team of girl songwriters in popular music history." The songs they wrote for Fleischer cartoons include *Play Safe*, *Be Up to Date*, and *Hold It*. They also authored songs featured in the big band era *Screen Songs* series including *Please Keep Me in Your Dreams* and *No Other One*.

Al Neiburg (1902–1978)

Lyricist Allan J. Neiburg was born in St. Albans, Vermont, and attended Boston University. While he is best known for his association with Jay Livingston and hits such as *It's the Talk of the Town*, his brief association with Fleischer Studios was as a lyricist for *It's a Hap-Hap-Happy Day* from the animated feature, *Gulliver's Travels*.

In addition to the music, the sound effects created by Maurice Manne and Milton Lustig were equally important to the aural atmosphere and branding of the Fleischer cartoons.

Maurice Manne (Birth–Death?)

Little is known about Maurice Manne other than the fact that he had a musical background, the foundation of most acoustical sound effects men. He may have been a brother or cousin to Musical Director Max Manne, who supervised the musical synchronization for Paul Terry's first sound cartoon, *Dinnertime*, and Max Fleischer's first *Screen Songs* in 1929. It is likely that this relationship brought Maurice to Fleischer Studios with a career lasting nearly 40 years as a sound effects editor and member of The Film Editors Guild, continuing on with Famous and Paramount Cartoon Studios into the late 1960s.

Milton Lustig (1916–1996)

Milton Lustig was born in Brooklyn and began his career in 1937 in the Fleischer Studios Music Department as an assistant sound effects man, music editor, and composer. He later became a music editor and member of The Film Editors Guild, and authored the book, *Music Editing for Motion Pictures* published by Hastings House, New York, 1980. He also was an Instructor of Music Editing for Motion Pictures at UCLA (1985), Los Angeles City College, and The University of the Pacific at Stockton, California.

8

The Popeye Plant

Ever since Popeye made his debut in Elzie Segar's *Thimble Theater* comic strip, he became the center of attention. And without question, the acquisition of the animation rights was the greatest business move taken by Max Fleischer. On November 17, 1932, he secured the character licensing from King Features Syndicate and approached Paramount about developing a series. The executives had doubts about the screen appeal of such a grotesque character, so Fleischer arranged an on-screen tryout in a *Betty Boop* cartoon, titled appropriately, *Popeye the Sailor* (1933).

Popeye was unquestionably an instant hit and became one of the most successful adaptations of a comic strip character primarily because the Fleischer animation style was a natural fit. The Fleischer *Popeye* cartoons are not only memorable, but remain among the best comedy short subjects in cinema history. Part of this success can be attributed to an "unleashing" of the animators who had been confined by the more "sissy" *Betty Boop* cartoons. Now they could let loose with greater adventure with a broader male character. And because of this the *Popeye* series moved Fleischer Studios forward artistically with strong plot lines and well-defined characters that were perfectly matched to their voices.

The original voices for Popeye and Olive Oyl were William "Billy" Costello (1898–1971), a.k.a. "Red Pepper Sam," and Bonnie Poe. Costello had already appeared on the N.B.C. *Betty Boop Radio Show* using his trick raspy voice as Gus the Gorilla, which was first used as a mounted policeman speaking "Ga-bye, John!" in the *Screen Song* cartoon, *Boilesk* (1933).

Bonnie Poe originated the oafish-sounding Olive heard in the first eight cartoons, *Popeye the Sailor*, *I Yam What I Yam*, *Blow Me Down*, *Season's Greetinks*, *Wild Elephinks*, *Let's You and Him Fight*, *Can You Take It?*, and *Strong to the Finich*. Mae Questel added a ZaSu Pitts impersonation beginning with *I Eats My Spinach* (1933), and became the permanent voice starting with *Shiver Me Timbers (1934)*, continuing until *A Date to Skate* (1938) when she took a hiatus to raise a family. She was replaced by Margie Hines starting with *I Yam Love Sick* (1938). Oddly, *Plumbin' Is a Pipe* and *The Jeep* released during this period feature an unidentified Olive Oyl substituted with an annoying, squawking nasal voice. Margie Hines returned as Olive in *Cops Is Always Right* (1938), and continued in the role until 1944. After a period of adjustment, Miss Hines settled into the more realized ZaSu Pitts voice, becoming more wildly comedic and original.

Costello's career was accelerated as the voice of Popeye, and he was aware of it. His ego took over, demanding vacations at inconvenient times, sometimes arriving late for recording sessions. When he finally showed up drunk for the recording session for *Be Kind to Animals*, Dave Fleischer fired him. Floyd Buckley was called in as a temporary replace-

Above: The Popeye animation unit (author's collection). *Below:* Animation by "Doc" Crandall from *Sock a Bye Baby* (Ryan Englade).

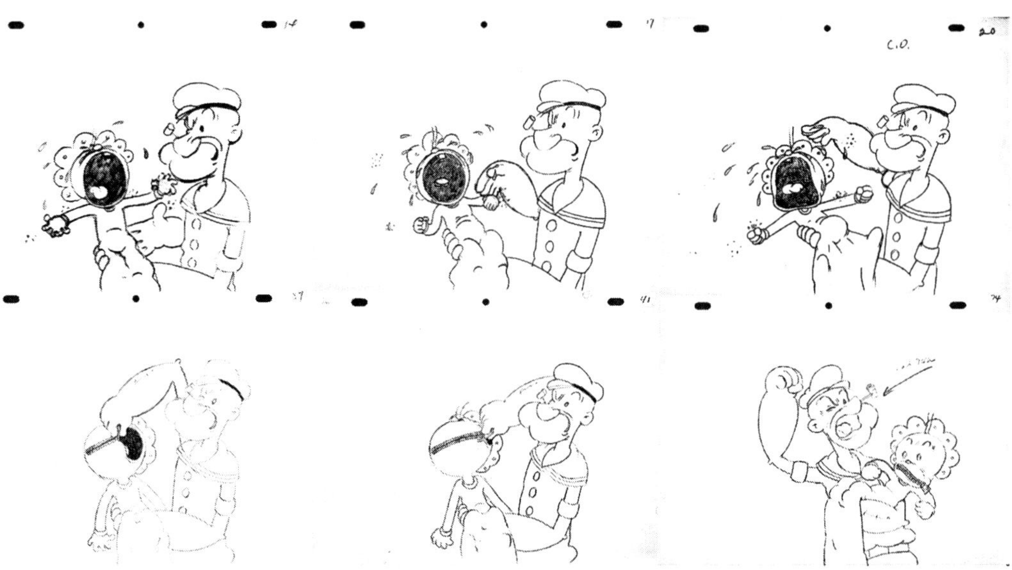

ment for the one cartoon. How Buckley was recruited is a mystery since he did not become the radio voice of Popeye until seven months later. Regardless, this explains the odd Popeye voice sounding as if he had a bad cold. What is more puzzling is that this cartoon was released February 22, 1935, and Costello's voice continued to be heard in the next six cartoons, his last being *You Gotta Be a Football Hero,* released August 31, 1935.

William "Red Pepper Sam" Costello (Virginia Kneitel-Mahoney).

Costello continued to capitalize on his connection to Popeye as he performed in vaudeville and on novelty records claiming to be the voice for the cartoons produced after he was terminated. Because there were no screen credits for voices, and the fact that he did originate the Popeye voice, his claim was credible to the general public even if he was no longer recording for the cartoons.

The Fleischers obviously needed a better replacement. That replacement was right under their noses in one of their own staff members, Winfield "Jack" Mercer (1910–1984). Mercer came from a theatrical family, having had some vaudeville and legitimate stage experience. In Mercer's interview with Mike Sporn, he explained how he came to be discovered:

> I was in the Inking Department when I first started doing the voices of the characters I happened to be inking at the time. The other Inkers seem to get a kick out of it and sort of egged me on. Well, after a while I was advanced to the Inbetween Department, and one day I was given a scene of Popeye to work on. Yeah, you guessed it, I began to imitate the Popeye voice.[1]

While walking through the studio, Lou Fleischer heard Mercer and was quick to ask, "Who is that? Who's doing the Popeye?" Lou was obviously excited about what he was hearing and after making his way through the aisles located the source. Jack was asked to audition over the telephone for Paramount's short subjects head, Lou Diamond. Diamond was impressed, but the vocalization became a strain on Mercer's throat. He was given mints and various throat remedies until his voice finally "cracked" for the necessary transition. Mercer continues:

> I don't know if Dave Fleischer was aware of my potential at that point. I didn't think I did it well enough. A short time after that I started to do some incidental voices on some of the cartoons as a sort of "breaking in" period. Then one day I was informed that I was going to do a *Popeye* cartoon.[2]

Jack Mercer debuted as Popeye in *King of the Mardi Gras* (1935) and became the studio's most versatile voice actor and story man. The introduction of Mercer brought about greater depth and humor to the *Popeye* character. Where the Costello portrayal was more gruff and grim in the sense of the comic strip, Mercer's take was more comedic, with a sensitive and sympathetic element. In addition, the teaming of Mercer and Questel was perfect since they were both clever ad libbers, contributing to many of the aside remarks heard without animated mouths. This impromptu approach to unanimated dialogue can be best described as "audio thought balloons" with the characters' thoughts being heard without the benefit of being spoken on screen. This practice continued until 1939. By 1940, all dialogue was pre-recorded and animated to the soundtrack, as was the industry standard by this time.

Rounding out the *Popeye* cast was the villain, Bluto. Due to the lack of screen credits and surviving of studio records, much confusion has resulted over which actor provided the voice. Two names surface in the 1930s, William Pennell (1889–1956), and Gus Wickie (1885–1947). Pennell, who was a member of a Paramount Quartette, joined the Fleischer stable of voice actors playing "heavies" starting in 1931. He was first heard in *Jack and the Beanstalk*, and again as the lecherous Ring Master in *Boop-Ooop-A-Doop*, then Betty's Germanic father in *Minnie the Moocher*, followed by the pirate captain in *Swim or Sink*.

Pennell was Bluto for the first two years of the *Popeye* cartoons, and was replaced with August "Gus" Wickie starting with *Choose Yer Weppins* in 1935. While both actors had low-pitched voices of similar tone, Wickie was a truer baritone, able to sing in a lower register with greater ease. He was a member of the Bill Hardy Gay 90s Quartet, which included Spike Harrison, Fred Bishop, and an alternating fourth member. Wickie continued as a voice performer until 1938, his last work as the Indian Chief in *Big Chief Ugh-A-Mug-Ugh*. With the loss of Wickie, the studio developed stories without their established villain for one year, then brought the character back in *Customers Wanted* (1939). By this time, the relationship between Bluto and Popeye was less threatening, neutralized by the absence of the strong voice by Wickie. A substitute was used in both *Customers Wanted* and *Ghosks Is the Bunk* until Pinto Colvig took on the role starting with *Wotta Nightmare* (1939) and ending with *Fightin' Pals* (1940). For Colvig's final voice work, he used his "Goofy" voice for the Mailman in *Popeye Presents Eugene, the Jeep* (1940). Following Colvig, story man Ted Pierce and Dave Barry were the voice for Bluto until 1944.

The *Popeye* series quickly hit its stride with a number of classics, many built around songs. *Barnacle Bill the Sailor* had been featured in the 1930 *Talkartoon* of the same name, noted for the second screen appearance of what was becoming Betty Boop. The song was used again to greater effect in *Beware of Barnacle Bill* (1935), which is one of the all time *Popeye* classics. *Popeye* was extremely popular and financially successful for both Paramount and Fleischer Studios. Polls indicated that *Popeye* had become more popular than Mickey Mouse.

> Walt Disney has a rival. Until I saw Popeye I could name no rival to Mickey Mouse or the creatures of the *Silly Symphonies*; but Max Fleischer has a fine sense of visual rhythm and a delicious sense of humor, although he lacks the authentic Disney touch. Nevertheless, he is a box-office winner, and a programme of Fleischer cartoons has been planned by Paramount for the coming season. I have discussed the question before, but it is worth repeating that the secret of the appeal of these animated cartoons is the exquisite balance they achieve between sound and movement—a fascinating question of visual rhythm, which should be more carefully explored by producers, particularly in musical films."[3]

This competition with Disney did not go unseen. Paramount ordered cartoons in packages of twelve, one each month. To meet these requirements, the *Popeye* unit was divided into four sections, each working on a separate cartoon simultaneously. In the first year, a large share of the *Popeye* cartoons came from the section headed by Seymour Kneitel and Roland "Doc" Crandall.

When asked who the best animators were, Dave Fleischer named in descending order of preference, Willard Bowsky, Seymour Kneitel, and Dave Tendlar. Bowsky was Max's favorite as well. While the pattern appears that each unit retained the same animators, some were rotated according to need, and the most senior received screen credit. Each unit had from four to eight animators according to complication, availability, and deadlines.

Key animation was typically in production from two to three weeks, with scenes going to the Inbetween, Ink and Opaque, and Camera Departments once completed. With several units working in tandem, an industrial management of the "trafficking" was necessary, with production numbers assigned to scenes to maintain order. As scenes would come back from the film lab, Dave Fleischer would review the footage and assemble the work print. Once all scenes were assembled, the post-production recording session would be scheduled. And because the studio was producing other series at the same time, these same units would rotate onto those other series on alternating weeks. With all of this footage being produced and assembled, indications are that several cartoons would be recorded within one day or in one week. The evidence of this can be found in the sound of the orchestrations and arrangements having a similar sound or tone regardless of series. But without question, it was the *Popeye* cartoons that were Fleischer Studios' "A List" product.

The Kneitel Unit

Seymour Kneitel (1908–1964)

Seymour Kneitel was educated in the New York Public School System, graduating from the High School of Commerce with a Commercial Art degree, followed by night courses at the National Academy of Design. He began his career at age 16 at the Bray Studio as an inker on the *Colonel Heeza Liar* series. Anxious to make animated cartoons, he went to the L.F. Cornwell Company in 1924. He worked his way up from office boy to animator within one year, becoming one of the three staff animators on *Ebinizer Ebony*, which was produced in the early Kelly Color process. He came to Max Fleischer's Inkwell Studios in 1925, working as an inbetweener.

In 1927, Kneitel left New York to become a title card writer at MGM.

A year later he was out of a job when sound films became permanent. He returned to New York and worked as an inbetweener at Loucks and Norling, which produced industrial films and *Mutt and Jeff* cartoons. Six months later, he returned to Inkwell Studios as an inbetweener, was promoted to animator in 1929, and by 1931 he was a head animator and director of a number of industrial and military training films, as well as *Talkartoons, Screen Songs*, and *Betty Boop* cartoons. Teamed with Berny Wolf, Kneitel was instrumental in the human transformation of Betty Boop into the full human character as she is known. He was then teamed with veteran Roland "Doc" Crandall on the first three years of *Popeye* and continued on the series, becoming its production Supervisor starting in 1939. Kneitel loved his work and had a studio set up in the maid's quarters at home where he did some freelance cartooning under the name of "Knight." Kneitel remained during the transitions under Paramount management until his death in 1964.

Eli Brucker (1887–1982) Uncredited

Brucker worked in the Kneitel unit, then the Tendlar unit after 1935.

Roland "Doc" Crandall (1892–1972)

Roland Crandall was the most "seasoned" animator on staff, having been with Max Fleischer from the beginning. Crandall was teamed with Seymour Kneitel as lead animator on *Popeye* for the first three years of production starting with *Popeye the Sailor* (1933) and ending with *Never Kick a Woman* (1936). The two credited animators were the lead animators, the one with top credit billing being the actual director. In the teaming of Crandall with Seymour Kneitel, it was Kneitel who essentially directed the cartoons, providing stories, layouts and a share of the animation as well. Since there were no formal Model Sheets defining details on the characters, they varied in the way they were drawn from one scene to another due to the individuality of each animator. Where Kneitel drew Popeye with a larger, rounder head and more articulated fingers, Crandall drew him with a smaller head and sausage-like fingers. The most glaring of these examples can be seen in *The Hyp-Nut-Tist* (1935) which not only displays blatant shifting "on and off model," but also shows some poor drawing in several scenes that may have been done by lesser animators or trainees. Crandall's work can be identified by a solidity of form. He also handled the detailed, handsome close-ups featuring thick and thin lines-a reflection of his illustration background.

While an industry veteran, his approach was becoming old-fashioned and expressionless in light of the advancements being made by the younger animators who were introducing more personality animation to the *Popeye* series. From 1936 until 1938, Crandall was assigned to the *Screen Songs* series when it adapted a mock newsreel format.

Crandall animated on *Gulliver's Travels* and *Mr. Bug Goes to Town.* He also animated *Popeye* one last time, for *Shakespearian Spinach* (1940). Crandall left the business at the end of the studio and returned to his native Connecticut doing commercial illustration until his retirement in the 1950s.

William Henning (1896?–?)

William Henning began animating in 1931. He had been with the Fleischer Studio for six years by the time he was moved to Seymour Kneitel's unit. He had previously been one of the Inbetween Department supervisors and ran it in a militaristic fashion. His drawing ability may have been less than that of his peers, but he worked fast.

> William Henning ... unlike the other animators in the New Wave, was a man of thirty-five who had been a captain of machine gunners in World War I... After the war, he came to New York, and Max rescued him from a job as a car washer. Unlike most Prussians, he was not stiff-necked around the kids in the studio. While his drawing ability left much to be desired, he managed to do acceptable animation.[4]

In 1939, Henning was given his own unit, directing *Ghosks Is the Bunk, Hello-How Am I?, It's the Natural Thing to Do,* and *Never Sock a Baby.*

Dave Hoffman (Birth?–Death?) Uncredited

Hoffman also worked in the Tom Johnson *Screen Songs* unit starting in 1935.

Abner Mathew Kneitel (Birth?–Death?)

Abner Kneitel became an animator at Fleischer Studios in 1931. A cousin to Seymour Kneitel, he joined the Kneitel unit in 1934 and took the name Abner Matthews when credited with Seymour. He also crossed over to the Dave Tendlar and Henning units when needed. Abner animated on the features, *Gulliver's Travels* and *Mr. Bug Goes to Town.* He enlisted in the Navy during World War II and returned to live in Florida, having left the animation field.

The Bowsky Unit

Willard Bowsky (1907–1944)

Willard Bowsky was a colorful character, outspoken and open with anti–Semitic remarks. Skilled with complicated perspective scenes, his group was assigned such scenes when they came up. When the *Popeye* series began there were two teams, one headed by Kneitel and Crandall and the second by Bowsky and Bill Sturm. Although a prolific animator, he left the Fleischer Studio shortly after the declaration of World War II, volunteering for combat duty in the Army and was killed in a tank in France in 1944.

Orestes Calpini (1911–1974)

Information on Calpini is obscure. While already an established animator at Fleischer Studios, his first *Popeye* screen credit was on *Let's Get Movin'* (1936).

George Germanetti (1908–1967)

Joined the Bowsky unit in 1936.

Charles "Tex" Hastings (Birth?–Death?)

Charles Hastings received his first screen credit on *Be Kind to Animals (1935*). Hastings had been an animator for Walter Lantz in the early 1930s before coming to Fleischer's.

Ed Nolan (Birth?-Death?) joined the unit in 1935.

Jack Ozark (Jacob Ozarkowitz a.k.a. Jake) (1914–2000)

Ozark joined the unit in 1936, uncredited.

Graham Place

Place joined the unit in 1936, uncredited. Place worked for the Tendler, Kneitel, and Johnson units also.

Lod Rossner

Rossner joined the unit in 1935, uncredited.

Gordon Sheehan

Sheehan joined the unit in 1936, uncredited.

Bill Sturm (1906–1981)

William A. Sturm was born in New Jersey and attended the Art Students League. He began his career at the Bray Studio while still a teenager. He animated *Felix the Cat* in the 1920s and is credited with the iconic twisting of Felix's tail into a question mark. His name surfaces in early 1934, receiving second line screen credit as a lead animator. He was one of the major staff members at Fleischer Studios, and during World War II, did technical animation for both Walt Disney and Jam Handy under Max Fleischer. He worked for the Fletcher Smith Studios and later operated a successful commercial production company, Bill Sturm Productions.

Nicholas "Nick" Tafuri (1913–1990)

Born in the Coney Island section of Brooklyn, Tafuri became a lead animator beginning with *The Two Alarm Fire* (1934). He continued on the staff of Fleischer Studios and its successors, Famous and Paramount Cartoon Studios until its closing in 1967. He continued to freelance in New York City on commercials and was one of the major animators on Ralph Bakshi's *Fritz the Cat* (1972).

Harold Walker (1904–1994)

Harold Mitchell "Hal" Walker was born in Ossining, New York. Some sources state that he had done some silent film acting before he entered the cartooning field. Sources also claim that he served in the Navy during World War I, but this is impossible since he would have been 12 or 13 years old at the time, and was 37 at the time of World War II, making him too old for the draft. He began his career as a cartoonist and soon entered the animation field at age 16 when he worked on the early *Mutt and Jeff* and *Felix the Cat* series. Walker's career in animation is difficult to trace other than to say that he appears to have been assigned to the Willard Bowsky unit, with screen credit on *Popeye* cartoons, beginning with *Beware of Barnacle Bill* (1935). While Walker remained with Fleischer Studios, animating on both features, he seems to have disappeared from the industry after World War II.

The Waldman Unit

Myron Waldman (1908–2006)

Myron Waldman was born in Brooklyn and attended Pratt Institute. He became an animator at Fleischer Studios in 1930 and became associated with sensitive and cute characters. Due to his formal art training, Waldman opposed the tendency to animate in the "rubber hose" fashion, choosing a more skeletal foundation. Ironically, he was placed in charge of a *Popeye* unit, directing the violent comedy, *Can You Take It?* (1934). Waldman remained with the transition to Famous and Paramount Cartoon Studios, later becoming animation director for Hal Seeger Productions' *Out of the Inkwell* television series (1961–62).

Frank Endres

Endres joined the unit in 1936, uncredited.

Lillian Freidman

Freidman joined the unit in 1934 and animated the opening scene in *Can You Take It?*, uncredited. She received screen credit on the *Betty Boop* cartoons, *Pudgy Takes a Bow-Wow* and *Pudgy and the Lost Kitten.* Lillian also animated Betty Boop rope-skipping and taking a bow in *Betty Boop and the Little King*, uncredited.

Tom Johnson (1907–1960)

Thomas Johnson began as a newspaper cartoonist and entered the animation field at the Fleischer Studios in late 1930. His first assignments were on the *Screen Songs.* He was eventually promoted to the *Popeye* series, placed in the Waldman Unit, and became one of the studio's Lead Animators. In 1936, Johnson was placed in charge of a unit that included Charles "Tex" Hastings, Saul Kessler, and Don Figlozzi. Johnson animated on both features, *Gulliver's Travels* and *Mr. Bug Goes to Town,* remaining during the changeover to Famous and Paramount Cartoon Studios until his death in September 1960. He also did occasional freelance work for Jam Handy.

Hicks Lokey

Lokey joined the unit in 1936, uncredited.

Ed Nolan

Nolan joined the unit in 1936.

Sam Stimson

Stimson joined the unit in 1936.

Ted Vosk

Vosk joined the unit in 1936.

The Tendlar Unit

Dave Tendlar (1909–1993)

David Tendlar was born in Dayton, Ohio and got his first job in animation when his family moved to New York in 1926. He started out as an errand boy and inker on *Krazy Kat* along with veteran Berny Wolf. He was hired by Max Fleischer as an inbetweener on *Out of the Inkwell* around 1927 or 1928, and promoted to animator in 1931. Because of his skilled drawing and realization of personality animation, he soon became one of the lead animators in the Bowsky unit and was promoted to supervising animator/director beginning with *Choose Yer Weppins* (1935), remaining with the series when it was taken over by Paramount. He later worked for Terrytoons, Hal Seeger Productions, Filmation, and Hanna-Barbera.

George Germanetti (1908–1967)

Credited lead animation for the Tendlar unit in 1935.

Graham Place (1903–1981)

The background of Graham Place is also obscure. He is first recognized as an animator under Dave Tendlar starting with *King of the Mardi Gras* (1935) and later worked in the Kneitel unit. From appearances, it seems that Place was influenced by Disney character design and was put to use when Paramount requested more of a "Disney look" in the cartoons. Place handled the 1939 redesign of Betty Boop, as well as the character designs for the Fleischer feature *Mr. Bug Goes to Town.* He remained active as an animator with Famous Studios, continuing with Paramount Cartoon Studios and Hal Seeger Productions until 1967.

Demand and Supply

The tremendous demand for *Popeye* cartoons presented many more challenges. The allocated advances from Paramount were not enough, and cost-cutting measures were always sought. One was found in the "recap" film, or "cheater," using clips from previously released cartoons. While the credit to this goes to Seymour Kneitel, this had been done in the *Out of the Inkwell* series.

Thanksgiving (1925), consists of a series of clips taken directly from the old negatives for *The Cure* (1924), *The Masquerade* (1924), and *Up to Mars* (1924), spliced to the new live action footage under the premise of showing "home movies" to the dinner guests.

The problem was that the original negatives to the cartoons were sacrificed. With the introduction of duplicate negative films stocks and the optical printer in the 1930s, original negatives could be duplicated without harming them. But taking random sections of scenes with locked-in sound presented editing problems especially when sequences were cut shorter than in their original versions. This would cause obvious jumps in rhythm, which is why the sound was dubbed for these flashback films.

The first and best of these was *The Adventures of Popeye* (1935), which uses a live action foundation to integrate the animation in a manner reminiscent of the *Out of the Inkwell* films. *The Adventures of Popeye* is largely a live action film with a seemingly normal premise of a little boy dressed in a frilly summer suit buying a *Popeye* book at a newsstand. As he is walking along enjoying the book, an older boy calls him a "sissy" and starts bullying him. During a minor scuffle, the *Popeye* book falls back against a row of produce baskets. The cover with a portrait of Popeye comes to life. And seeing the little boy left crying, *Popeye* consoles him by recalling highlights of his dealings "with guys what thinks they're tough." Popeye then turns the pages and stills from previous cartoons come to life through the insertion of matched duplicate negative footage from *I Eats My Spinach* (1933), *Popeye the Sailor* (1933), *Wild Elephinks* (1933), and *Ax Me Another* (1934).

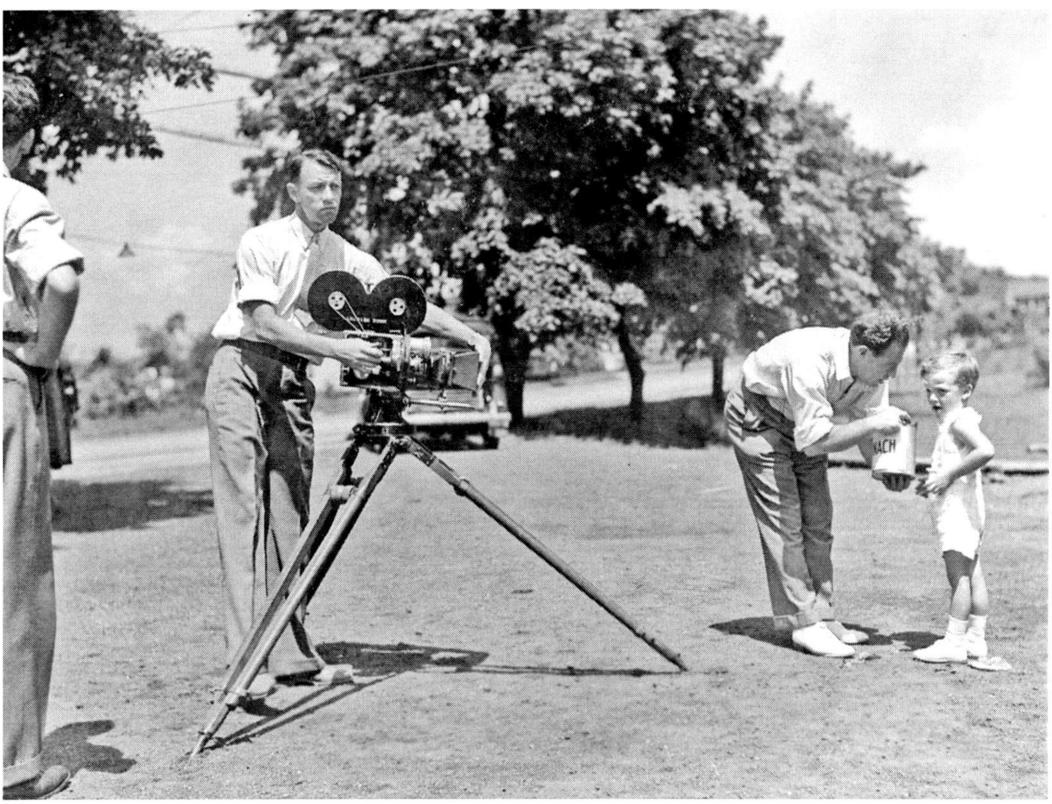

(*Left to right*) Unknown, Charlie Schettler on camera, Dave Fleischer directing child actor for live action portion of *The Adventures of Popeye*, 1935 (Todd Levine).

Nov. 14, 1939. J. E. BURKS 2,180,194

PHOTOGRAPHIC APPARATUS

Filed July 23, 1937 5 Sheets-Sheet 2

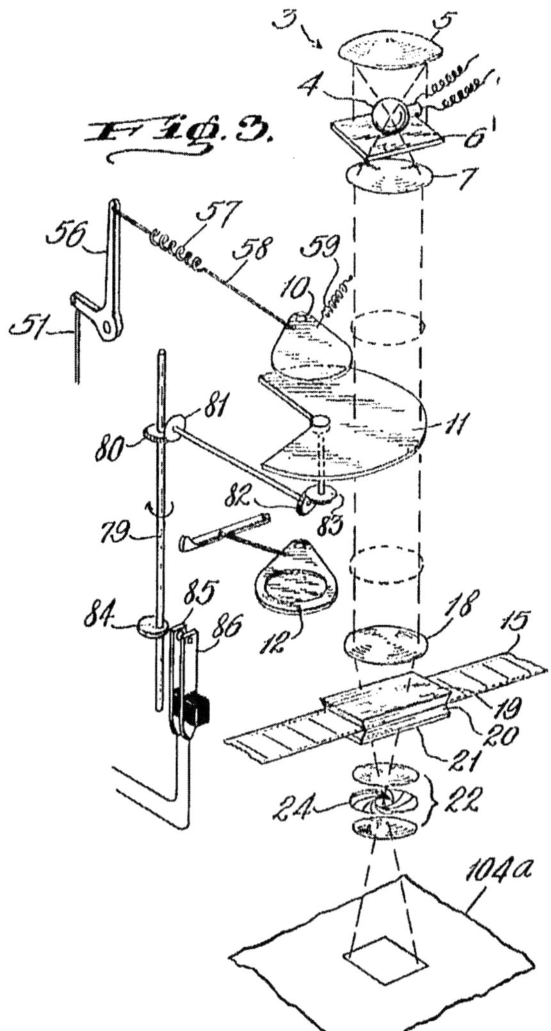

INVENTOR
JOHN E. BURKS
BY Horwidge and Dowd
ATTORNEYS

Burks' Optical Printer patent (U.S. Patent and Trademark Office).

To address the technical issues of capturing still images for the transition to moving footage, Max worked with John Burks in the development of a type of projection printer allowing the images from a motion picture negative to be exposed onto photographic paper. This served two purposes. It acted as a type of enlarger to produce still photographs of live action scenes used as backgrounds for cel overlays, as in scenes with Popeye interacting with the live book. The other purpose was to provide stills from cartoon footage integrated into the animation artwork. As the camera moves in on them, there would be a match. And when the new footage was spliced together with the dupe negative, the transition would appear as a continuation of the action. The effect essentially worked, although there is a slight shift in tone and contrast between the original and dupe footage. This process was first used in *The Adventures of Popeye* (1935) and following "flashback" cartoons, such as *I'm in the Army Now* (1936), and *Customers Wanted* (1939). Coincidentally, the concept in *Customers Wanted* uses the old amusement park arcade Mutoscopes, which both of Max's rotating drum patents were based on.

The Fleischer studio had a large staff producing four series with a new cartoon in theaters every week, which brought their yearly production output to an average of 52 releases. To meet this production schedule, a regimented production system came into use. According to John Gentilella, everything was planned right down to the exact number of drawings required. Gordon Sheehan mentioned the footage quotas placed on animators. Animators working with assistants were required to produce 30 feet a week, and animators working without assistants, 22 feet a week. With 35mm film running 90 feet per minute, an average *Popeye* cartoon running seven minutes came to 630 feet. With four animators assigned, this averaged five weeks to animate a single cartoon. While the quality of the animation was stressed, it was obvious that the focus was on quantity. These requirements forced the animators to follow formulas and footage shortcuts to meet their quotas. Cycled actions, holds, slow-ins and cushions to accent poses on holds, and animation levels such as mouths or arms over hold cels of bodies, a staple of limited animation for television, were among the production shortcuts used extensively combined with full animation where permitted.

The work of certain animators can be identified by the way characters were drawn or the way the animation was approached, many times using formula walks and other actions. Seymour Kneitel had a calculated approach that reduced the risks of error in light of the need to meet footage quotas for fast turnaround of production. While there were rules in production procedures at Fleischer Studios, there were no set rules for the animation of the characters as at the Disney studio.

> What had become central to Disney animation by the late thirties, the exploration of character through animation, was incidental at best in the Fleischer scheme of things because of the threat it posed to the steady flow of production. That flow could best be maintained by adhering to formula. Here again, it is probably the voices of the lower-ranking animators that convey the studio's priorities most clearly. Ed Rehberg said for instance, of Seymour Kneitel … "he had a stock formula for walks and runs, and you either did it his way or it was wrong. There was never any experimenting." He'd say, "You're stupid if you do it that way."[5]

For two years, Max Fleischer had been petitioning Paramount executives about expanding production into feature length animated films. Fleischer had already explored feature concepts in the *Color Classics*. And because of *Popeye*'s strong box office draw, Paramount authorized an expansion of the format in the 1936 epic, *Popeye the Sailor Meets Sindbad the Sailor*. *Sindbad* was an instant success and proved that there was an audience for longer animated pictures. In *The Miami News*, December 25, 1936, Max was quoted: "We have an eye on an eight-reel feature, which in production expense will vie with some of Hollywood's most elaborate pictures. There will come a day when audiences can go to a theater and see only a cartoon feature, for the possibilities of the medium are limited only by the imagination of our artists."

Starting with the first two-reel *Popeye* Special, Paramount began promoting the Fleischer cartoons in competition with Walt Disney for Academy Award consideration. In 1937, Paramount nominated *The Educated Fish*, and in 1938, *Hunky and Spunky*. *Popeye the Sailor Meets Sindbad* lost to Disney's *The Country Cousin*. This was a disservice since *Sindbad* was the first two-reel cartoon ever produced, and a precursor to longer format feature cartoons that were to come. Had Paramount petitioned aggressively, *Sindbad* could have received a "Special Achievement for pioneering the long format cartoon." It was unfair to pit this minor epic against a one reel Disney cartoon of a different type and category even if it did qualify as a "short subject" by being under one hour in length.

Animation Drawing of Sindbad, *Popeye the Sailor Meets Sindbad the Sailor* (Todd Levine).

Color callout drawing, *Popeye the Sailor Meets Sindbad the Sailor* (Todd Levine).

Although Fleischer Studios produced better cartoons in their *Popeye* series, they were in black and white. Paramount management mistakenly reasoned that their color cartoons emulating the sentiment of Disney could compete for the coveted Oscar. And while Disney continued to develop and refine with each year, Fleischer remained static for five years due to the emphasis on commercial production over artistic advancement. For this reason, the color Fleischer cartoons looked years behind Disney, giving them a great disadvantage by comparison. As a result, *The Educated Fish* lost to Disney's *The Old Mill* in 1937, and *Hunky and Spunky* lost to Disney's *Ferdinand the Bull* in 1938.

While an attractive product, the process of producing animated cartoons on a commercial scale tended to be a combination of excitement and tedious frustration due to its very nature. Much of the work, especially at the entry level was repetitive and impersonal. Conforming to character model sheets and set drawing styles was necessary. Any creativity originated in the story department and was largely in the hands of the directors and animators. This system of rigidity required an artist to duplicate characters exactly as designed and make in-betweens matching the quality of animator's drawings. Such a worker was highly desired since these were the requirements for this assembly line procedure.

Every animation studio operated on a 45-hour week. And while there were no paid vacations or sick leave, Fleischer Studios offered paid overtime when others did not. The

Inbetweener's room (author's collection).

wage scale at Fleischer Studios was considered the best in New York. In the early 1930s with salaries beginning at $12 per week for cel painters, $16 for inkers, and $22 for inbetweeners. The next steps up were assistant animator at $50 per week, and animator at $100 per week and higher. Everyone at Fleischer Studios started at the lower ranks, and it was among the lower levels that the studio looked for talent.

In the 1930s, women were tasked with inking, opaquing, timing, and matching. The most they could hope for was managerial positions. The goal for beginners was to become an inbetweener since this was a step away from being an animator. While opportunities for women to become inbetweeners were non-existent at studios such as Disney's, Fleischer Studios was an exception, promoting three women, Lillian Freedman, Lillian Oremland, and Edith Vernick.

Lillian Freedman became the first female animator at $65 per week—at least $25 less than her male counterparts. To a degree, there was a certain sense of glamour associated with working on these popular cartoon films even though many of the workers were not earning very good salaries. The age range among the lower positions was between 18 and 20. Many of them were single, still living with their families. Inbetweener Alden Getz described the situation:

I suppose, in a sense, it was a seduction. I can see where people would be attracted to working in a studio with Popeye and Mickey Mouse and think they were really doing something great and disregard the fact that they were not making very good salaries.

There were two types of people in the Studio: those who had to live on what they made, which was tough; and there were the other type who were subsidized—they either lived with their families or they had a spouse who was working. Because they were young, most of them were 18, 19 or 20, a lot of them did live with their families. Therefore, the paying of those low salaries was possibly only because of that set of conditions. You couldn't, for instance, hire 30-year old people because they had to make a living.[6]

Dan Glass was a young artist from Harrison, Arkansas, who started as a cel painter in 1932. He was a good worker and was well liked by everyone. He supplemented his income by painting signs. He also attended night courses at the Art Students League. He was quickly promoted to the assistant department and earned $22 per week. Then he started working a lot of overtime. Max Fleischer was aware of Dan's activities, and cautioned him about over-extending himself to the risk of his health.

Dan Glass (Harvey Deneroff).

One day that fall Dan did not show up for work. After a few days of not hearing from him (he did not have a phone) my father paid him a visit to see what was the matter. Dan, it seems, had come down with a severe case of pulmonary tuberculosis. This came as a shock to everyone in the Studio, as he had always been so quiet and reserved. His friends in he Inbetween Department tried to take care of Dan as best they could, taking turns feeding and comforting him.

Max Fleischer paid for a week's stay for Dan at a New Jersey resort. However, his condition worsened, and his prognosis was not good; there seemed to be no point in hospitalizing him and it was felt that it was best that Dan be sent home to Harrison. A collection was taken up, and a delegation saw him off at the train station—this was probably in late November, around Thanksgiving time. Max Fleischer paid for his ticket home, though the fact that he did not show up to see Dan off irked some who had blamed Dan's low wages and poor working conditions for his plight."[7]

Dan Glass died in his parents' room on January 17, 1935. Dan's death started talk about unionizing the studio. But other events contributed to the growing discontent, motivated by a similar occurrence with Inbetweener Lillian Oremland, which began in 1931. Miss Oremland started complaining about stomach pains. Following an examination, a scar was discovered on her lung resulting from tuberculosis, which had entered her stomach. She spent a summer in a sanitarium in Liberty, New York and remained sickly. The studio took her back on several occasions with an absence of about one year. The studio then refused to take her back for fear that her illness was contagious in spite of doctor's notes denying this.

Lillian Oremland was hospitalized afterward, eventually dying in late 1935 or early 1936. The growing suspicions connected the crowded Inbetweening Department of confined cubicles with the lack of air-conditioning as a breeding ground for disease. But Fleischer Studios was not alone in growing labor problems. Across the street at 729 Seventh Avenue,

Animation Drawing from *Betty Boop for President* by Dan Glass (Harvey Deneroff).

The Van Beuren studio had become a hotbed of labor unrest since the arrival of Burt Gillett as its new director. Gillett arrived in May 1934 having directed Walt Disney's most successful cartoon of the previous year, *The Three Little Pigs*. The appointment of Gillett was intended to upgrade the quality of the Van Beuren cartoons and improve its box office returns. And because of Gillett's association with Walt Disney, management was assuming that the studio would be in a position to duplicate the Disney successes. But Gillett's presence had varying impressions and affects.

Animator Bill Littlejohn recalled Gillett as a "...fantastically talented man, and I got along with him. But others sort of thought he was a wild man and mad.... He was a very nervous guy and very dynamic. He was erratic, he would get flashes of ideas and he would throw out what he had before and take off on another tangent."[8]

Animator Isidore "I" Klein regarded him as a lunatic, "...constantly firing people.... Gillett told me he hired a wonderful young artist to do backgrounds. He turned out to be a very capable young painter I knew. Three days later I found out he was fired. There was a constant revolving door."[9]

A good share of Gillett's erratic behavior was due to alcoholism. Within six months, he had fired 50 highly experienced people who found employment with Fleischer and Terrytoons. There had been talk of organizing at Van Beuren, and some staff members were fired for alleged union talk. One of them was Hicks Lokey, who eventually was hired as an animator at Fleischer Studios when an opening became available.

Sadie Bodin had been a paint matcher for Fleischer Studios since mid–1929. By 1933, she felt exhausted and asked studio Production Manager William Gillmartin for an eight-week vacation, substantiated by a doctor's note. Bodin was granted a temporary leave of absence with the assurance, "You will be hired again. Don't worry, just go away and have a good time."[10]

Gillmartin left shortly afterward to work for Van Beuren, and Sam Buchwald was promoted from Assistant Production Supervisor to Production Manager. Then on September 1, Buchwald sent Bodin a registered letter informing her that her position had been filled "due to the pressure of production," and she was therefore laid off. She found work as a librarian in a settlement house for a year and was then hired as a "matcher" at Van Beuren in September 1934 at $18.40 a week. She did planning and inking, and following layoffs a month later, did opaquing "when there was a call for it."[11]

The Animated Motion Picture Workers Union began to organize at Van Beuren in late 1934. The membership consisted of animators and assistants. Sadie Bodkin was the Union's recording secretary when she joined on January 22, 1935. Gillett was aware of the Union's presence in the studio and on March 22 fired Sadie Bodin without notice. Her firing seemed associated with rumors that she had spoken against working overtime and also for her union association. Management claimed Mrs. Bodin was uncooperative and denied her union affiliation as grounds for her dismissal. On April 17, 30, and May 1, Sadie Bodin and her husband, Paul, a painter, picketed Van Beuren themselves. They carried signs reading:

> "Van Beuren violates Sec. 7-A, N.R.A. by firing Union Labor for Union Activity." Van Beuren fires for Union activities. Do not patronize theaters where Van Beuren animated cartoons are shown—*Tattletales* and *Rainbow Parade.*

The Bodins picketed during the noon hour. The rest of the workers crossed the line going to and from lunch with the understanding that the picket was advertising a firing for union activity, which was in violation of National Recovery Act rules. All of the Fleischer people witnessed this, the first picketing of an animation studio being carried out by two people. The next event prompted Van Beuren workers to take this more seriously.

The Van Beuren cartoons were distributed by RKO. After a four-year association with United Artists, Walt Disney signed with RKO. Having struggled for half a decade to compete with Disney, RKO had the real thing, which prompted the closing of Van Beuren at the time when Fleischer was expanding due to increased production brought on by Paramount's demand for more *Popeye* cartoons. Many of the Van Beuren people who were hired were placed in positions lower than they had previously held. Marty Taras, who had been a $30 a week assistant animator at Van Beuren had to return to doing in-betweens at Fleischer. Taras recalled:

> Before we went there, there was a friendly rivalry between Van Beuren people and the Fleischer people. However, the Fleischer people somehow or other held themselves (as if) they were an elite group of artists, which was not necessarily so. Van Beuren people were held in mild contempt because we didn't work our way up the ranks as others did in Fleischer. We were held (despite our ability) as somewhat second-class citizens.... We Inbetweeners, especially from Van Beuren, tried to be friendly ... ask Opaquers and Inkers for dates. A fairly good camaraderie all around there. But the Animators and the Directors? Forget it! Everybody had to kiss the ground wherever they walked.[12]

Before this, it was not unusual for those with talent and ambition to be promoted to the position of animator before the age of 21. But by 1936 the animation ranks at Fleischer Studios had been filled. Bill Carney, who came from Van Beuren, was impressed with the Fleischer operation. It was an efficient operation with attention to detail and quality, due largely because Fleischer had fully developed continuing characters and following model sheets had become important. This is not to say that the same practice was not in place under Gillett at Van Beuren, but procedures at Fleischer were quite definite. Lou Appet, who had begun working for Fleischer in the early 30s, remarked that when the entire studio was on one floor there was a friendly atmosphere, "It was pretty free-flowing.... And most people ... just circulated and met everybody including all the Animators. There was no such thing as a caste system. Everyone seemed to accept someone if you were in the business, you were in it."[13]

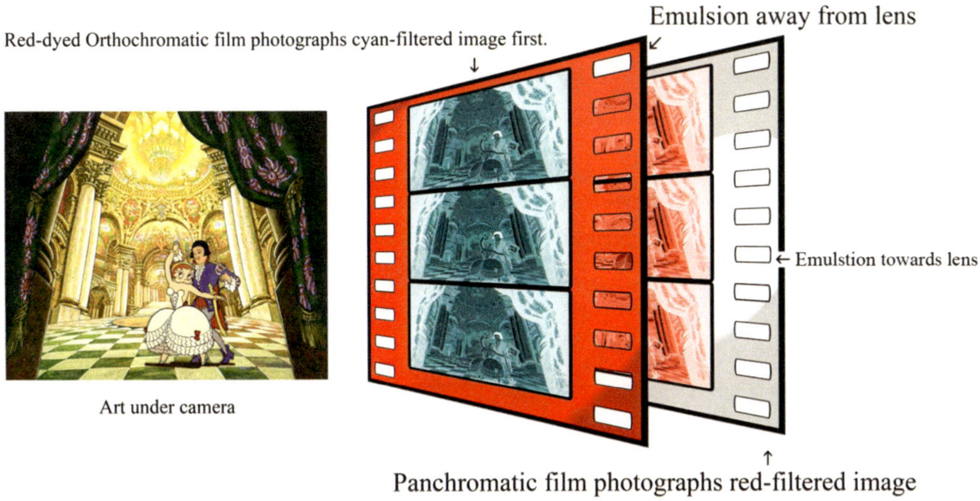

Illustration of Cinecolor Process.

The artwork had to be keyed to the range of red and blue that the system reproduced. But this was a two-emulsion system with red on one side of the print, and cyan on the other side. While Cinecolor produced saturated color, one of the colors always appeared out of focus because film has to be focused on the emulsion (image) side. Art directors generally avoided purple, lavender, or pink because they did not reproduce faithfully in printing. Cinecolor produced brilliant reds, oranges, blues, browns and flesh tones, but bright greens and violet were distorted and muted.

The original background painting for the master scene from *Kids in the Shoe* (1935) exceeds the color range that the two color process could reproduce, especially the use of orange and magenta. These colors tended to be compromised in greyed hues. Skies were purposely painted blue-green since cyan was used as a compromise of blue.

Color Classics trade ad—representative of the Two-Color Technicolor period (1934–1935).

Dye Composited Image

Illustration of Two-Color Technicolor Process.

Similar to the process of Cinecolor, art work was keyed to red and blue, and photographed using red and cyan onto a single negative and single emulsion. This produced saturated color with consistent sharpness, and was the color process used until 1936, when the Three-Color Technicolor Process became available in 1936, resulting in full spectrum color reproduction.

Glory and David (Ryan Englade).

These original cel set-ups were designed to take advantage of the full range of color in the Three-Color Technicolor process, though color accuracy would vary. The grey used on King Little's hair appears light brown in most Technicolor prints.

"There's a giant on the beach!" (Todd Levine).

Gulliver's banquet (Todd Levine).

David and Glory reunited (Todd Levine).

Gulliver gathers the Navy of Blefescu (Todd Levine).

Honey Shop concept painting (Ryan Englade).

Honey Shop fire concept painting (Ryan Englade).

Background from the burning cigar sequence (Ryan Englade).

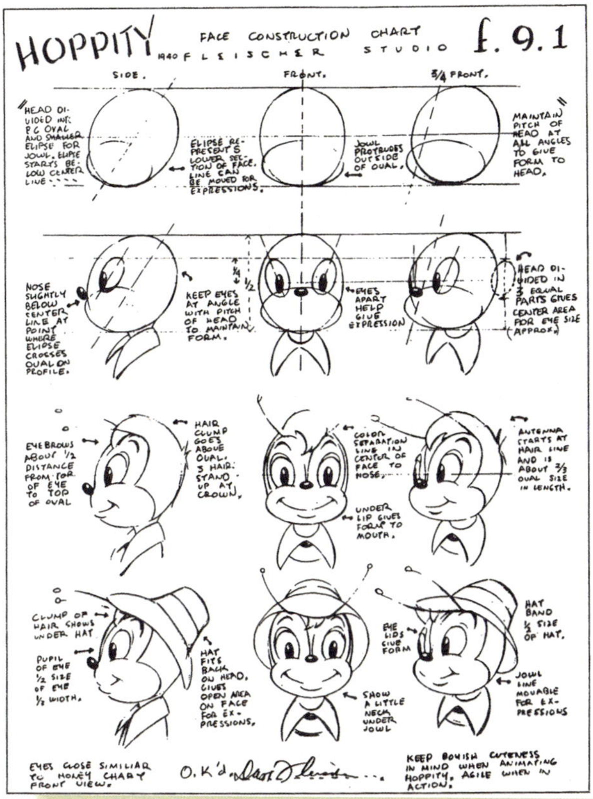

Hoppity model sheet and concept sketches (Fleischer Studios).

Noveltoon Jack (author's collection).

Trade ad for the new *Out of the Inkwell* series (author's collection).

9

The Spinach Lid Blows Off

The Fleischer studio was now producing four series with a new cartoon released to theaters each week. And this volume of product demanded more workers.

> Fleischer Studios kept leasing more space at 1600 Broadway. They had one floor originally, and when it went to four cartoons (series) they had to take four stories and they were up to 650 employees. It was a very, very large organization.... Fleischer Studios was the "big" animation studio.[1]

The demand for *Popeye* cartoons brought about a production speed up. Inbetweeners who normally produced 25 drawings a day were pushed to 45, which resulted in a slowdown to the normal load, and internal problems continued to brew.

> The people at Paramount had great difficulty understanding the problems created when they would ask them (Fleischer Studios) to produce two cartoons in the same period of time that they used to do one. And they would not give them enough money generally to do it right.... And so the staff was just frazzled.[2]

After failing to organize Van Beuren, the Animated Motion Picture Worker's Union attempted to interest the Fleischer staff. Tom Johnson received one of their pamphlets referring to the Dan Glass affair as being cause for action. Max Fleischer addressed the issue of the attempts by the AMPWU to influence Fleischer staffers. The following response was posted on page 15 of the April 1935 issue of the in-house news magazine, *Fleischer Animated News*.

Tom Johnson found it impossible to resist revealing his own viewpoint and reactions and accordingly made it his business to write a letter expressing his opinion to the so-called union. Page 16 posted his letter to the AMPWU as referenced in Max's response.

> March 20, 1935
>
> Executive Committee
> Animated Motion Picture Workers Union
> 60 West 15th Street, New York City
>
> Gentlemen:
>
> You included me on the mailing list of your Bulletin and invited me to write you on the matter. The things that struck me more forcibly in your paper were your "black jack and brass knuckles," your Communistic, "let's take it" and your unfounded vicious attack on Max Fleischer in the Dan Glass case. DAN HIMSLEF WOULD CONDEM IT!
>
> Who said Dan made $12? His weekly check showed TWENTY-TWO. Why didn't you state that Dan, besides doing In-betweening, carried a very heavy night school program while at Fleischer's? He himself complained of the strain and gave up this outside activity. TWO years of night school averaging three nights a week. COULD THAT HURT HIM?
>
> And didn't you "forget" that Max urged Dan to take a week's rest at a New Jersey resort, which Dan did as Max's guest? And didn't you also "forget" that Max urged Dan to return home long before he did and at the time offered to send him?

FLEISCHER'S
ANIMATED NEWS

VOL. I. NO. 5 APRIL 1935. 10 CENTS.

***Flesischer's Animated News* (author's collection).**

I have a letter from Dan's mother. I knew her and she wrote me after his death. A quotation shows her attitude: "MR. GLASS AND MYSELF WILL ALWAYS FEEL GRATEFUL TO MR. FLEISCHER AND ALL OF DAN'S FRIENDS IN NEW YORK WHO HELPED HIM IN HIS RECENT ILLNESS." Dan and his family, it is obvious, had no complaint. His folks sincerely appreciate the thoughtfulness shown their son. I have a hunch they would feel deeply hurt in knowing you used Dan as a "SPEARHEAD" IN AN ATTACK ON MAX FLEISCHER, who really did all he could to help Dan. And with your logic and deductions you ask me to sign up with you?

> But to come back to my own case, WHAT CAN YOU OFFER ME? In the five years I have been here, I have had every opportunity to advance. (When) we saw a vacancy we *worked* for it. At one time fourteen of us competed for ONE opening in the Inbetween Department. The best one got it. These opportunities are still present. We went ahead that way instead of ganging up and putting the "squeeze" on Max. My salary advances kept pace with my added value to the company. This also is fair enough. In short, I am satisfied and have NO COMPLAINTS.

The Animated Motion Picture Workers Union faded away soon afterward, failing to acquire an affiliation with the American Federation of Labor (AFL). But another group, the Commercial Artists and Designers Union Local 20239, picked up where the AMPWU left off. The CADU was an outgrowth of the Artists Union created under the WPA Arts Projects to help unemployed artists. This evolved into the CADU of the American Federation of Labor under the newly elected President, James Hulley, who set out to organize Fleischer Studios. Union affiliation was not entirely absent at Fleischer's, however. First, the animation cameramen were represented by the IATSE Cameramen's Local 644 as of 1934. Second, Lou and Dave Fleischer were members of the Musicians Local 802.

As additional workers were taken on, more desks and cubicles were added, creating a crowded atmosphere that resembled a garment district "sweat shop." Tensions were aggravated by the management procedures of the Inbetween Department Supervisor Edith Vernick.

Edith was born in 1905 in Kiev, Ukraine, to an Orthodox Jewish family. Her family immigrated to New York when she was two years old, and she attended public school, studying art at Washington Irving High School. She started her career as a decorator of lamp shades, and entered the animation field in 1923 with Fleischer's original *Out of the Inkwell* films company where she made the cutaways used for the paper "slash and tear" method used as a substitute for the licensed cel process. When a formal switch was made to using cels, she cleaned them for reuse. She rose through a series of promotions from opaquer, to inker, to inbetweener, inbetween department manager, and finally assistant animator in 1937. She became very close to management and was not concerned that as a Manager, she was making only $28 per week, a dollar more that the top men in her own department and half of what other department heads were paid. Edith reasoned, "You must remember I was like family. I used to go to Sam Buchwald's house every Friday for dinner. I was like one of Max's daughters. It never occurred to me that I was making a hell of a lot less than I should have."[3]

Berny Wolf stated that Edith taught him to how to animate. He described her as a "rough and tumble gal who could hold her own with the boys, including the use of some 'salty language.' She had a 'mouth' on her—not the sort of girl you'd take home to mother." People working under her were afraid. If someone was not working hard enough to Edith's estimation, she reported that person to the boss. Workers had to raise their hands to request restroom breaks. She kept track of how long the person was in the restroom, and would send someone in to check after so many minutes. If she had nothing else to do, she went herself, never hesitating to enter the Men's Room if necessary, announcing loudly, "Hey, what's the matter, ya got diarrhea?"[4]

While Edith's tyrannical management style of the Inbetweening Department was resented, it seemed consistent with studio policy, having preceded her under William Henning, and continuing with her successor, Frank Paiker, who was promoted from manager of the Ink and Opaquing Department in 1937. Joseph Barbera confirmed the frustrating and pressured environment there. Fleischer Studios was in the first year of the production of *Popeye*, and he had been called by Willard Bowsky to try out. His impression of the studio was what he labeled "the Oliver Twist hotel" with the same "whip-cracking" environment in the Ink and Opaquing Department.

> They started me at the bottom of the heap: the Painting Department. The least-skilled and most tedious job in traditional animation.... *Oliver Twist*? It was more like *A Christmas Carol*, with a roomful of Bob Cratchits presided over by Ebenezer Scrooge in the person of Frank Paiker. He managed the studio underlings, and in fact, to compare him to Scrooge may be too generous. All he needed was to bare his chest, and find a whip and a guy to beat a drum, and he would have made a highly creditable slave master in a Roman galley...[5]

On his second day, Barbera was promoted to inker. He observed a female inker reaching into a little drawer, grabbing at a sandwich, taking a quick nervous bite, returning it quickly into the drawer and continuing to work. He asked her why she was doing this, and she replied that she couldn't take a lunch break because she had a quota to meet. On his second day as an inker, he saw a fellow about 35 years old inking cels. "How long have you been inking?" I asked. "Three years." "Three years of tracing over other people's work for what? Thirty-five dollars a week!"[6]

Barbera reasoned that the chance for advancement under these conditions might not be with Fleischer Studios and he left after one week. Ironically, Frank Paiker became an animation cameraman for Hanna-Barbera Productions 25 years later. This surely gave Mr. Barbera an amount of satisfaction, since, as the saying goes, "What goes around, comes around."

The continued overcrowding in the Inbetween Department compounded by increased production pressures bred more worker dissatisfaction. Hot summers without enough air circulation made conditions more uncomfortable.

> One very hot summer afternoon, it was unbearably hot, and the word got out that if it got to reach a certain temperature, we'd be given the afternoon off. Those who wanted to would go off to Park Central and have a swim. And it exceeded that temperature. I have a recollection of Dave Fleischer coming around and feeling the different desks to see if they were hot enough to let these people go. He went around putting his hand on the desks. He shook his head—it wasn't hot enough in his estimation.[7]

An effort was made to correct the heat problem by moving the Inbetween Department into the room occupied by the Opaquing Department, which was moved to the eighth floor. Obviously, management was aware that this expansion was causing crowded conditions, and the four floors were not enough since there was no more space left in the building. Shamus Culhane quotes recollections from Nick Tafuri from 1981:

> Max used to come around sometimes, but after a while he stopped altogether, so he never talked to the staff. He did go bowling one a week with some of the boys, and I was invited once or twice. I found out that they didn't really get together to bowl. Usually, it was only executives like Sam Buchwald, Seymour Kneitel, Izzy Sparber, and Frank Paiker. All they did was talk business, so I quit going.[8]

Tafuri's witness to this suggests that the key Fleischer men were aware of problems but were not telling Max. It is ironic also that Edith Vernick, with her loyalty and assumed position with management was in the very middle of the unrest. Considering this, the question is why Max was not aware of the complaints coming largely from Edith's department—especially since it was Max's policy that anyone could come to him about problems? The studio was still relatively small enough for word to reach management that talk of organizing was circulating. Management retaliated by firing Carl Wessler.

On March 31, a pre–April Fool's Day prank centered on Marty Taras and Phil Lepinsky. Taras, who was already known as a union activist, became the butt of several practical jokes. Taras recalled:

> Phil Lepinsky took a paper cup and put it just underneath my desk. As I sat down, the paper cone tipped over ... and all the water spilled all over my pants. It looked like I just "peed" in my pants. I saw Phil because he had walked away from my desk pretty fast.... So I figured, "Okay, I'll fix you!"
>
> There were ventilation openings at the bottom of the desks where people's feet would stick through. Taras waited a few minutes, and while Phil was busy working, stooped down and stuck a match in the sole of Lepinsky's shoe....
>
> I had just finished lighting the match, and I sensed that somebody was alongside me. So I just looked up and I made a very sheepish grin. And there was Edith Vernick just staring down at me, arms akimbo, on her hips and just didn't say a word, with a frozen expression on her face. And I says, "Well it's April Fools' Day, you know," which she didn't think was so humorous. So she went into a fast walk and went out of the room.[9]

Vernick went straight to Max Fleischer and reported the incident. Because of the presence of papers and highly flammable cellulose nitrate animation cels, open flames and smoking were prohibited by the city fire code. When Taras reported to work the next day, April 1, he was informed that he had been fired. Many felt this was due to his union activities and not the prank. When asked in 1980, Edith recalled that she probably reported Taras not so much because he was a union activist, but that his activities were against Max Fleischer. The center of union membership was in Edith's department with the bulk of the grievances based on her "drill sergeant" management tactics compounded by the frustrations of the lack of advancement. The inbetweeners pool sent Lou Appet to appeal to Max Fleischer and Sam Buchwald without success. More firings resulted based on union association. The department most difficult to recruit was the Animation Department.

The animators all worked under individual contracts and were not affected in the same manner as the lower level production workers. Dave Tendlar stated that the head animators tried to avoid the union organizers because they all had a tremendous loyalty to Max. "The animators felt not so much that they were independent artists ... but felt they were working for Max Fleischer. They were a group of 15 or 20. We were making ... anywhere from $90 to $125 a week. At that time, it was considered an excellent salary."[10]

Dave Tendlar (Todd Levine).

Lillian Freeman became a member of the Commercial Artists and Designers Union (CADU) and recalled at her first meeting 10 or 12 animators were present including Myron Waldman, Ed Nolan, and Nick Tafuri. Union organizers feared that the animators being so close to the boss would talk. Dave Tendlar was sympathetic to the cause and attended one of the meetings. Once he learned that one of the officers, Arthur Post, was a disbarred attorney, he determined that the organization was not legitimate. Other animators were outright enemies of unions from the start. One of them was the outspoken Willard Bowsky. Besides openly displaying anti–Semitic sentiments, he was believed to have been a supporter of the Nazi Party. While these matters were brought to Max's attention, they had no affect on him. Bowksy was one of Max's favored animators and Max could not allow such suspicions and rumors to influence his respect for Bowsky's work.

It is difficult to believe that Max was unaware of problems in the studio in spite of the "white-washed" reports he was given by department managers. Once the prospect of a strike became clear, Edith Vernick was quickly promoted to assistant animator, and Frank Paiker was considered as her replacement. Frank Paiker had risen through the ranks from inker, to head of the Inking Department, then manager of the Coloring and Planning Department. He was puzzled about being selected since he never liked the Inbetween Department. Paiker recalled:

> I was called into the office; Max and Dave were there with Sam Buchwald, Izzy Sparber, Seymour Kneitel, and Bowsky. Either Max or Dave said, "In view of your support, we're going to give you a promotion." I said, "What's that?," "We're going to put you in charge of the Inbetween Department." I said, "Come on, let's stop kidding each other. I know why you want me in charge of the Inbetween Department." [This was where all the union activity started.] "If you want me to go in there and police the place, alright, fine. But let's not kid each other. I am not an Inbetweener. If you want me to bluff my way through ... if one of the Inbetweeners comes up and has a problem on how to make an Inbetween, I can't sit down and show him how. The only thing I can do is send him into the Animator and let the Animator show him." So they started laughing. They said, "Okay." But it worked out fine.[11]

Even with the change in department managers, the approach remained the same and so did the sentiments about going on strike. After 13 union members were fired, the inbetweeners, inkers, and opaquers walked out. On April 4, Anthony Pinelli was fired. The CADU visited Max Fleischer, demanding a closed shop, and 35-hour work week, double time for overtime, paid sick leave and paid vacations, and a 12 percent increase in salaries. Max refused these demands and refused to recognize the CADU, who complained to the National Labor Relations Board. Fleischer was now represented by the famous Louis Nizer, Legal Council for Paramount, who met with NLRB attorney, Lester M. Levin. While skeptical, Nizer advised Fleischer to schedule another meeting, held on April 29. Interestingly, Animator Ed Nolan, who was one of the key participants in the CADU, went to Jam Handy in Detroit the following day to avoid the pending strike according to Don Figlozzi, as documented in the NLRB Fleischer-CADU files.

Max held his position not to recognize the union, and CADU claimed that Fleischer refused to negotiate. From the meeting, Nizer offered to open the books to the union to reveal company profits. From a business perspective, it was determined that the Union's demands would cost from $150,000 to $200,000, where CADU estimated between $65,000 to $70,000. The books showed the studio's gross annual income as $500,000 with a payroll excluding the salaries of Max and Dave Fleischer of $370,000. The Securities and Exchange Commission records reported the annual salaries of Max and Dave Fleischer as $33,000 each. With these figures, Fleischer was left with $64,000 before taxes, and claimed a profit of only $5,000 for 1936.

On May 3, the CADU filed a petition with the Labor Board requesting a certification for election. CADU's attorney Lester M. Levin spoke with Nizer regarding the petition. Nizer did not reply immediately due to the slowdown strike already in place. The CADU met again with Nizer who sustained Fleischer's position not to recognize the union. That same day, 13 more union members were fired. On the evening of Thursday, May 6, the union voted to strike. The strike started on Friday, May 7 at 6:30 p.m. Although there were three and a half hours left to work, no work was done. Other workers returning from their dinner breaks went home after seeing the pickets. On Monday morning, some 100 pickets kept everyone out.

While dissent was building up to the strike, Lou Fleischer had been hospitalized for near-fatal pneumonia, contracted from swimming in icy water off Coney Island during a men's club initiation. During his hospital stay, members of the studio sent hand-drawn get well cards that display the range of talent at the studio.

Cartoons by Tom Moore and Orestes Calpini (Bernie Fleischer).

Cartoons by Max and Dave Fleischer (Bernie Fleischer).

Ironically, the card from Charlie Schettler made a prophetic reference to a strike. On the day of his discharge Lou called the studio to say he was returning, only to be told, "Don't come in," with an abrupt hang up. Unaware, Lou brought his young son, Bernie along with him to visit the studio only to discover a picket line circling the building. Bernie Fleischer recalled:

> We came to 1600 Broadway and I saw all kinds of commotion and people walking around with signs. And my dad went over and he spoke with these people for a while and then he came back to me and said, "Bernie, were not going in the studio today. We're going to the (Brooklyn) Aquarium." And it wasn't until the next morning I guess that kind of all "Hell broke loose" because one of the papers, and I think it was *The New York Times* got a picture of my dad refusing to cross the picket line at his own studio.[12]

Cartoon by Charlie Schettler (Bernie Fleischer).

The strikers were seeking many of the benefits that other industrial workers of the Depression were fighting for:

1. A fair wage.
2. A 40-hour work week.
3. Paid vacations
4. Sick leave

To their credit, Fleischer's was the only studio with paid overtime. Picketers fought with police and studio personnel. Five workers tried crossing the picket line including Ink and Opaque Supervisor, Frank Paiker, and Camera Department Head, Charlie Schettler. They had just returned from the dinner break, as Paiker recalled:

> We just stood on the curb. Suddenly out of nowhere, we see all these pickets coming with the signs. So, we just stand there and we know what's going to happen. So what do they do? Right up against the building they formed a circle and started picketing. So we look at each other and say, "How do we get in?" Someone says, "I see only one way we can try it," which we did.[13]

They charged through the picket line and a fight started—fists and picket signs swinging. Paiker was thrown out into the middle of Broadway by one of the inkers in his own department, Gilbert Fox. Charlie Schettler's nose was broken when Sammy Robinson and Lou Appet stuck him with their picket signs. The fight lasted an hour and a half.

By the time the police arrived a crowd of nearly 2,000 people witnessed what resulted in a riot. Fourteen of the strikers were arrested, with ten cited for disorderly conduct and three for assault. Checker Ellen Jenson was arrested for biting a policeman after he knocked her hat off with his baton.

Saturday evening, everyone in the Animation Department was called to report to work on Monday. The head animators had no interest in representation by CADU. They were merely interested in doing their work in compliance with their individual contracts. Don Figlozzi recalled that Dave Fleischer called him, telling him the animators would have plenty of protection. But Monday morning the picketers had the entrances to the building blocked. Later that morning, a committee of 17 animators led by Myron Waldman, Hicks Lokey, and Dave Tendlar were allowed entrance to persuade Max Fleischer to accept impartial arbitration. Max responded with how "poor" the company was, having paid back only half of a $40,000 loan he had to make in 1935. Figlozzi remembered that 1935 was the year that Fleischer offered employees bonus service certificates as part of a savings plan.

Max agreed to negotiate on a cash basis, and agreed to reinstate all who were fired except for certain relatives, whom he "had great pleasure in letting go." The committee reported back to Post and Hulley of CADU. Post talked Waldman into having a Union representative present during talks with Max, stressing that the CADU had always been ready for impartial arbitration. When the Animator's Committee returned, Max had talked with his attorney. He had changed his position, willing to meet the Union's demands by cutting salaries of workers making over $50 per week. This harkened back to the Motion Picture Industry's plan for dealing with the cash flow crisis that followed Roosevelt's "Bank Holiday" in 1933.

Max told the Union that he would agree to arbitration if the wage demands "would be limited to the profits shown by the company's books for income tax purposes." The Union rejected Max's proposal. That same evening, Hulley sent a telegram to the animators' committee:

> Fleischer offer obvious attempt to split shop. Any negotiations must be conducted by your elected representatives. Therefore no one can pass picket line for any purpose. Urgent animators attend meeting strike headquarters 48 West 46th Tuesday 8 A.M.

Hulley allowed only four members from the Fleischer animators' committee to the meeting, including Waldman, Hicks Lokey, "Doc" Crandall, and William Henning. It was agreed that the Fleischer committee members and 16 other animators would be allowed to cross the picket line and return to work. Two days later, the pickets pretended to beat up Joe Oriolo and Ted Vosk to keep everyone out.

The following day, Thursday, the picket line was small, allowing the animators to cross, with only Figlozzi, Sidney Pillet, Frank Endres, Lillian Freedman, and Eli Brucker from the Animation Department, plus Al Windley and Jack Wilis from the Timing Department, still on the line. Friedman left the picket line that afternoon and returned to work after being called back by Lokey. The others returned the next day, Friday, except for Brucker, who stayed on the line for the duration of the strike. Fleischer Studios resumed production on a reduced scale by taking back its animators and hiring "scabs" to fill the voids left by the strikers, most of whom now felt betrayed.

Max reversed his decision on arbitration and stated that he would rehire only half of those who had been fired. And with the animators back at work, the strike turned to the NLRB for organizing a boycott. Publicity stunts were staged to gain public sympathy and embarrass Fleischer. Dave Fleischer's home was stink-bombed. The publicity triggered a boycott that started with the Musician's Union. On May 13, four studio musicians went to the Union with Jim Hulley, asking the local to support the CADU strike. The musician's local agreed to join the strike and threatened to bar Lou and Dave Fleischer from recording sessions until the strike was settled. At one point, Max was pleading for Lou to come in to work, but he refused to cross the picket line because of his loyalty to the Musician's Union.

Strikers planted in the theaters booed the appearance of the cartoons. Next, the IATSE Projectionists Local 306 refused to run any Fleischer cartoons, placing them on an AFL unfair list that kept them off screens in New York and nationwide. The boycott was also aimed at breaking up Paramount's block booking policy that forced theaters to take their features regardless of quality if they wanted *Popeye* cartoons. The Consent Decree of 1938 finally abolished this practice.

The strikers targeted the flagship of Paramount, the Paramount Theater in Times Square, on Saturday, May 22 during its peak hour of business, after 8:00 p.m. with 100 picketers circling the entrance. The picketers later proceeded uptown to the Roxy. This demonstration continued for several weeks with the picketers chanting the official strike song:

I'm Popeye, the Union Man, Toot-Toot!
I'm Popeye, the Union Man, Toot-Toot!
I'll fight to the finish
'Cause I wants my spinach
I'm Popeye the Union Man!

Picketers outside of the Paramount Theater (Corbis Archives).

THE ARTISTS WHO DRAW US

ARE ON STRIKE!

Because though our drawings make the whole world laugh, we are forced to work at less than even a factory wage. Some of us get as low as $15 a week for work that requires great skill and a strain on eyes and nerves.

Because our employer, in complete defiance of the Wagner Act, fired 18 of us for joining a union !

Because in further defiance of the Wagner Act he refuses to recognize our Union which has attempted to negotiate with him peacefully.

Because we have been forced to work without vacations! Some of us have worked for 6 or 7 years without time off.

Because we do not get sick leave. We can't afford to take time off at our own expense...so we work while we're ill !

Because during the depression our wages were cut more than half. Now, our employer admits business has improved,but he hasn't restored those pay cuts!

Because of all these reasons, we ask your support! Help us win a decent American standard of living by writing to your local theatre manager or the Max Fleischer Studios. Tell them that you object to having any Fleischer pictures shown while this firm is unfair to its employees and refuses to recognize their labor union as specified under the Wagner Act.

Commercial Artists and Designers Union
Local 20329 • American Federation of Labor
155 East 34th Street• Caledonia 5-4970

--------------------------- Tear off and Mail at once ---------------------------

Manager of----------------Theatre

Address-----------------------------------
----

or

Max Fleischer Studios
1600 Broadway,N.Y.C.

I object to having any Max Fleischer pictures shown (Betty Boop, Popeye, Color Classics, etc.) at my local theatre while Mr. Flei- ver is unfair to his employees and refuses to recognize their union.

Strike flyer placed in theater lobbies (author's collection).

For the most part, Paramount had dictated how the strike was to be handled. The Hollywood studios were in essence blackmailed into accepting the IATSE (International Alliance of Theatrical Stage Employees) as the recognized labor representative of the motion picture crafts, technicians, and supportive laborers when IATSE representative Willie Bioff, threatened to shut down all production after successfully acquiring representation of the sound technicians. For this reason, Paramount and Fleischer refused to recognize any other labor organization. But after five months, and a major upset to its distribution revenue, Paramount directed Max to end the strike.

Settlement came on October 12, 1937. By now, Max was nervous and emotionally drained. He had always taken a paternal attitude towards his employees, and the idea of a labor strike conflicted with his Victorian values and work ethic. He took it all personally and developed an ulcer.

Dave was definite in wanting to "crush the Union." While Max was trying to handle the strike strategy, Dave was heard yelling at Max to "Shut up" when he expressed his thoughts. Before the strike, Fleischer Studios was considered "one big happy family." Afterward, it was split in two, with the studio and its guiding spirit being the biggest casualty.

The Fleischer strike was the first major labor strike in motion picture history. It demonstrated all the tactics and problems that would dominate labor-management conflicts in animation for the next sixty years: employee anger over working conditions but apathy about joining organizations to do anything about the conditions ... employers trying to stay friends with their staff while acting tough behind the workers' backs; official rhetoric about "free choice" masking strong-arm tactics. Like all conflicts, the Max Fleischer strike could have been avoided.

> Many said afterward that if Max had simply recognized the union and offered a token raise or agreed to arbitrations, the strike would not have happened. But that would be asking for some pretty forward thinking from a businessman of those times, even one as well loved as Max Fleischer.[14]

Max felt betrayed by his employees, causing him to enter into a state of depression. This mental state seemed to contribute to his questionable business decisions from this point on. He saw the success of *Popeye* as the cause of the strike, and off-handedly remarked to Dave that he looked forward ceasing their production once their license with King Features expired in 1942. In their place, he was in favor of making "serious films" without being clear about what he meant. Dave found this ironic. He argued that it was the comedy cartoons that should continue, especially since they made Max rich. Disgusted by this, Dave scoffed at the thought of throwing it all away on the assumption that Max wanted to make "boring" educational films. This was the beginning of the disintegrating relationship between the two brothers, the seeds of it planted during the strike.

Max and Dave had several discussions about the future of the studio. Although Dave was against labor being controlled by the Union, he was sympathetic to the plight of strikers and their right to fairer wages. It was at this time he started reappraising his worth to Fleischer Studios. According to Dave, Max was earning $750 per week while he received only $500. This seems to conflict with what the books indicated at the time of the strike since they revealed equal annual salaries at $33,000 each, or $634.62 per week. It should be understood that this did not constitute their entire income. As the major stockholders of Fleischer Studios, they received annual dividends from the corporate profits.

It was at this time that Dave asked Max for a raise, feeling just as valuable to the studio. Max argued that he was the one deserving the higher salary since the studio was built upon his concepts, beginning with the Rotoscope. Dave reminded him that the Rotoscope was a collaborative effort involving all of the brothers, and specifically that he was "The Clown" that was the foundation of their initial success, *Out of the Inkwell.* By this logic, Dave argued that he was the actual origin of the studio. Max argued that he was the one with the credentials, having the education and artistic accomplishments that led to the forming of the organization, much of which was built upon his intellectual input, mainly his inventions. Based on this, Max refused Dave's request for a raise in spite of the mounting pressures created by the continued production of the *Popeye* cartoons and preparations for their first animated feature. These pressures seemed to have had an effect on Dave's marriage and continued to fester as the studio resumed activity.

10

Picking Up the Pieces

Fleischer cartoons returned to theaters starting in November 1937 beginning with the second *Popeye* two-reel featurette, *Popeye the Sailor Meets Ali Baba's Forty Thieves.* The Studio picked up speed into 1938 due to the backlog of unreleased cartoons, which reflect the end of their New York zenith. *Film Daily* reported numerous publicity items and reviews, perhaps the most in the history of Fleischer Studios.

Film Daily Reviews

April 7, 1938

"Thanks for the Memory" (Screen Song Series)
Paramount 7 mins.
Fair Musical Number

The song, "Thanks for the Memory," is a delightful piece of music, but it has been spoiled by the addition of a lot of jumbled ideas that purportedly are funny. The reel opens with a series of gags about trailers and their owners and then swings into the tune that gives it its name. Bert Block and his orchestra provide a tuneful interpretation of the song. Bill Johnson, a singer with the band, handles the vocal part neatly. The bouncing ball appears to lead the audiences in singing with the orchestra. Too much trailer and too little attention to a swell musical number sum it up.

"I Am Love Sick" (Popeye)
Paramount 7 mins.
Funny Antics

When Popeye makes a social call on Olive, she ignores him as she reads her love story. Popeye finally pretends to be awfully sick and throws fits on the floor to attract Olive's attention. He is more than successful. She sends for an ambulance, and he is carted off to the operating room. Here many exciting things take place as the surgeons and interns try to work on him, but Popeye eludes their efforts. Finally, he laughingly admits to Olive that he only wanted to test her love for him. Olive starts to work on him, and when she gets through, he is really ready for the hospital and the operating table. Produced by Max Fleischer.

Trade ad for *Popeye the Sailor Meets Ali Baba's Forty Thieves*. Note the title error, "and the Forty Thieves" (author's collection).

"Honest (Love) and True" (Betty Boop)
Paramount 7 mins.
Amusing Cartoon

This cartoon is an amusing take-off on the mustachioed villain era of the gay '90s, with a whip-cracking villain. Our heroine, Betty, is a poor but honest actress. Hungry and cold, she gets a job as a singer in a dance hall. The villainous owner annoys her and slaps her around a little until our hero arrives, a neat young man in Mounties' clothing. The villain flees with Betty in his dog sled, drawn by a dachshund. The hero dons his skis and after a wild chase Betty is rescued and the villain is laid low, never again to worry innocent young ladies. Max Fleischer produced.

Film Daily Reviews

April 20, 1938

"Big Chief Ugh-Amugh-Ugh" (Popeye)
Paramount 7 mins.
Exciting Fun

Popeye is again the hero in the eyes of Olive Oyl. While Popeye and his sweetie are wandering over the plains, a band of Indians appears, and the chief wants to take Olive for his squaw. But Popeye takes on all the tribe in feats of skill and tests of strength and licks 'em all. Then he tackles the chief, and conquers him in a battle that is a wow for laughs. So Popeye and Olive become the heads of the tribe.

"Out of the Inkwell" (Betty Boop Cartoon)
Paramount 7 mins.
Clever Animation

Betty Boop falls flat in the latest of her inkwell comedies. A porter cleaning up a studio stumbles on a book dealing with hypnotism. He makes a pen come to life, and the pen brings Betty into the picture. Betty hypnotizes the porter after he teases her. The porter becomes a veritable buzz saw at his work and Betty takes a dive back into the inkwell. The animation is clever. Short was made by Max Fleischer.

"Hold It" (A Color Classic)
Paramount 7 mins.
Weak Cartoon

The adventures of a number of stray cats late at night provide the subject for this number, but it fails to have anything novel or very amusing. The leader of the cats assembles his yowling cohorts and leads them in a song called "Hold It." The song causes numerous things to happen, it shakes apples off a tree that wake up Bowser the Hound and also wakes up the neighborhood. The dog chases the cats and the cats practically annihilate him, but they are chased to cover by a barrage of missiles hurled by irate dwellers.

June 2, 1938

"You Leave Me Breathless" (Screen Songs)
Paramount 8 mins.
Novelty

A combination of cartoon skits and actual photography, showing Jimmy Dorsey and his "ork." The idea is to show what the television sets of the future will display. The cartoon skits cover some gags such as a shower-bath type street cleaning apparatus, a fountain of youth operating in Turkey, chill-proof overcoats for Eskimos, football player harnessed up with a stove, invention for a cow to mow a lawn and feed at the same time. Then the television set brings in Jimmy Dorsey and his band. Bob Eberle is the vocalist, singing the theme song, "You Leave Me Breathless." The film finishes with another cartoon skit, presenting the modern trend in caring for infants by mechanical contraptions.

June 3, 1938

"Swing School" (Betty Boop Cartoon)
Paramount 7 mins.
Musical Animated

A day at the school for pets conducted by Betty Boop. She is conducting the class of animals in a singing lesson, but Pudgy, the little pup, always hits a sour note and spoils the harmony. Finally, the teacher is forced to send him up on the dunce's chair, where his little sweetie comes to console him. As the cutie puppy kisses him, Pudgy gets a new slant on life and music. He jumps to the platform and leads the class in a swing rendition of Betty Boop's song, and they all go to town with the number.

"Plumbing Is a Pipe" (Max Fleischer Cartoon)
Paramount 7 mins.
Lively Cartoon

A Popeye cartoon, with the sailor visiting Olive to find she is struggling with a broken water pipe in the kitchen. While waiting for the plumber, Popeye goes to work. The more Popeye works, the more pipes burst. Finally, he gets mad, eats his can of spinach and ties the pipes up in knots. The plumber arrives after it is all over. As Popeye is bragging to Olive over his work, the pipes burst in fresh places, and the flood is worse than ever.

On the heels of the second *Popeye* mini-feature came the much- anticipated Walt Disney production of *Snow White and the Seven Dwarfs.* While industry cynics referred to it as "Disney's folly," it became the biggest box-office attraction of the time. *Snow White* received a big Hollywood premier at the Carthay Circle Theater on December 21, 1937, and premiered at Radio City Music Hall in New York on February 4, 1938. The location of the showing of Disney's masterpiece was most ironic since Radio City Music Hall was built on the very location where the Fleischer family first lived. Dave remembered Max's reaction while walking up the street, refusing to look at the marquee or see Disney's name on it. Bernie Fleischer recalled:

Of course we were invited to the premier of *Snow White*. And I was just a little kid and of course I loved it. I thought it was just sensational, and I had a great time. But I remember going home how depressed my parents were by it because they felt that this was a great work of art. That they had really seen somebody take animation to a different plateau than Fleischer Studios had taken it to. And my mom said, "Disney is doing art, and you guys are still slapping characters on the butt with sticks!"[1]

While Max had been proposing the concept of an animated feature for three years, Paramount did not show great confidence. An internal memo from A.M. Botsford to Russell Holman dated January 19, 1938,[2] substantiates this:

> With reference to your enquiry in the night wire about the colour cartoon feature, from all I can gather from the executives here there seems to be grave doubt about Fleischer's ability to compete against the *Snow White* idea. As for the four subjects mentioned, the following are some of the ideas here…

Among the titles proposed by Max were *Peter Pan*, which Paramount owned the rights to, *The Bluebird, Captain Kid*, and *Neptune's Daughter*. Also mentioned was an "unnamed project" that suggested *Gulliver's Travels*. Paramount executives objected to each of these. The memo continues:

> The whole doubt here is whether Fleischer has the imagination and the ability to compete with the Disney idea. He has never developed a Mickey Mouse, Donald Duck, or a Dopey. His most famous characters were handed to him from comic strips. If he could make a fairly cheap feature, it might get by, but suffer badly by comparison. We doubt a venture that would leave us playing second fiddle to Disney with *Sorcerer's Apprentice*. Of the four subjects mentioned, *Gulliver's Travels* seems to be the closest, but even this has to do with people, not fairies, sprites, elves or animals. Eugene Zukor is of the opinion that if we want to go in for this sort of thing, we should get Russell Patterson and Fleischer together and go into a cartoon extravaganza musical comedy sort of thing using the Patterson girls and developing a complete show. Another suggestion made is that perhaps there is something in *Funny Page* that would lend itself to this cartoon feature. *Funny Page* has a definite story outlined in the script, which I am sending under separate cover, and it might be read and analyzed with the view to considering it for a cartoon feature. It may be that we no longer own some of the rights to the cartoons in *Funny Page*, but these might be secured or others substituted. Personally, for this project I think that the idea of getting Fleischer and Patterson together is the best way.

In spite of the suggestions from Eugene Zukor, doubts continued to be expressed. On February 15, Bogart Rogers wrote to Botsford:

> Seeing that Disney is so far ahead of Fleischer in every respect—originality, colour, music, scoring, story conception, and writing, established characters and national popularity and presage—then any attempt to follow *Snow White* would be decidedly second rate at best. I just don't think that Fleischer has what Disney has—and that any feature picture that he might attempt might suffer badly by comparison.… If Fleischer can make a fairly cheap feature, it might get by. However, it seems to me folly to undertake a venture that would leave us playing second fiddle and there's no question in my mind that Fleischer would be playing that particular instrument—perhaps even fourth clarinet.

Jeff Lazarus to Botsford, February 16:

> Answering your enquiry of the 15th, I do not feel that I can qualify as an expert on the "feature" cartoon subjects and I furthermore have a great question mark in my mind as to whether Max Fleischer or his organization are equipped to turn out anything that will compete with the genius of Walt Disney. My opinion is that we are all getting into a field we know nothing about and are headed for disaster.

The phenomenal success of Walt Disney's *Snow White and the Seven Dwarfs* was apparent within the first three weeks at Radio City Music Hall. This sent an important message to Paramount—animated features are big box office. Now Paramount reversed their sentiments, targeting Christmas 1939 for a release of their own. An internal memo dated March 1, 1938,[3] stated:

> Fleischer has been urging Paramount for at least three years to permit him to make a feature cartoon. And one of his chief motives in making the two-reel *Popeye* subjects has been to convince Paramount that the longer length cartoons would be popular. These two-reel *Popeyes* have made substantial profits. Fleischer's plans call for more imagination and fantasy than Disney has shown. More amazing and startling new uses of the cartoon medium. He estimates that the picture would cost about $500,000 and would take a year to a year and a half from start to final delivery. Fleischer's past reputation and experience, and his very successful results to date entitle him to the opportunity that people here feel to fulfill his long cherished ambition of making a feature picture.

From Max's perspective, Paramount had stood in his way too many times for too long. He continued to build a mental wall between himself and Walt Disney that prevented him from seeing what was happening, denying that Disney was making major advances that Fleischer Studios was not. Max Fleischer, one of the major pioneers in the field, was being eclipsed by this "Johnny-come-lately," this "interloper" who was striving for higher quality and in the process driving costs up as standards continued to be raised.

One of the elements that contributed to the success of *Snow White* was its skillful handling of the naturalistic human figure. While the use of Rotoscoping was generally denied, the Disney Studio had indeed used it for decades. Disney used the technique as far back as his silent *Alice Comedies*, where live action photography of a real girl was combined with cartoon action. Although this use of Rotoscoping was not used to animate Alice, it was used to determine the action areas of the animation. It was also used on rare occasions to switch from the live action Alice to an animated version as an animated special effect substitute in long shots.

The starting point for Disney's *Snow White* is cited as the *Silly Symphony* cartoon, *The Goddess of Spring* (1934). Disney decided this was the point where his staff would be able to graduate to the standards he was reaching for in his first feature film. While a lot of exploring and awkwardness was experienced animating the goddess Persephone, there were some crude attempts at using Rotoscoped tracings in two long shots near the end. It was realized that the imagination of animators alone would not be enough to create naturalistic animated characters. So references to models and actors would be crucial.

While the Disney Studio claimed it used photostat copies from the reference footage, the final product indicated very clear applications of the Rotoscope technique. Max and Paramount considered suing Disney for infringement of patent. In a letter to the author, Max's friend, Frank Goldman, wrote the following account:

> I got a call here in Detroit from a Paramount attorney. He knew of my previous association with Max and my knowledge of the patent situation. He asked me if I would appear as a Star Witness for Max. I told him I'd do anything I could to help Max, and the most helpful thing I could do was to suggest that they drop the idea of a suit against Disney. Then I told him something I had never told Max because I like him too well to hurt him. An Animator, who worked for me showed me a still picture of the equipment for the Rotoscoping Process, which was developed several years before Max's patent application. A small outfit in Wilkesbarre, Pennsylvania by the name of Bosworth, Defresenes, and Felton had been making cartoon sequences for Burton Holmes, the great travelogue producer for many years. I gave the attorney the information and the name of the artist who had the picture, and that was that—no suit![4]

Since Max Fleischer gained fame as the first to apply this concept, his technique was assumed exclusive. While Max's original patent was granted in 1915, this evidence would have substantiated his claim as "first to invent." But the major issue was that the term of Max's patent had expired in 1932. Although the original model showed the projection on an inclined board, indications are that the process was modified by the 1930s. According to Berny Wolf:

> One day I was sent into the Camera Department to do some Rotoscope tracing and I realized I was working on something with Cab Calloway and it turned out to be a thing called *The Old Man of the Mountain*.... I was working along with the film projected from overhead...[5]

There is no record of this variation on the Rotoscope as an improvement on the original patent. Had this revision of the process been filed, Fleischer and Paramount might have had a case with a pending renewed patent. But Paramount dropped the idea of a Disney suit for another reason, fear of generating anti–Semitic sentiments among the Paramount audience.

Walt Disney was the "darling of Hollywood," with a worldwide following. One of the reasons for this was that his films conformed to the Production Code, which encouraged more "wholesomeness" in content, a quality valued in Disney's largest U.S. audience, the Midwest. In an industry dominated by Jewish owners, Disney, a Protestant Christian, as well as a small independent producer, was unique. Any attack on this revered producer by a large Jewish-controlled production/distribution/theatrical corporation such as Paramount would have had serious negative effects on their business, making Paramount and Max appear as corporate bullies and "bad sports" in the eyes of the public. This was also a time when the Hollywood moguls sought to assimilate into American society and not attract attention to their Jewish roots especially with the rise of anti–Semitic policies under Nazi Germany, which was already threatening war. It was for these reasons that Paramount ceased its actions on a Disney suit, and Max was once again placed as the loser to Disney's triumph.

Disney dominated the field with publicity and industry-recognized awards. While Max dismissed it all by saying "you can't eat awards," this was a tremendous blow to his ego. Ironically, Max was experiencing what had happened to Winsor McCay just ten years earlier—seeing the field he pioneered pass him by. Now that an animated feature was definitely ordered to compete with Disney, Max had the opportunity to gain his just deserts, and Paramount agreed to Max's demands. One of them was to build a new studio to produce features.

11

Setting Sail for Miami

The plans of the diligent lead surely to abundance, but everyone who is hasty comes only to poverty.—Proverbs 21:5 New American Standard Translation

Everyone was caught by surprise when Max announced that he was going to actively compete with Walt Disney by moving to a more "ideal climate" for producing animated features. After operating in New York for 20 years, and surviving the first major labor strike in the motion picture industry, Max was tired and eager to leave New York. The Florida real estate boom of the 1920s made Miami a popular vacation site for many New York residents. But the premature land speculation led to the first major housing bubble of the 20th century, which burst just prior to the 1929 Crash, making many luxurious homes affordable at low prices.

Max's first summer home at 944 Meridian Avenue reflected his interests in technology and showmanship with its garage-sized central air conditioning system—a revolutionary concept at the time. In 1938, Max purchased a Mediterranean style house on Biscayne Bay at 2324 North Bay Road. Max was well known in the Miami circles and became reunited with Johnny Gruelle (1880–1938), creator of Raggedy Ann. Max knew Gruelle when he was on staff at the Bray Studio. And through this personal relationship, he managed to obtain screen rights to the Raggedy Ann stories just prior to the author's passing in early 1938. Max also became acquainted with Louis Jambor (1884–1955), the famous illustrator of Louisa May Alcott's *Little Women*, and recruited him for the studio's Scenic Department.

Due to the availability of cheap land and low taxes, it appeared that building a facility in Miami would be the best and most economical solution. The land was purchased at the cost of $5,000, and Miami offered an attractive tax exemption. The city of Miami had courted the film industry for years, eager to benefit from its activities to boost its economy.

Lilliput village layout by Louis Jambor (Todd Levine).

Best of all, it offered a similar tropical climate as California with the absence of labor unions. This relocation seemed to have a double purpose, coming five months following the settlement of the strike.

> ... The chief factor in Paramount's backing Max Fleischer in his decision to move to Florida ... was a test by Paramount as a way of curtailing or destroying the growing union tide ... although moving a studio the size of Paramount to Miami would indeed have been extremely costly, moving an animation studio ... might have been seen as relatively cheap. Unlike a live-action facility, a studio like Fleischer's had only minimal capital investment in equipment and facilities—its main investment being in labor.[1]

While the strike seemed the major motivation for the Miami move, evidence shows that it had been anticipated much earlier. The April Fools' Day 1935 issue of *Fleischer's Animated News* mentioning a move to Miami was regarded largely as a joke. But an article in *The Miami News* dated September 2, 1934, indicates that Max was already considering relocating then:

Betty Boop, star of the animated cartoons is thinking seriously of moving headquarters to Miami Beach—but there's just a little matter of her creator, Max Fleischer giving his approval. Mr. Fleischer hasn't yet decided, but meanwhile he's keeping his hand in with a few drawings while vacationing at Miami Beach. Local business builders will readily agree that it's more important that Miami see Betty than that Betty see Miami, for these 140 artists who assist Mr. Fleischer are not working for their health. Mr. Fleischer's annual payroll for these assistants is $225,000, so it's easily understandable that the business leaders would have more than a passing interest in Mr. Fleischer and Betty. As for the Miami angle, Betty, according to her creator, will at any rate tell 50,000,000 Americans about Miami and the Beach whether she moves or not.

Betty's all set to make the change, said Mr. Fleischer, for "after all as an artist she can appreciate the improved working conditions under the palms." But Mr. Fleischer is figuring the various ramifications of the plan, the least of which is a $12,000 moving expense before he definitely decides. Meanwhile, he's enjoying the summer at the Beach. Temporarily located at 911 Washington Ave., Mr. Fleischer and his family, which includes his wife and his son, Richard, a battalion commander at the Peekskill Military Academy, are planning to move into their recently purchased home.

From a logical perspective, Max claimed that the additional space for an expanded staff would have been too expensive to rent in New York. Also the presence of flammable paper and animation cels required a specially constructed fire-proof building. Max could have considered a site on Long Island, which would have kept the studio close enough to Paramount headquarters, yet operate in a newer and larger facility while maintaining their ties with established resources such as laboratories and talent pools. But this was not the case. By this time, the desire was strong to escape the stigma of the strike and its lingering aftereffects.

The concept of working in a vacation paradise was very attractive in theory but came without careful planning. And the selection of Miami as a production site had certain psychological elements at work as well. Allowing for Paramount's interest in the "experiment," this east coast location was a means for Fleischer Studios to operate in a vacuum outside of the Hollywood influence and the dominant presence of Walt Disney. If Max was seriously interested in meeting Disney on his own turf, he needed to arrive with an understanding of the Disney financial history and business structure. Had Max made the effort to build a bridge with his competitor, he may have gained valuable insight to the Disney business model, which was based more on its assets and financing independent of his distributor.

When Walt Disney acquired a formal distribution contract with Columbia Pictures in 1930, the cost for his short cartoons was $5,400. The following year his production had more than doubled to $13,500, and he was barely breaking even on their returns. The lack of profit made it difficult for Disney to maintain a steady payroll with Columbia being late on payments. This forced periodic layoffs with both Walt and Roy taking pay cuts until the next wave of finances came in. Walt and Roy realized that the studio could not produce cartoons at a perpetual loss and asked Columbia to increase the advance on each cartoon to $15,000. Columbia declined.

The veteran producer Sol Lesser had become a friend of the Disneys, and he mentioned their distribution problems to Joseph Schenck, president of United Artists. Schenck told the Disneys', "You are producers; we are a company of producers. We will sell your cartoons on their own. We don't sell any other shorts, so your product won't be released with a bunch of others in block-booking. We'll give you $15,000.00 advance on each cartoon. We also have a close connection with the Bank of America, and we can help you get financing."[2]

Following the expiration of the Columbia contract in 1932, Disney signed with United

Artists, who not only advanced $15,000 per film, but also offered a 60 percent return on the box office gross.

> His advances were raised to more than $20,000 a film. Under this contract, which ran until 1937, Disney was obliged to turn out twenty shorts a year.... On a typical color film the economics went something like this: Disney spent about $27,500 to produce each of them, added another $17,500 for prints and another $5,000 for advertising, shipping, taxes, foreign duties and other miscellaneous costs, bringing the total expense of a short to $50,000. He expected each picture to gross about $80,000 in its first year of release, $40,000 in its second. After UA's distribution fee was deducted, his receipts in the first year amounted to about $48,000, which meant he did not begin to take a profit until the second year. Then he might expect to receive profits of $22,000 (remember that starting the second year of each film he would typically still be $2,000 behind on that film). Once this cycle was functioning fully, Disney was spending about one million dollars on current production and taking in about $440,000 above that figure in profits on the United Artists arrangement. To this he could add about $20,000 on receipts from older films still being handled by Columbia and income from a third source—merchandising...
>
> In all, it was estimated that by 1934, he was taking in $660,000 a year in profit, most of which he was pouring back into the studio. Even so, it is clear that he had accomplished something of an economic miracle, for it must be remembered that the years of this stupendous growth in profitability were the years during which the rest of the country was wallowing in the deepest trough of the depression.[3]

Clearly, the association with United Artists afforded Disney the means to make his greatest artistic advances in spite of this complicated financial structure. And the year 1936 would have been Disney's best financial year if he had not been in full commitment to *Snow White*. While the relationship with United Artists provided him with the means for his greatest artistic growth, he went to RKO for the most lucrative deal of his career.

> Without the killing overhead *Snow White* added to their operations, the Disneys would have been—temporarily at least—as secure as it is possible to be in the motion-picture business. On the other hand, they would have achieved stability at the price of future growth, and they knew—better that many of their crucial competitors—that they dare not stop growing. At first they had financed *Snow White* out of the accumulated earnings of the studio, but Disney's first cost estimate of $250,000 was soon surpassed, as was the $500,000 figure next projected.... Racing to get the picture into the theaters in time for the 1937 Christmas season—traditionally the best movie-releasing time—Disney finally had to turn to his principle backer, The Bank of America, and request an additional $250,000. By the time the shooting was done, the negative cost of the film was to be in the neighborhood of $1.7 million and the total gross needed before it would become a Disney asset was placed at $2.5 million.[4]

Paramount was privy to certain financial details of reported box office receipts of its competition. Knowing the production cost history of Disney and the projected potential earnings, it is puzzling how management agreed with the Fleischer plan without entering into a more formal business plan or solid joint venture. In fairness to Paramount, they knew nothing about running an animation studio and left that up to the people managing it so long as the product was delivered. Accordingly, the decision to produce *Gulliver's Travels* was made impulsively based on the first month's box office earnings of *Snow White*. Much of this payoff was due to the three years Disney spent preparing his staff for the production, with the majority of actual production work occurring within the final weeks before its premier. Even with the rush, the scene of the Prince kissing Snow White was seen unfinished at the premier, but was completed for the New York premier and general release two months later.

The Fleischer staff had not prepared for such an undertaking in the way that Disney had. Although their two-reel *Popeye* features suggested a growth into longer formats, these were essentially extensions of their short cartoons without further developments in refined drawing and character animation. Max entered into *Gulliver* simply on the faith of the concept alone without considering the "bigger picture" and the chance for failure, which Paramount feared from the start. Had Max followed the Disney model, he would have secured his financing independent of Paramount. But he seemed unwilling to cut his ties, continuing to have faith in his long-standing relationship with his distributor, unaware of the reservations expressed by the executives.

FILM DAILY, April 4, 1938

Fleischer to Make "Gulliver's Travels"?

Miami—Max Fleischer's first cartoon feature is understood to be "Gulliver's Travels," it was learned here Saturday. Rights to the story are said to have been cleared and production probably will get under way immediately at the New York studio. Paramount will distribute. Work on a new studio here is progressing. Efforts to confirm the Miami report that "Gulliver's Travels" would be the subject of Max Fleischer's first cartoon feature were unveiled Saturday.

Disney built a new facility in Burbank, California from the profits of *Snow White*. Just as he had proposed the initial financing for his first feature film from his assets with additional financing from the Bank of America, he did so with limited borrowing. By comparison, Max was working under several handicaps. The total assets of Fleischer Studios were appraised at $300,489.32. These assets were applied as collateral for the construction loan over a 10-year term through the Delaware Mortgage Company. While its construction cost was reported as $300,000, the actual cost was $167, 653.21. $132,836 remained, applied to the relocation of studio equipment and personnel, leaving a near zero balance.

Max worked closely on the design of the new Fleischer Studio with C. Sheldon Tucker and John M. Lyell, who contracted with the Ware Construction Company, using the new poured-concrete techniques to aid in rapid completion. The Miami Fleischer studio was the first building specifically designed for animation production. It was equipped with three-point air conditioning and an air re-circulation system combining fresh air with filtered recycled air. Air from restrooms was returned through the ventilation exhaust fans in the ceilings "to avoid circulating obnoxious odors in the corridors." Venetian blinds on the windows were kept in a downward angle to eliminate glare. Additional measures were taken to minimize glare in corridors through deflected 25-watt lighting units recessed along the edges of the floors.

Starting a new studio for the production of animated features required more workers. Max sent invitation letters to everyone on the staff, including those who participated in the strike to come to Miami. Additional workers were hired following training at the local Miami art schools. The move was initiated with the groundbreaking ceremony on March 1, 1938. Story work on *Gulliver's Travels* had begun in New York, and the overlap of production and moving combined with training additional workers in Miami presented many challenges especially with a December 1939 deadline to meet. With a commitment to exploit the Disney market, Paramount waged a saturation campaign in the trades.

New Miami studio floor plan (author's collection).

FILM DAILY, June 8, 1938

Fleischer to Start Work on Cartoon Feature Here

Max Fleischer's first feature-length cartoon for Paramount release, "Gulliver's Travels," gets under way immediately in New York but a greater part of it will be made at the new Miami studios, Fleischer announced yesterday. Picture will require about 18 months to complete and will be released on Paramount's 1939–40 program. Fleischer said yesterday that he expected to have his new plant in operation early in September.

It was only natural that Max held to his ideas to enjoy creative satisfaction since *Gulliver* was his concept from the start. In spite of the impact of Disney's *Snow White and the Seven Dwarfs*, Max dismissed it as being too "arty," and declared that *Gulliver's Travels* would be a "real cartoon" without the horror elements of *Snow White.* Max's remark about "horror elements" was ironic considering the nightmarish surrealism prevalent in his early 30s cartoons that made them a standout among the competition. But surely the policies imposed by the Production Code and Paramount had a great deal to do with a neutralization of the

MIAMI DAILY NEWS, MARCH 1938

GROUND BROKEN FOR MOVIE STUDIO

—Miami Daily News photo.

Ground was broken today for a proposed $250,000 studio in which Max Fleischer movie cartoons will be produced. The studio will be at N. W. 17th st. and 30th ave. Miami Chamber of Commerce, city and county officials attended, with County Commissioner N. P. Lowrey breaking the ground. Shown above are, left to right: John H. Ware, jr., of the Fleischer company; Mrs. Fleischer, Mrs. H. Goldberg, Abe Aronovitz, attorney; Mrs. Dave Fleischer, Miss H. Goldberg, Lowrey, Mel Fossey, A. D. H. Fossey, John Morris and Mrs. Seymour Kneitel.

Groundbreaking news article (Virginia Kneitel-Mahoney).

Fleischer cartoons—especially since Paramount was expecting Fleischer to equal Disney. In Max's 1939 autobiography he states his reason for selecting *Gulliver's Travels*:

> Swift's story of *Gulliver's Travels* was selected for our first cartoon feature because of its great reputation, and because it was not really a fairy tale. It is a story, which might have actually happened—that is, it could have happened. It wasn't based on mystic or miracle, and behind it, in spite of its great humorous aspect, is its political satire. I believe that a picture should have universal appeal. A child will enjoy every second of it without the slightest realization that behind it was political satire. On the other hand, the adult can enjoy the picture and read through the humor, and there find its political satire, nevertheless entirely free of propaganda. It shows the smallness of human beings regardless of how great they think they are.[5]

In his good intentions, Max was not thinking on the larger scale, conceiving his feature as a serious motion picture as Disney had. There was an anxious desperation in Max to see this production through as a means of regaining ground lost to his greatest competitor. Production on the cartoon shorts was reduced in order to channel all efforts towards the feature. The *Screen Songs* had been discontinued the previous year, and *Betty Boop* was retired by the summer of 1939, mostly because the series had long been exhausted.

Popeye continued with supervision given to Seymour Kneitel. Jack Mercer, the voice of Popeye and an active member of the Story Department, followed the staff to Miami. Teamed with Jack Mercer on the *Popeye* cartoons, Margie Hines also followed the staff, filling the void left by Mae Questel. Interestingly, this teaming led to the real life marriage of "Popeye and Olive Oyl" on March 3, 1939.

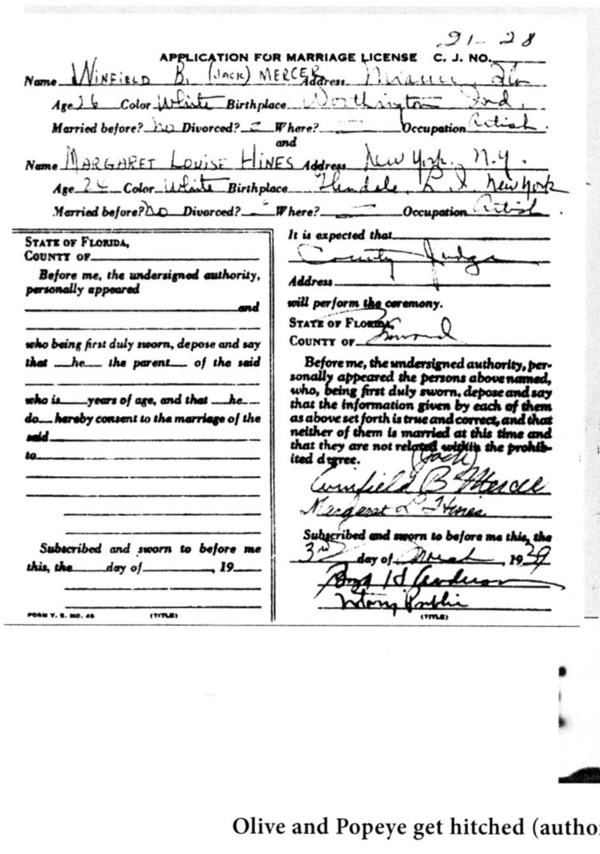

APPLICATION FOR MARRIAGE LICENSE C. J. NO.

Name WINFIELD B. (JACK) MERCER Address

Age 26 Color White Birthplace

Married before? No Divorced? Where? Occupation Artist.

and

Name MARGARET LOUISE HINES Address New York, N.Y.

Age 24 Color White Birthplace New York

Married before? No Divorced? Where? Occupation Artist.

STATE OF FLORIDA,
COUNTY OF

Before me, the undersigned authority, personally appeared ____ and ____ who being first duly sworn, depose and say that ____ he ____ the parent ____ of the said ____ who is ____ years of age, and that ____ he ____ do ____ hereby consent to the marriage of the said ____ to ____

Subscribed and sworn to before me this, the ____ day of ____, 19__

It is expected that County Judge

Address ____ will perform the ceremony.

STATE OF FLORIDA
COUNTY OF

Before me, the undersigned authority, personally appeared the persons above named, who, being first duly sworn, depose and say that the information given by each of them as above set forth is true and correct, and that neither of them is married at this time and that they are not related within the prohibited degree.

Subscribed and sworn to before me this, the 3rd day of March, 1939

Olive and Popeye get hitched (author's collection).

FILM DAILY, May 16, 1938

Fleischer Miami Studio May Be Ready by Aug. 1

Work on Max Fleischer's new studio in Miami is progressing so rapidly that it is expected to be opened August 1, far ahead of the date originally planned. Equipment will be shipped immediately so that operations can begin as soon as the studio buildings are completed.

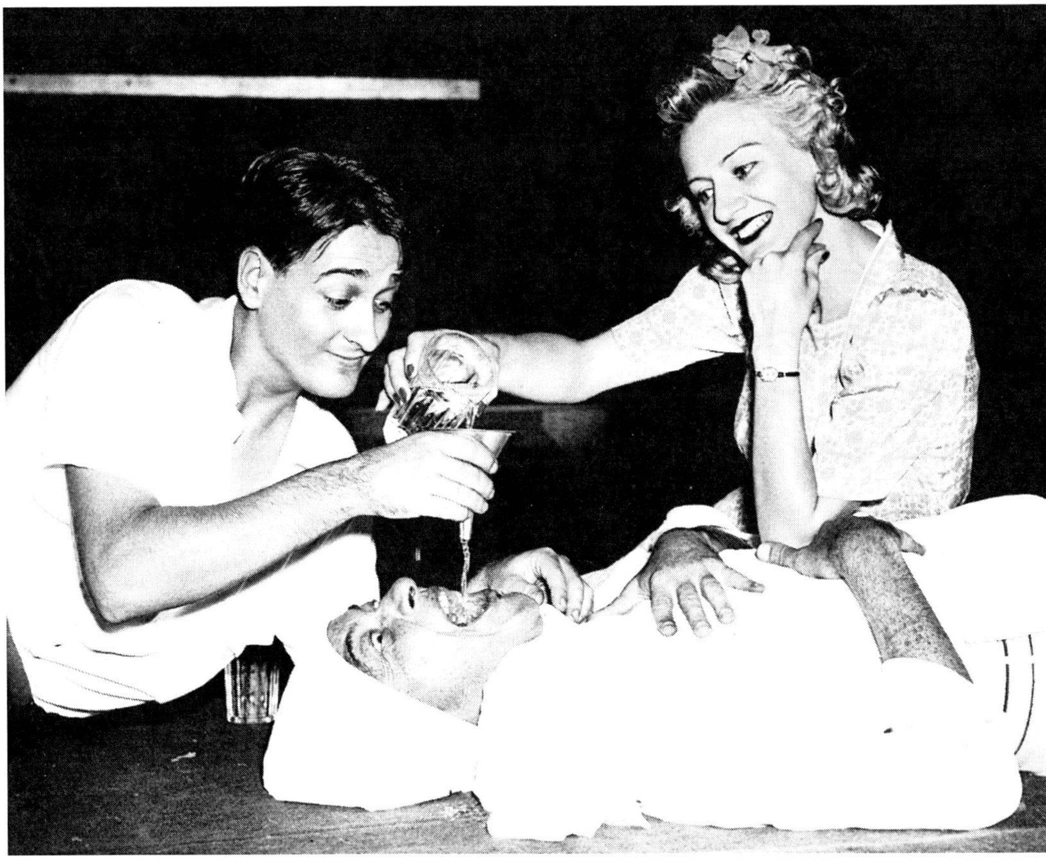

Mercer and Hines "clown" with Pinto Colvig (Paramount Pictures).

In order to fulfill Max's vision, it would take some 80 Animators, 2,000 reams of paper, and four tons of ink and color. Max was clearly in the "driver's seat," and selected popular radio stars, Lanny Ross and Jessica Dragonette for the singing voices of the prince and princess. And for the town crier of Lilliput, Pinto Colvig was cast as "Gabby." Colvig, best known as the voice of Walt Disney's Goofy, was also the voices for Grumpy and Sleepy in *Snow White and the Seven Dwarfs*. He had also worked with fellow Disney voice artist Billy Bletcher, providing the voices for the speeded up technique used for the Munchkin City Manager and Coroner in *The Wizard of Oz*. This same technique was used on Colvig for the character of Gabby.

While money was tight in New York, Fleischer was now offering the highest salaries in the industry to attract Animators to Miami. Grim Natwick, Al Eugster, and Shamus Culhane were among the former Fleischer animators returning from the west coast. Culhane received a warm welcome from Max, with an invitation to join him in the commissary. Once he entered the commissary, he noticed the isolation of the Hollywood and New York people with particular attention drawn to those who had participated in the strike.

> When I went to Max's table, there was the Palace Guard: Bowsky, Sparber, Paiker, Buchwald, and Kneitel. Max sat at the head, looking like an old, wounded lion, with Bowsky at his elbow. Between copious mouthfuls, Bowsky kept up a running fire of comment as he glared at one section of the com-

missary, "Look at them, Max, eating your good food!" Of course, he was talking about the strikers who, even after this long time, were still shunned by the Loyalists. The fact that they had paid for the lunch did not seem to be a factor. The monologue was sheer glucose: "Don't worry, Max, we still love you." Max seemed to lap it up, but Kneitel shot me an embarrassed glance when the going got really sticky. Buchwald was looking at Bowsky with open disgust, but the rest of the table beamed approval at Bowsky's snow job.[6]

Operating in Miami was costing more than it would have had the studio remained in New York paying Union wages. Even in Miami, the issues of the strike and those who participated in it continued to be an issue of division. So the matter of unionization was not entirely escaped. But it was full speed ahead with *Gulliver's Travels* regardless.

Originally, Paramount seemed interested in a live action and animation combination, the type of technological development that was of great interest to Max. According to Gordan Sheehan, Gary Cooper was considered, but a stronger possibility for a musical fantasy would have been Bing Crosby, who was becoming Paramount's biggest musical star. While Max had pioneered the combination of animation and live-action 20 years earlier, the task of compositing live action photography in Technicolor was an entirely new and pioneering process that even Disney had not yet broached. A brief announcement in the *New York Times* indicated that the Stereoptical Process seen in the short cartoons would be used, and *Gulliver* was announced as being in "three-dimensional Technicolor" in its pre-release advertising. This concept was in Max's mind from the very beginning.

Third-dimensional feature-length animated cartoon movies will be offered the theater-going public in the not very distant future, according to Max Fleischer, creator of the famous *Betty Boop* cartoons, who is now spending the winter at Miami Beach. Fleischer, whose producing company in New York employs some 22 artists to give life to Betty and Popeye the Sailor, revealed yesterday he holds the exclusive patent rights on a photographic process that gives animated cartoons depth, or third dimension, and that his plans include the production of a full-length cartoon feature picture to cost $750,000.[7]

Since Paramount was set on its deadline of Christmas, 1939, many compromises had to be made, resulting in a fully animated approach. The original story work began in New York. One version cast Popeye in the role of Gulliver with a purely comedic flavor.

As the concept took on more momentum, it went in other directions. After re-reading *Gulliver's Travels*, as described in "A Giant Comes to Town," *Good Housekeeping*, February 1940, Max stated, "The fellow's self-centered, to say the least. I wonder how the poor Lilliputians felt when Gulliver picked them up by the scruff of the neck and dangled them on his thumb? Gulliver's had his say. It's time for the little men to speak up. I'll take a five-inch citizen-of-Lilliput's view of the adventure."

One of the initial story conferences for *Gulliver's Travels* went along these lines, with Bill Turner leading the discussion:

TURNER: Who do you suppose found Gulliver? He's the hero of our story, I should think.

FLEISCHER: Gulliver doesn't tell who found him. After all, Gulliver didn't wake up until the Lilliputians had already tied him down. And quite an engineering feat that must have been, too!

TURNER: I know! The Town Crier found Gulliver.

FLEISCHER: Of course. It was a stormy night, and the Town Crier was sleepily making his rounds.

Unidentified voice: Singing "All's Well" and in a rather bored voice, I'll bet. He was sure nobody'd be about on such a gloomy night and doubtless he wanted to go home himself.

TURNER: When suddenly he bumped into something. Some huge object was stretched on the beach. The Town Crier raised his lamp.

FLEISCHER: A human finger he'd bumped into, and lifting his lamp, he saw five giant fingers spread fanwise on the beach, and attached to a human hand about twice the size of a full-grown Lilliputian! Lifting his lamp still higher…

TURNER: (Jumps in) He saw the giant! Oh, boy! What an opening!

FLEISCHER: What's the Town Crier's name?

TURNER: (Thinking for a second) His name is Gabby, of course. He was born with the gift of gab and knew and told every happening that had ever happened in Lilliput back to, and even before the First Great War with Blefuscu.

At the next story conference it was decided that Gabby had not been stricken dumb with terror on spotting the giant, though many a lesser man might have been, but had run lickety-split through the town, crying: "There's a giant on the beach! There's a giant on the beach!" And he successfully rounded the whole population.

TURNER: "Surely he went to tell the king."

Everyone agreed that he had indeed made a special trip to King Little's palace to inform His Majesty that a giant had come to town. It was also unanimously decided that Gabby had personally organized and directed the binding up of the sleeping giant's body. Gabby, the ingenious, had suggested that the workmen dig tunnels under Gulliver's back and carry ropes through these tunnels and hurl them over his monstrous chest by means of the very rock catapults that the Lilliputians customarily used to defend their North Wall from attack by the folk of Blefuscu.

As the story conferences proceeded and the script took shape, it became obvious that Gabby—garrulous, bossy, braggart—was nabbing the lion's share of the drama for himself—a modern David who would overcome Goliath and steal the show. When all the principals were safely down on paper full of life and vigor and loud with words, Seymour Kneitel, chief animator and his assistants were asked to make convincing sketches of them.

KNEITEL: Gabby should be short and dumpy. His feet should be flat and his head large.

UNKNOWN ASSISTANT: He has a bulbous nose.

ANOTHER ASSISTANT: His hair is unruly.

EDITH VERNICK: You can't be too mean to Gabby.

KNEITEL: Princess Glory is the glamour girl of Lilliput, and I wonder what her dimensions should be?

VERNICK: Ideally, she'd be about three and a half inches tall. That would make her about one and twenty-nine one-hundredths of an inch through the middle, with an ankle…

KNEITEL: We'll draw it, but we'd better not try to compute it.[8]

The first version of *Gulliver* was more slapstick and deliberate, lacking in subtlety and continuity. While the level of drawing was not up to the standards required for feature animation, it improved throughout production. To ensure the success of Fleischer's first feature, Paramount appointed Edmond Seward, an experienced live action feature film writer to fashion the original adaptation from the Swift original. Once in Miami, the Seward screenplay was reworked by Dan Gordon, along with Cal Howard and Ted Pierce. The new crew thought the story begun in New York was too slapstick and weak in continuity. They refashioned the script into a romantic musical fantasy that even the most steadfast Fleischer veterans saw as vastly improved, fashioning songs that were key to the plot, especially the two national anthems that become the center of the war been Lilliput and Blefescu. Gulliver's

Early *Gulliver* story sequences (author's collection).

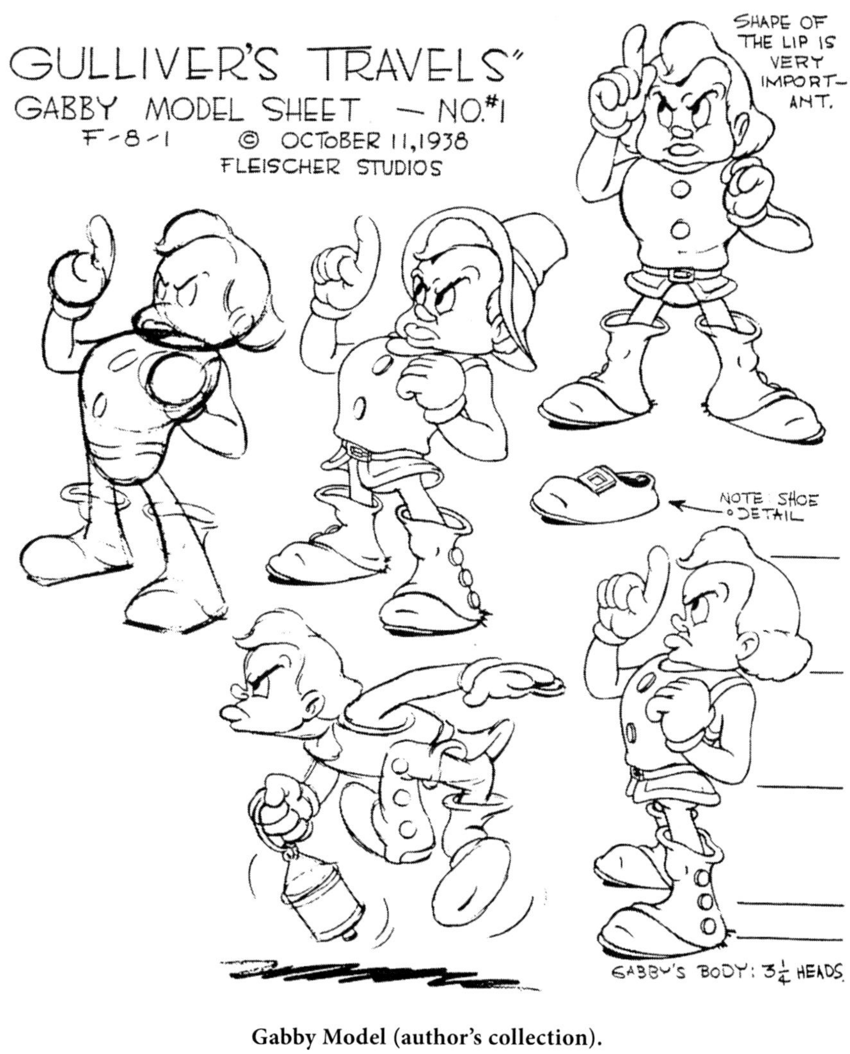

Gabby Model (author's collection).

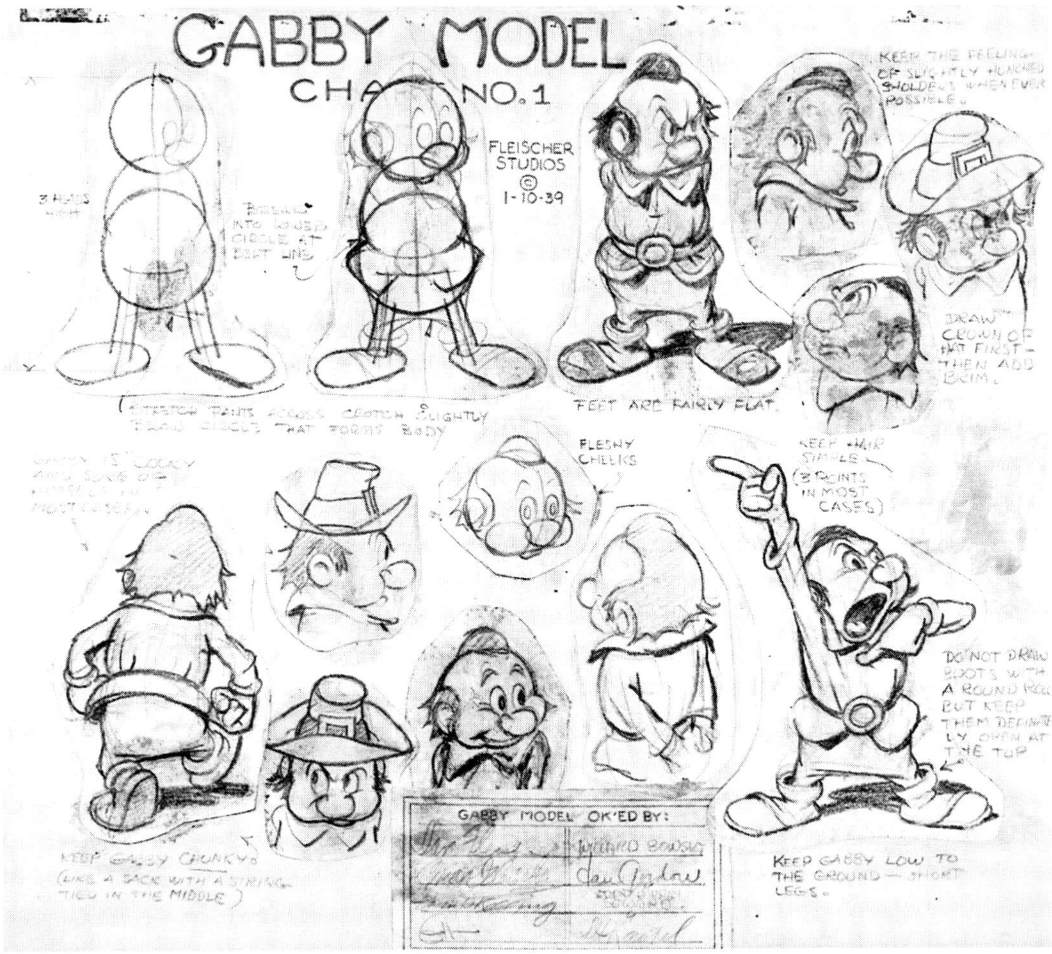

Final Gabby model original pasteup (Ryan Englade).

design was not quite defined when production began with his face purposely left vague and turned away from the camera for the first three reels.

While attention was given to the Lilliputians, the role of Gulliver remained uncast.

Once in Miami, Max started a public search for a tall, dark, and handsome model. Sam Parker, announcer for the Miami CBS radio station WIOD, read the announcement, requesting a letter and photograph from all applicants. After a few days, Seymour Kneitel went to the station to look over the responses, and he found the perfect candidate right in the station—Sam Parker. Parker's image was used for all of the scenes where Gulliver's face is finally revealed the next morning and for the remainder of the film.

Several West Coast techniques were used to introduce better animation and greater personality in the characters. Some animators adapted while others did not. Pencil tests were unheard of in New York but were soon embraced as a tool for improving production methods. The rushed schedule seemed to take precedence over quality, and overtime was the order of the day. Even with the rush, deadlines were compromised with Paramount considering canceling the film. Relations with the Technicolor lab were strained due to

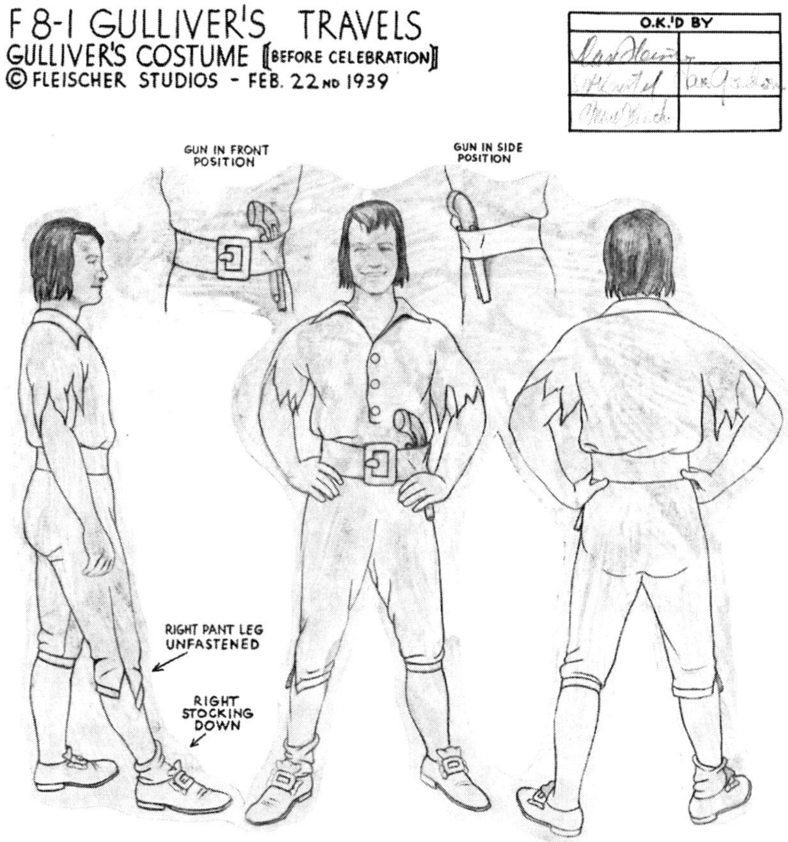

Above: **Early Gulliver model (author's collection).** ***Below:*** **Gulliver model hoisted for live action reference (Todd Levine).**

Left: Live action models Lovey Warren, Sam Parker, and Cal Howard (Todd Levine). *Below:* Gulliver model sheet (author's collection).

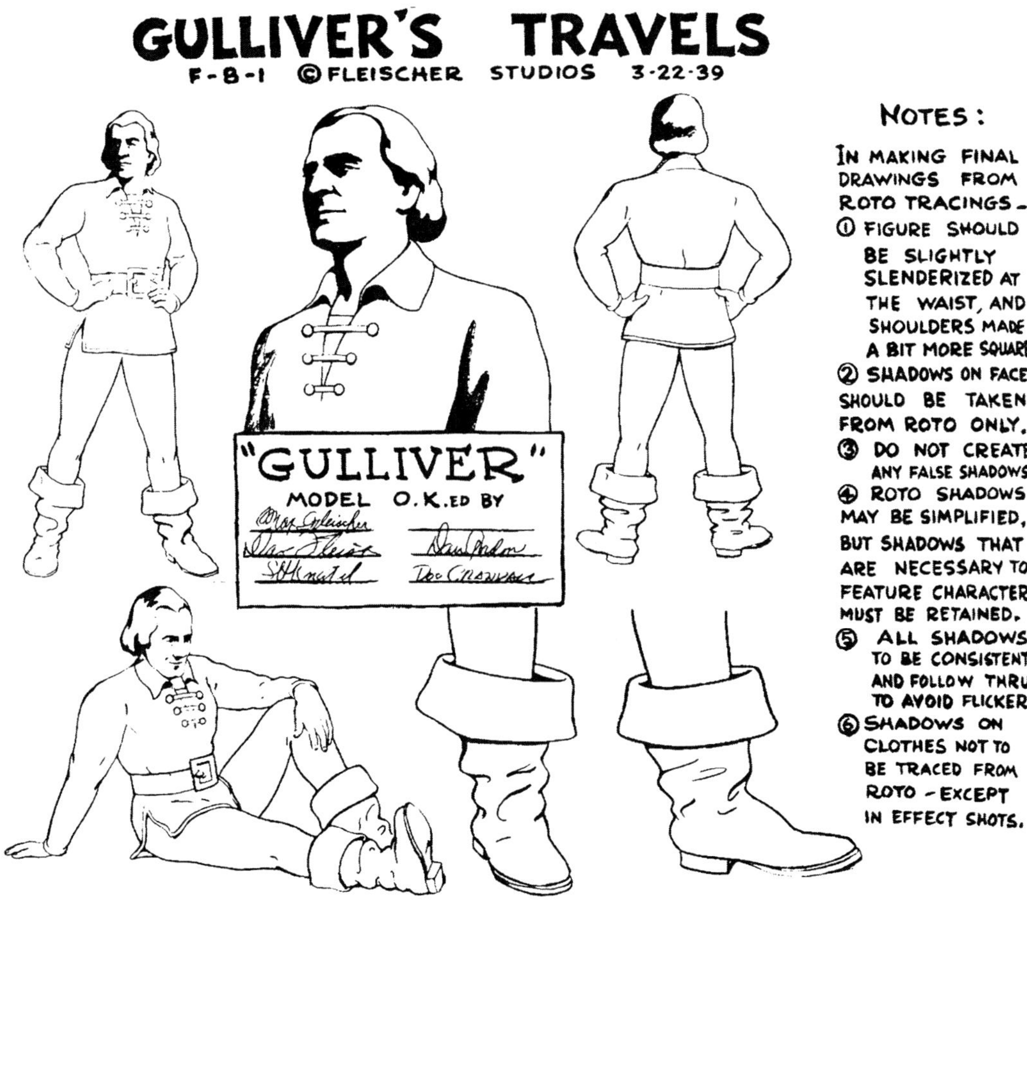

Above and right: **Dave Fleischer directing live action reference footage for *Gulliver's Travels* (Todd Levine).**

these constant delays largely associated with the remote location of Miami.

Paramount had a major investment with the production of *Dr. Cyclops*, the first horror film produced in full Technicolor, and the labs were already working at capacity to make 100 prints. With all this drama, it looked as though Fleischer would never meet the delivery date. *Gulliver's Travels* premiered in Miami on December 18, 1939, to an eager public. The crowds were so large that the premier was held at both the Sheridan and Colony Theaters to packed houses.

Fleischer Studios delivered *Gulliver* for Paramount's planned Christmas release schedule, opening in New York on December 20, 1939, going into general release on the 22nd. Considering the potential demonstrated in the two *Popeye* specials, *Gulliver's Travels* seemed a lesser experience. This much-anticipated feature produced by Max Fleischer was still met with an eager public and started out well, breaking box office records in spite of the inevitable comparisons to *Snow White*. As Film Reviewer Frank S. Nugent cited, *Gulliver's Travels* had more of a juvenile appeal and performed as predicted in the internal Paramount memos.

New York Times, December 21, 1939

Review

Unlike Disney's "Snow White," which was preeminently a fairy tale for adults, Max Fleischer's feature-length cartoon of "Gulliver's Travels" is a fairy tale for children and for children almost exclusively. As such we have no hesitation in recommending Paramount's new film as a pleasant and diverting animated picture-book, drawn in the brightest Technicolor, happily free from ogres, hobgoblins and other nightmare-breeders, and so broad in its humor that the littlest four-year-old can scarcely miss its jokes.

But, by any other standards than those of the juvenile audience, the film is so far beneath the level of Mr. Disney's famous fantasy that, out of charity, we wish we did not have to make the comparisons demanded by professional responsibility. If it were only possible to soften the blow by suggesting that the second feature cartoon automatically loses the novelty—value of the first, we should be cushioning our typewriter with the excuse right now. But it is far more than novelty that "Gulliver lacks": the wit, the freshness, the gayety and sparkle, the subtlety, the characterization and, for that matter, the good drawing that are the trademarks of the Disney factory.

Pointedly enough, the best parts of the Fleischer show are those which are most reminiscent of Disney: the comet-like course of the lamp-bearing town crier of Lilliput when the first sight of Gulliver sends him rocketing through the city to spread the alarm, the Lilliputian methods of repairing the human giant's wardrobe, the music-box effect of the harmonic snores of King Little and other members of his court. And pointedly, too, the worst parts of it were Disney stumbling blocks also: inability to make a little Prince and Princess anything but expressionless dolls, to crease a natural human face into a smile or frown without the lines and shadows performing a square dance.

For comic cartoon purposes they have used only the roughest outline of the Jonathan Swift satire about Lemuel Gulliver, the shipwrecked sailor who came ashore in Lilliput, where the folk were only thumb-high but just as cantankerous and warlike as full-grown members of the race facetiously known as human. That is the beginning and virtually the end of the synopsis—since animators have material aplenty just in the notion of a working crew of Lilliputians trying to capture a man seventy times their size—but, for good measure, they have tossed in the Prince of Blefuscu and the Princess of Lilliput whose wedding is called off, and war declared, because King Little insists that his anthem, "Faithful," be sung at the wedding and King Bombo is adamant about the singing of his anthem, "Forever." Some parts of it are amusing enough to adults, even by Disney standards. The capture of Gulliver, with block and tackle and monumental Lilliputian energy, is chuckling fantasy; the behavior of Bombo's three spies is good burlesque in the Three Stooges tradition, and we enjoyed the sequence when Gabby—the would-be Dopey of "Gulliver"—is blubbering about his indigestibility, his wife and kids—"millions of em." The score is fair enough, thanks to Lee [*sic*] Robin and Ralph Rainger and to Jessica Dragonette and Lanny Ross, who sing their tunes; but even the score is familiar, a blend of "Snow White" and "The Wizard of Oz." The children, of course, won't be so critical: whether it's Disney, Fleischer or Mervyn LeRoy, fantasy in picture-book form is just what they want for Christmas.

Comparisons of *Gulliver's Travels* to *Snow White* were a matter of relativity since the two films are nothing at all alike. *Gulliver* is a far more complicated feature from a production standpoint. There are more characters, several crowd scenes, contrasting scale and dramatic perspective. Also, there are many technical and special effects animation scenes involving mechanisms and construction processes. Clearly Dave Fleischer had a lot on his hands. But in many respects the realizations that Walt Disney had in shaping *Snow White* were just not present in *Gulliver's Travels*. As animation historian John Canemaker cites, Walt Disney was a ruthless story editor—a trait that was absent in both Max and Dave Fleischer. Interestingly, Dave recalled an awareness of needing to cut a sequence due to the length of the picture.

> It was a little too long when I got finished with it, which I did intentionally. I wanted to cut in places. Each room was on a sequence, and we had four or five animators per room. We had seven sequences in the whole picture. Sequence three had the weakest animation, little originality. I didn't like it. I wanted to cut it out after the picture was finished, but I knew if I did, I would cut the boys' hearts out. I didn't know what to do. I didn't sleep all night. I couldn't just go and clip it and not say anything. So I got the animators from all the sequences into the projection room, and I said, "Boys, the picture's too long. Where can I cut?" So they all started to pick little short parts in their own sequences. I said, "That won't do me any good. I've got to cut a whole section out. I wish you boys would talk it over without any favoritism, and if you see another sequence is better than yours, please be honest because I want to get a good picture." And they got together, and they cut out sequence three. I didn't have to do a goddamn thing.[9]

The film does struggle with its point of view and suffers from confused editing in places. While the initial story conferences suggested a more interesting approach from the Lilliputian perspective, this was not quite realized. The opening scene of Gulliver's ship's log is very impressive, suggesting something that the viewer does not come to see. Orestes Calpini animated the storm at sea with great difficulty, having no references or established models to follow. The animation looks more like figures from a stained glass window at times, and *Gulliver's* proportions are incorrect as he struggles with the sails. The handling of the rain and water is crude compared to the effects appearing later in the film as well.

Gordon Sheehan animated the scenes of Gulliver coming out of the water. For this, live action reference was filmed of animator Nelson Demorest struggling onto the beach and dropping down. This entire opening sequence appears to have been done during the early stages of production with Gulliver's face purposely obscured. Aside from the mediocre animation in this sequence, the major problem is that these scenes are literal and unnecessary, giving away the surprise. The simpler and more dramatic solution would have been to create an entire storm sequence in special effects, ending with its clearing as Gabby announces, "All's well," leading up to the discovery of the giant hand fanned out on the beach, as Max described in the initial story conference. The elimination of Gulliver falling onto the beach would have been a better decision since the animation is better with the introduction of Gabby in a good song sequence.

Following the discovery of Gulliver, the sequence is slowed down by too much repetitive business. Once Gabby arrives at the castle to tell the King of his discovery, he is told that the wedding contract between Prince David of Blefuscu and Princess Glory of Lilliput is about to be signed. Much attention is given to the two kings here with the introduction of a secondary sequence to integrate the song of Lilliput through Princess Glory. This is the first revelation of the "love interest," which needs a sequence to establish these characters. Instead of going directly to the kings, it might have been better to establish a little cuddling scene with dialogue between David and Glory to establish the song of Blefuscu, *Forever* sung by David followed by *Faithful* from Glory.

Perhaps dialogue about the young couple in love since childhood would have been an interesting way of setting up the two songs as the kings sign the wedding contract. King Little could give a sigh of satisfaction, saying, "Ah, Faithful, the song of Lilliput. It'll be played at the wedding tomorrow." This would be a more credible set up for the argument than the one in the film since it doesn't make sense that this would have been the first time that Bombo has heard the national anthem of Lilliput. Introducing *Forever* after Bombo stomps out, having declared war, stops the film at that point. Oddly, it is heard in the underscore behind Bombo's argument for it before it is sung and established in the film.

While the scene of Bombo sitting and reminiscing in the doorway of the coach is a technical achievement of optical printing, it is unnecessary, suggesting that he is considering apologizing and calling off the war. But he changes his sentiment when he realizes that his spies are seeing him in a moment of sensitivity. The better cut would have been to continue Bombo down the steps, and seeing his spies in the shadows, remark, "Don't look now gentlemen, but it's war," to which Snitch reacts with glee, "War? Whoopie!" David, who looks longingly towards Glory's balcony, would be urged into the coach, and they drive away.

Since the audience is seeing the spies for the first time here, this would have been an ideal spot to place a character developmental song establishing Sneak, Snoop, and Snitch especially since the audience is never told their names, which have the potential for being characters like the Seven Dwarfs. Unfortunately, one does not physically "sneak," one does not "snoop," and the other does not "snitch"—in fact, he is mostly mute, reminiscent of *Snow White*'s Dopey, whose antics seem modeled somewhat after Harpo Marx. They have the potential of being like the Three Stooges but lack individual personalities and mannerisms. Instead, they work together as a unit. Interestingly, the voice of Sneak, the lead spy, is Jack Mercer's second use of the raspy wheezy voice he later used as the Professor in the *Felix the Cat* television series; his first use was for the Spider in *The Cobweb Hotel* (1936).

The call to alarm in the middle of the night is an exciting sequence. But it slows down when Gabby loses sight of the giant under the cover of night. The sequence where the Lilliputians do not realize they are on Gulliver's chest is too long, running over four minutes. It also has some of the worst animation in the picture with characters the most grossly off model. Although better animation precedes this, its entire purpose is merely a repeat of Gabby falling into the brook, which interferes with the progression of the story. This sequence could have been improved by shortening the business and dialogue by half, and cutting from the Low Angle march across the bridge to Gabby saying, "Shhh, we're almost there," and climbing onto Gulliver's chest.

The cart building sequence for moving Gulliver is very detailed and long, taking seven minutes from construction to getting the horse-drawn conveyance moving. This would have been a good place for a work song led by Gabby to help shorten the process. A misdirected bit of dialogue comes from Gabby running along Gulliver's chest, barking contradictory orders, then turning to camera to say, "I don't know what they'd do around here without me!" This joke would have been better delivered as a self-realization as he sits down with disgust.

The Lilliputians work all through the night, and by next morning the details on Gulliver's face are seen after being awakened by the accidental firing of his pistol. The Close-Up on his eye opening is perhaps one of the most dramatic images in film history, followed by the scenes of him breaking loose from his bindings, which are equally as impressive with the skillful use of airbrushed shadows. It seems odd from an acting perspective that Gulliver does not register surprise about waking up, finding himself tied down before he starts to break loose. Going directly into this seems too deliberate.

The scenes for the introduction of Gabby to Gulliver do not quite connect since they lack direct points of view between the characters. As Gulliver supposedly sees Gabby pounding on the closed balcony door, he turns seeing Gulliver but does not look in the correct direction—to camera, which is Gulliver's point of view. When Gulliver reaches into the balcony, he does not appear to be feeling around for Gabby, but "fishing around" with his fingers too close together for picking up something. This could have been staged more interestingly seeing Gulliver's hand come in from above, giving Gabby more opportunity to crawl around, dodging the giant fingers until they grasp him. It is reasonable to assume that the choice of the low angle was a short cut to simplify the animation and limit it to just the action of the hand. But this choice makes the scene appear as action for its own sake and not for the drama and sake of the character.

Once Gulliver does pick up Gabby, his reaction is not genuinely amazed. There is a great close-up of Gabby dangling from Gulliver's fingers as he begs him not to eat him. But this scene stays on too long. A Close-Up of Gulliver speaking to Gabby, or a Long Shot of Gulliver sitting up, saying to Gabby, "Hold on mate, nobody's going to hurt you." would have established a better sympathetic connection between the two characters. As Gabby continues pleading to be put down, King Little suddenly rushes out onto the balcony without opening the door. There was an opportunity to have the King slowly open the door in Close-Up to peek out, motivated by Gabby's cries, then rush out in the Long Shot and say, "Drop that, drop that!"

When King Little calls for the archers to surround the giant to entice him to release Gabby, there is no real sense of being surrounded. Gulliver, amused by the audacity of the tiny people, gently deposits Gabby onto the balcony with King Little, who starts a long call for "ready, aim, fire" at the giant. Having Gabby interrupting with "aim, fire" does not make sense and wastes time. Also, Gabby would still be in a state of shock, not quite so composed. But the King's attempt to "surround the giant," with his archers interrupted by Bombo's sudden attack with arrows hitting the turret spelling "Forever," is a good story device leading into the shower of flying rocks and arrows from the Blefuscuian Navy.

While Gulliver would have been sitting up, he would have ducked down to avoid the projectiles. Once he does sit up, the sailors see him and jump ship. The scenes of the sailors and Bombo seeing Gulliver do not make sense, however. They appear out of order and violate film grammar and rhythm. Although there is a good continuity cut from Gulliver sitting up from the flying pebbles, the image size of the close-up here does not connect with the sailor's point of view. Then, when Bombo in medium long shot sees Gulliver in a medium long shot, his point of view is diminished, as if from further back from the position of the sailors. It would have been legitimate to continue Gulliver laughing or looking at Bombo saying "Hello!" in close-up to represent his point of view, motivating the retreat of his fleet with greater strength. This calls for a cut back to Gulliver looking in the direction of the retreating ships. Instead, the film cuts directly to Gulliver turned, addressing the Lilliputians who are still hiding from the attack, asking, "Where's everyone gone? This is no way to treat a harmless visitor." The better cut would have been to King Little pushing off the accumulated rock pile in the balcony and exclaiming, "Look Gabby, we've won!" Then Gulliver needs to enter sooner, saying, "Hello there!" as a reminder that it was his presence that was responsible for the assumed "victory." Perhaps this should have been followed with the scene of the people cautiously opening their shutters. Too much time is spent getting to this point, and too much time is wasted in this sequence, especially with King Little's reaction, only to rush back into his chambers peeking out, and Gulliver leaning in to say, "Come now, don't let my size frighten you." As wonderful as this animation is, the obvious problem here is that Gulliver does not look directly at King Little and Gabby, but looks around haphazardly. This also takes too much time. This scene would have made better sense if preceded by the residents peeking out of their homes. Then Gulliver's looking around would have been more logical followed by his addressing the King, "You, Your Majesty. Surely you aren't afraid of me." This scene cuts too soon and should have lasted through Gulliver's entire line, then cutting to the King's reaction.

The sequence picks up pace as Gulliver introduces himself. As King Little welcomes Gulliver to Lilliput, this is followed by a clichéd action of pausing, placing the finger to the side of the head to register thinking. This could have been more effective with a subtle facial expression to register the King's realization. These things are the point of view that Max was looking for and were unfortunately missed.

The film picks up momentum with the delightful *It's a Hap-Hap-Happy Day* sequence where the Lilliputians construct a new suit of clothes for Gulliver. From this point on, *Gulliver's Travels* looks like an entirely different film becoming easier to look at. However, there are minor problems with some crude character designs and mediocre animation of the Lilliputians—including the Shoe Shine Boy—who looks like an unrefined version of Pinocchio polishing Gulliver's fingernails. The cut from the finger polishing to Gulliver picking Gabby out of his breast pocket comes too soon, with the polishing music continuing ahead of the triumphant fanfare that concludes the sequence. This scene calls for displaying the entire hand with polished fingernails, which ties in with Gulliver's fanned out fingers on the beach at the beginning of the picture. An interesting touch would have been to show the nails shining with the boy looking at his reflection in one of them, nodding with approval for the final two beats, then cut to Gulliver with the fanfare.

There is a continuity error with the disappearance of the scaffold from Gulliver's shoulder at the end. But most of all, the sequence ends without an obvious connection with the Lilliputians. When Gulliver stamps his boot and stands up, there needs to be a scene of the crowd cheering, and then cut back to Gulliver looking about as the cheers continue, ending the sequence. In spite of these discrepancies, this is one of the bright spots of the picture, as it displays one of the key Fleischer components, the preoccupation with construction processes.

The banquet sequence framed by the song *Blue Birds in the Moonlight* is another highlight of the film, memorable for Gulliver's "finger dance" with King Little. This sequence is paralleled with the spies who receive a message from Bombo via the goofy carrier pigeon, Twinkletoes. The message reads, "Dear Spies, Get rid of that giant or else." This is a direct order to kill Gulliver that is repeated later. What the message should have said was, "Dear Spies, Find a way to assassinate Gulliver." This gives more meaning to their worrying until

Snitch; the little mute spy comes up with the solution—Gulliver's "Thunder Machine," which is on public display.

The following song sequence of *Come Home Again* set beside the moonlit shore seems unnecessary. On the one hand, Gulliver looking out to sea as he smokes his pipe does give him a moment as the chorus sings the song in the background, bringing the evening to a close. But his singing stops the progress at this point, seeming unnecessary or out of place. It takes up too much time and interrupts the flow from the climax of the previous scene.

The next sequence with Gulliver carving out a sailboat and the accompanying business between Gabby and Gulliver is a nice light-hearted touch that supports the relationship between Gabby and Gulliver. It connects better with the ending of the banquette sequence with the spies waiting in the nearby mill where they have hidden Gulliver's pistol. The spies now have the means of killing Gulliver, and they only have to wait for instructions on the proper moment. It would have made better story sense to cut to Snoop dictating the letter to Sneak as he pats the pistol, "Dear Bombo, say the word, and the giant is a dead duck. P.S. What do we do with the body?" Then having Snitch see Gulliver approach, and having them cover the pistol and hide makes better sense. This would retain the nice sequence of the mill catching fire and Gulliver putting out the fire by scooping up the water with his hands.

The next sequence with David singing *Forever* to Glory in the garden is followed by a senseless sword fight against three palace guards. This is made more senseless with Gabby flailing his sword around in the air, dropping it several times for the sake of a laugh. But what is more senseless is the set-up. Gabby, the town crier, is in the process of going to bed when he overhears David singing in the garden. Apparently it was forgotten that Gabby works nights and should be on patrol. Also, the appearance of David is unexplained. Imagine Glory hearing David's singing coming from somewhere near the garden. She approaches the gazebo area, which is on a cliff. She looks out and sees David standing on some steps leading up to the garden with a rowboat in the background. The two lovers would then rush towards each other, Glory singing parts of *Forever* in answer to David. Hearing the song of Blefuscu, Gabby starts looking around, following the direction of the singing, which leads him to the gazebo on the cliff. He sees the two lovers and calls for the guards. Perhaps the three spies would also hear the singing and get tangled up in the chase, attempting to help David in the escape. While the singing surely exposes David as it did in the film, this might have been a better set-up, working into a dramatic chase to be scooped up in Gulliver's hand and reunited with Glory at the amphitheater.

An improved transition might have been a dissolve to a close-up on the spies' message, "King Bombo, say the word, and the giant is a dead duck." Then cut to Bombo as he repeats the last few words in gleeful realization, "And the giant is a dead duck!" Twinkletoes, perched near Bombo's desk, mocks a dying duck in a silly faint and making a sickly duck call would seem a better gag than Bombo's malapropism, "Now we are getting at somewhere!" Bombo would then proceed with the order to kill Gulliver, writing, "Dear Spies," then looking upward thinking of the words, "obliterate ... annihilate..." then registering satisfaction in finding the right word, writes, "KILL HIM!" From here the remaining sequence builds with excitement as Bombo launches the attack at dawn.

The spies' attempt to shoot Gulliver is stopped when Glory and David see the pistol being rolled into position at the cliff, and David rides off on horseback, knocking the pistol over the side, crashing on the banks below. This blocks the attack, and Gulliver brings the realization of the harm that this silly quarrel has caused. Then he suggests the songs as they might be sung. Ironically, Robin and Ranger had difficulty combining the two songs, and Lou Fleischer solved it by random rearranging. This is the big moment of the film, reestablishing the romantic aspect of the prince and princess held in Gulliver's hands. Gulliver's solution revealed at the amphitheater earlier is unnecessary since it spoils the climax.

The sentiment of the song needs to continue throughout the sequence. Cutting away to two unnecessary and mediocre scenes unfortunately mars it, particularly the crowd and its awkward dancing. The two kings singing together is a logical choice as well as the spies, and the entrance of Gabby still tied up in the feed sack, cut loose by Snitch, leading into the rumble is a logical comedic ending for the sequence.

Out of appreciation for uniting the two countries, they build Gulliver a boat for his return home. This ending seems rather pedestrian, suggesting that something more was intended. The record album contains dialogue between Gulliver and Gabby, suggesting a reprise of *Come Home Again* was to be followed by this dialogue:

GULLIVER: "Farewell, little Gabby. It's time to part, for the call of the sea has reached my heart. And it bids me sail to a distant shore, to my land, my people, my home once more. So to you and Lilliput, may I...."
GABBY: (interrupting with tears) "I know, You've got to say Good Bye."
GULLIVER: "Gabby, are you crying?"
GABBY: "No, it's something in my eye."
GULLIVER: "My, my, my."

According to Dave Fleischer, this extension was dropped in order to meet the looming deadline. This is unfortunate since the picture would have benefitted greatly by including this passage of dialogue in the ending.

Gulliver's Travels started out well, breaking box office records at the Paramount Theater alone. The 3,664-seat theater was consistently packed, mostly during morning and matinee showings, with respectable attendance in the evenings. With admissions ranging from 25 cents for children and 90 cents for adults, Paramount executives were excited by the box office earnings. Approximately 265,000 people had seen *Gulliver* at the Paramount alone, with only 73,000 being children's admissions.

Following its two-week run at the Paramount, *Gulliver* was moved uptown to the Roxy where it continued to do record business, and went into general release throughout the U.S. and Canada during the Christmas 1939/1940 season. Collectively, it can be determined that between 6,500,000 and 10,000,000 people saw *Gulliver's Travels*. With the New York attendance figures representing between 5 percent and 7 percent of the national gross, it can be determined that the total earned revenue for *Gulliver's Travels* came to $3,000,000 in gross rentals, as determined based on "Balaban's Law" of box office computation ($2.85 × base film rental = net profits). Taking the round figure of $3,000,000 divided by an average adult admission of 90 cents equals an average of 3,333 patrons per day. Dividing this amount by the average total attendance of 10 million equals an average admission price of 33 cents. Although the production of *Gulliver* was originally estimated at $500,000, its final cost was nearly $1,500,000. Based on the overwhelming business of *Gulliver's Travels* in its opening run, Barney Balaban immediately ordered another feature for a 1941 Christmas release. In spite of running over the original budget, Paramount made a profit of at least $1,000,000 domestically. Dave proudly remarked:

"It was such a big hit that Buddy de Silva called me in and congratulated me and shook my hand and said, 'We've got a great picture here, Dave, and I want to compliment you.... You know how I know it's good? My wife likes it!'"[10]

The public response to *Gulliver's Travels* is still remarkable considering its limitations, not just in terms of production time and inherent flaws, but in its limited distribution of 50 prints. Due to this and a one-month run, many parts of the country did not see *Gulliver's Travels.* And while *Gulliver* was intended as Paramount's holiday "A" feature, *The Great Victor Herbert* was offered as a substitute when prints of *Gulliver* were not available. But most of all, Paramount had definite plans for a short-term domestic release to capitalize on the large children's market during Christmas vacation.

An all-out effort was made to advertise *Gulliver's Travels* with full-color magazine ads, following the Disney example of merchandising, including books, fine china, and a four-disc 78 rpm Decca record album conducted by the film's Musical Director, Victor Young, using sound-alike cover artists Wynne Davis for *Faithful*, Bob Stevens for *Forever*, and Harry Stanton as Gulliver.

The year 1939 was a banner year for quality movies with the release of *The Wizard of Oz, Gone with the Wind, The Hunchback of Notre Dame, The Little Princess, Stagecoach,* and *Mr. Smith Goes to Washington* to name just a few, with Paramount seeing *Gulliver* as its "A" picture of this tier. But *Gulliver's Travels* had reached its peak by February 1940, earning three-eighths the business of *Snow White*, which continued in release for two years. Then, with the release of Walt Disney's *Pinocchio* in February, *Gulliver's* domestic run had played out. But Paramount had enough faith to offer Victor Young's score and Robin and Ranger's *Faithful Forever* for Academy Award nomination. It lost out to *The Wizard of Oz* for best score, and *Over the Rainbow* as best song.

12

Stormy Seas Ahead

As Max was so determined to see his feature length vision come to fruition, a serious price was paid, both economic and personal. One of the sensitive realities of this issue is that in the pursuit of success, Max and Dave lost their sense of direction, which affected their personal lives and how they handled them. Max had experienced marital problems several years before, with Essie attempting suicide. Charlie and Joe had come to Max's house on Union Street one evening, surprised to see an ambulance out front. Richard Fleischer speaks frankly about the incident:

> Theirs was a long marriage but not a particularly smooth one. In fact, it sometimes got pretty rocky. There were some good shouting matches, with my mother doing by far most of the shouting. I seem to remember a dent in a kitchen wall that was made by a coffee pot that she winged at my father. These contretemps were usually brought on by Essie's violent fits of jealousy. She was very much in love with Max, and there were fairly frequent accusations of his 'making eyes' at some young lady.... One day when I was six or seven ... she attempted suicide. She went into the bathroom one morning and tried to swallow a bottle of iodine. It was a very poor choice of lethal weapon. As soon as the liquid hit the inside of her mouth, it burned like hell. She spat it out and started screaming in panic. My sister, Ruth, a teenager at that point, rushed into the bathroom and also started screaming. My mother was flailing around, with Ruth trying to find out what had happened and keep Essie from hurting herself. Neighbors started rushing into the room yelling, "What happened? What happened?" Ruth, or a neighbor, called an ambulance. By the time it arrived, Essie had rinsed her mouth and calmed down and was insisting that it was just an accident, that she had mistakenly picked up the wrong bottle of medicine. But who takes medicine right out of the bottle?[1]

Max's business status and professional success placed him as the patriarch of the family, although he was the second born. Because of this, Essie placed value on her position, and the stigma of a divorce in her mind would be a social and family disgrace. Instead, she resigned herself to a more liberal attitude with Max, which is how she came to regard the business relationship between Max and his secretary, Vera Coleman. Vera was very devoted to Max, seeming to understand him as well, or better than Essie. In essence and spirit, Vera became in effect Max's "professional mate," a role that Essie came to accept.

Dave's wife, Ida, became suspicious of his spending more and more time "at the office." At first Dave denied any infidelity, then finally relinquished, warning of the power of suggestion, which led to an open relationship with his secretary, Mae Schwartz. The relationship seemed motivated by two things: To satisfy Ida's insistence that Dave was being unfaithful, and more importantly, to strike back at Max. Ida had indiscreetly told Essie about her problems with Dave, real or imagined, which in turn Essie relayed to Max. When Max consulted Dave on what he had heard, advising him to cease this affair, Dave took offense to these lectures in light of his perception of the relationship between Max and Vera Coleman. In

Dave's mind, this was hypocritical since he claimed that he was going to divorce Ida and marry Mae. From here on Dave ignored anything that Max said, and he set out to prove that he alone was the guiding force of Fleischer Studios.

In many ways, Dave carried an inferiority complex due to Max's professional credentials and education. In the beginning, the opposite personalities of the brothers complimented each other. Max was dignified and articulate. Dave had a street-wise Damon Runyon "thug" personality, which men like him developed as a defense against limited education and a Bogart-like lisp combined with a slightly effeminate sounding voice. The 20 years of comparisons between Dave and his more intellectual brother had reached their climax. Now in the Miami paradise, this professional "match made in heaven" had descended into hell. If they met each other in the hall, it was with hate-filled glares, passing without speaking. The brothers took offices on opposite sides of the studio and avoided interacting. They communicated only through interoffice memos. And the friction continued to escalate through Dave's cavalier actions designed to irritate Max. This was the basis of the feud that escalated in Miami, posing a threat to other family members. Richard recalled with candor:

> This situation was starting to put Ruth and me in an uncomfortable position. The problem was that we loved Dave, and he was genuinely fond of us. He had a wonderful sense of humor and was great fun to be with. We asked Max if it bothered him when Dave would hire a pleasure boat and invite Ruth, Seymour, and me to go fishing with him in the Everglades. Max always pooh-poohed the idea that he might be offended, but if he had been, he would never have let his children know.[2]

Saddled with delivering Paramount's "A" Picture for the 1939 Holiday Season, Dave Fleischer was in a position to ask again for an increase in salary. Max reasoned this time that Dave deserved the raise for enduring the pressures associated with bringing his personal project to fruition and moving the studio in a new direction. On May 2, 1939, in a special meeting with their corporate attorney N. William Welling, an official agreement was made placing Max as president in charge of all business matters, and Dave as vice president/secretary in total control of production. This came three weeks before the renewed Paramount contract for the 1939–1940 season, which included continued financing for the completion of *Gulliver's Travels.*

In this agreement, each party was entitled to make creative suggestions to the other. But a serious strategic mistake was made by generously giving Dave 50 percent ownership and total charge of production in addition to the raise. With this new business arrangement, Max and Dave Fleischer were named as equal producers responsible to Paramount. This equal partnership neutralized Max's power to fire Dave should he fail to perform his duties. Dave clearly had the advantage, and he knew it. On the one hand, Max's generosity seemed a means to end the feud by giving Dave what he wanted. But one can only question the wisdom of making Dave an equal partner under the advice of their attorney since the deteriorating relationship between the brothers was accelerated further by this action. According to Bernard Fleischer, this was demonstrated in a production meeting where Max attempted to make a suggestion and Dave dismissively responded, "Oh, Max why don't you just shut the Hell up and go back to your office and sign some contracts! Dave began to take over much more of the production chores, relegating Max to sitting in an office working out and signing contracts. And Max was an extremely creative person and he just couldn't stand it."[3]

Max admitted that he disliked conflict and used creativity as an escape. After being barred from participating in the production of the cartoons, he found satisfaction in research and development projects. One of these was an improvement of the time-consuming and inconsistent cel inking process. Even with the most skilled inkers, the original vitality and flexibility of the pencil drawings could not be captured. The first concept was realized in his patent filed December 14, 1936. This patent calls for the original drawings to be photographed in high contrast with a positive print loaded in contact with the camera's raw stock. The coloring, or "opaquing" of the figures would still be painted on cels using the original drawings as an outline guide. The painted cels would be placed over the painted background and shot as before except that the image of the outlines would already be inside the camera. While the basic intent was to retain the quality of the drawings, this method was obviously more complicated and impractical for production. Photographic line transfers to sheet film already existed for printing processes, but they were too expensive for the thousands of animation cels required for an animated feature film. Max continued to explore other means of replacing the inking process.

A second line transfer method was attempted using a special pencil and a press. Unfortunately, the lines came out squashed and distorted. While Max was ahead in his thinking, his solutions were not suc-

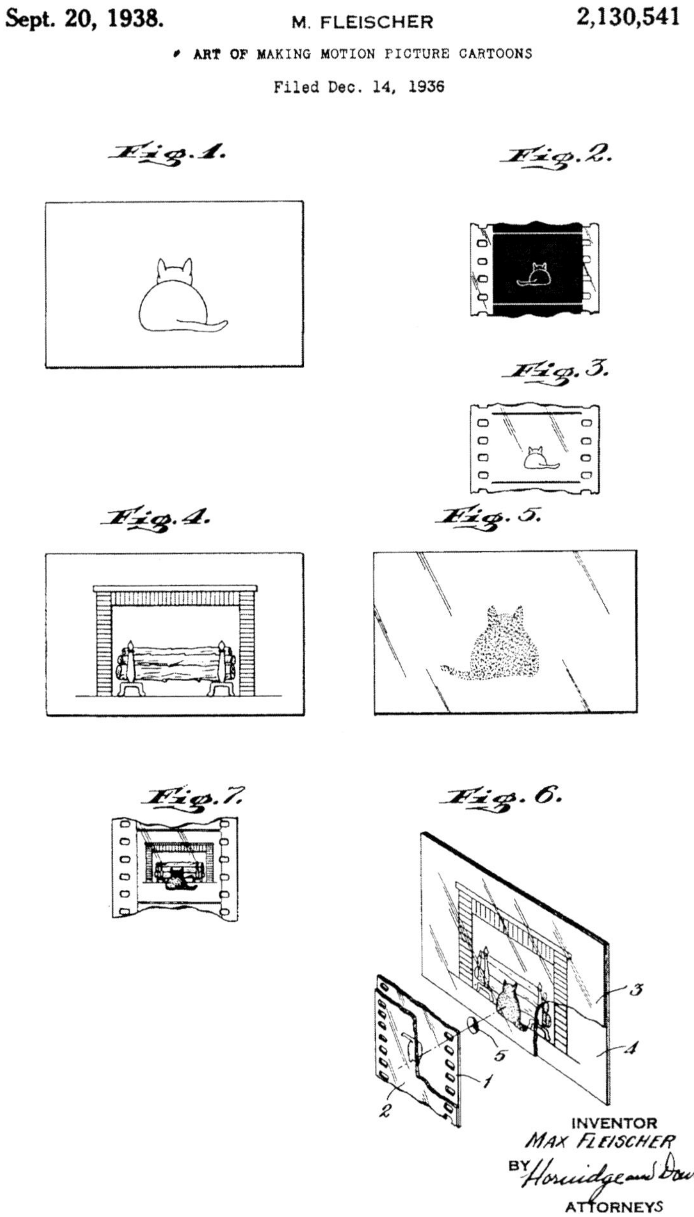

Max's first line transfer patent (U.S. Patent and Copyright Office).

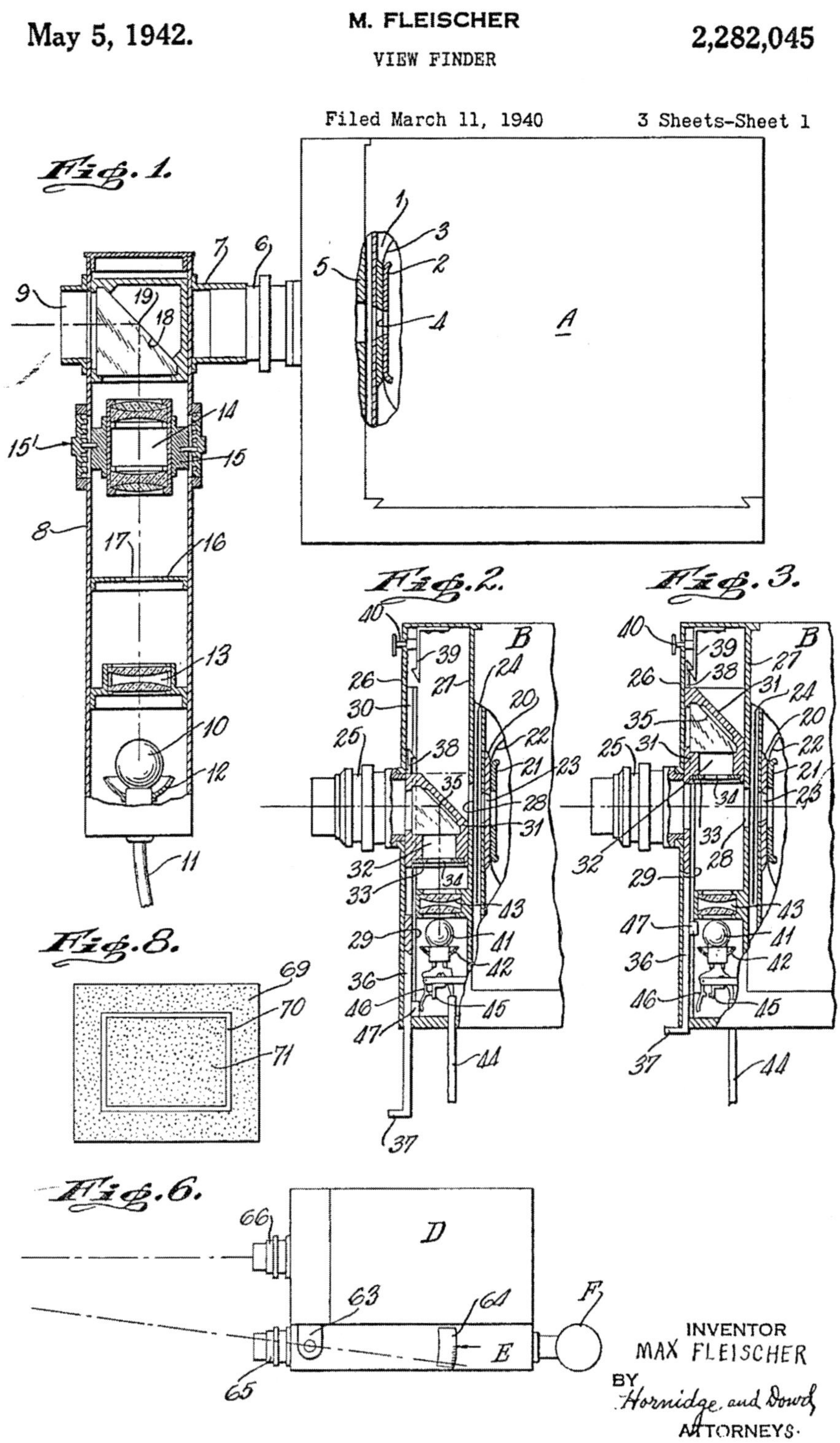

Fleischer's Viewfinder patent (U.S. Patent and Trademark Office).

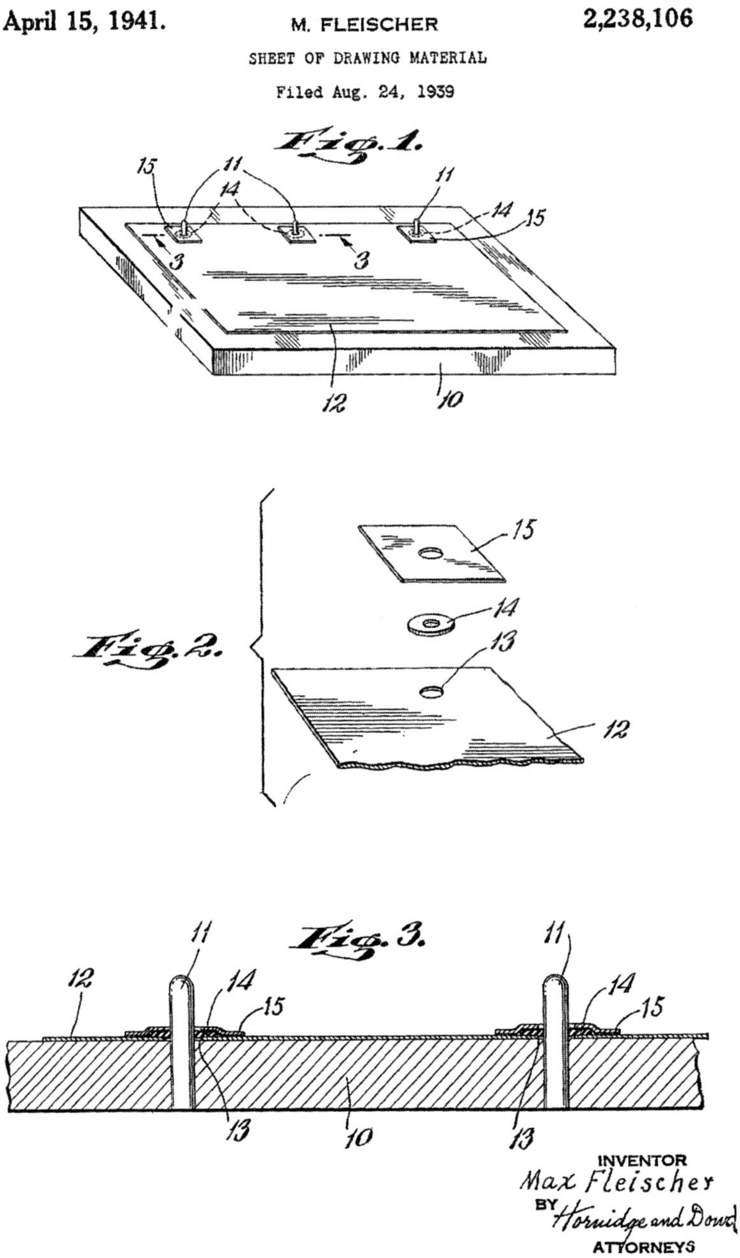

Fleischer's Cel Reinforcement patent (U.S. Patent and Trademark Office).

cessful. The image transfer concept in animation would not be realized for another 20 years, with the introduction of line transfer processes by the Jam Handy Organization and the Disney studio in the late 1950s.

Concerned about accurate registration for the feature, Max filed a patent for an adhesive reinforcement to lessen the wear on punched animation paper and cels. While Max had a close connection with the animators in the past, he was now spending more time in the Camera Department, which led to his invention of a Reflex, "through-the-lens" camera viewfinder. The patent specifically refers to its application to motion picture cameras and was perhaps Max's one invention that had the most potential for licensing to camera manufacturers.

Aside from his technical abilities, Max's role in the production of the cartoons has been greatly underestimated. Following the move to Miami, Dave Tendlar was in charge of the third *Popeye* special, *Popeye the Sailor Meets Aladdin's Wonderful Lamp* (1939). It was taking a lot of time to complete, and Max suggested the use of an inter-title to eliminate a long sequence introducing Aladdin to the sorcerer, which advanced the plot in an economical way. This substantiated Max's value as an effective production problem solver

Above: **Princess Olive model sheet (author's collection).** ***Below:*** **Charlie Schettler shooting a scene from *Popeye the Sailor Meets Aladdin's Wonderful Lamp*, 1939 (Todd Levine).**

which changed under the new agreement. Once Dave was in charge, he set out to prove himself more important than Max. Dave's name started appearing larger on the screen than Max's. Dave also arranged all sorts of oddball publicity plants in the newspapers. An article in *The New York Herald* dated September 19, 1941, read:

> Dave Fleischer, head of the studio that makes animated cartoons, says that 52 percent of the 700 cartoonists employed by him are left-handed. "Considering that only 11 per cent of the population of the United States is left-handed," (don't ask us how he found that out), he says, "I naturally deduce from my studio survey that southpaws must be inherently artists."
>
> Fleischer, who is somewhat of an expert on useless facts, claims that 73 per cent of the master animators currently working on *Mr. Bugs Goes to Town* employ the left mitt in doing everything but shaking hands. Among other left-handed artists (not employed at his studio), he names Leonardo da Vinci, Titian, Rodin, Immanuel Gaspaya, Henner, and Fra Angelico. Fleischer himself is not. Neither is Walt Disney. Charlie Chaplin is. So was Gyp the Blood. What does that prove, Dave?

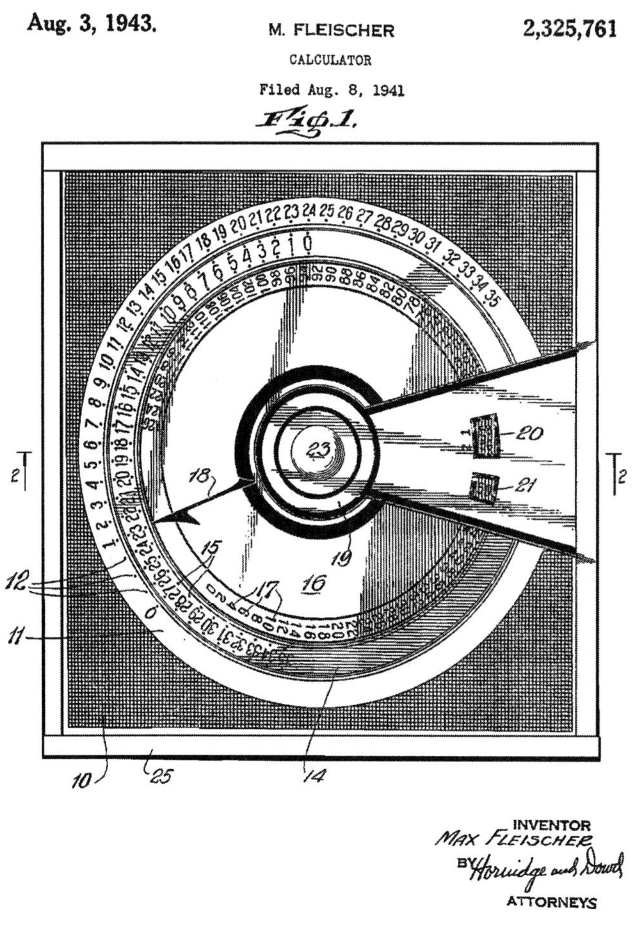

Fleischer's Betting Calculator (U.S. Patent and Trademark Office).

Dave continued to do outrageous things. He took on the role of a playboy, dressing and acting the part. He drove around in a late model Packard, arriving at the studio with a liberal use of the horn to announce his presence. He arranged to have his New York bookie moved to Miami, and his office was a betting parlor more active than in New York, complete with a ticker tape machine. But Dave was not alone in playing the horses. Several of the key animators, as well as Max's wife, Essie, partook of the "sport of kings." This popular Miami pastime motivated Max to develop a "betting calculator" to aid in handicapping horse races.

In spite of the improvements in the appearance of the cartoons, problems continued brewing under the change of command as the studio moved into the 1940s. And the studio needed to develop new short subject product to keep the large

Seymour Kneitel (center) with unidentified friends at Hialeah Park, Florida (author's collection).

staff busy while the next feature was being prepared. But with Dave Fleischer at the helm, the studio was steering off course into troubled waters with the cartoons produced under his stewardship.

Sally Swing was originally planned as a replacement for the *Betty Boop* series. This had been announced in the trades two years before. While Russell Patterson, the famous magazine cartoonist, was originally engaged to develop the character, none of his ideas were used. The early Sally Swing model is bland, displaying weak, unrefined drawing. The original concept was brunette, but changed to a blonde character with a larger forehead and longer hair. These revisions were still too timid for a potential college "sweater girl" character. If the Fleischer artists weren't held to the blandness imposed by Paramount's adherence to the Production Code, a character of the type developed by Tex Avery at MGM would have been a sensation.

> FILM DAILY, April 18, 1938
>
> *Washington Bur*
>
> A new character, Sally Swing, joins the Paramount short subjects group, replacing Betty Boop in 12 cartoons.

Original Sally Swing concept (author's collection).

Perhaps if the original Russell Patterson concepts had been adapted the character would have had more impact. Unlike Betty Boop, Sally Swing's personality had no foundation in an established entertainer. The fact that now 15-year-old Rose Marie had been the original voice was not enough. By this time, another Betty, Betty Hutton, was on the rise as Paramount's new star of the Swing Era labeled "The Jitterbug Girl." But the Fleischer development team did not take the initiative to follow Betty Hutton as a model and Paramount did not promote the concept as they had with Betty Boop. In this case a series based

"They put HER in the right department."

***Left:* *Sally Swing* theatrical poster, 1938 (author's collection). *Right:* Russell Patterson cartoon, ca. 1940 (author's collection).**

on star-on-the-rise Betty Hutton would have actually complemented and accelerated her career since there would have been no deliberate attempt to compete with her audience or exploit her personality as in the Helen Kane case. *Sally Swing* had great potential for a series in the mode of the college musical, *Good News*. In spite of the potential, Dave changed plans at the last minute to produce a prehistoric parody concept.

Twenty years before the debut of *The Flintstones*, the Fleischer studio produced the *Stone Age* series. The visual gags of contemporary life placed in the Stone Age presented many cartoon opportunities, but the character designs by Charles Thorson were unappealing and old-fashioned. There was no effort made to develop "star characters," and the studio was looking for audience reaction to find one. Aside from a lack of central characters, the voice work was not outstanding, further limiting their appeal.

The first *Stone Age* cartoon, *Way Back When a Triangle Had Its Points* was released in February 1940, with the last, *Way Back When Women Had Their Weigh* released in September. Aside from the ugly, unappealing designs, the series had little value in black and white when the competition had already gone to all color production. Dan Gordon worked on several of the story sketches on *Stone Age* and would draw on this experience later when he did storyboards for the Hanna-Barbera television series 20 years later.

Many thought that Gabby stole the show in *Gulliver's Travels*. As a result, he was given a series of eight cartoons in Technicolor. While his established personality of a complaining, frustrated self-important character was considered amusing in the feature, he became a

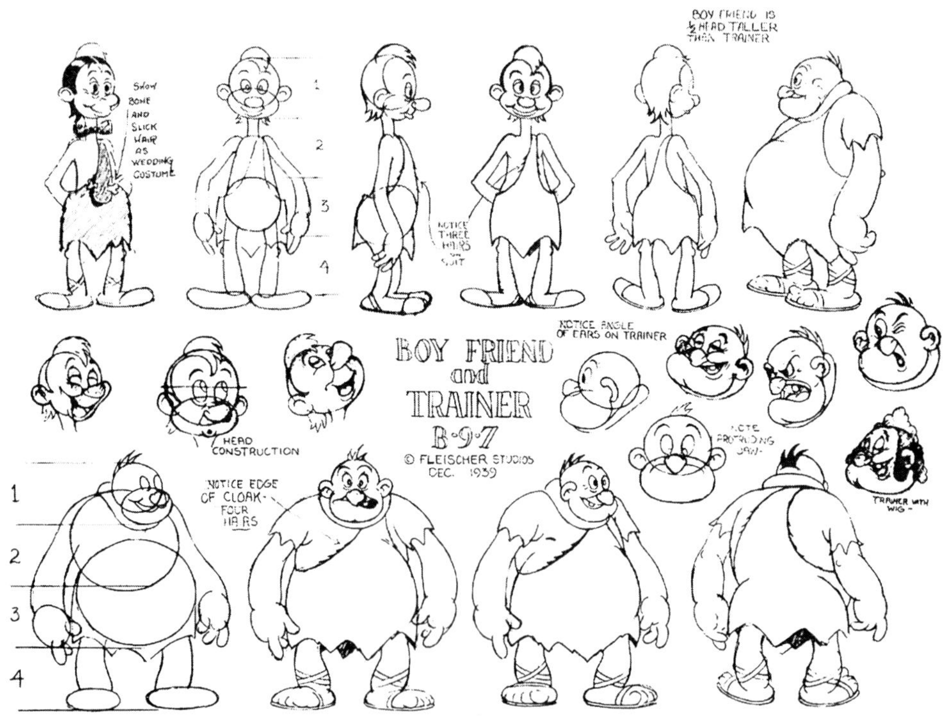

Top and bottom: **Stone Age model sheets (Todd Levine).**

Top and bottom: **Stone Age model sheets (Todd Levine).**

meddlesome know-it-all, far more abrasive than humorous in these cartoons. Theater owner C.L. Niles of Anamosa, Iowa, complained to Paramount headquarters, "Certainly a weak sister! Why this series?" Paramount had a pattern of ordering cartoons in groups of 12. But the *Gabby* series was canceled after the delivery of the first eight. Reviews in *Film Daily* substantiate an unevenness of the series.

FILM DAILY, February 17, 1941

"Two for the Zoo"
Paramount 7 mins.
Amusing Cartoon

Gabby, the town crier, insists upon delivering a newly arrived rare baby specimen to the royal zoo. However, Gabby doesn't notice that the baby animal has hopped out of its mother's pouch when he starts his journey and when he turns around and discovers that he is leading a full sized specimen he is surprised, to say the least. Gabby has plenty of trouble before he gets himself out of his jam. Cartoon is a Max Fleischer production. Subject is in Technicolor, which helps make it bright and visually appealing. There is not much individuality to this one but as comedy it gets by okay.

FILM DAILY, April 18, 1941

"Swing Cleaning" (Gabby Cartoon)
Paramount 7 Mins
Gets by Okay

Folks who annually go through the pangs and pains of Spring cleaning will find lots to smile o'er in the antics of Gabby, who gets permission from the King of Lilliput to personally supervise putting the castle in slick shape. The intention is perfect; the results ghastly, for the stupid Gabby wrecks the handsome joint and is reprimanded thoroughly. He wasn't content to give the orders, but to demonstrate just how each job should be done. The carnage to carpets, pictures, china, draperies et al., is immense.

FILM DAILY, June 24, 1941

"Fire Cheese"
Paramount 7 mins.
Fair Cartoon

This quick-paced Technicolor cartoon has a fair amount of laughs. Gabby butts into the fire department organization and before they get rid of him a building is destroyed from what started out to be a small fire.

FILM DAILY, August 1, 1941

It's a Hap-Hap-Happy Day"
Paramount 7 mins.
Some Amusing Moments

Cartoon features the Max Fleischer character, Gabby. This time Gabby gets in the hair of the town mayor when he invites himself along on the mayor's fishing trip. He attempts to show the mayor how to do everything, naturally with disastrous results. End has Gabby up a tree with the owls.

Animated Antics, a black and white anthology series with subseries starring supporting characters from *Gulliver's Travels*, were also a disappointment. Even though the entries with The Three Spies and Twinkletoes may have had potential, these characters failed to sustain interest.

> FILM DAILY June 24, 1941
> **"Twinkletoes—Where He Goes—Nobody Knows"** (Animated Antic)
> Paramount 7 mins.
> Weak Cartoon
>
> A not-very-funny reel showing the adventures of a messenger pigeon who is engaged to carry a time-bomb. Losing the address, the bird goes back to the sender where the package blows up.

To fill out the *Animated Antics* schedule, Paramount bought independently produced films such as *Mom and Pop in Wild Oysters* (1940) by the Stop Motion Animator Charles Bowers, and the first *Speaking of Animals* short, *Down on the Farm* (1941), from Jerry Fairbanks, which won the Best Short Subject Academy Award in 1942 and spawned its own short subject series. *Speaking of Animals* was a concept ideal for Fleischer Studios with the trick of composited live action animal footage with animated mouths appearing to sing and make comedic remarks. Unfortunately the studio was too mired in its own problems to realize this on its own.

While Fleischer Studios had hit their stride in New York by 1936, they were now on a downhill path. Dave let the studio run on its momentum while he frequented Hialeah Track with his secretary, Mae Schwartz, which angered Max, since these "pastimes" were conducted during business hours, resulting in confrontations to which Dave became abusive and unreasonable.

Mae, becoming increasingly uncomfortable about being the center of the gossip and the focal point of the feud between the brothers, moved back to New York. Because of this, Dave took "extended vacations" continuing to visit her, leaving work unattended. In a memo to Dave, Max became direct about the details of an unfinished film: "If you are too busy to give this picture several days of your personal attention, let me know and I will consult with the cutters and editors assigned to the film."[4]

It is essential to consider the six to eight month gap between initial production of cartoons and their release dates in order to understand the timeline at this point. Therefore the evidence indicates that these problems followed the delivery of *Gulliver's Travels* in early December 1939 following the recording of the score in Hollywood. Subsequently, Dave's absences threatened the delivery dates of the shorts, and Paramount was raising questions. On January 2, 1940, Max sent a complaint letter to Austin Keough at Paramount about Dave's "extended vacations" that were affecting production. This letter seems to imply a request to fire Dave for breach and non-performance.

> January 2, 1940
>
> Dear Mr. Keough:
>
> Dave's vacation ends on February 12th, 1940. I have no way of knowing whether he intends

to return to Miami. Our last conference with him indicated that he would return, although he did not actually say no.

I assure you I shall closely guard every necessary move for harmonious result and will consult with Dick and be guided by his advice in doubtful situations.

I make the suggestion above because I believe it is important in this situation that you be informed as to my progress in handling this matter in a manner I believe to be entirely satisfactory to Paramount.

There are a number of reasons why Dave may hesitate to return to Miami.

1. His domestic affairs here are hopeless.
2. The direct cause of his domestic troubles resides in New York, where he prefers to remain.
3. Permission for the girl to come to Miami cannot be entertained.
4. Dave may go so far as to abandon his position and income in order to defeat Judge Gomez's verdict rendered in Circuit Court last Thursday.
5. His shocking abuse of my character and ability in his desperate effort to write music and lyrics for the next feature has not resulted in Paramount's permission for Dave to write such material.

The above facts make his return doubtful in my mind. However, in the event he fails to return, I should like to have Dick Murray here anyway, as changes and replacements in our organization will be made and I would like Dick to know when and why they are made.

Sincerely,
Max Fleischer

Max's last paragraph makes a strong implication calling for the firing of Dave, but it never happened. While the annual stockholder's meeting was scheduled for the last Wednesday of January, Dave was still on "vacation." This seemed a deliberate action on Dave's part, and the shared ownership once again stood in the way of moving ahead with changes in the board of directors. Technically the shared ownership amounted to 49.5 percent each of Fleischer Studios Common Stock, with 1 percent owned by Izzy Sparber. This came about when the studio moved to Miami, and under Florida law, corporations could not be totally owned by relatives. And the presence of a third stockholder was essential as a tie-breaker in the election of officers. On the other hand, if Max had acquired Sparber's 1 percent he would have had 50.5 percent and gained the position of majority stockholder, giving him power over Dave. But he was prohibited by Florida law from doing this.

It is unclear as to why the stockholder's meeting could not have been delayed until Dave's return, since he was still under contract until May 24, 1940. What is puzzling is why action was not taken on "lack of performance of duties." It is also puzzling as to why Dave was included on the renewed contract considering the poor quality of the cartoons under his supervision. Buying him out was awkward and uncertain. And with the diminishing assets of the studio, the stock held less value by this time. Still, Dave would not sell.

In Paramount's eyes, things were out of control and they acquired the services of George Pal for the production of his delightful *Puppetoon* series. Had Max secured these contracts, he could have controlled the supply of the short subjects that Paramount wanted, especially since the novelty of these series was fresh and generated the revenue that was desperately needed. So where was Max's attention?

Max became more and more concerned about Dave's unreasonable attitude and refusals of his suggestions. He surely was aware of the poor quality of the current product, and rightfully embarrassed in having his name associated with it. But he held fast to his agreement, being more concerned about Dave's mental state. Along with the obvious trouble they were having, he was struggling with the issue of dismissing Dave since there was cause. But most of all the 50 percent agreement prevented him from doing this, and there was no clause addressing failure to perform.

Max's son, Richard, was in the pre-med program at Brown University, preparing to become a psychiatrist. Dave recalled that during a school break, Richard visited him at the studio on the premise of demonstrating what he had learned at school. Dave surmised that Max sent Richard in to administer the Rorschach (Ink Blot) Test to determine his sanity. The results were inconclusive and business continued as usual, or as best it could under the circumstances. With their first feature film under their belt, Fleischer Studios was looking for its next project.

The Raggedy Ann character was already an established icon worthy of a screen adaptation. This was the same concept that Disney followed, adapting classics of popular recognition to ensure box office success. Since Max obtained the rights to three Raggedy Ann stories before the death of author Johnny Gruelle, only one was produced, limited to the two-reel format.

Story adaptation was by Bill Turner, with production under the supervision of Myron Waldman, who had a feel for gentle, sensitive material. While Gruelle's son Worth was credited as a story consultant, his input was largely ignored. From development to completion, Max tried to maintain a professional relationship with Dave, attempting to open the channels of communication with his comments on the finished film, "The two-reeler, *Raggedy Ann* is an admirable piece of work and probably the best cartoon made in our Studios in some time. The result as a whole is entirely satisfactory and deserving of comment."[5]

Dave failed to respond to these compliments, which was unfortunate. *Raggedy Ann and Andy* had enough story material and charm for a successful animated feature.

Raggedy Ann model sheet by Charlie Thorenson (University of Manitoba Archives).

Raggedy Andy model sheet (University of Manitoba Archives).

But the finished production suffers from a rushed and compressed story that does not allow enough time for character development. In addition, the film could have been strengthened by a live action wrap around, using the animation as the fantasy imagined from looking at a storybook. Regardless, Max was so pleased, it is strange that he did not think to develop it into their next feature. It would have been relatively inexpensive to produce, being a simple story with fewer characters, and most of all ideal for a Christmas 1940 release with the obvious merchandize tie-ins.

While the model sheets show a May 1940 date, apparently it was under consideration in late 1939, perhaps during the initial release of *Gulliver's Travels*. Had Max sold the idea of *Raggedy Ann* as the next feature, it is likely it could have been ready for Christmas. The extension of five reels would have reached a completion by fall, allowing enough time for post-production and making prints for a wider distribution. Considering that the final scenario for *Mr. Bug* was not ready until October, this would have easily folded into the schedule. A *Raggedy Ann* feature the type that Fleischer Studios was capable of producing with the added value of Paramount's Music Department could have been the answer to their financial problems—an inexpensive, commercially successful feature with automatic marketing tie-ins. Oddly, the final release date for the two-reeler was 11 months later, on Easter weekend, April 11, 1941—A YEAR LATER!

Max was in the position to approach Paramount with this easy sale. Instead, he let *Raggedy Ann* remain on the schedule as a two-reeler with hopes of rekindling the Fleischer magic, failing to see things on a larger scale. He continued to put his faith in the established reputation of his studio and his long-time relationship with his distributor, taking for granted that the future was guaranteed based on the past. But the tone set by Walt Disney in the 1930s was changing. In 1941, tradition was broken when the Academy Award went with MGM's *The Milky Way* for best animated short. MGM and Warner Brothers were now taking the lead, leaving Fleischer behind the competition once more.

Fleischer Studios advanced from failure to failure under the direction of Dave Fleischer with the shorts losing nearly $250,000 for the year of 1940. Theaters only wanted the *Popeye* cartoons and refused the others. The cartoons of lesser value were packaged with Paramount's "B" pictures as a "no cost bonus." To compensate, the *Popeye* earnings were used as a cross-collateralization to

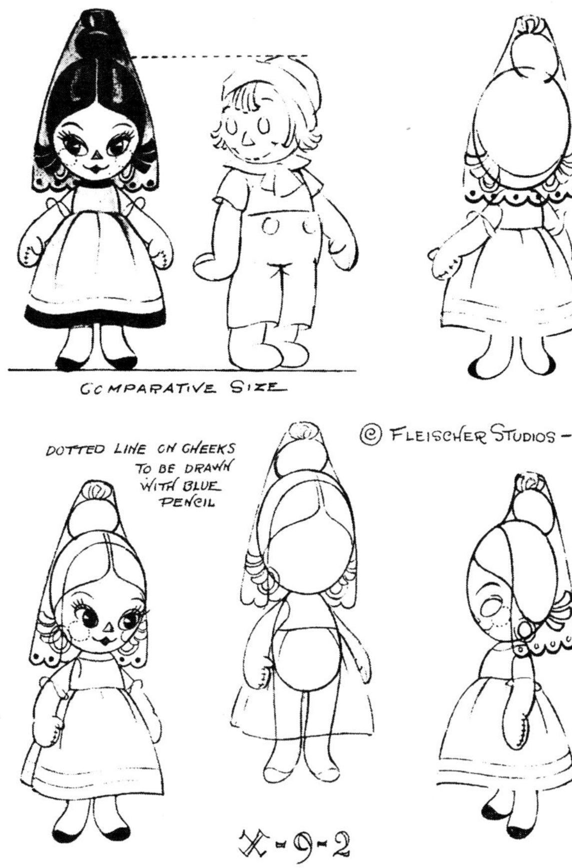

Left: Spanish Doll model sheet (University of Manitoba Archives). _Below:_ Little girl (University of Manitoba Archives).

recover the losses from the rejected cartoons—revenues shared in thirds between Fleischer, Paramount, and King Features. But Fleischer Studios no longer received their share due to the losses of 1940. Max Fleischer's gamble on a Miami production facility proved to be an expensive enterprise in need of sophisticated management to stand up to the machinations of Paramount, which continued to work away at the studio.

It should be understood that as Paramount advanced Fleischer Studios production funds, the anticipated returns on these advances were based on the projected earnings, which normally earned more than the production cost. After the dismal year of 1940, it was a wonder that Paramount continued doing business with Fleischer. While the studio had been producing highly profitable cartoons in the 1930s, it was now in trouble. Miami proved not to be the profitable "movie maritime province" that was expected, and this vacation paradise was not influencing creativity. Emulating Disney and Warner Brothers was not working, and they needed to turn in a new direction unlike that of the competition. Paramount wanted another hit to duplicate the success of *Popeye* and make Fleischer Studios relevant to the new decade.

The Man of Steel, Superman, first appeared in Action Comics in 1938. This single creation by high school students, Joe Shuster and Jerry Siegel, quickly developed into a major property, spawning a comic book series and a radio drama that same year. *Superman* had been optioned to Republic Studios for a live action serial. But Republic supposedly passed due to the complicated and expensive special effects that were necessary. The general story states that Paramount bought the rights from the publisher, Detective Comics, and presented the concept to the Fleischers in the fall of 1940. *Superman* was the biggest challenge to be faced since entering feature production due to the naturalistic nature of the subject with its dramatic camera angles and realistic human figures. All of this was costly, requiring great drawing skill and time to animate effectively compared to the comical cartoon characters that had been produced up to this time.

According to Dave Fleischer, he wanted to discourage Paramount by quoting a price of $90,000 to $100,000. In light of the debt already hanging over Fleischer Studios, it is puzzling that Paramount would propose such an expensive endeavor. At the same time, Dave's account of the situation does not sound logical for two reasons. First, Max handled business matters. Second, the science fiction element of *Superman* appealed to him, which raises the question of who expressed interest in the property first, and whether it was Max who proposed the acquisition of *Superman*. According to a legal filing by Republic, the rights were "given" to Fleischer by the publisher.

FILM DAILY, June 27, 1941

Republic Demands $50,000 in "Superman" Balm Action

Suit for $50,000 damages was filed yesterday in the New York Supreme Court by Republic Productions, Inc., against Detective & Superman, Inc., owner of the comic strip "Superman." Republic claims that in April 1940, it made a contract with the defendant who gave it the right to make a film serial based on the "Superman" cartoon. Subsequently, according to the complaint, the defendant breached the contract and gave the film rights to Fleischer Studios.

This contradicts the story that Republic dropped their interest due to the complicated special effects. The article states that Fleischer Studios acquired the license, which supports the idea that Max negotiated the acquisition, substantiated by the list of Fleischer Studios' licensed properties including Popeye. With the previous year of poorly received cartoons, it was clear to the front office that Fleischer Studios was not successful in developing new original characters since their greatest success, *Popeye* was a pre-existing property. By this logic, Paramount was confident in duplicating this success with *Superman*, agreeing to half the reported production price.

The 1941 contract reveals an allocation of $50,000 for the first *Superman* cartoon, with the following cartoons produced at $30,000. By comparison, the *Popeye* cartoons in black and white were budgeted at $16,500 each. The original intent was to produce *Superman* in black and white to keep costs down. But plans changed in an official announcement posted in *Film Daily.*

FILM DAILY January 15, 1941

Technicolor Treatment for "Superman" Series

Shift of plans to make the series-picture, "Adventures of Superman," in Technicolor instead of in the originally planned black-and-white, has necessitated the postponement of the productions release until the spring; it was learned yesterday from sources close to the situation. Originally, release was announced for December or the present month. The film is currently before the color cameras at the Fleischer Studios in Miami, Fla., with the staff there concentrating on the initial "chapter," of which there will be 12 when the entire series is completed. Production is based upon the comic strip character, "Superman," and the first chapter of the adventures will deal with his advent on earth from the fictitious planet, Krypton. Paramount will distribute the film.

The January 15, 1941, *Film Daily* announcement confirms that *Superman* was already in production before the Republic lawsuit, placing the starting date in September 1940. This is also substantiated by its inclusion in the new May 1941 contract. Development art was created to determine whether the studio could handle the first naturalistic animated series. The lessons learned about staging and layout from *Gulliver* prepared them well. The first story was assigned to Seymour Kneitel and Isidore Sparber, with detailed story sketches and layouts following. Since realistic human animation was necessary for *Superman*, Max Fleischer's Rotoscope was once again the solution. For Rotoscope footage reference, wrestler Karol Krauser was hired as the live action model for *Superman*. And because *The Adventures of Superman* radio drama had such a popular following, the original radio cast was used including Bud Collier as Clark Kent/Superman, Joan Alexander as Lois Lane, and George Lowther as the Narrator, with Jackson Beck as Perry White in the first cartoon. The story line of the first *Superman* cartoon is easily communicated through the intricate 16 field layouts by the Fleischer studio artists.

Superman was a dramatic departure in the field of animated short subjects and brought the Fleischer studio the last of its Academy Award nominations. The science fiction tone put the studio back in its element with futuristic gadgetry and fantastic action. It also defined the studio's maturing and transition into the next decade. This type of "serious"

Karol Krauser, live action model for Superman (author's collection).

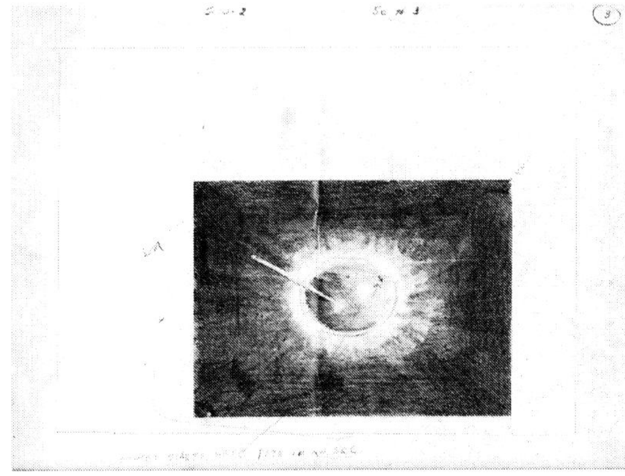

The rocket launch from the planet Krypton (Ryan Englade).

Krypton exploding (Ryan Englade).

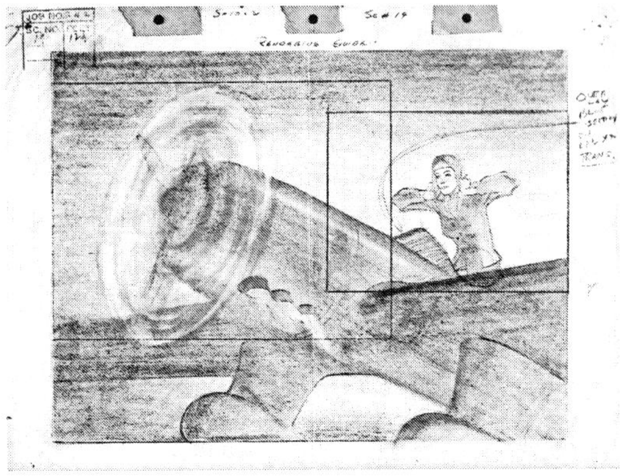

Above: The *Daily Planet* building (Ryan Englade). *Left:* Lois Lane in plane with field and camera move indications (Ryan Englade).

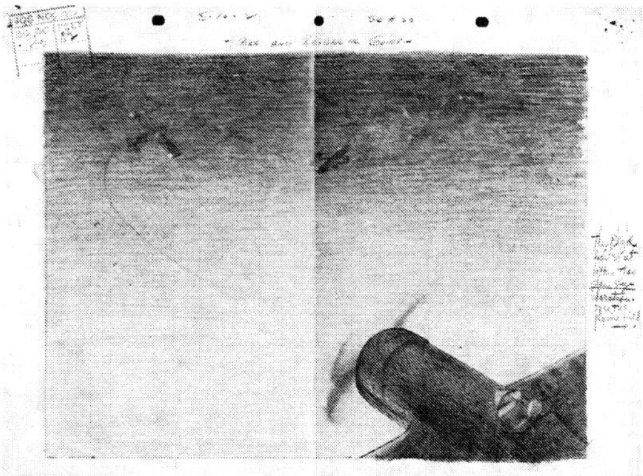

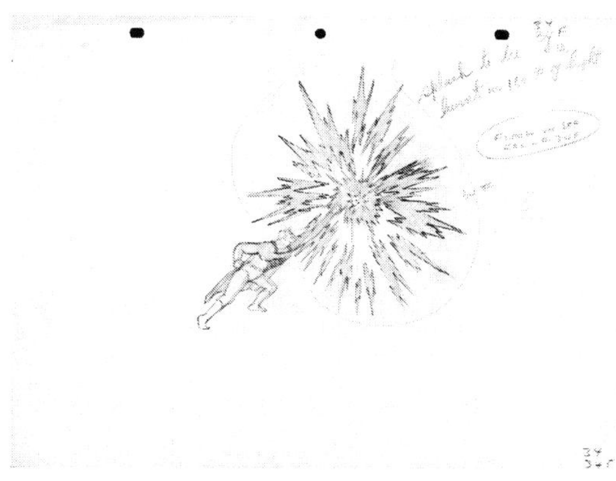

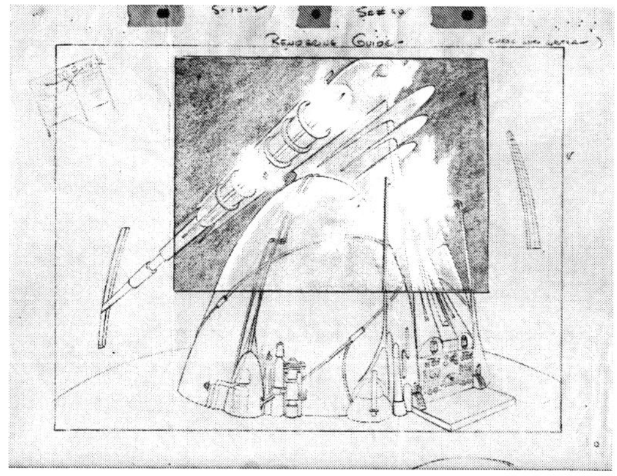

Top, left: **Plane take off.** ***Top, right:*** **Lois outside the Scientist's tower.** ***Second row, left:*** **Mad Scientist waiting inside at the door.** ***Second row, right:*** **Mad Scientist at the "Electrothanasia-Ray" console.** ***Third row, left:*** **Destructive Ray emanating from tower.** ***Third row, right:*** **Superman punches Ray.** ***Bottom, right:*** **Long Shot "Reference Guide" of tower interior and console (all photographs, Ryan Englade).**

film was the sort that Max was interested in making. Accordingly, *Superman* became a top flight hit as documented through the end of the year in *Film Daily*.

FILM DAILY, August 1, 1941

"Superman"

Paramount-Fleischer 11 mins.

Cartoon Newcomer Is Super-Duper

Latest entry in the animated cartoon field is the well-known comic strip character, Superman. He makes his bow under auspicious circumstances. All he does is save a city from destruction by a mad scientist. Possibilities for the new series catching on are very good. Superman here as in the strip certainly taxes the imagination, but that should make for more fun. It is a Fleischer Technicolor cartoon.

FILM DAILY, October 28, 1941

Offer "Superman" Trailer as Outright Exhib. Buy

One of the few trailers ever made for a short subject has been prepared by Paramount for "Superman," its series of 12 Technicolor cartoons, produced by Fleischer Studios. Trailer, a combination of Technicolor and peach blow film (tinting) is available to theaters for outright purchase.

FILM DAILY, December 19, 1941

"The Mechanical Monsters" (Superman)

Paramount 10 mins.

Top-Flight Cartoon

Fleischer Studios, Director Dave Fleischer, and Paramount offer herewith the second of the Superman shorts in Technicolor. The reel is well delineated, highly imaginative, and crammed with all those exciting elements which have made the character, Superman, a byword among the current generation of Americans, and a "buy" word among all exhibitors seriously interested in adding something new and colorful to their screens, as well as profitable to their box-offices. This adventure recounts the visitation on the "House of Jewels" of a phalanx of weird mechanical monsters, controlled by their arch-villain inventor by means of radio waves. Clark Kent, suspecting that Lois has been abducted by a mechanical monster, changes into the form and raiment of his other self, Superman, and pursues the robot scourge to the inventor's lair. There he annihilates the array of robots and rescues Lois, incidentally reclaiming the lost jewels, and, of course, destroying the inventor. Short is highly exploitable and every bit as engaging and novel as its predecessor.

13

The Ship Wreck

The year 1941 was a major turning point on several levels. Fleischer Studios was now reduced to producing just two series, *Popeye* and *Superman*. With a staff of over 700, survival was now hanging on a profitable second feature. The studio was hit with an additional casualty in March when Seymour Kneitel suffered his first heart attack—the result of his workload as head of the *Popeye* unit combined with a steady diet of beef and potatoes, compounded by chain smoking. It was because of his several months' absence that his name does not appear in the credits of the next feature. The loss of Seymour was certainly felt by Dave, confirmed in a letter written during the Post-production of *Mr. Bug* with a handwritten post-script to "keep healthy from now on." While it is difficult to determine to what extent the Popeye unit suffered from his absence, a number of the cartoons from this period seemed to miss the mark.

> FILM DAILY, January 22, 1941
>
> **"Problem Pappy"**
> Paramount 7 mins.
> *Fairly Amusing Cartoon*
>
> Popeye has trouble again with his Pappy in this reel from the Max Fleischer studios. Pappy is spied by his son, sitting on top of a flagpole. Pappy refuses to come down, so Popeye goes up, but Pappy refuses to be rescued until there is a lightning storm. It's fairly amusing.

> FILM DAILY. March 15, 1941
>
> **"Quiet! Pleeze"**
> Paramount 7 mins.
> *Weak Cartoon*
>
> The kids may like this one, but it is not up to the standard of other Popeye cartoons. Popeye walks in on his Pappy and finds he is suffering from a terrific headache, actually a hangover. Immediately Popeye starts quieting all the noises in the neighborhood by ingenuity and brute strength. However, when he returns from one of his anti-noise campaigns he hears a riotous party going on in his own apartment house and discovers Pappy performing as the life of the party. Reel is a Max Fleischer production.

Popeye Meets William Tell, directed by Shamus Culhane a year earlier, was a misguided concept. Culhane described the challenge, "*Popeye Meets William Tell* was a good example of my efforts to take a typical lusty Fleischer Popeye script and superimpose some Holly-

Top and bottom: **Model sheets for William Tell and the Gov'ner (author's collection).**

wood finesse in acting and cutting. The result was something like putting a lace sunbonnet on a wild boar."[1]

The problem with *Popeye Meets William Tell* is its content totally misses the fantasy/adventure potential. Unlike the epic two-reelers such as *Sindbad* and *Ali Baba*, this one-reel black and white short places Popeye in a silly and embarrassing role, pretending to be William Tell's son. Imagine the possibilities if it had been played straight as "Popeye Tell." The obvious casting would place Swee' Pea as his "son," and Bluto as the evil governor. The supporting characters could have been cast as well. But the main problem is that the Culhane version contains no real sense of threat or motivated revenge that was the root of the best *Popeye* cartoons.

In the original story, William Tell was a Swiss peasant from Bürglen who opposed Austrian authority. Due to his extraordinary skill with the crossbow, he was forced to shoot an apple from his son's head. Hitting his target in true Robin Hood style, Tell vowed that his next target would be the governor. Tell was arrested for making this threat, saved the governor's life en route to prison, escaped, then killed the governor in an ambush, leading to the Swiss uprising against Austrian rule. Since the issue of death would have been out of character, the reversal of imprisonment would have been the desired solution, with Popeye Tell appointed governor by the people with a satisfying heroic ending.

Adapting this story would have made for great entertainment worthy of the Popeye formula. At the same time, an interesting parallel between the original story and the Fleischer's ancestral background would have been realized had they taken this course. Instead they went for comedy in the worst way, mocking the character and the story.

Original Rip Van Winkle cel over mismatched background from *Stealin' Ain't Nice* (Fleischer Studios).

Popeye Meets Rip Van Winkle (1941), directed by Myron Waldman is another missed opportunity for a great adventure cartoon. Popeye taking the displaced Van Winkle home resulted in a cartoon that was more uncomfortable than funny.

FILM DAILY, May 5, 1941

"Popeye Meets Rip Van Winkle"
Paramount 7 mins.
Just Fair

Popeye meets up with Rip Van Winkle just as the old gent is being dispossessed for 20 years non-payment of rent in this fair cartoon. He takes Rip home to finish the famous nap but, after a round of wild adventures with a gang of dwarfs, the old man accuses the sailor of robbery and blazes away with his musket.

The original Washington Irving story offered greater opportunities. The logical choice would be casting Poopdeck Pappy in the role of Rip Van Winkle, and Popeye as his son. The original story has Van Winkle walking out on his nagging wife, headed for the woods when a thunderstorm starts. He then comes across a group of gnomes engaged in a game of nine pins bowling, which is the source of the thunder. The gnomes offer him some of their "homemade brew," which causes him to sleep for 20 years. During Van Winkle's sleep, the American Revolution has occurred. When he wakes up, he is unaware of the passage of time, although his beard has grown. Van Winkle returns to the village and doesn't know anyone. The villagers become concerned about this stranger and alert the authorities after Van Winkle innocently declares his allegiance to King George. He is then arrested for treason and insanity. His son, Rip Van Winkle II is returning home from the Revolution to his wife and son played by Olive and Swee' Pea. Van Winkle II hears of the eccentric old man and realizes he is his father who disappeared 20 years before. This gives Popeye a big heroic rescue sequence leading to the resolution of the confused issues.

While this plot is similar to the original comic strip adventure, *The Quest for Poopdeck Pappy*, and condensed in the classic short, *Goonland,* it offered far better situations. Instead, a routine and passable vehicle was produced that is not as remembered as the earlier adventure-themed cartoons. Regardless of the economic issue, another Technicolor *Popeye* special of *Rip Van Winkle* would have been a superior choice to the two-reel Technicolor production, *The Raven,* which was allocated $54,000.

While the reputation of *The Raven* lent itself to interesting possibilities, the actual production bore no resemblance to the gothic Edgar Allan Poe work, resulting in a total waste of time, effort, and money. *The Raven* was a confused travesty about a crooked wolf plotting to "clean out" the castle of a Scottish Terrier. To carry this out, he engages the assistance of the Raven, who poses as a vacuum cleaner salesman. This was a lost opportunity to produce an eerie, surrealistic cartoon that would have put Fleischer Studios back in familiar territory. It is conceivable that Max realized the obvious advantages in both a Popeye epic or a faithful adaptation of the Poe classic only to have it vetoed by Dave who stubbornly held to his position as head of production and his continued rejection of Max's input.

FILM DAILY, August 1, 1941

"Pest Pilot"
Paramount 7 mins.
Only Fair

A Popeye cartoon that dives as far as the laughs are concerned. In this, Popeye's seagoing father is anxious to fly a plane. After being turned down by Popeye, he hops into a plane and goes on a wild flight. He cracks up and that is about all. It is mostly for the kids.

Further reviews of the Popeye cartoons indicate a slipping of content.

FILM DAILY, November 28, 1941

"The Mighty Navy"
Paramount 7 mins.
Average Cartoon

Popeye joins the Navy and accomplishes a number of unusual feats. He shows his officer what an old time gob can do. Ideas just leap harum-scarum in the realm of implausibility. A certain amount of inventiveness is always necessary in cartoon subjects but the type of situations developed for Popeye do not fall in this class. The climax, which has Popeye ramming into a battleship as a human torpedo, is a good example of stretching a point.

The Mighty Navy was the beginning of placing Popeye in the World War II Navy. While the actual declaration was a week away, it had been anticipated. By the time this cartoon was in general distribution, the United States was fully committed. This attempt to modernize Popeye made use of the contrast and irony of the old salt and modern sophisticated methods. This was the start of Popeye's white uniform, which he continued to retain throughout the remainder of the series, with occasional attempts at showing him in "dressed-down" blues. In these wartime cartoons he was a "fish out of water" in the modern Navy, resorting to his talents for physical resolutions for the strong "finitch."

Seeing Popeye out of his element was jarring with this sudden change in formula. But it was a reflection of the change in people's daily routines brought by the war. Interestingly, the last of the *Popeye* cartoons featuring his traditional black shirt and captain's cap was released next, *Nix on Hypnotricks*, revisiting the premise of *A Dream Walking* with Olive Oyl walking a hazardous path while in a trance. Although paling in comparison to the original, it was better received than *The Mighty Navy*.

FILM DAILY, December 24, 1941

"Nix on Hypnotricks" (Popeye)
Paramount 7 mins.
Unusually Funny

Short but sweet from the standpoint of laughs, this newest adventure of the spinach-guzzling Popeye ranks among the best of the Fleischer series. The sentimental sailor is reading Romeo and Juliet to the waiting-to-be-petted Olive Oyl. She answers the ringing telephone, the call coming from an East Indian hypnotist who, seeking a human subject on whom to practice his scientific stuff, has picked her name at random from the phone book. His Svengali "passes" are even effective over the wire, and she heads at once for the mystic's apartment. In her trance, she has hair-raising escapes from death, as does the frantically following Popeye. Latter at length, after swallowing a goodly swatch of spinach, mops up the mystic, and is in turn mopped up by the indignant Olive whom he has handled roughly to end her trance.

It is difficult to determine whether the presence of Seymour Kneitel would have made a difference since the team of story men and animators were already veterans with the series and surely knew the material. But in an effort to take the series in new directions, they seemed to lose their way. These were two such examples. To be fair, the realities of fulfilling contractual obligations and keeping an important product fresh can overwhelm one's thinking when deadlines have to be met. So finding new situations for Popeye was a constant challenge.

In spite of the friction between Max and Dave Fleischer, production had to continue focused on a new feature. While the studio still had story material, a Greek mythology theme was discussed. Then Maurice Maeterlinck's *The Life of the Bee* was considered. The title and subject matter seems to suggest that it originated from Max. Maeterlinck had written screen treatments for a number of his books, *The Blue Bird* and *The Life of the Bee* among them. But according to Dave, the rights could not be attained, or more rightly, Paramount was unwilling to purchase them from Samuel Goldwyn. Instead they fashioned a modern story loosely based on the book. Dave Fleischer recalled:

> Maeterlinck's story is a very famous story about bugs. People were called "The Human Ones." And the bugs were having so much trouble existing with The Human Ones who'd step all over their houses. That's the kind of story it was. I like the very end of it, where they had no place to go because The Human Ones were building buildings and destroying all the lots and all their homes and everything, so they finally worked their way to the top of a building in the penthouse, and the little child bug would go to the edge of the building and say, "Look at all those 'Human Ones.' They look just like a lot of little bugs!"[2]

Tremendous artistic growth and refinement is reflected by the concept art for *Mr. Bug*, indicating a maturing of Fleischer Studios as it entered the 1940s. It is similar in concept to *Gulliver's Travels* with its large cast of characters, complicated crowd scenes, and the contrasting scale of tiny characters against the gigantic human world. In *Mr. Bug*, the environment is central to the picture. While the lead characters, Hoppity the grasshopper and Honey Bee, do not lead the story as Disney characters do, it is the situation that propels the plot combined with colorful supporting comical characters. The villain, C. Bagley Beetle, is no real threat, more conniving and vain than truly evil. Perhaps a greater villain concept would have been in a pretentious, flamboyant character named C. Reginald Roach with a Vincent Price type of voice.

The character designs by Graham Place bear a strong resemblance to the lead characters in Disney's *Silly Symphony—Moth and the Flame* (1938). Even the insect fire brigade concept was taken from the Disney short, but with less meaning or invention. Instead it is meaningless action that is neither amusing nor productive as they chop needlessly away at the Honey Shop while the burning cigar is the problem.

The entire premise of the cigar is missed since it presents more of an air pollution threat than one of fire because the Honey Shop does not catch fire. Instead, it is a set up for a cliché, the "blackface powder burn gag," the result of the explosion from the gasoline thrown into the burning end of the cigar. In reality, a thimbleful of gasoline would not trigger such a large explosion, but on an insect level, it is credible. Interestingly, the blackface

Top: **Dramatic low angle views were key to *Mr. Bugs Goes to Town. Bottom:* "She can't hold a candle to a certain honey-bee" (both photographs, Ryan Englade).**

gag appears in only two short scenes when Hoppity is atop the Honey Shop and tumbles off the roof and through the scene. The blackface is then missing in the next scene where Hoppity has landed, legs and arms crossed over. While issues of "political correctness" were not a concern in 1941, these two short scenes could easily be cut without losing logic. Sacrificing this cheap-shot gag would not have hurt the sequence since it is weak comedy even by 1940s standards. There is also a poor logic to the gag.

Hoppity throws the gasoline straight into the burning cigar. The impact of the explosion would have propelled Hoppity out of the scene, screen left. The explosion would have left all of the characters coughing while the smoke dissipates. As they recover, Honey could wonder what happened to Hoppity and go looking for him, lead in his direction by his eccentric belch-like cough. She could then discover him in the weeds upside down, arms and legs interlocked. The original lines would still work with Honey saying, "Oh, Hoppity, you make everything so complicated." Then Mr. Bumble could enter, the two of them untangling Hoppity, with Mr. Bumble saying "Same old Hoppity!" One can only wonder if this might have been one of Max's suggestions ignored by Dave. On October 8, 1940, Max offered an extensive and detailed analysis of the screenplay for *Mr. Bug Goes to Town* in a most professional tone. Dave replied dismissively on October 16:

> "Max: I received your communication of October 8th, and wish to advise you that I have read its contents very carefully. Since the story is now quite complete and ready for animation, it is quite late for any real changes. However, I will consider your suggestions carefully as I again go through the story. Dave"[3]

It is apparent that Dave's response coming a week later was a deliberate stall to justify his rejection of Max's suggestions. Dave boasted of developing a "story chart" to guarantee a successful cartoon. But based on the results of the 1940 shorts, it did not seem to work.

Much was learned in terms of production planning and layout since *Gulliver* because the story sketches demonstrate greater skill and care, many done in charcoal. Backgrounds were better planned as well, with thumbnails done prior to finals. The use of color and special effects is superior, the highlight being Hoppity's neon Jitterbug exhibition accomplished through Bottom Lit photography. Most of all the opening title sequence is breathtaking with its use of a New York skyline miniature, designed by Background Artist Robert Little, whose architectural background was put to great use. This was one to two places where Max Fleischer's Stereoptical Process was put to use in the film. The second was for the water can interior where Hoppity and Mr. Bumble rock forward and back as Mary picks it up in the garden. This was the last use of the Stereoptical Process, and the only time it was applied to a feature film.

Mr. Bug Goes to Town was the first animated feature to display screen credits for the voice actors and shows an interesting mixture of professional and amateur performers. For some unexplained reason, the lead characters of Hoppity and Honey are not given top billing.

Dick Dickens	Kenny Gardner
Mary	Gwen Williams

Dave Fleischer posing at the Stereoptical model of New York City for the opening titles for *Mr. Bug Goes to Town* (author's collection).

Mr. Bumble	Jack Mercer
C. Bagley Beetle	Ted Pierce
Swat the Fly	Jack Mercer
Smack the Mosquito	Carl Meyer
Hoppity	Stan Freed
Honey	Pauline Loth
Buzz the Bee	Mae Questel (uncredited)
Mrs. Lady Bug	Jean Rhys (uncredited)
Mr. Creeper	Pinto Colvig (uncredited)

Kenny Gardner (1913–2002) received top billing even though his character is incidental. Gardner was a vocalist with the Guy Lombardo Orchestra and sings the film's key song, *We're the Couple in the Castle*. Kenny Gardner sounded like Bing Crosby, who may have been considered due to his name value, but unavailable since the part was not large enough and his services too expensive. Because these were the only "professional performers" engaged, they garnered top billing, even though their parts, central to the story, were relatively small.

Gwen Williams (1888–1962) was a stage actress who appeared in films between 1918 and 1921, including *Lead Kindly Light* (1918), *The Breed of the Treshams* (1920), and *The Wonder Year* (1921).

Little can be found about the voice actors for the lead characters.

Stan Freed (Hoppity) had only one other film credit, an independent crime drama, *The Devil's Sheep* (1949).

Pauline Loth (Honey) may have been employed in the Inking and Opaquing Department and thought to have a pleasant voice for the role, which did not require a great deal of acting ability.

As in the production of *Gulliver's Travels*, the animation staff provided the more interesting character voices. Ted Pierce returned to the microphone to portray the sinister C. Bagley Beetle. Pierce was a story man from Leon Schlesinger's "Termite Terrace" group and lent his talents as the evil sorcerer in *Popeye Meets Aladdin's Wonderful Lamp* (1939), and King Bombo in *Gulliver*. Fellow Storyman Carl Meyer was the voice for Smack the Mosquito with a slight hint of Jimmy Durante. He remained with Famous Studios and was the voice of the Superman imposter in *Showdown* (1942) using a version of this same voice.

Paramount had built up a big campaign for *Mr. Bug Goes to Town* as their Christmas release for that year. On May 19, 1941, Fleischer Studios renewed its contract with Paramount—just five months away from recording the post-production score. The contract issued by Austin Keough, Vice President of Paramount included funds of $600,000 carried over from 1940 for completing *Mr. Bug*, *The Raven* at $54,000, the first *Superman* cartoon at $50,000, with an additional eleven at $30,000, and 12 *Popeye* cartoons in black and white at $16,500 each. This brought all production advances for the 1941–1942 season to a total of $852,000. Five days later, on May 24, Dick Murray, Paramount Short Subject representative presented Max with a complicated, confusing, and contradictory amended contract referencing transfer of ownership of Fleischer Studios.

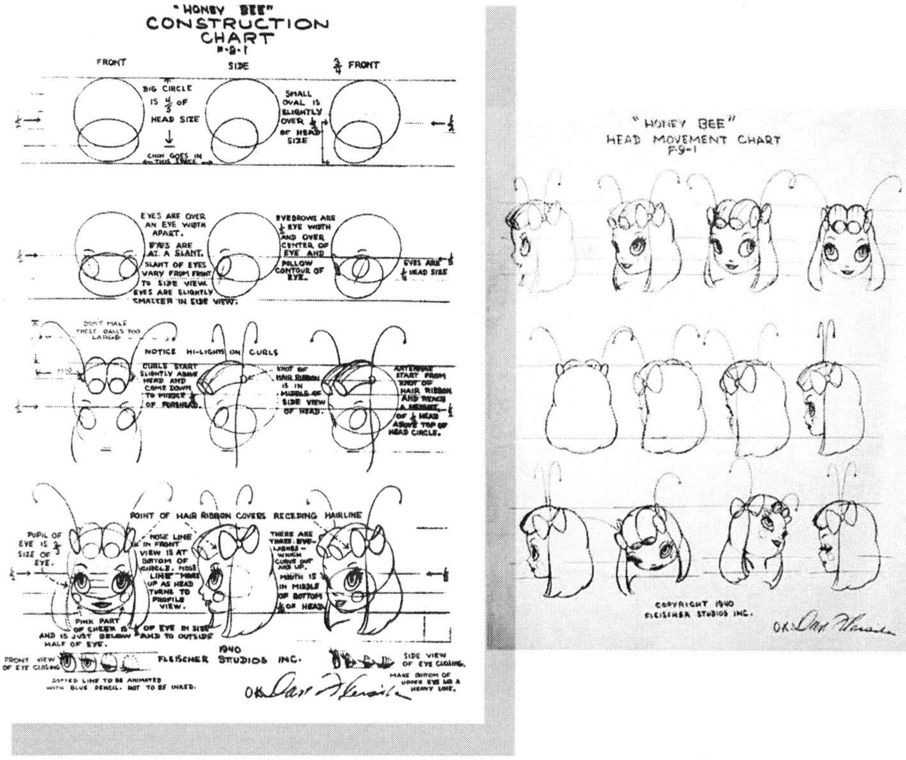

***Above:* Honey Head model sheets (author's collection). *Below:* Swat and Smack watch Hoppity and Honey enter the Night Club (Ryan Englade).**

Top: **Swat misses Hoppity.** ***Second row, left:*** **"Well, the boss said to follow 'em."** ***Second row, right:*** **C. Bagley Beetle's Fountain "Castle."** ***Third row, left:*** **C. Bagle Beetle's Bedroom.** ***Third row, right:*** **Smack "knocks" on Swat's head after entering Beetle's bedroom (all photographs, Ryan Englade).**

Fleischer Studios was most vulnerable in the way that Paramount allocated the finances, issuing them weekly. With the losses of 1940, they were not receiving their royalties and were dependent upon the continuation of these "allowances" to remain in business. With this amended contract, Murray threatened to withhold finances until Max and Dave signed it, canceling all previous agreements.

Above, left: **"What did they do?"** ***Above, right:*** **"Ya mean, what didn't day do-Woo-Woo!"** ***Right:*** **Animation key by Nick Tafuri (all photographs, Ryan Englade).**

> FIRST: All understandings and agreements of whatsoever nature between Paramount (or any one or more of its predecessors in interest) and the Producer (or any one or more of its predecessors in interest), and all options exercised or exercisable thereunder (including but not limited to the option exercised by Paramount dated May 19, 1941), shall be and hereby are terminated and cancelled as of May 24, 1941, and Paramount shall have no further obligation after said date to make payments whatsoever including but not limited to the payment of any amounts accrued but unpaid as of May 24, 1941, under any of said understandings, agreements or options, to the Producer or any others by way of advance payments, down payments or percentage or share of receipts, or otherwise; provided, however, that the obligation of the Producer to repay to Paramount all amounts owing by the Producer to Paramount as of May 24, 1941, shall survive.

Max was clearly shocked in reading the first paragraph because all of this came without warning. The dialogue between Max and Murray went as follows:

MAX: What does this mean?
MURRAY: All I know is that you are to read it and sign.
MAX: The first paragraph is shocking. Who wrote this?
MURRAY: I don't know.
MAX: Have you read this contract?
MURRAY: No. I didn't read it.
MAX: Did Lou Phillips (Paramount Attorney) hand it to you for delivery?
MURRAY: Lou is out of town, and I'm not authorized to say who handed the contract to me. Why don't you read it through?

MAX: You surprise me, Dick. The whole story is in the first paragraph. Didn't you even read that?
MURRAY: All I can say is, they want me to bring the contract back signed ... this week, or else.
MAX: Or else, do they mean bankruptcy?
MURRAY: You can take it that way, but you better get it signed; otherwise the next payroll won't come through.
MAX: Do you mean to tell me that Paramount won't even give me enough time to secure another distributor?
MURRAY: Definitely not.[4]

The wording demanded immediate payment of monies owed Paramount coming after the signed contract already in place. On the one hand, Max was in a position of power and succumbing to his own philosophy, but he failed to use it. Here he was the producer and license holder to Paramount's most valuable short subject commodity, *Popeye the Sailor*, and he failed to use that power. Murray's threat in effect would have been a breach of the standing contract signed on the 19th by stopping the payroll and interrupting production. Max could have called Murray's bluff since he had a legitimate signed contract specifying funds for the fiscal year. Any interruption of funds would be a breach of exponential proportion.

Since Fleischer Studios had individual contracts with its animators, they would be in the position to sue Fleischer Studios for breach if they were not paid, and Fleischer Studios and the animators could in turn join in on a class action lawsuit against Paramount. This, of course would have resulted in an interruption of production, placing Fleischer in breach, negating the original agreement, giving power to the amended contract.

Murray admitted that Paramount was losing money, and so was Fleischer Studios. Max recalled the quarterly royalty checks personally delivered by Murray or Lou Diamond averaged $14,000, or nearly $60,000 annually. Then the royalty fell to $9,000 per quarter, then stopped. So if Popeye was so lucrative, why was Fleischer Studios in debt to Paramount? What did Fleischer Studios owe Paramount, and why did Paramount continue doing business with Fleischer?

For decades, it has been thought that an immediate demand of $483,922.83 was called for. But the contract does not make reference to this amount. What it does refer to is Paramount's payment to the "Producer" the amount of $151,212.57, the result of the "Net Consideration" deducted from the studio's assets, which was to be applied to the assumed "debt," but does not reference any outstanding debt than the mortgage with Delaware Housing Association. As part of the contract, Paramount was assuming the mortgage on the building, which had a ten-year term with a balance of $149,066.23. If this were the case, that would have left Fleischer Studios with $2,146.34. All of this does not explain the figure of $483,922.83.

SECOND: (a) The Producer shall and hereby does sell, transfer, assign and convey to Paramount, its successors and assigns, absolutely and forever, all of its real and personal property of whatsoever kind, nature, and character and wheresoever situate (such of said property situated in Miami, Florida, being sold, transferred, assigned and conveyed subject to a Mortgage Deed dated January 6, 1939, as supplemented and amended, executed and delivered by the Producer as Mortgagor, to Delaware Housing Association, Incorporated,

> as Mortgagee but without any assumption by Paramount of any liability or obligations thereunder whatsoever), free and clear of all liens, encumbrances, pledges, hypothecations, claims and demands whatsoever except for said Mortgage Deed dated January 6, 1939...

The most important issue of the second clause is the transfer of ownership. But the contract implies an assumed large debt accumulated over the past two years. So how did a debt exceeding $400,000 happen? One explanation may be connected to the $300,000 penalty for going over budget on *Gulliver's Travels* combined with the poorly performing cartoons of 1940.

While the shorts lost money the previous year, it was recoupable through the *Popeye* cartoons and other forms of cross collateralization such as block booking, which was supposed to be illegal due to the Consent Decree of 1938, yet still practiced. So it would appear that Paramount grouped these figures together.

The studio's assets were only in excess of $300,000 as reported in 1938. According to Paramount, *Gulliver's Travels* continued to show a loss 18 months after release and they were holding Fleischer Studios accountable. With a commitment to a Christmas 1939 release, Paramount continued advancing the funds. Although the final cost was three times its original estimate, Paramount was banking on its foreign releases to recover the cost overruns, with England being its biggest market.

It has been thought for decades that the outbreak of World War II cut off Paramount's foreign releases of *Gulliver's Travels.* But it has been discovered that *Gulliver* was released in Brazil on January 22, 1940, in Sweden on April 26, 1940, Denmark on May 17, 1940, the Netherlands on July 19, 1940, Finland on September 1, 1940, then in Portugal on February 7, 1941, and Hungary on April 8, 1941. This proves that *Gulliver's Travels* continued earning profits through these foreign releases and continued doing so a month before the renewal of the Fleischer contract.

While Paramount made a domestic profit of $1,000,000, it is not clear as to how much of the total cost was dedicated to publicity and merchandising. But most of all, it is unclear as to what percentage of the profits were due Fleischer Studios. If it had been 50 percent, then the penalty for going over budget would have been absorbed by Fleischer's cut, leaving them nearly $16,000. But with the foreign release of *Gulliver's Travels*, Paramount was continuing to make money for nearly two years. So the sudden demand for the penalty payment even with accumulated interest was certainly unexpected and puzzling.

Paramount took advantage of a detail in the Fleischer contract that excluded them from participating in foreign box office earnings. Under these circumstances, Paramount was not obligated to report these figures and continued to hold Fleischer Studios responsible for going over budget even though they had for all practical purposes balanced the books. While Max was in the position to call for an audit, he refused, continuing to have faith in his history and position with Paramount. Had he done it, the fiscal health of his studio would have been protected. But this was not the case. Max was a team player, and his greatest fear was in "offending Paramount," or more specifically, Chairman of the Board Adolph Zukor.

In essence, *Gulliver's Travels* was Paramount's movie and Fleischer Studios was the hired contractor. An option that Max failed to consider in financing his features was to set them up as Chattel Mortgages separate from the short subject production contract in order to protect ownership. By that plan, all profits and losses on the features would have been attributed to their own accounts. The features would have been collateral with Paramount assuming ownership until the advances were paid back. This would have protected Fleischer Studios from the over budget penalty especially since it was Paramount, or specifically Barney Balaban who ordered *Gulliver's Travels* and approved the continued advances for its completion. But the established arrangement of financing and distribution gave ownership of all of the cartoons produced by Fleischer to Paramount. So the issue of the mounting debt and the sudden action taken by Paramount does not seem entirely logical. However, it was clear to Paramount that things were suddenly out of control with the apparent slipping of quality coming from Fleischer Studios that resulted in their first major loss in 1940.

> When Max made inquiries into what was happening, he was told that the cartoons were getting harder and harder to sell, that, in fact, Paramount was in the red as far as the cartoons were concerned. But still they kept releasing them. Max asked if Paramount had any idea of discontinuing the cartoons. The answer he got was, "No, the exhibitors want them, but they don't pay much for them…." One of the broadest suggestions that something was amiss came from William Brandt, a good friend of Max's. Brandt owned and ran a chain of fifty theaters, loved the Fleischer cartoons, and wanted them for his theaters but couldn't get them. One day he phoned Max complaining about this situation. Brandt told him that even after he offered Paramount more than the other chains paid, he was still turned down. Max asked his Paramount contact, Lou Diamond to investigate. According to Max, Diamond came up with this: "You better keep your nose out of distribution and tend to your productions if you don't want a bellyful of trouble." If anything ever screamed out for an audit, this was it.[5]

Emanuel Cohen's predictions were coming true. Max was facing the prospect of another bankruptcy. He called his attorney, who surprisingly seemed to have full knowledge of Paramount's crudely amended contract, and advised Max to sign to avoid the embarrassment of missing payroll. The other detail of concern was the surrender of ownership for six months while the deficit was settled. Attorney Welling assured Max, "We can take care of that matter later on and have the ownership returned to you." This advice raises questions that are crucial to understand how the studio was lost and becomes more confusing from here on.

One source states that the amended contract was not signed until July. This belies the sense of urgency implied in Murray's visit, and is impossible to determine for two reasons. The copy of the contract made available to the author is missing two key elements: a signature page referencing the 26 week term and signature date. The only signature page is at the end of the original contract and it does not have a date of signature either. In spite of it all, there was no interruption of funds as Murray threatened, and the staff was unaware of what was happening.

Regardless of when it happened, Max signed the 31-page document, and upon sending it to Dave for signature, it was returned in less than 20 minutes. Dave obviously signed without reading it. Max and Dave had surrendered their stock and became employees of Fleischer Studios under the management of Paramount for a period of 26 weeks, with weekly salaries of $750.00 each. Paramount owned the name to Fleischer Studios as well as the names of Max and Dave Fleischer, which meant that they did not have the right to use their own names in the formation of a new studio. There could be no "Max Fleischer Studio," or "Dave Fleischer Studio" during the term of this contract, which in essence was a subcontract obligating both Max and Dave to remain for the completion of *Mr. Bug*. From that point, Paramount allowed for either brother to submit his resignation 30 days prior to the expiration of the six-month term. At the same time, Paramount was in the position to terminate either of them within the term of the main contract, which extended to May 1942. But the main point of order was to complete *Mr. Bug*.

The six-month period should have expired on November 24, 1941, but the amendment did not indicate this. The only expiration date was May 24, 1942, indicated on the last page of the original contract. Between October and early November, Dave was at Paramount in Hollywood supervising the post-production recording for the *Mr. Bug* score. Once the recording was completed, Dave resigned on November 22. The question is what motivated his resignation in light of the positive responses reflected in his letter to Seymour Kneitel dated October 14?

> "I think we have got a real good feature on our hands, Seymour, because when I ran it for the publicity group they liked it very much, and if anyone could like it in the shape it was in then I know that when it is seen in completed form that it will be a hit. So now the only thing I am worried about is what shall we make for the next one?"

The prospect of Dave's termination did not seem likely since he had survived the six months without being fired. Max wanted to see Paramount handle Dave's dismissal. Lou Fleischer was present during the month-long scoring in Hollywood, which wrapped on Tuesday, November 3. Following the three-day train trip, Lou reported to Max the next morning, Friday, November 7, to learn that Max had sent a telegram to Paramount stating "I can no longer work with Dave Fleischer." Max had been waiting patiently for the completion of *Mr. Bug* to have Paramount terminate Dave now that the recording of the score was completed and the terms of the 26-week agreement were nearing an end. In this, he was premature since Dave had another two weeks to see *Mr. Bug* through to the answer print. So the picture was not considered "wrapped" until November 21. Lou and Joe tried to reason with Max on this point and when he came to realize his error it was too late. The telegram had already gone out. In fairness to Max, he may have been acting on the implication of the agreement which gave both parties the right to resign "within" 30 days of the expiration date. While it is unknown as to whether Max followed legal advice or his understanding of the contract, he was looking forward to being through with Dave. But he may not have considered the underlying trap.

In the eyes of Paramount, Max was giving up. A more direct wording in his telegram would have been, "In accordance with our 26-week agreement, we have fulfilled our obligations, and it is realized that the services of Dave Fleischer will no longer be needed." Had this message been sent to Paramount, Paramount in turn would have notified Dave prompting his resignation. It is reasonable to believe that Max's telegram signaled a termination of the joint agreement between the brothers, which resulted in Paramount's request of Dave's resignation.

As a result, Dave Fleischer resigned on Saturday, November 22, 1941, two days before the expiration date of the 26-week agreement.

Aside from the stigma of termination, Dave did not return to Miami because authorities were waiting for him regarding his pending divorce, which was finalized in 1944. According to Dave's account, while on his way to California for the recording of *Mr. Bug*, he was stopped at the airport and served with a subpoena. Appearing before the judge, he was questioned about his leaving Miami, which he explained was business-related. When asked about how much money he had, he answered, "Just what's on me." The judge accepted this generalized answer, not suspecting that Dave may have intended to leave town permanently, having emptied his bank account. Regardless of the resignation, it seems that Dave had no intentions of returning to Fleischer Studios. After the wrap of *Mr. Bug*, he rented a car for a cross-country sight-seeing tour prior to Thanksgiving. The trip was interrupted in New Mexico.

FILM DAILY, November 25, 1941

Fleischer and Secretary Hurt in Triple Crash

Lordsburg, N. M.—Injured in a three-car auto crash here, Dave Fleischer, cartoon director, and three others, including his secretary, Mae Schwartz, are under medical treatment. Fleischer, who suffered two fractured ribs, will fly east when his hurts permit.

Mr. Bug Goes to Town was completed on schedule and went into prints for delivery within 30 days for a Christmas release. In spite of its potential for success, its optimism offered no protection against a greater threat that surfaced. The release was interrupted by two events. The first was the enforcement of the Consent Decree, which required previews to theater operators in advance of release dates. There were 16 films waiting for prerelease previews, and *Mr. Bug* was one of them. Surprisingly, theater exhibitors rejected it, firmly convinced that it would not do business. The New York opening on Friday, December 5 was ruined further by Japan's attack in the Pacific two days later. A disturbed and frightened public stayed home, attached to their radios as all attention shifted to the war. The timing of the opening was devastating in spite of positive reviews.

FILM DAILY December 5, 1941

"Mr. Bug Goes to Town"
Paramount 78 Mins.

FEATURE CARTOON IN TECHNICOLOR
RATES AS DELIGHTFUL HOLIDAY PACKAGE

Max Fleischer's studio has created a delightful fable about the struggle of a little community of insects. Skilled animation and a fine musical score tend to make this Technicolor cartoon feature a sock favorite for the juvenile trade and a delightful novelty for adults. Hero of the comic fantasy is a pleasant little fellow known as Hoppity. He is a good-natured chap and like his name, Hoppity is concerned about the welfare of his neighbors and although his attempts for their welfare go awry, Hoppity succeeds in the end. C. Bagley Beetle is the scoundrel, and his character is a clever bit of make-believe. Like all scoundrels, Beetle has designs on Honey, Hoppity's sweetheart, who refuses to marry him. Beetle's henchmen, Swat and Smack, are liable to be the most popular Fleischer creations. They are a comic pair. Swat and Smack have no scruples and are always at Beetle's beck and call.

An adjacent garden appears to be the only safe spot for the community because the humans are always intruding. The couple living there is waiting for a check from a music firm so they can repair the garden. Beetle and his aides steal the check. The house is foreclosed and a skyscraper is erected in its place. Hoppity discovers Beetle's secret and helps the couple get the check. Hoppity then leads his friends to the penthouse garden of the young couple for a happy finish. Cartoon highlights are the trek of Hoppity and his friends to the top of the building, the tidal wave caused by the sprinkler system, Hoppity and Bumble's experiences during their visit to the garden, the preparations for Honey's wedding to Beetle which is broken off in time and the scene where Hoppity catches hold of a live wire. There are four songs worthy of note. Easily outstanding is "We're the Couple in the Castle" by Hoagy Carmichael and Frank Loesser. "Katy Did, Katy Didn't" and "I'll Dance at Your Wedding" are two other tuneful compositions by the composers. "Boy Oh Boy" is another good number by [*sic*] Herman Timberg and Frank Loesser.

CREDITS: Producer, Max Fleischer, Director, David Fleischer
CAMERAMAN, [*sic*] George Schettler
SOUND EFFECTS, Maurice Manne
MUSICAL DIRECTOR, Leigh Harline.
DIRECTION, Grade A.
PHOTOGRAPHY, Excellent.

Back in Miami, everyone was celebrating the successful completion of Fleischer Studio's second feature. Max's spirits were high at the annual Christmas party because the film was finished. But most of all he was relieved being finished with Dave, who was conspicuously absent. Everyone assumed that the picture was doing well, but this was not the case. Because of the bad New York opening, Paramount canceled their 1941 Christmas release following the huge yearlong campaign. Considering that the holiday season was three weeks away, one can only wonder why a greater effort was not made to go forward with a release since the theme of *Mr. Bug* with the invasion of humans and the threat to the lives of the insect community bore an interesting parallel to current events. Hoppity's plea to "stick together" for survival could have been a marketing device and the kind of optimistic motivation needed at this time. But Paramount did not see this, and lacked the imagination to market the film effectively in the light of the situation.

While the 26-week term was over, Paramount still controlled the studio and the name

Fleischer Studios until May 24, 1942, the expiration of the 1941 contract. Accordingly, Paramount's actions in canceling *Mr. B*ug made them responsible for the losses, not Fleischer Studios. Fleischer had fulfilled its obligations to Paramount by delivering *Mr. Bug* on time and at cost. Barney Balaban was concerned that the canceled release of *Mr. Bug* in turn canceled any prospects of cross-collateralization to recover the remaining Fleischer debt. Looking to the immediate future, the Florida venture would no longer be affordable. The cancellation of *Mr. B*ug and the accumulated debt affected Balaban directly since he ordered the features and supported the Miami experiment. As a result, he was responsible to Paramount for these expenses mainly for wanting to duplicate Disney's successes without totally understanding them and their financial structure.

Balaban and Paramount were acutely aware that they were already in second place to Disney and carefully planned the Fleischer feature releases when they would not be in competition with Disney. This again motivated their release of *Gulliver* for Christmas, 1939, knowing that Disney was going to release *Pinocchio* in February 1940. But *Pinocchio* performed poorly, failing to earn its $2.6 million cost in its initial release. Then in November, Disney released the groundbreaking *Fantasia*, costing $2.28 million, which also failed. But Disney was financed through a line of credit with the Bank of America and not his distributor, RKO.

Seeing that Disney's returns were not successful in 1940, Balaban had a chance to cancel *Mr. Bug* before a full commitment was engaged since it did not start production until late October. He failed to cancel, and Fleischer Studios continued in good faith. Even as late as the final contract of May 1941, the feature could have been canceled before any more funds were committed to its completion. In spite of the economic warning signs, the commitment to *Mr. Bug* continued in full earnest, and Fleischer Studios lived up to its contractual obligation only to be victimized by Balaban's focus on the anticipated business of the 1941 Christmas season. From this point on, the order of events becomes confused.

According to Richard Fleischer, Balaban called Max to the boardroom of Paramount in New York on December 28. But internal communications indicate this event occurred five days earlier, on December 23. Max arrived with his secretary, Vera Coleman, on time after the overnight trip from Miami. The discussion went as follows:

> BALABAN: Max, we have decided to accept your resignation.
> MAX: (dumbfounded) This is all very puzzling. What is the purpose of all this?
> BALABAN: That's our decision.[6]

Balaban's opening remark implies references to the telegram Max sent six weeks before. So this raises questions about Max's response in not understanding. Regardless, the issue was that after a solid 14-year relationship with Paramount, Max deserved the courtesy of a detailed explanation. The dialogue in this meeting seems unusually cold and incomplete since there is no reference to the cancelation of the release of *Mr. Bug Goes to Town* or the associated losses accumulated over the previous two years affecting Paramount's interest in continuing to do business with Fleischer Studios in spite of the success of the *Superman* series. At the same time, there is no mention of previous concerns, discussions, or warnings about these problems, which should have been addressed when they were beginning.

On one level, the accepting of Max's resignation was a means for Balaban to save face with Chairman of the Board, Adolph Zukor. Corporately, Paramount had lost confidence in Fleischer Studios based on the accumulated debts, which were largely Babalan's responsibility. So the appearance and purpose for this meeting would seem to make Max the "fall guy" for Balaban's mistakes. Richard Fleischer suggests that Max scheduled a return visit with Paramount's Legal Department following this meeting. But the events at this point also become confused and contradictory.

During the trip from Miami to New York and back, temporary porters supposedly came in and purged the files of Fleischer Studios. The timing of this was ideal since the studio was shut down for Christmas with no one in the building—so they thought. Charlie Fleischer's son, Ozzie, was a maintenance worker at the studio and saw Dick Murray, the same man who delivered the fatal contract directing the temporary workers to dump large piles of papers into the incinerator. For two days all corporate records, including bank statements, tax filings, production and film delivery records, laboratory invoices, payroll, and social security records of some 700 employees, as well as all other corporate history of Fleischer Studios, went up in smoke. This event was later denied by Murray. Moreover, the date of December 28 figures in being 30 days prior to the anticipated Fleischer Studios stockholders' meeting, when Max's reinstatement was to be considered.

With Dave out of the picture, Paramount managers then approached Seymour Kneitel about assuming the position of production supervisor, and he assured them that production would continue without interruption. Further discussions were taking place about the final state of Fleischer Studios as revealed in a letter to Max's attorney, N. William Welling, from Bernard Goodwin dated December 23, 1941:

> As you know, the annual meeting of the stockholders of Fleischer Studios, Incorporated is set for January 28, 1942. Hence Dick (Murray) would like to postpone the election of the new board of Fleischer Studios, Incorporated until the annual meeting, at which time the new board can authorize the execution of an amending letter agreement to the employment agreement between Max Fleischer to use his name in the manner set forth in the proposed agreement between Max Fleischer and Paramount Pictures, Inc. dated December 23, 1941. <end extract>

The reference to the "proposed agreement" of December 23 seems to indicate a return to the previous conditions, terminating Max's status as an "employee," and returning his ownership of the studio with his services to be determined in the upcoming stockholders' meeting. But this understanding seems contrary as implied in the letter, which makes reference to "assignment" documents dated this same day indicating a transfer of ownership from Max Fleischer to Paramount. The following paragraph sums it up.

> At the time you return the above documents to me, I understand that you will also deliver to me the resignation signed by Max Fleischer under his employment agreement with Fleischer Studios, Incorporated dated May 24, 1941, addressed to both Paramount Pictures, Inc. and Fleischer Studios, Incorporated, such resignation to be effective immediately as of the date of the signing of the same, waiving the thirty-day clause provided for in said employment agreement and in Article TWENTY-FOUR of the agreement dated May 24, 1941 between Paramount Pictures, Inc. and Fleischer Studios, Incorporated.

While the official resignation came December 23, it should be remembered that the reference to the letter of resignation dated May 24, the date of the 1941 contract, signaled Max's surrender of ownership and acceptance of employment under Paramount management for six months. The Goodwin letter references this, which relieved Max of pending or remaining financial losses during that period. This was of particular importance regarding the unreleased *Mr. Bug Goes to Town.* What is missing is a declaration from Paramount confirming that the 26 week agreement had been met, and all conditions and understandings were to return to the way they were before May 24. This is the source of confusion over Max's resignations under two different agreements—one before May 24 and the other after November 24.

Dave's resignation became official on December 22, 1941, and seems to be the motivation of these actions taken with Max the following day. Dave's resignation was announced in the *Miami Herald* on January 2, 1942.

> **Cartoon Head Quits Studio**
> *Dave Fleischer Resigns as the Director General of Miami Organization.*
> Miami, Fla., Jan. 2—The Fleischer Studios, Inc. announced today the resignation of Dave Fleischer as director general of the organization. He will retain his stock interest in the company. Sam Buckwald, who has been an executive with the Fleischer Studios since its organization, has been appointed executive general manager of the company. The present executive production staff, which is headed by Seymour Neitel [*sic*] and Isador Sparber has been augmented by the addition of Dan Gordon. Other additions are also being made to the present story staff.
> The Fleischer Studios recently completed work on its second Technicolor feature cartoon, "Mr. Bug Goes to Town," which has been highly praised at its advance showings to date and which will be released by Paramount in February. The Fleischer Studio is engaged at present in a heavy production schedule of Superman Technicolor cartoons and Popeye cartoons for the current releasing season. An even more extensive program of cartoons from the Miami plant is planned for the 1942–43 season.

On January 6, 1942, Bernard Goodwin issued a letter to Dick Murray:

> Bill Welling has delivered to me today Max Fleischer's signed resignation, effective December 20, 1941, under his employment agreement of May 24, 1941, with Fleischer Studios Incorporated, addressed to both Fleischer Studios, Incorporated and Paramount Pictures, Inc., and also an assignment from Fleischer Studios, Incorporated to Paramount Pictures, Inc. of rights under the former's agreement with King Features Syndicate, Inc. and Superman, Inc. in respect to the "Popeye" and "Superman" cartoons, respectively, and also the letter agreement between Max Fleischer and Paramount Pictures, Inc. concerning the use of Max Fleischer's name. I will deliver a fully signed copy of the last named letter agreement to Bill Welling for forwarding to Max Fleischer.

It should be noted that the date December 20 may have been a typographical error since all associated correspondence is consistent with the date December 23 as the official resignation of Max Fleischer as an employee of Paramount. This letter confirms that the character license for *Superman* was originally in the name of Fleischer Studios. It also sets to rest rumors that the Fleischer *Popeye* license was "burned" along with the rest of the office records.

With the transfer of ownership combined with the resignation, Max was indeed giving up as Balaban concluded. Upon the return to Miami, Max was preparing to make a case with the Paramount Legal Department only to discover that the company files were indeed emptied. Oddly, the necessary papers for "transfer of ownership" existed, perhaps kept in a safe. Max had no choice but to surrender, thinking not of himself, but of the sake of the others he had brought up in the business. On this same day, January 6, 1942, Max sent the following telegram confirmed in his letter to William Welling:

> PLEASE DELIVER TO PARAMOUNT RESIGNATION AND ASSIGNMENT PAPERS. I CONFIRM THAT THERE IS NO UNDERSTANDING WHATSOEVER RELATIVE MY RETENTION OF PRESIDENCY. "REGARDS."

This statement alone, issued on January 6, confirms Max Fleischer's resignation from Fleischer Studios, Inc. Paramount continued to abide by the conditions of the 1941 contract, keeping the names of Max and Dave Fleischer in the credits over the remaining five months even though they were no longer present. Fleischer Studios continued to operate for five months, finishing the contracted cartoons led primarily by Sam Buchwald. Then on May 21, 1942, Max, Dave, and Welling were given official notification of termination on the letterhead of Fleischer Studios.

> May 21, 1942
>
> Attention: Mr. Max Fleischer, President
>
> Dear Sirs:
>
> I thought I should write to tell you that on my trip to New York this week I was told by Paramount Pictures that they did not intend to exercise their option under their present agreement for another year after May 24, 1942. This means, of course, that Fleischer Studios will stop operating at these Studios after the close of business on Saturday, May 23rd.
>
> Under the circumstances, you can well understand that I was concerned about the future and that that was true of some of the other employees of the Company. Consequently, I and some of the other employees have gotten together to organize a new company which will begin operations on Monday, May 25th, 1942, at these Studios under a new agreement with Paramount, and we will, of course, feel free to hire such employees of Fleischer Studios as we may wish to take on and who may wish to resign prior to that time.
>
> Not knowing your plans, I think it advisable and the other employees with whom I intend to associate think it advisable, that we put a copy of this letter on the bulletin board at the Studios, as well as to circulate a copy of this letter among all of the employees through the various department heads, so that everybody can be fully aware of what is going on and determine their own actions in respect to the future.
>
> Yours sincerely,
> *Sam Buchwald*,
> General Manager
>
> cc: Mr. Dave Fleischer
> Mr. N. William Welling

Max received a letter from Russell Holman of Paramount dated May 21, 1942:

> Dear Max,
>
> I think I should inform you that Paramount does not intend to exercise its option to extend the present agreement with Fleischer Studios beyond May 24th, 1942. Included in our plans for the future will be the completion of pictures now in production. With every good wish for your health and prosperity in the future, I am
>
> Sincerely yours,
> *Russell Holman*

Max responded on May 25, 1942:

> Dear Russ:
>
> You probably realize how deeply I regret Paramount's decision not to renew the agreement with Fleischer Studios. However, I wish to thank you for the good wishes expressed in your letter of May 21st.
>
> Sincerely,
> *Max*

After 22 years of activity, the Fleischer Brothers were finished. Max was officially removed on May 24, 1942. In accordance with the provisions of the 26-week agreement, Max and Dave's Fleischer's stock was returned after its assets were stripped, leaving it valueless.

On the surface, this all might have seemed designed to "steal" Fleischer Studios as fans might wish to believe. But after the "ship wreck" of *Gulliver*, Paramount had to take action to protect the fate of its top ranking sailor, *Popeye.*

While Max's business decisions seemed short-sighted, consideration should be given to the legal advice he was given through his attorney, N. William Welling. The first issue of consideration would be the 1940 agreement arranged by Welling that gave equal partnership to both Max and Dave which started the breakup of the studio. But the most crucial issue being Welling's advice to Max to sign the amended contract that surrendered control. His assurance, "We can take care of that matter later on and have the ownership returned to you" was left open-ended. A specific answer as to exactly *how* ownership would be returned was never explained, nor were details on protecting Max's rights or alternative solutions discussed. While Max should have asked for the details, he placed his trust in his advisors, never suspecting the possibility of collusion.

Having regained the right to use his name commercially, Max planned to start another studio to produce armed forces training films. With the war in Europe already in its second year, it was inevitable that the United States would eventually be engaged, and it was now a reality. Some of the staff were already members of the Miami Army Reserve Unit. Demand for training films was great, and this was a field that Max had pioneered. A new studio devoted to instructional films would have suited Max very well by this time. While animating on *Mr. Bug*, Shamus Culhane approached Max about a subcontract he had acquired to produce *The Strategy and Tactics of the Battle of Chancellorsville* for the U.S. Army.

> Max Fleischer allowed us to use the recording room and cutting equipment. None of us realized what a monumental job this was. Very soon we were working forty hours a week on *Mr. Bug* and more than forty hours on *Chancellorsville.* Many of the inkers and painters gave hours of their time, too. Most of them were paid, but others worked for nothing with the proviso that if we sold the picture they would be paid double wages. Even with this help I had to pay three thousand dollars for materials and services, making a sizable dent in my savings.
>
> *The Battle of Chancellorsville* was finished just before my contract with the Fleischers ran out, which was the main reason we had all put in so many long hours. It was a very dramatic moment when we screened the film and watched units break their geometric shapes and assume new ones as the battle progressed ... nobody had ever made such a teaching film before.[7]

With war priorities, money and resources were scarce. Film was among the necessities that was rationed, and regardless of Max's reputation, he could not find the necessary back-

The Fleischer Studios Army Reserve Unit. *Kneeling:* Charles Fleischer (1), Myron Waldman (2), Ruben Grossman (3), Nick Tafuri (4). *Standing:* Dave Tendlar (5), Tom Johnson (6), Ellsworth Barthen (7), Abner Kneitel (8) (author's collection).

ing. Shortly after his dismissal by Paramount, his friend from the Bray days, Jamison Handy, paid him a visit in Miami. Max confided in Handy about many of the issues resulting in the Paramount takeover. Handy had a large industrial film company in Detroit, the Jam Handy Organization. And because of their ties to the Bray Studios and Max's background in training films, he was invited back into the arena he had pioneered.

With the demise of Fleischer Studios, Max and Dave Fleischer went their separate ways, starting new careers in the 1940s. While the remaining brothers were outside of the problems with Paramount, they were still affected. The role of Lou Fleischer had been a mystery to Paramount executives even though he was largely responsible for the precise synchronization in addition to supervising the musical scores for the shorts. In spite of his contributions, he was terminated as well. Lou suspected that the people at Paramount were eager to learn his secrets and raided the trash bins during the final scoring of *Mr. Bug* to figure out what he did. But Lou's dismissal seems most likely associated with a conflict with Dick Murray.

Murray started making suggestions about the use of certain song material for the scores of the cartoons. His reasons for doing this are not clear unless it was for some personal gain with the main office or Paramount's Famous Music Company. According to Lou, Murray requested the use of a song about John Dillinger. Lou did not think this was a good selection and argued the point. As Murray continued to insist, Lou responded by reminding him that John Dillinger was an arch criminal and that this form of glorification would be in the worst of taste. Murray continued to push the issue and Lou finally said, "I score for Paramount and its audience, not myself!" Those in attendance later remarked to Lou that he should not have said that since this suggested that Murray was receiving a "kickback." The incident may have struck a nerve, and Lou was eventually dismissed through orders from Paramount delivered by Sam Buchwald. While Lou thought it odd that Max did not come to him directly, it should be considered that this came after Max's dismissal. And with Max out of the picture, he was not obligated.

Joe Fleischer was the only brother who remained with the new studio and moved with it back to New York, continuing to work in the machine shop until returning to Florida where he worked as an electrical contractor until his retirement in 1968. Of all of the brothers, Joe was affected largely by disappointment in all of the time and effort put into the building of the studio only to see it deteriorate the way it did. In spite of that, the other brothers seemed to put it all behind them, as did their respective families.

14

The Change of Command

FAMOUS Studios

MIAMI • FLORIDA

On May 27, 1942, the change from Fleischer to Famous Studios was official, although in practice it had been so for a year. Sentiment over the end of the Fleischer era has colored perceptions about the studio changeover. The demise of Fleischer Studios was a combination of events, some avoidable and others not. With the absence of Max and Dave Fleischer, it was business as usual. The core staff remained, including writers Jack Ward, Joe Stults, and Bill Turner, background artists Robert Little, Anton Loeb, Robert Owen, Robert Connavale, and Shane Miller; as well as the key Fleischer animators.

Seymour Kneitel was the Lead Director, having nine years with the *Popeye* series as a head animator/director. Izzy Sparber, who had come up through the ranks from Max Fleischer's personal errand boy to becoming traffic manager of the Camera Department, was now a director, in spite of the fact that he didn't draw. His qualification was as a writer, and he depended largely upon the artists under him. Dan Gordon, who was a major contributor to the Fleischer features and shorts, left after one year due to presumed disagreements with management. He was replaced by Bill Tytla, one of the important animators of the Disney "Golden Age" who was banned from the Disney Studio after the 1941 Strike.

From a business point of view, Paramount needed another cartoon producer when Fleischer was no longer meeting satisfaction. Since there were no other cartoon studios to contract with, they created their own out of what was left from their long time association with Fleischer. And contrary to popular assumption, the quality of the cartoons did not immediately deteriorate with the change to Famous Studios. Except for a change in the

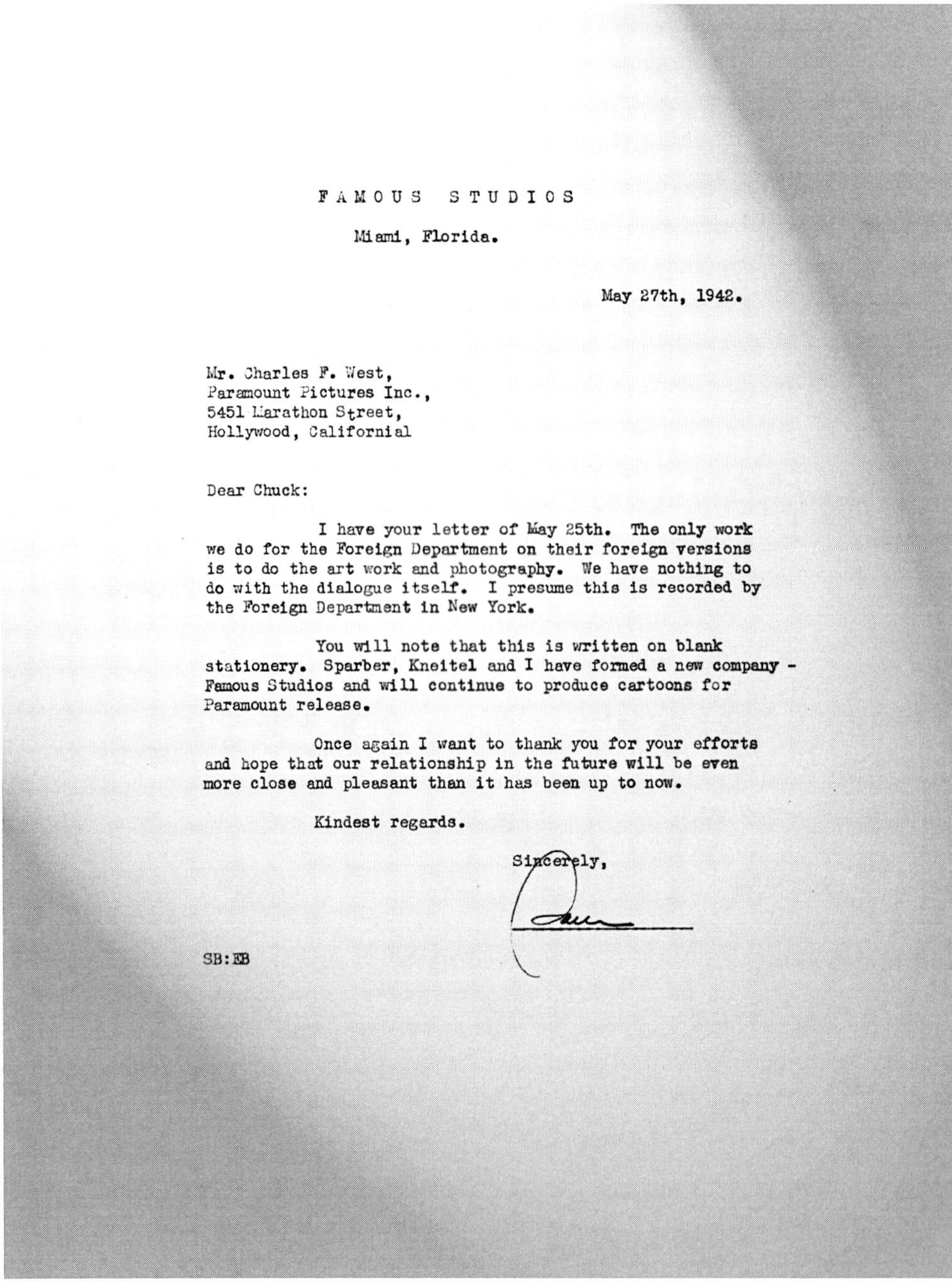

F A M O U S   S T U D I O S

Miami, Florida.

May 27th, 1942.

Mr. Charles F. West,
Paramount Pictures Inc.,
5451 Marathon Street,
Hollywood, California

Dear Chuck:

I have your letter of May 25th. The only work we do for the Foreign Department on their foreign versions is to do the art work and photography. We have nothing to do with the dialogue itself. I presume this is recorded by the Foreign Department in New York.

You will note that this is written on blank stationery. Sparber, Kneitel and I have formed a new company - Famous Studios and will continue to produce cartoons for Paramount release.

Once again I want to thank you for your efforts and hope that our relationship in the future will be even more close and pleasant than it has been up to now.

Kindest regards.

Sincerely,

SB:EB

Letter from Sam Buchwald (author's collection).

screen credits, the transition was seamless, virtually unnoticed by the public. The only noticeable change was "in name only."

Famous Studios did not become public until August 1942 when their cartoons started hitting the screens. The inevitable question is what would Fleischer Studios have gone on to if Max had remained without Dave? For the most part, exactly the way it went during the war, continuing on what had been built upon Fleischer's most important character, Popeye.

A clause in the Popeye licensing agreement stipulated that final ownership of all subsequent films were to become the property of King Features after 10 years—a flaw in the Fleischer relationship with Paramount since all copyrights were registered by Paramount, leaving Fleischer out of the picture regarding future ownership. This was another area where Disney had an advantage since he owned everything he produced from 1928 on. In essence, Fleischer was a service company to Paramount, providing it with it greatest short subject series. And it was in Paramount's interest to protect this important commodity. But a key issue in the Popeye license was the fate of the finished films. A stipulation in the original Fleischer license with King Features was that the negatives to the cartoons be destroyed at the end of the license, which was due to expire in November 1942. The backlog of 109 *Popeye* cartoons produced over the previous nine years was extremely valuable, and Paramount wanted to continue production with an eye on the future—television. Now that Paramount had the license, it was in the position to renegotiate the terms, retaining ownership of the negatives, and save the most successful cartoon series in cinema history.

The new team quickly developed the very thing that was needed—a fresh approach in step with the times. But this did not materialize until the reorganization. So in many ways, the early period of Famous Studios represents the direction Fleischer Studios might have taken in the 1940s under the right circumstances.

> Everyone seemed to care a lot more in the 1940s—theater owners, moviegoers, and the people who made the films. One of Famous' first jobs was to spruce up its image and stimulate new interest in its product. *Popeye* was still the company's major breadwinner, but exhibitors were complaining that the novelty of the *Superman* shorts had worn off. So Paramount announced a major over-haul of the 1943–44-movie season.... Henceforth all Famous Studios cartoons would be made in Technicolor, including *Popeye*.[1]

Paramount valued short subjects as program warm-ups for its feature packages. For this reason, it wanted production to continue with efficiency. Operations in Miami proved to be awkward and costly. As the newly formed Famous Studios entered production for the 1942 season, it initiated its plans to move back to New York by January 1943 to 25 West 45th Street. At the point of the takeover, only two series were being produced, *Popeye* and *Superman*. Famous Studios ceased production on *Superman* in 1943 on two counts. Exhibitors claimed that the novelty was worn out, which is hard to imagine since *Superman* continued as a successful radio drama and was revived as a 13-chapter serial by Columbia Pictures in 1948 and 1950. But the main reason was the complication and cost of production, which made Paramount eager to drop it in favor of simpler characters. As a replacement, Famous licensed *Little Lulu*, the mischievous little girl with the deadpan face created by Marjorie Henderson Buell.

When Carl Anderson's *Henry* moved over to King Features in 1935, the *Saturday Evening Post* picked up *Little Lulu* as a replacement. In the spring of 1943, Dick Murray arranged the licensing for an animated series. The terms of the first contract paid Buell $500 for each cartoon produced with an additional 5 percent of the profits. The *Lulu* series enjoyed a successful four-year run. It was a lucrative arrangement for Buell since she did not contribute artistically. Fortunately, *Little Lulu* was a success and helped launch an enterprise

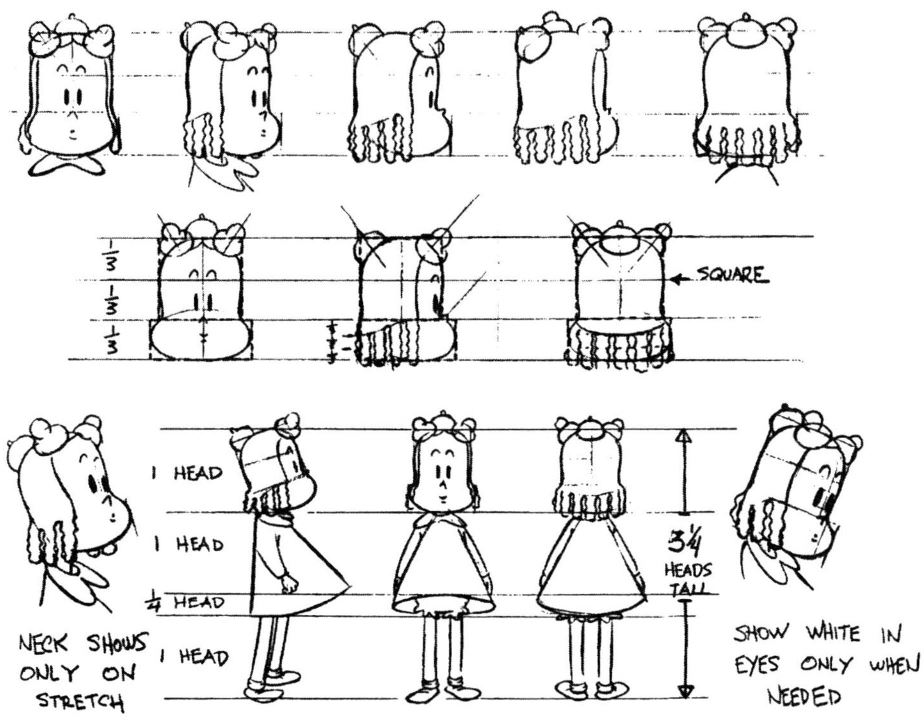

Little Lulu model sheet (author's collection).

for Buell with an equally important advertising campaign for Kleenex tissues lasting until 1960. While the *Lulu* cartoons were hugely entertaining, several of the entries are marred by black stereotypes, largely in the form of Lulu's maid, Mandy, who is established in the first of the series, *Eggs Don't Bounce*. Even with the addition of the "black characterizations" there is believability in the vocal performances that elicit warmth and realism in spite of the negative perception by a contemporary perspective. In spite of this, the stories are clever and the animation first rate.

The cartoons under Famous took on a vast improvement in design and direction, putting them more in tune with the 1940s. *No Mutton fer Nuttin'*, the first Noveltoon, was as good as any MGM Tex Avery cartoon and set the stage for greater things from the new group. This cartoon gives top credit billing to Dave Tendlar as lead animator, and was most likely the director.

The quality of the music and orchestrations improved with the collaborations of Sammy Timberg and Winston Sharples, whose arrangements set the aural tone for the Famous and Paramount Cartoon Studios for the next 20 years.

Famous Studios

Along with the creation of new characters, Famous Studios was refreshed with an expanded stable of voice actors that included Arnold Stang, Jackson Beck, Sid Raymond, and Cecil Roy. And with the return of Mae Questel in 1944, the talent group was quite versatile.

Arnold Stang (September 28, 1918–December 20, 2009)

Broadway comedian and radio star, Arnold Stang provided the voices for Fatso/Tubby in *Little Lulu*, Shorty—a caricature of Stang in his last Popeye short, *Movin' Away*, and most famously, Herman the Mouse. Stang's career began as a juvenile on New York radio shows including *The Horn and Dardart* and *Let's Pretend*. He graduated to teenaged roles by the 1940s, performing on *The Goldbergs*. He continued in character roles on the Eddie Cantor and Milton Berle radio shows and also did a short stint as the voice of Jughead on *The Archie Radio Show*.

Stang's popularity led him to a number of movie roles including *Seven Days Leave*, *My Sister Eileen*, *So This Is New York*, and *They Got Me Covered*. He also appeared on Broadway in *Sailor Beware*. During the "golden age" of Television, Mr. Stang was a regular on the DuMont Network's *The School House* in 1949. He also appeared on Milton Berle's *Texaco Star Theater* and *The Colgate Comedy Hour*. His most memorable film appearances include *The Man with the Golden Arm* (1955), starring Frank Sinatra and Kim Novak, and *It's a Mad, Mad, Mad, Mad World* (1963), teamed with Marvin Kaplan as gas station attendants. Stang appeared in commercials as "Shorty" for Chunky candy, with the slogan, "What a chunck-a chocolate!" He is best recognized for his later voiceover work for *Top Cat*, and *Catfish* for *Mister Jaw*. He also was the voice of the *Honey Nut Cheerios Bee*.

Jackson Beck (1912–2004)

Jackson Beck was one of the major radio and voice performers from the 1930s to the 1990s. During the peak of his career, he was doing as many as 20 to 30 radio shows per week. After several years of replacements for Gus Wickie, Beck's portrayal of Bluto was without a doubt the most satisfying, lasting 18 years. Beck began in radio in the 1930s and played Bluto on the *Popeye Radio Show*. His first voice work in a *Popeye* cartoon was as a juvenile Bluto in *The Football Toucher Downer* (1937). Once hired by Famous Studios, Beck became the permanent Narrator for the *Screen Songs* as well as the standard "heavy," in the Noveltoons and *Little Lulu* cartoons.

In 1943, Beck replaced George Lowther as the announcer for *The Adventures of Superman* radio show, remaining until 1950. He reprised the roles of Narrator and Perry White for the Filmation animated series of 1966. Besides becoming a major performer in the Famous Studios stable of actors, Beck continued successfully as a major voice-over artist for television cartoons and commercials. He was heard as the ominous narrator for Woody Allen's films *Take the Money and Run* (1969) and *Radio Days* (1987). Beck had a long and lucrative career and continued to be active until his death in 2004 at age 92.

Beck was sometimes favorably compared to Orson Wells, who responded by saying, "I appreciate the compliment, but you obviously have never heard Jackson Beck. He is a king, and all the rest of us who labor in this business are commoners."[2]

Sid Raymond (January 21, 1909–December 1, 2006)

Vaudevillian Sid Raymond was the voice of the Wolfy character in the early Noveltoons featuring Blackie the Sheep. His Wolfy voice was a spot-on impersonation of Bert Lahr right down to his signature reaction, "Ehh-Nahhhng-Ehh-Nahhhg-Ehh-Nahhhg!" His Bert

Lahr voice was used on a few other occasions as well. Raymond was used as secondary characters in several Famous Studios cartoons, but was most know for the characters Baby Huey and Katnip.

Born Raymond Silverstein in 1909, he was also a character actor for television, films, and stage for several decades. Some of his appearances include *The Honeymooners* with Jackie Gleason, *The Hustler* with Paul Newman, *The Pajama Game* with Liza Minnelli, *Let it Ride* with Richard Dreyfuss, *Folks* with Tom Selleck and Don Ameche, *Making Mr. Right* with John Malkovich, and *Big Trouble* with Tim Allen. Always the consummate performer, Mr. Raymond was called back into service for the new *Baby Huey* series of 1994 and remained active until his death.

Cecil H. Roy (October 2, 1900–January 26, 1995)

Cecil Roy was a female radio performer well known in radio in the 1930s and 1940s as "The Girl of a Thousand Voices." She had the ability to portray a wide range of characters, shifting with ease from an elderly woman to a crying baby. Born in St. Paul, Minnesota, she grew up in Oklahoma. She started her acting career with a Chicago stock company but soon entered radio during the 1930s, appearing on *Ma Perkins*, *The Rise of the Goldbergs*, *The Henry Aldrich Show*, and many other programs.

Miss Roy began performing voice work for Famous Studios in 1944, providing the voice of Little Lulu. She was the main voice of *Casper, the Friendly Ghost* in the 1950s series and provided various child voices for the other Famous cartoons as well. By the late 50s and early 60s, the height of Casper's popularity, various performers took on the role, including Norma McMillian and Julie McWhirter.

Gilbert Mack (1912–2005)

Gilbert Mack was an active character actor whose first voice work for Famous Studios was as Billy the Kid in the *Popeye* cartoon, *The Hungry Goat* (1943). Mack occasionally appeared in films such as *Sorry Wrong Number* and later in television series including *Fearless Fosdick* in the 1950s, as well as guest spots on various series throughout the 1950s. During the 1960s, he was active in cartoon voiceover work for the dubbing of the Japanese imports *Astro Boy* and *Gigantor*, and returned to Paramount as Mike the Masquerader in *Disguise the Limit* (1960), as the Robot Salesman in *Electronica* (1960), and Moe Hare in *Turtle Scoop* (1961). He continued to be an active actor until his death, his last cartoon work for *Casper and Wendy's Ghostly Adventures* (2002).

The animators were back in their element of "cartoony" characters not just with *Popeye* and *Little Lulu*, but in a new concept, Noveltoons. The Noveltoons spawned several minor neglected classics that include two Raggedy Ann stories inherited from Fleischer Studios, *Suddenly It's Spring* and *The Enchanted Square*. Also in the Noveltoons series was *Teacher's Pest* and *Land of the Lost*, which had great series potential. *Wee Men* was another "charm" cartoon about leprechauns that introduced *Start the Day with a Song*, which became the theme used to introduce the revised *Screen Songs* series. Paramount ran a trade ad stating, "The public wants NOVELTY and COLOR. This NEW series gives them both." Paramount clearly was selling the fresh approach by Famous Studios with emphasis on "new," "novelty," and most of all "color." Variety was the thinking behind this omnibus series that combined one-shot cartoons with a few recurring characters. Herman the Mouse was introduced in *The Henpecked Rooster* (1944), teamed with Henry Rooster. The pair returned in *Scrappily Married* (1945) and *Sudden Fried Chicken (1946)*.

Casper the Friendly Ghost

The most valuable new character to emerge from the Noveltoons series originated from a a children's book written in 1939 by Seymour Reit and Joe Oriolo about a boy ghost named Casper. The story remained unpublished for six years until it was picked up by *The Saturday Evening Post.* Joe Oriolo then sold it to Famous Studios, and Casper was first seen in *The Friendly Ghost (1945)*.

> No one regarded it as anything more than a one-shot premise about a ghostly little boy who wants to make friends with people, and not scare them. Sam Buckwald like the idea and suggested another go-round two and a half years later. *There's Good Boos Tonight* was released April 1948, and a follow-up with practically the same plot called *A Haunting We Will Go* came out in May 1949.[3]

Casper the Friendly Ghost became a regular series starting in 1950 and became the most valuable cartoon for Paramount since *Popeye*, especially since they owned the Casper character, which enabled them to license him for comic books, toys, and various novelties. The gentler tone of the *Casper* cartoons was endeared to children because they focused on the child's point of view. The visual gags were more naturalistic, and the use of wild takes and exaggerated reactions were used more sparingly than the violent gags seen in many of the Noveltoons.

Following a four-year run, Famous replaced *Little Lulu* with its own character, *Little Audrey,* who was different in manner and voice. This time Mae Questel became the voice of the lead character first introduced in *Santa's Surprise* (1947). Instead of a mischief maker, Audrey was an adventure character placed in cute moral stories. She became a regular entry in the Noveltoons series starting with *Butterscotch and Soda* (1948), and like Casper, was given a series in 1950.

The *Screen Songs* were brought back through the Noveltoons starting with *When G.I. Johnny Comes Home* (1945), became a regular series starting in 1948, and continued until 1951. The song films were a great morale booster for the G.I.s during the war. Paramount realized their value, continuing them as a goodwill gesture as the country embraced the traditional American values and culture that these songs represented. And due to advanced animation techniques, the "bouncing ball" effect was accomplished by a combination of double exposures and mechanical moves before the animation camera, specifically the use of animation cycles on pan cels that replaced the live action method originated by Max Fleischer.

Famous Studios cartoons in the late 40s seemed aimed at three audiences. The *Screen Songs* were nostalgia. The Noveltoons with characters such as Casper and Little Audrey were aimed at children, and of course Popeye was aimed at both audiences, having been the foundation of the Paramount cartoon package for a decade. Famous continued to develop more characters aimed at juvenile audiences and introduced Buzzy the Crow, Moe Hare, and Tommy Tortoise in 1953. With these new original characters Paramount licensed them for merchandising and made a lucrative comic book deal with Harvey Publications.

After a prolific period in the 1940s, the renaissance of Famous Studios had reached its ebb by the end of the decade with weaker stories and an increased focus on sadistic cartoon violence—an issue with many of the *Herman and Katnip* cartoons in particular, which was Famous' answer to MGM's *Tom and Jerry* with the addition of dialogue voiced by Arnold Stang and Sid Raymond. The cartoon violence exercised in these cartoons was many times unmotivated and inserted for its own sake. Perhaps the one exception was its application to *Baby Huey*.

Baby Huey was "hatched" in *Quack a Doodle Doo* (1950). Huey seemed well suited to the deliberate violence gags of this period. In this case, Huey being hit on the head with a pipe forming his contour without feeling pain worked since the "thick-headedness" of the character is understood. It is uncertain how audiences took to cartoon violence of this nature, but Paramount never ordered it to stop.

The full effect of the 1938 Consent Decree was enforced in the 1948 case *United States v. Paramount Pictures, Inc.* This final action forced the separation of production and distribution from theatrical operations in addition to the elimination of block booking. This action resulted in lowered production budgets for cartoons, which affected their quality in the 1950s since their financing was now limited to their rental income. Even if the Consent Decree had not happened, cartoons still would have suffered due to the emerging competition with television.

During the period 1951 to 1953, Famous fell into a pattern of mundane stories. For a period, Famous was remaking a number of the Fleischer shorts to save on developing new material. Starting in 1949, Famous reissued cut-down versions of the Fleischer two-reel *Popeye* specials framed with new animation sequences. The first was *Popeye's Premier*, the edited version of *Popeye the Sailor Meets Aladdin's Wonderful Lamp*. This was followed by *Popeye Makes a Movie* (1950), an edited version of *Popeye the Sailor Meets Ali Baba's 40 Thieves*, and lastly, *Big Bad Sindbad* (1952), a shortened version of the epic *Popeye the Sailor Meets Sindbad the Sailor*. Because the there were no separate music, dialogue, and sound effects tracks saved from these cartoons, the sound had to be re-recorded to fit the new edits. But most obvious of all was the mismatch of the quality of the new animation and the old. The budgetary limitations prevented the full animation of the Fleischer era, which used more drawings shot on single exposures, forcing Famous to animate with half the number shot on "twos." Much of the blame for the short cuts and compromises in quality has been placed on Seymour Kneitel, who has been labeled a "so-so" creative person and mediocre director. This is a great disservice to a man whose heart was in his work and essentially held the studio together through its ups and downs. This he did, remaining professionally disciplined while dealing with issues in his personal life, including witnessing the problems associated with his father-in-law Max Fleischer, surviving a heart attack, and coping with problems within his family. In 1946, his sons Tom and Kenny contracted polio. Fortunately they recovered two years later, although Ken retained a limp in his walk. In spite of this, Kneitel carried on.

A major turn of events affected Famous Studios in 1952 when Sam Buchwald, the enthusiastic force behind Famous Studios, suddenly passed away of a heart attack while riding home on the subway. He was replaced by Seymour Schultz, who remained with the studio into the 1960s. Then on October 1, 1956, Famous Studios became Paramount Cartoon Studios. With this change in name came a change in production standards with budgets

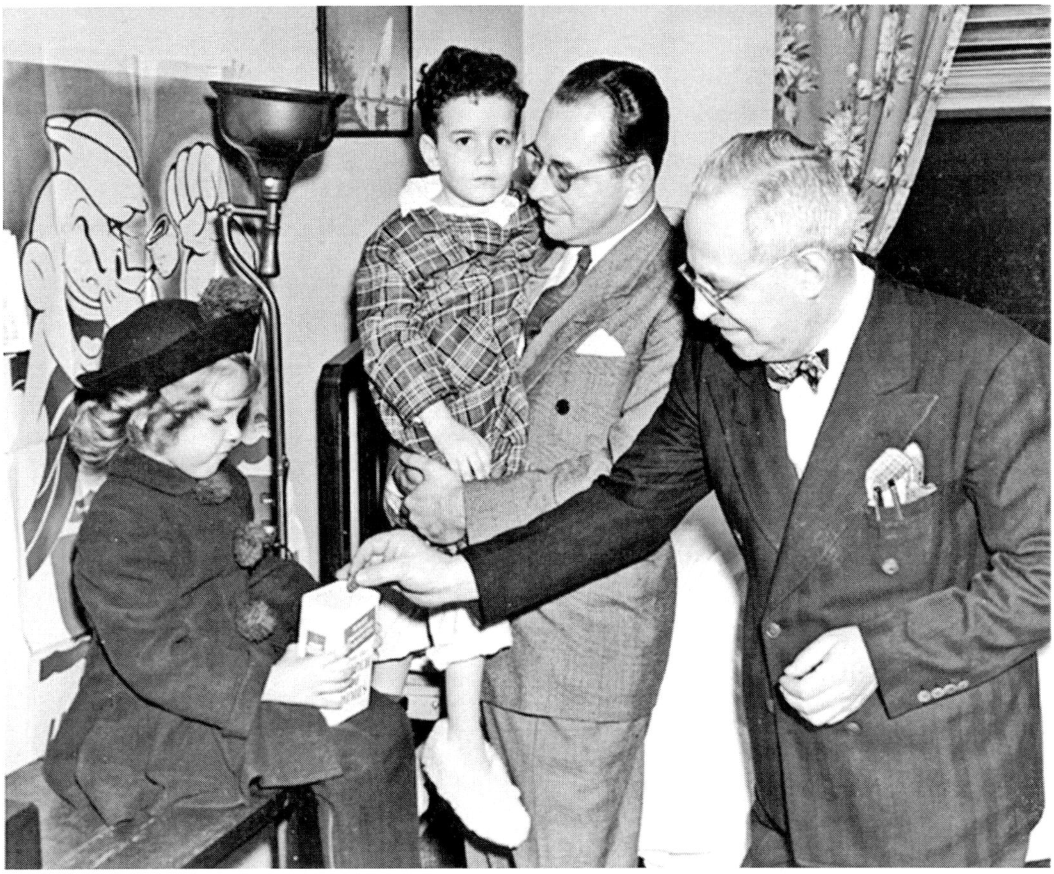

continually lowered with the adaptation of UPA-influenced designs. Paramount continued production of its established characters in the new stylized look to play to juvenile audiences while developing one-shot story cartoons aimed at adults such as *Finnegan's Flea*, a reworking of the Chuck Jones classic, *One Froggy Evening*, and *Le Petite Parade*. Juvenile-oriented stories such as *Pedro and Lorenzo* (1956), reminiscent of Disney's *Ferdinand the Bull*, were also produced.

Top: **Max Fleischer donating to the March of Dimes, Seymour Kneitel holding Kenny.** ***Right:*** **Tommy and Kenny Kneitel, 1946 (Virginia Kneitel-Mahoney).**

The last *Popeye* cartoon, *Spooky Swabs*, was released in 1957, ending a 24-year run as a box office champion, only to be an even larger hit when the series was sold to television the year earlier. Then in 1959, Paramount sold its remaining 1950s cartoons to Harvey Publications for television licensing while retaining theatrical rights. Harvey secured a deal with the Mattel Toy Company for a cartoon package titled, *Matty's Funday Funnies*, running on Friday evenings at 7:30 p.m. on ABC in its first run. It was an instant hit, and the most-liked characters were Little Audrey, Baby Huey, and most of all, Casper. The Casper character became the major merchandising property for Harvey and ABC, which lead to the production of a show of all new cartoons in 1963, produced through Paramount Cartoons Studios. The *New Casper Cartoon Show* featured the supporting comic book characters including Spooky, Nightmare, and Wendy. The show also included a selection of the later Paramount theatrical cartoons from 1959 to 1962. Their modern designs with limited animation played well on television and with television budgets.

In 1959, Paramount executives directed Seymour Kneitel to terminate Izzy Sparber as another cost-cutting measure. Seymour was too loyal to his associate, having grown up in the business with him and sharing an office. He refused to fire Izzy, leaving notice to come

Harveytoons trade ad (author's collection).

from the front office. Sparber passed away shortly after his dismissal, leaving Kneitel as the sole director of Paramount Cartoon Studios. While Kneitel loved his work, his job became more unpleasant with the continued pressures of producing television product with continually lowered budgets.

Ruth and Seymour Kneitel, 1955 (Tom Kneitel).

The 234 *Popeye* cartoons produced from 1933 to 1957 were a huge success on television, and were becoming exhausted after three years. Starting in 1960, King Features Syndicate commissioned 220 new *Popeye* cartoons to be produced over a two-year period. In order to meet this volume, production was contracted out to several studios simultaneously, and Paramount was one of them, producing 62 cartoons directed by Seymour Kneitel. The elements of the stock Winston Sharples music cues, combined with the original voices, director Kneitel, and the former Fleischer/Famous animators gave this series a sense of continuity and integrity in spite of the smaller budgets compared to their theatrical versions. These elements made for perhaps the best of the new *Popeye* cartoon package due to the experience of the staff.

Following the completion of the new Popeye cartoons, Paramount produced the majority of the King Features Trilogy for television, and distributed theatrically as *Comic Kings*. This series included 49 *Barney Google and Snuffy Smith* cartoons, 33 *Beetle Bailey*, and two *Krazy Kat* cartoons, *Keeping Up with Krazy* and *Mouse Blanche*. Two new *Little Lulu* cartoons, *Alvin's Solo Flight* (1961) and *Frog Legs* (1962), were also released under the Comic Kings titles but never went to full series.

Seymour Kneitel continued directing theatrical cartoons for Paramount under the *Modern Madcap* and *Noveltoons* titles, adapting to the new production conditions of low budgets and short production schedules for the next two years. He developed a series, Swifty and Shorty that ran through the entire year of 1964. Then in July 1964, Kneitel passed away from a second heart attack, bringing a close to what was left of the original Fleischer foundation.

15

Separate Courses, New Directions

When Dave arrived in New York, he met with Jack Cohn at Columbia Pictures. He had frequented Cohn's office during his trips from Miami to New York while he was still seeing Mae Schwartz. This time, Cohn offered him the position of producer for their cartoon division, Screen Gems. And in April 1942, he assumed the position with a salary of $500 per week—$250 less than his salary at Fleischer Studios. Dave served as producer of *The Fox and Crow* and *Lil' Abner* series in addition to the *Phantasies* omnibus series.

Song of Victory, an animal analogy of the World War II Axis Powers, was nominated for an Academy Award. *Imagination* was another Oscar nominee somewhat reminiscent of *Raggedy Ann and Andy* released three years before. While Columbia's executives were impressed with Dave's past reputation, the staff was not, feeling his approach was old-fashioned by 1940s standards.

In spite of the Oscar nominations, Harry Cohn fired Dave in 1944, replacing him with Henry Binder. Determined to reinvent his career, Dave reached back to its very beginning and approached Republic Pictures with an elf-like version of Ko-Ko the Clown named Snippy. The character was tried out as a novelty at the end of their low-budget nightclub musical, *Trocadero*. Sitting alone, Dave is introduced by bandleader Eddie LeBaron as having "drawn" *Gulliver's Travels*. Once Dave's presence is established, radio comedian Cliff Nazarro proceeds to tell Dave in a lot of nonsensical double talk what is wrong with his cartoons. Becoming bored with this "blabber mouth," Dave takes out his fountain pen and draws Snippy on the tablecloth. In classic *Out of the Inkwell* form, the character jumps off the tablecloth and up to a seltzer bottle, spraying Nazarro in the face, effectively squelching his annoying banter. This sequence appears designed to generate a *Snippy* cartoon series that never materialized.

Dave was an Associate Producer of the minute-long animation sequence for another Republic "B" movie, *That's My Baby*. While the sequence was skillfully handled, Republic made no further commitments to producing animation, with the exception of *It's a Grand Old Nag* (1947) from Warner's veteran, Bob Clampett.

Dave Fleischer's career from 1944 to 1950 becomes difficult to trace. For a short while he reportedly produced a comic strip for the *Hollywood Citizen News*. In the early 1950s, trade ads promoted a series of Technicolor theatrical advertising trailers known as "snipes" as animated by Dave Fleischer, "producer" of *Popeye the Sailor, Betty Boop, The Bouncing Ball, Superman, Gulliver's Travels,* and *Mr. Bug Goes to Town* for the Filmac Trailer Company of Chicago. One of the most recognized in recent years, *Let's All Go to the Lobby* is now among the collection in the National Film Registry as representative of American culture, along with the Betty Boop version of *Snow White*.

Dave Fleischer overlooking production on sequence for *That's My Baby*, 1944 (La Cinémathèque Québecoise).

Following a series of oddball assignments, Dave landed a permanent position as a "specialist" at Universal through animation veteran Walter Lantz. While Lantz was abundantly aware of Dave's connection in the animation field, it is ironic that he had no place for him in his own animation studio. Perhaps in Lantz' wisdom, his arranging a position outside of his own operation was the better move since Dave's career in animation was essentially finished.

Filmack trade ad (author's collection).

At Universal, Dave applied his story chart to structure the post-war *Francis the Talking Mule* series starring Donald O'Connor, served as a special effects consultant, and post-production dubbing supervisor. He also supervised the animated title sequence for *Abbott and Costello Meet Frankenstein.* While it was assumed produced by Lantz, he had broken with Universal by this time, releasing his product through United Artists. Now in the eve of his career, it seems that Dave was relentless in remaining active with animation in some form or another.

The JAM HANDY Organization

2821 EAST GRAND BOULEVARD

DETROIT 11, MICHIGAN

TRINITY 5-2450

The Jam Handy Organization, Detroit, Michigan (author's collection).

While Max's presence at the Jam Handy Organization in Detroit brought credibility to clients, his film activities were select. Jam Handy had a large animation department consisting of two divisions, cartoon and technical. There was an amount of conflict and misunderstanding between the two departments, and Max's presence was intended to bring them together for a more balanced existence. At the same time, Max would be free to invent for the company:

1. Gong-less slide film projector
2. Copy Reader: a means of assisting galley-proof readers
3. A method for using paper film for projection
4. Record timing device

In addition, Max worked on several top secret government projects for the war, one of them being a sighting system for Army Air Corps Bombers.

Max was in his element, but his arrival was badly timed since he had not recovered from losing his studio. Matters were made worse when he learned that he was being audited by The Department of Internal Revenue. He called on his secretary, Vera Coleman for assistance.

> If ever there was a perfect secretary, Vera was it. She had been Max's personal secretary for at least twenty years and was totally and irrevocably devoted to him. She knew everything there was to know about his private and public life, the studio, what he liked and disliked, how he thought. She knew him inside out, backward and sideways, so much so that she chose to follow "the boss" to Detroit and remain his secretary. If anyone could find out what happened to the papers, it would be Vera. And eventually she did.[1]

Vera Coleman (author's collection).

Vera did extensive detective work, but it was too late. All of Max's tax records were destroyed along with the rest of the Fleischer Studios papers. This detail was entered into an affidavit Max presented including his accounting for his income. Following a thorough investigation of Paramount by the IRS and FBI, it was concluded that Max's figures were correct.

Having survived an IRS audit, Max considered building his case against Paramount because his contract contained renewal options running until May 23, 1947, which were breached by Paramount's actions. But a suit of this magnitude had great repercussions affecting his son-in-law, Seymour Kneitel, who was in a vulnerable position appointed as production head of Famous Studios by Paramount out of both practicality and deliberate strategy. Seymour was privy to the details that affected the changeover, making him a star witness for Max, complicated by being in the employ of the defendant, Paramount.

This was complicated further by his having had a heart attack the previous year, and any such case would endanger his livelihood with a wife and three young children to support. While Ruth and Seymour encouraged the suit, Max looked for another angle. Ultimately, Fleischer Studios as a corporation was eventually dissolved in 1946.

Max was obviously confused, frustrated, and distracted, and his abilities for solving production problems were affected. When Max first arrived, the animation department was producing a technical illustration segment for International Harvester Tractors. Too many cel levels were employed, due to the lack of efficient scene planning, and no thought of combining them onto the same levels. As a result, the scene was dense and dusty and totally unacceptable. Bob Kennedy, a young staff member, eliminated some of the cel cycles, replacing them with cutouts to be manipulated between exposures. When Max saw the results, he was surprised and asked Bob how he came up with the idea. Bob said, "Why,

Max, you did this years ago!" Once again, Max's solutions were found in his forgotten past.

Many of the Jam Handy industrial films of this era displayed elaborate uses of animation techniques that seemed overly embellished, lacking in focus and direction. Max felt strongly that educational and training films should be entertaining in order to keep audiences interested. But...

> he soon became aware that the writing staff at this company didn't have a clue about how to do this. He immediately wrote a 34-page "bible" applying the theory and practice of motion picture script techniques to the presentation of industrial and educational films. The scriptwriters lapped it up like parched wolves. Their screenplays took on a new and improved look.[2]

Max's metaphoric semi-autobiography (author's collection).

While the prestige of Max's presence commanded great respect, he was clearly ill and in need of therapy. In 1944, he published *Noah's Shoes* as a semi-autobiographical account of the Florida studio gamble. The book reflected Max's paternal attitude, placing himself in the role of Noah. Noah's sons are metaphors for his assistants, Seymour Kneitel, Izzy Sparber, and Sam Buchwald, with the animals boarding the ark representing studio personnel. His reference to a contract with the "Rattel" is a metaphor for his sense of betrayal by Dave. With the ark filled, he feels his job is complete. He stands on the bank, bidding farewell as the ark drifts towards the rainbow, a symbol for the crest of stars in the Paramount trademark. While feeling unworthy for the journey, he is satisfied that the ark is in good hands.

After the war, Max and Essie moved back to their old apartment, number 11 in the Windermere Hotel. Back in New York, he worked out of the local Jam Handy office in the development of television engineering and commercial production while commuting between New York and Detroit. He also supervised several corporate-sponsored cartoon productions including the now-famous animated *Rudolph the Red-Nosed Reindeer*, produced for the Montgomery Ward department stores. Max called upon some of his old contacts including Joe Stultz for story adaptation, backgrounds by Shane Miller, animation by Fletcher Smith, Bill Sturm, Robinson McKee, and Howard Kakudo, and photography by Charlie Schettler.

Starting in 1949, Max was on the lecture circuit, speaking for groups such as the Junior Advertising Club at the Fort Shelby Hotel in Detroit on the topic of television advertising. He returned a year later with a lecture on the development of animation before the Greater Detroit Film Council at the Jam Handy Organization. The following year, Max issued a considered appraisal to Mr. Handy regarding his continued presence.

> Dear Jam:
>
> My full knowledge and ability to assist JHO in many directions have never been utilized. Will the future offer such an opportunity?[3]

16

Recommissioned

Max's presence at Jam Handy was becoming less, appearing as more of a consultant than a department head. In 1951, Gene Deitch was recruited from the New York office of UPA to take charge of the Jam Handy Animation Department in Detroit. Gene's influence brought on a smart, modernized look that was in step with current advertising trends, which was also more economical to produce. Max met Gene following the completion of his first film, *Building Friends for Business*. They had a pleasant chat and Max left, never to be seen again.

Max resigned from Jam Handy on March 2, 1953, and signed a contract with John R. Bray to form the Bray-Fleischer Division for extended technical research, and development of film projects for television and industrial film production. The last page of the contract interestingly includes a list of Max's patents from 1917 to 1948, most of which were now expired or nearing expiration as indicated on Exhibit B. Only the patent for his "Gong-less Slide-Film Projector," developed at Jam Handy, was still in effect. It was during this time Max created a mail order animation course that was featured in a continuing ad in *Popular Science Magazine* throughout the 1950s.

Part of Max's return to New York was to plan a lawsuit since in essence his contract with Paramount had been breached. While the 1941 amended contract supposedly cancelled the conditions previously agreed upon, this was supposed to relate to the six week period. After that, all previous agreements should have been reinstated. Max had annual renewal options continuing to May 23, 1947, so in essence his contract was still in effect until 1948.

But his resignation worked against this issue, canceling these options.

Starting in 1950, a selection of *Out of the Inkwell* films were syndicated to local television stations. Many of these from the mid to late 1920s were packaged by Stuart Productions, which acquired the original music tracks composed and conducted by Winston Sharples for the *Van Beuren Rainbow Parade* series from 1935 to 1937. New titles omitting his name were added, such as *Koko's Treasure Hunt* substituting for the original title, *Ko-Ko Hot After It*, or *Koko in Reverse* instead *of Ko-Ko Back Tracks*.

The Bray studio also packaged a selection of their silent cartoons, and the surviving *Out of the Inkwell* films were among them. In the process of making their television titles, they gave credit to Max but misspelled "Fleisher." Then in 1955 Paramount sold its short subject library to television syndicators.

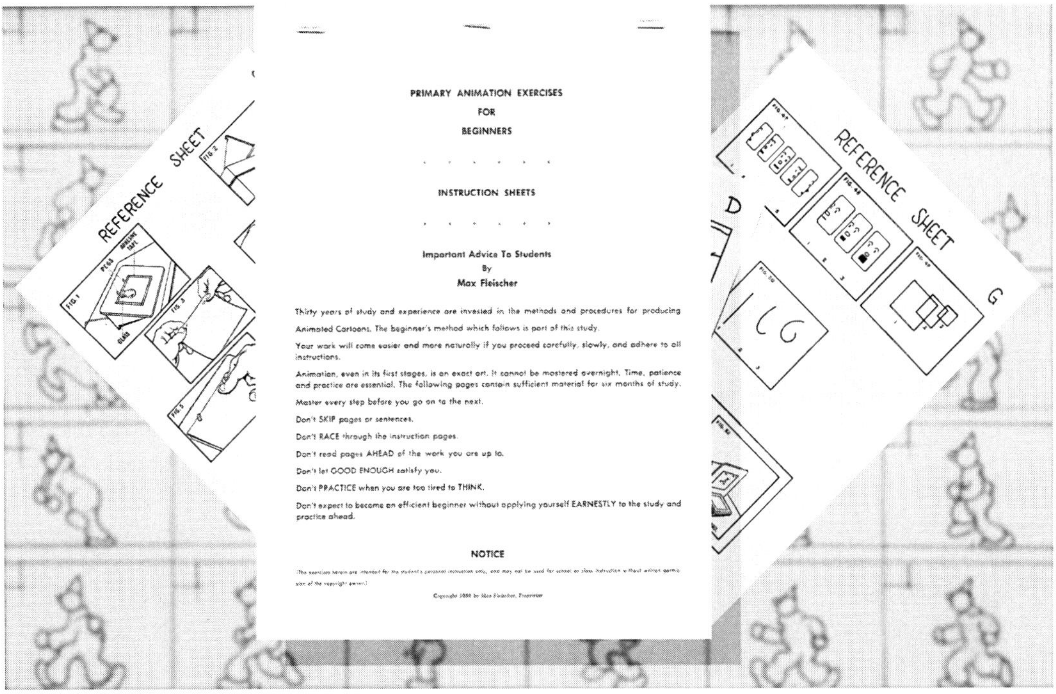

Max Fleischer's animation course (Cam Ford).

"Paramount Pkg. of 2,000 Shorts Up for Video"

In one of the most extensive such deals yet, Paramount is engaged in negotiations of the sale of nearly 2,000 short subjects for television. Basis of the talks is a price of about $4,500,000. A.W. Schwalberg, who resigned six months ago as Par Vice President in charge of domestic distribution now operating on his own as producer and artists' representative in the theatrical film field, is representing the prospective buying group. Both Schwalberg and Par Execs are clamming on the details, preferring to await conclusion of the arrangement before making any announcements. Chances are the buyers, presuming the deal goes through would license the shorts to various TV outlets instead of peddling the entire package to one network. The films represent virtually Par's entire library of back-number reels. They're mostly one-reelers and include about 200 "Popeye" subjects along with other cartoons and musical and sports items.

Variety, November 2, 1955

While the Popeye cartoons were featured as a sales enticement, Paramount held off their sale for two more years. The bid at $4,500,000 for the Paramount shorts from 1927 to 1950 went to U.M.& M. T.V. Corporation, the partnership of United Film Service, former employer of Walt Disney, MTA (Motion Picture Advertising Service of New Orleans), and Minot TV.

Of the many short subjects in the library, the cartoons, stop motion George Pal *Puppetoons* and live action novelty *Speaking of Animals* series were of greatest value, with the cutoff release date of September 22, 1950. These included: *Inkwell Imps* (1927–1929); *Talkartoons* (1929–1932); *Betty Boop* (1932–1939); *Screen Songs* (1929–1938), (1948–1951); *Color*

Classics (1934–1941); *Gabby* (1940–1941); *Stone Age* (1940); *Animated Antics* (1940–1941); *Raggedy Ann and Andy* two-reel feature (1941); *The Raven* two-reel feature (1942); Noveltoons (1943–1950); *Little Lulu* (1943–1948); *George Pal Puppetoons* (1940–1947); *Speaking of Animals* (1941–1944).

Paramount provided mostly 35mm nitrate prints from which safety film duplicates were made of the black and white cartoons prior to making 16mm reduction negatives for television prints. Paramount retained the 35mm negatives as well as the theatrical rights, continuing to reissue a selection of the cartoons well into the 1960s. However, certain theatrical rights were granted in the sale of *Gulliver's Travels* and *Mr. Bug Goes to Town*.

A condition of the sale was that all references to Paramount be removed in the main and end titles, which resulted in the removal of the Paramount trademark, replacing it with the U.M.&M. T.V. shield, and NTA logos. And because black and white and Eastmancolor prints were made, all references to Technicolor, Cinecolor, and Polacolor also had to be removed because they were trademarked processes not used in the making of these prints.

U.M.& M placed their logo shield at the head and optically altered the original main title frames, adding a still frame with their name placed on the copyright line. Many times this freeze frame was held for the entirety of the opening music, obscuring the credits. This process did not entirely eliminate references to Paramount on *Betty Boop* cartoons from 1932 to 1934, which used the Paramount mountain as an art element framed by a stage proscenium. During the process of altering the main titles, the name of Max Fleischer was sometimes omitted. The Max Fleischer screen credit was a condition in his contracts, and its omission was enough grounds for suing. On June 26, 1956, Max launched a suit for $2,750,000 based on the following issues:

1. Paramount had continued production that was founded on concepts and techniques originated by him and his organization.
2. The cartoons were being shown on television in violation of the original contracts, which stated that his name was to appear on the main titles of the cartoons.

The suit named several parties in addition to Paramount, made complicated by Paramount's interest in the fledgling DuMont Television network, which was airing the cartoons. Also named in the suit were U.M.&M. T.V. Corporation and Flamingo Films, Inc., which had television distribution of the *Superman* cartoons. U.M.& M. was still in the process of making 16mm reduction negatives and prints when they sold the library to National Telefilm Associates the following year. It was during this time that Max visited the office of Inventors Intermediaries in an effort to sell his patent on a new type of slide projector using images compressed on a disc. And it was through this company that he met the young attorney, Stanley Handman, who had recently graduated from Harvard Law School on the G.I. Bill. Handman knew who Max Fleischer was, and having completed his business there, waited to meet him. During his course of study, he had become familiar with the Fleischer/Paramount affair and was interested in knowing what had happened. He invited Max for coffee to talk about the matter, which led to a dinner invitation at home where Max went into additional details, with subsequent meetings for lunch and dinner. In spite of all of the ethical issues involved, they were still faced with the inevitable. Without documents to prove Max's case, it was impossible to win.

At this point, the films were being telecast, reedited or displayed with his name removed. Handman realized this matter as actionable. But they needed proof, and with the cartoons starting to play on television, the evidence was in the open for all to see. For days on end, two and then three television sets were operating in Max's apartment, with Max and Vera making records of the cartoons that were shown, noting titles, channels, and time slots along with distributor, credited producer, deletions, and edits. In addition, records were made of the names of all advertised products associated with the cartoons. After approximately three months, they had accumulated a large volume of records sufficient enough to go to court.

Handman assisted in re-establishing Fleischer Studios, Inc. on June 17, 1956, and a suit was filed against Paramount, U.M.&M. T.V. Corporation, National Telefilm Associates, Flamingo Film Sales, and DuMont Broadcasting. Action was filed in the New York State Supreme Court seeking $2,750,000 in damages for the display of the films "without proper credit and authority." Two days later the press announced "Popeye's Papa Sues Paramount" with the following statement issued by Max Fleischer:

> It is my intention to prevent the improper exploitation of my reputation and the films, which I produced. In certain instances, credits have been inserted which mislead the public by giving credit to people who never had anything to do with the production of my films. I will not consent to being relegated to anonymity by allowing others to reap the artistic prominence and financial reward of my lifetime of creative work in the motion picture field."[1]

While the court ruled in Max's favor, no actual money was awarded. The infringement on his name was however corrected on all subsequent prints exhibited on television, and Max's name was saved for future generations to discover.

The year 1956 was perhaps the most eventful in Max's later career. It began the historic meeting with Walt Disney on January 4 following Max's 50th wedding anniversary, December 24, 1955. Walt hosted a special luncheon with previous Fleischer employees now working for Disney. This meeting of the former rivals became a press event. As Walt was taking pride in the recent opening of Disneyland, Max, now 72, modestly remarked that he was very happy to be making educational films. The catalyst of this event was Max's son, Richard, who was directing Disney's first domestically produced all live action film, *20,000 Leagues Under the Sea.* The selection of Richard Fleischer as director was a combination of irony and providence. Richard was initially puzzled by being contacted, particularly because the name "Disney" was a "dirty word" in his parents' home. But his initial meeting with Walt was warm and open. He recalled Walt's reaction to *The Happy Time*, which featured former Disney child star Bobby Driscoll in a teenage role. Disney remarked, "Anybody who can make an actor out of Bobby Driscoll has got to be a great director."

> All of us burst into laughter. Walt got up from his desk and walked over to me. "How about it? Are you coming to work for us?" I got up, too, and studied him and the others in the room for a moment, trying to get a clue from their faces. Then I said, "You do know who I am, don't you?" Walt chuckled. "Yes, we know. That doesn't make any difference." "That's wonderful, because more than anything in the world I want to do this picture. But I can't accept it without talking it over with my father first. I'm afraid he might think I'm disloyal, or something. If he did, I just couldn't do it." "I understand," Walt said as he walked me to the door of his office. "You're absolutely right. You talk to your father tonight and call me tomorrow morning." I phoned my father in New York as soon as I got home, told him the whole story, and held my breath. "Of course you should do that picture," he reassured me. "You didn't have to call me. You go right ahead and take the job." "You sure?" "Absolutely. And tell Walt one thing from me." "What's that?" "You tell Walt that I said he's got great taste in directors."[2]

Walt Disney hosting a lunch honoring Max. *Left to right:* Gerry Geronimi, Walt, Ben Sharpsteen, Ted Sears, Max, Dick Huemer, George Strallings, Richard Fleischer, Andy Engman, and Disney Animation Director Wilfred Jackson (author's collection).

Due to the publicity of Max's lawsuit, Dave went forward with his own on October 14, 1957, against A.A.P and Paramount. Ironically he named Max as a defendant, attempting to prove that Max worked in collusion with Paramount to destroy his own studio. But this claim proved counterproductive, working in Max's favor. Key to the case was testimony from Dick Murray who stated:

> During the course of production of *Gulliver's Travels*, a great and disruptive personal conflict arose between Dave Fleischer and his brother Max. Their personal animosity grew to such an extent that they were not even on speaking terms with each other. This feud between the brothers was a matter of general knowledge in the Studios. Morale suffered and any effective operation of the Studios was rendered impossible.[3]

Lou Phillips, Legal Representative for Paramount, added further clarification of Paramount's actions by stating:

> By 1941, it had become apparent that the Fleischer Studios operation was unsuccessful and in financial straits. Very heavy advances by Paramount were unrecouped. Max and Dave were at loggerheads, and their feud was disrupting their operations. The Fleischer Studios difficulties were further complicated by the fact that the Studios had been moved from New York to Florida.[4]

Walt Disney, Max Fleischer, and Richard Fleischer (Los Angeles Public Library/*Herald Examiner*).

Lou Phillips was consistent in the details pertaining to the difficulties and the apparent source of the problems. The rebuttal to Phillips' affidavit was very revealing of Dave's perceptions and accusations in naming him as a co-conspirator to the loss of the studio.

> I am met with a torrent of abuse, offensive personalities, improper speech and malevolence by Mr. Phillips. Some of the epithets applied to me are "hysterical and incoherent," "baseless attack," "scandalous and false attack," "expose distortions and inaccuracies," "sheer nonsense," "false issue," "manifest bad faith," "monstrous concoctions," "complaint confusion and incoherent," "patent nonsense," "vague confusing references," "elliptically and haphazardly jumbled," "absolutely preposterous shabby cross-motion," "snide impertinency," "spiteful origin," "torrent of abuse," "inflammatory cross-motion," utter nonsense," "plaintiff's sorry performance," all of which add up to a clear violation of the Canon dealing with the treatment of litigants (Cannon 18). An epithet is not an answer to charge of professional misconduct, which in the vernacular is double cross or the stiletto in the back by a lawyer of his former client.[5]

In fewer words, Dave was calling to have Phillips taken off the case. Dick Murray reiterated the situation related by Lou Phillips adding further explanation for the demise of Fleischer Studios.

> The unpleasant developments between Max and Dave Fleischer were communicated to Louis Phillips. It was thought that since Louis Phillips had always been a close friend of the brothers, he could perhaps

serve as a peacemaker. I recall that Mr. Phillips visited the studio in Miami for a few days for that purpose, but to no avail. Matters went from bad to worse. The advances by Paramount to the Fleischers were steadily mounting. Paramount's executives decided that this critical impasse could no longer be tolerated. With the brothers at war with one another, the situation clearly appeared disastrous. The contract of May 24, 1941, was made in order to avert complete disaster.[6]

Based on Murray's testimony, the following statement sheds tremendous light on Dave's reasoning based largely upon denial of the obvious facts.

I have been advised that Dave Fleischer now claims that Paramount was responsible for the destruction of the Fleischer Studios and that Paramount had forcibly confiscated the business. Nothing could be further from the truth. Fleischer Studios was destroyed by two factors: 1: the extremely unwise decision of the Fleischers to remove the studio from New York to Miami, and 2: the feud between the brothers.[7]

By all accounts, Max made extensive efforts to cooperate with Dave in spite of his apparent unprofessional conduct. Therefore, the difficult conclusion to face is that Dave Fleischer was central to the studio's demise, secondary to the questionable move to Miami. While Dave continued to pursue his case, he failed to recognize the facts already presented and claimed that his suit reached the United States Supreme Court in 1963, only to be can-

Dave Fleischer reviewing photostatic storyboard panels for *The Snow Queen* (La Cinémathèque Québecoise).

Dave Fleischer posing with theater poster for *The Snow Queen*, 1959 (La Cinémathèque Québecoise).

celled due to the Warren Commission's investigation of the Kennedy Assassination. But Dave's case did not carry enough merit to reach this level. Having lost this exhaustive battle as well as his fortune, Dave Fleischer continued to work in obscurity for the next several years.

When Universal bought the American rights to the Russian animated feature, *The Snow Queen* (1959), Dave supervised the English language dubbing, with the voices of Sandra Dee and Tommy Kirk as the lead characters, along with voice-over veterans Paul Frees and June Foray. As a Production Specialist, Dave created a lobby kiosk display for Alfred Hitchcock's *The Birds* (1963), and concluded his career doing special visual effects and a sing-along sequence with the "bouncing head" of Beatrice Lillie for *Thoroughly Modern Millie* (1968) before retiring, living in the same apartment in Hollywood, drawing social security.

17

Raising the Inkwell

In 1958, Max's career turned full cycle. He returned to his original position as production manager at the Bray Studios in New York. After 40 years of activity, the Bray film library contained a vast selection of technical and scientific film footage. Max set out to develop several television projects using this material, but nothing sold. Then on January 14, Max re-established Out of the Inkwell Films, Inc. with the intention of entering television production. His first interest was to produce new cartoons for television with Betty Boop. While Betty was held among the Fleischer Studios assets acquired through the Paramount takeover, Koko was available. Then, Max was approached by his former animator Hal Seeger about producing *Out of the Inkwell* for television. Max was once again President, Seeger, Vice President, Myron Waldman, Production Manager, with Stanley Handman and Israel Seeger Legal Representatives. Seeger graduated from being an animator to becoming a clever businessman. Seeger recalled his approach to Max:

> "I want to do *Out of the Inkwell*." He said, "Everybody wants to do *Out of the Inkwell*. Bill Sturm, Shamus Culhane, everybody wants to do Koko." So I said, "But with me it's different, Max. I'll put my money where my mouth is. I just spent $2,500 on a presentation. I'd like you to come up to my office and see it." He saw it and said, "This is fantastic!' And then (he) added, "You got it, that's it!" This presentation was a storyboard, not a film yet. The whole wall, I had the whole studio filled with it. I wanted to do *Out of the Inkwell*. He said, "Why?" I said, "Because I think a lot like it. Every time I think of an idea for a cartoon series, *Out of the Inkwell* keeps popping into my head. Now it hasn't been done in 30 years and I want to do it in color with sound. It will never be like you did it."[1]

Limited animation was the production method for television, due to its speed and economy, making good writing an important element, which was realized in Seeger's pilot. Max returned to the beginning of his career, in front of the camera and back at the drawing board. He dyed his hair to help reverse four decades, interacting with the animated characters as before, this time in color. There was even a bouncing ball song sequence. It was all very nostalgic.

> Jack Mercer ... wrote the script ... he was a good writer, but he was a Fleischer-type writer, and it wasn't enough. It wasn't funny enough. It was good, but it wasn't what sold it for me. It sold me the series, but everything I did after that was funnier and wilder, and I got really crazy, zany writers. So when I started doing it, I used Max Fleischer in the film, my first film. And the clown jumped out and he pushed the clown back in. I did the whole "shtick," the cost was exorbitant. That film was never released as part of the TV package because it was too expensive, and we just had to bury it because there was no way we could do that for five thousand dollars for five minutes.... That was the price of each cartoon. That is what I did them for, 100 cartoons at five thousand dollars apiece. I had to use cutouts and I had to use still photographs. And I hired all the people that ever worked for me.... Shamus Culhane.... Orestes Calpini.... Myron Waldman.... George Ruffle.... Tommy Golden.... Marty Taras, Dave Tendlar, I mean all the top guys.[2]

The situation was substantiated by Shamus Culhane.

> The Koko series had a budget so small that the animation had to be very limited. The resulting pictures bore no resemblance to the entertaining cartoons that Max Fleischer made in the early 1920s. Even so, it was more interesting than doing one-minute TV spots. Like Walt Lantz, Hal Seeger was able to work with small budgets without yielding to the temptation to wring more work out of his employees than their salaries were worth. But working with Koko after these long years, I remembered with nostalgia when Dick Huemer's animation of the clown was matchless, and Koko was the most popular character on the screen. It is one thing to do a primitive type of animation from ignorance, and quite another to deliberately turn your back on knowledge painfully acquired. For my own satisfaction, I spent far more time drawing good poses of Koko that the job called for.[3]

The key element in limited animation is good dialogue, which required talented voice actors.

Hal Seeger (Mindy Seeger).

> Larry Storch did all the voices for all the men, and one day we recorded in my office on 48th Street, and Larry came up one day and I interviewed him and said, "Look, Larry, I want you to do Max Fleischer because Max is a little too old and his voice shakes a little bit. I really want you to do an imitation of Max." "Well," he asked, "What does Max Fleischer sound like?" I said, "I don't want you to

MAX FLEISCHER
PRESIDENT

CIRCLE 6-4939

Out of the Inkwell
incorporated

200 WEST 54TH STREET

NEW YORK 19, N. Y.

Max's last business card (Todd Levine).

sound like Max Fleischer, I want you to sound like me. Do me!" He said, "Well, I can't do you, your voice isn't distinctive enough. I gotta do people that have distinctive voices." I said, "Well do you!" And he did himself, and he sounded just like Larry Storch. He can't do a straight voice. He says, "Well, why don't you do Max Fleischer? Why don't you be Uncle Max?" And I said, "Well, I'd be happy to do it, but I can't direct myself." So he said, "Well, you'll direct me when I'm doing my voices, and then I'll direct you." So we did 100 cartoons and I was Uncle Max.

Now we needed a woman to play Kokette. So my wife was an actress before we got married ... her stage name being Beverly Arnold.... So I said, "Beverly will do it, but she can't come to the city with those five kids.... I have a recording studio at home... and Beverly will do the Kokette voices at home." I'd bring 'em in, and we'd do a mix and you'd swear they were in the same room.[4]

Everything about the new *Out of the Inkwell* series seemed like a reunion right down to the sound of the cartoons thanks to the Winston Sharples music cues and Maurice Manne's sound effects library. These elements so closely related to Fleischer and Paramount belied the interruption of Max's career in cartoon production. While the concept began in 1958, it was four years before the series went into full production. All copyrights on the 100 cartoons have dates between 1962 and 1963. Due to the passage of time, Max was becoming too ill and fragile to participate as he had in the pilot. His presence was created by substituting Myron Waldman in a waist to chest shot, with his hand dipping the pen into the inkwell, and closing it in the end. One can only wonder what the pilot footage was like and whether any of it could have been used to create more of a presence with the real Max Fleischer. Instead, "Uncle Max" was relegated to an ominous off screen voice. The small budgets and limited animation of the new *Out of the Inkwell* made it a pale reflection of the original series produced 40 years earlier. And because of this, the cartoons were difficult to sell in light of the standards set by Hanna-Barbera, the dominant force in television animation of the 1960s. Considering that Max had built his career and reputation on producing fluid, life-like animation, he was surely disappointed in having his name associated with these compromises.

Seeger's original backers were the Berger brothers, who had a company called Video House. Once the cartoons were produced, they sold their interest to Seven Arts on October 23, 1963. Seven Arts was not terribly successful in selling the cartoons, which finally landed in a few markets five years later. The new *Out of the Inkwell* ran on WXYZ, Channel 7 in Detroit, the same channel that ran the original black and white series the decade before. They ran for one season in the original 7:00 a.m. time block, but on Sunday mornings. While the past reputation of *Out of the Inkwell* was the attraction, the new cartoons were disappointing. Out of the Inkwell, Inc. was finally dissolved on December 3, 1964. In spite of the meticulous licensing and profit sharing arrangements made on behalf of Max by Licensing Corporation of America, the proceeds were short-lived. Max was now subsisting on social security. Richard Fleischer faced the difficult challenge dealing with the truth about his father.

As soon as I learned of the financial situation, I insisted that I help my parents and Vera.... It was simply unthinkable that he should be in such financial straights. How could such a thing happen?

I certainly wasn't one of Hollywood's highest-paid directors, but I knew I had to do something. Ruth and Seymour had done all that they could afford, but it wasn't easy for them.... In any event, in spite of strong protests from my father, I worked out a monthly budget for my parents and Vera. They could now stop worrying about the rent, food, utilities, and other expenses. It wasn't lavish, but it was enough.[5]

Richard's frankness becomes more direct:

> Time was not being kind to Max. He never fully accepted the reality that his case against Paramount was over.... Max never left the apartment except to go to one of his doctors. Slowly he began to withdraw within himself. He was speaking less and less. That brilliant, creative, inventive mind was slowing down. With what he had been through, it was a wonder that it had lasted as long as it had.
>
> Essie, my mother, was always much more extroverted than Max and given to short bursts of furious temper. A kind of cabin fever was developing. She loved being outdoors, traveling, going places, playing poker with her friends. Now she was all but locked in, taking care of her husband, staring out the windows, looking at the hard, concrete canyons of Manhattan instead of the grounds and gardens of her beloved Miami Beach home. Eventually, she began to talk of suicide, of jumping out one of the windows of their eleventh-floor apartment. She would frighten my sister, Ruth, with hysterical phone calls that, day or night, would bring Ruth in a panic from the other side of town.
>
> It was becoming more and more apparent that a retirement home would be the next step. And then The Motion Picture Country House (Home) came into our lives.... I knew it was a retirement home meant exclusively for people who worked in the industry in any capacity. It didn't matter whether you had money; if you were eligible, you would be accepted. Although I'd supported the MPCH, I'd never visited it or even seen it. That changed dramatically when a location survey for a film I was preparing took me to the San Fernando Valley and the MPCH ... I knew that this was the place for my parents, and I immediately started the process to get them admitted.[6]

Richard arranged for two adjoining cottages, one for Essie, and the other as an office where Max could work and sleep. They found an apartment for Vera that was on a bus line that passed in front of the MPCH, and she continued acting the role as secretary while they went through the motions of writing scripts for a proposed nature series that would never sell.

Max never gave up on the crusade to vindicate himself and regain the ownership of Betty Boop. Starting in 1959, Max began the decade-long pursuit based on a technicality associated with copyright renewal. When Paramount sold its stock of characters to Harvey Publications in 1958, the initial 28-year term on *Betty Boop* was about to elapse, which would have placed her in the public domain. This meant that Max, as the original "author" was free to renew the copyright. A new law stated that if the original author had not assigned renewal rights and was still alive, the rights would reverse to the author. Max's attorney, Stan Handman, assisted in the recovery of these rights and re-established Fleischer Studios for the sole purpose of exposing Betty Boop to the public through merchandising. Several companies expressed interest but the deals failed to materialize and the 11th hour was approaching.

The year 1972 was significant on two levels. On August 1 the merchandising licensing arrangement was signed with King Features Syndicate, with Ruth Kneitel and their attorney, Stan Handman, representing Max. By this time, Max was deteriorating, bed ridden from a bad fall. When Ruth came to deliver the news of the deal, he had suffered a stroke that affected his ability to speak. Seeing a pile of magazines beside his bed, she noticed one with a picture of Walt Disney on the cover. She picked it up, showing it to him and said, "Look, Pop, your old friend, Walt Disney!" Surprisingly, Max responded saying, "Son of a bitch!"

For his remaining months, Max lived in a vegetable-like state, confirmed in a letter dated May 15, 1971, sent to the author by Dave Fleischer. It is obvious from this letter that Dave was aware of Max's state in spite of the breach that occurred between the two of them three decades before. While it is unclear as to whether he had been visiting Max, it is likely that Richard kept him informed. What is a credit to both brothers is that in spite of the horrible circumstances between them, they kept their feud to themselves and avoided bringing their respective families into it. Because of this, Ruth and Richard continued to stay in contact with Dave.

On September 25, 1972, the press announced the passing of Max Fleischer, "Dean of animated cartoons." His untimely death preceded a national retrospective of *Betty Boop, Popeye,* and *Out of the Inkwell. The Betty Boop Scandals of 1974* started the Fleischer Renaissance with new 35mm prints of a selection of the best Fleischer cartoons made between 1928 and 1934. Included were *Minnie the Moocher, Betty Boop's Rise to Fame, Snow White, Bimbo's Initiation, Ha! Ha! Ha!, Stoopnocracy, Boilesk, When the Red, Red Robin Comes Bob, Bob, Bobbin' Along, Koko's Earth Control,* and *Swing You Sinners.* This was followed a few weeks later by *The Popeye Follies,* consisting of *Popeye the Sailor, A Dream Walking, Goonland, Popeye the Sailor Meets Sindbad the Sailor, and Popeye the Sailor Meets Ali Baba's Forty Thieves.* These special programs generated interest in the Fleischer studio and the people who made the cartoons, spawning a new wave of film research devoted to animation beyond what had been dominated by the Disney history for decades.

The first general history of animation, *How to Make Animated Cartoons: The History and Technique* by Nat Falk was published in 1940 as well as the French publication, *Le Dessin Animé* by Lo Duca. That same year saw the first Walt Disney Studios book, *The Art of Walt Disney* by Dr. Robert Field. For 18 years no other histories had been written until *The Art of Animation* by Bob Thomas, designed for promoting Walt Disney's *Sleeping Beauty.* It was another 15 years before animation art and history were revisited on a serious level with the 1973 publication of *The Art of Walt Disney: From Mickey Mouse to the Magic Kingdom* by Christopher Finch, which ushered in the era of the "coffee table book" with quality large color reproductions, giving birth to a new category of book publishing devoted to the subject of animation. While there is no argument about the place and impact of Walt Disney in the field of animation, the fact is that his accomplishments were built upon the pioneers who preceded him and these people deserved greater recognition.

Due to the broad exposure of old theatrical cartoons on television, the post–World War II generation received a virtual animation history lesson—including myself. We realized the importance of animation beyond its perception as trivial juvenile entertainment and raised it to a level of serious appreciation, making it a major part of the art, science, and cultural history of the 20th century. In 1968, Joe Adamson conducted a series of oral history interviews while a student at UCLA. One of them was with Dave Fleischer. Following my 1971 letter from Dave, I took him up on his invitation and visited him, gaining a great deal of insight and understanding on both historical and psychological levels. Contacting him was very easy since he had been listed in the Los Angeles telephone directory for years. I called him, and he asked me where I was. At the time, I called from where I was staying. Dave was brief.

One Sunday, I had lunch near Hollywood and La Brea and called him again. Dave asked me where I was and I told him. Since I was in the vicinity, he gave me explicit directions to where he was living. His address, 7253 Hollywood Boulevard, was an apartment complex called Peyton Hall that was once inhabited by many industry people and aspiring actors and actresses. Shelley Winters had lived there in the early years of her career, for one.

Dave directed me to enter the large courtyard where he said he would be seated by the fountain. As I went up the stairs and entered the court, there was the fountain on the right. Seated at it was Dave Fleischer in a white and gray striped shirt and gray trousers, wearing black-framed glasses. To my cinematic mind, his light bulb shaped head immediately dissolved to the image of Koko the Clown, complete with his black cone-shaped hat with white pom-poms. Dave greeted me warmly and led me to apartment #2 in the right-hand corner of the east end of the court. The inside looked as if it had remained in 1942, the year that he and Mae took occupancy. While it was clean, the furnishings were old and the apartment small. The walls were institutional green, and on the north wall of the living area were three rather crude acrylic paintings of outdoor scenes done by Dave. They were framed in cheap, light colored wooden frames, and the colors raw from the tubes, looking rather gaudy, orange being most dominant in one of an autumn scene. Dave introduced me to Mae, who graciously served me iced tea as I sat down to visit with him at the dining room table, which was covered with a simple white-laced tablecloth.

I told Dave about a cartoony experience I had at the restaurant just before I arrived. The top on the ketchup bottle was wet and looser than I expected and flipped out of my fingers, spinning up in the air, landing on my right leg top side up and bouncing into the air, leaving a splatter of ketchup on my navy blue slacks, then landing on the floor to the right of my foot and onto the tiled floor flipped over, inner side up. To this, Dave responded, "Did it hurt ya?" I was a bit stunned at first with a swallowed laugh, then realized the meaning of his "joke."

In many ways, Dave Fleischer reminded me of my grandfather, which helped me in handling him. At a certain point in our conversation Dave got up and went to another room, returning with a small black portfolio. He showed me highlights of his career, many things never publicly seen including original inked character model cards for the *Popeye* characters, as well as publicity shots of himself after his years at Fleischer Studios. In essence, he gave me the same interview he gave in 1968, which I was familiar with. I was cautious about bringing up Max and focused on him. In the process, I gained great insight to the man. While he was in stages of senility, I sensed a tremendous regret and guilt having lost so much and never regaining the position he had in the business with his brother. He was living on social security and still driving a 1959 Desoto in 1976. After talking to me the first hour, he summarized his career by saying, "After all I've done, I'm still just a clown." As I left, Dave shook my hand and said to me, "Thanks for coming to see me. I've made a friend."

I paid Lou Fleischer several visits, and he was most forthcoming in his recollections. Apparently he was in contact with Dave and mentioned Mae's complaining about the state of Dave's mind. Lou suggested that they consider moving to the Motion Picture Country Home. Mae was resistant to the idea, stating, "As long as he can open his eyes and see me, I won't take him there." Somehow in Mae's mind the MPCH was something like an asylum, and her resistance seemed based more on the fear of Max's presence there and the stigma associated with her influence on Dave which contributed to the issues related to the loss of the studio. What is more interesting to consider is the "motivation" behind the affair since it was a matter of two consenting adults. While Dave's motivation is realized, one might consider Mae's intentions knowing that he was a married man at the time.

Before the move to Miami, Mae was a roommate with Edith Vernick. According to Edith, Mae remarked, "When we go to Miami, I'm going for one of 'the big fish.'" There must have been some element of truth to this since Mae scoffed at the mere mention of Edith's name—evidence of guilt and denial. Working so closely with Dave during the move to Miami and the pressures to deliver *Gulliver's Travels*, it is reasonable to imagine that Mae started building up Dave for her own gain, convincing him that he was more important than Max. This is supported by her remark to me that "Dave was the whole thing," while she bitterly dismissed Max as insignificant.

Mae had sealed her fate by marrying Dave in 1945, and it was apparent she realized the reckless mistake she had made having nowhere to go. Together, Dave and Mae lived a life of pretending, masking the reality of a destroyed career that was self-imposed. This situation was made more uncomfortable when Dave's middle daughter, Doris, who was born with congenital hypothyroidism, was assigned to live with them as a condition of the divorce. Doris eventually passed away on August 17, 1963, while in her 40s.

Mae left Peyton Hall following Dave's passing on June 25, 1979, and lived with her sister near me in Sherman Oaks. She was broke and desperately attempting to find some means of getting money based on Dave's past work. Knowing that I had a lot of research material, she called me several times hoping I could help her. But there was nothing in my findings. The problem was that she had destroyed all of Dave's papers the day after he died, discarding any last proof that might have helped her. As she sat on the foot of her bed, she lamented, "I miss the picture business." The sad and inevitable truth was that neither of the brothers regained their professional positions once they were separated. And were it not for television, their names and place in animation history would have been completely forgotten.

After the loss of the studio, Max's older brother Charlie remained in the Miami area doing electrical contracting work, passing away in 1956 following a fall from a ladder. Joe Fleischer seemed to harbor the greatest resentment over the loss of the studio even though he was the only Fleischer brother retained by Famous Studios for a brief period. He then returned to Hollywood, Florida, working as an electrical contractor, passing away in 1979.

When Paramount sold the Miami studio building in 1943, it became a production center for the war effort. Lou went back to work in the very building where he was a department head, this time as a lens grinder. Soon after he made bouncing ball song films for the Army Signal Corps in New York, then moved to Redondo Beach, California, where he did scoring for George Pal, taught music, and tuned pianos.

Lou continued to be amazed at the accomplishments of the five brothers during their heyday, but took it in his stride. Once the era of Fleischer Studios was over, Lou faced reality and reinvented himself for a new era, never feeling sorry for himself, or placing the blame on anyone for having his life upset. Lou spent his final years at the Motion Picture Country Home, where he entertained residents with his piano playing until his passing on November 16, 1985.

Fleischer Studios Resurrected

In the early days of television, it was soon realized how quickly film material was consumed, creating a demand for newer product. Color television was making more of an appearance by 1958 and the market was interested in new cartoons in color. By the mid-1960s the majority of the Fleischer cartoons went off the airwaves largely because they were in black and white, which left just the 36 Color Classics included in the NTA package, along with the Famous Studios and George Pal color films. Thanks to the rediscovery of Betty Boop in the 1970s, NTA contracted with the Fred Ladd organization to remake the cartoons in color in order to sell them to a new television audience. But they were not well done. The animation was traced from film prints, skipping every second frame, resulting in a misrepresentation of the timing and fluidity of the originals. The backgrounds were painted in a heavy, opaque manner, lacking the skill and care of the original wash techniques. The use of color was haphazard, very garish and lacking in any real color scheme. Most of all there was sloppy camera work that added technical flaws, creating the gross misrepresentation, "Did people actually watch these in theaters? No wonder Disney cartoons were better!"

While the cartoons were available in color by the mid–1970s, NTA was unable to sell them and attempted to compile them as a feature, *Betty Boop for President* in 1976, which was reshaped by Dan Dalton into *Hooray for Betty Boop*, and sold to New Line Cinema for airing on HBO in 1980. A new soundtrack was created featuring Victoria D'Orazi as Betty Boop and Tom Smothers as the voice of Pudgy. It was an atrocity and an insult to the memory of the "original animation produced by Max Fleischer" as the credits stated. It clearly did not reflect the quality that Max spent his life creating.

While Fleischer Studios now existed for the sole purpose of licensing the image of Betty Boop for merchandise, there was interest in re-establishing Fleischer Studios in the animation field. Through its affiliations with the Hearst Organization and its own affiliate, King Features Syndicate, Fleischer Studios had a video rights option with Viacom, resulting in the production of the television special, *The Romance of Betty Boop* in 1985. Produced by the Bill Melendez Studio, it was telecast over CBS only twice, its last airing on New Year's Eve 1987. Although of interest to fans, it was a disappointment, failing to capture the spirit of the original cartoons on many levels. It was hampered by the limited budget, mediocre animation, misappropriated stylization, and most of all, a lack of understanding of the character.

Richard Fleischer took on the full-time role of Chief Executive Officer in Fleischer Studios following his last film, *Call from Space* in 1989. In that same year, a second television Special, *The Betty Boop Hollywood Mystery* was produced by Colossal Pictures in San Francisco with Art Direction by Timothy Berglund and Animation Direction by John Hays. This production made more of an effort to capture the original cartooning style and surrealistic environments, but also failed to recapture the essence of the original fluidity and timing that was a large part of the originals. Furthermore, the use of color was distracting, seemingly influenced by the color remakes with their garish and unharmonious color combinations.

After a 49-year absence from the silver screen, Betty made an impressive cameo appearance in the Robert Zemeckis hit, *Who Framed Roger Rabbit?* (1988). This time Betty was animated with great skill by Roger Chiasson, which generated interest in a feature vehicle. And with the wave of highly profitable Disney animated features of the 1990s, interest was renewed in duplicating the Disney success once again.

Richard Fleischer made a deal with the Zanuck Company, releasing through Metro-Goldwyn-Mayer. After exhaustive research of the old contracts to substantiate ownership and clearances, the project was "green lit" by Alan Ladd, Jr., Steven Leiva and Jerry Rees were assigned to produce a lavish animated musical with Rees' script placing Betty as a rising star of Hollywood's Golden Age. The music and lyrics were by jazzman Bennie Wallace, with Bernadette Peters cast as the voice for Betty Boop. Tests indicated that she captured all of the nuances of Betty's voice, retaining the tone established by Mae Questel. Then, two weeks before recording was to begin, Alan Ladd, Jr., left MGM. He was replaced by Frank Mancuso, Jr., who had just resigned from Paramount. While at Paramount, Mancuso, Jr., had approved two animated features, Ralph Bakshi's *Cool World*, and the Robin Harris-inspired *Bebe's Kids*. Both features were erroneously scheduled for release in July 1992, two weeks apart, with *Cool World* coming out first. *Cool World* was a box office failure. *Bebe's Kids* was next on the schedule and was pulled from release after two weeks in spite of positive reviews including a "thumbs up" from Roger Ebert. Both features lost money for Paramount due to bad executive judgment. Once Mancuso Jr. saw an animated feature on MGM's schedule, he quickly cancelled it stating, "Animated features don't make money." In spite of the cancelled feature, the popularity of Betty Boop continues.

Betty was a featured balloon in the annual Macy's Thanksgiving Day Parade beginning in 1985, in commemoration of her 75th birthday, and has returned every year since. She was parodied in an episode of *Animaniacs* as "Googily Goop," with Desirée Goyette reprising her role as the voice of Betty, and was the inspiration for the character "Boopsie" in the popular comic strip, *Doonesbury*.

In 1996, Richard Fleischer pitched a television venture with Betty Boop as an interplanetary travel hostess. Great effort was put into the production "bible" with authentic period style Hollywood caricatures of "the Golden Era" done by a studio in France. In spite of the name value of Betty Boop, it never came to fruition due to inadequate budgets. In retrospect, this was a wise decision based on Max's television experience with Koko the Clown.

In spite of failed attempts at a return to the screen, the image of Betty Boop continues to be of interest. In 2008, a series of Betty Boop photographs taken in the style of the 1930s were made of the Russian model Olya by the Retro-Atelier Studio. These photographs hit the Internet via Instagram, erroneously claiming to be Esther Jones, Helen Kane, and "the Black Betty Boop," entertaining the concept of Betty's origins in Black culture. While intended to honor the memory of Miss Boop, they have been the source of further historical inaccuracy. Nevertheless, Betty continues to live in the eyes of the public. In 2010, Betty became the honorary cheerleader for the United Football League. In addition, a Broadway musical with music by David Foster and book by Oscar Williams and Sally Robinson has been in development.

The recognition of Betty Boop in the last generation has been largely through the various merchandise items and not the original cartoons in spite of their exposure on cable television, video, and DVD releases—bootlegged and official. Because of the success of the merchandising, Harvey Publications challenged Fleischer Studios in 1995, claiming ownership rights and an entitlement to a portion of the earned revenue. These claims were defeated.

Part of the challenge surrounding Betty Boop was that she had been considered a dormant character for three decades. Some of the cartoons had fallen into the public domain. This raised the question about ownership of the images on posters and advertising art displaying the name Betty Boop, an issue prompting a lawsuit launched in 2010 by Fleischer Studios against Art & Vintage Entertainment Licensing Agency (A.V.E.L.A) for trademark infringement.

The case reviewed in exhaustive detail of the complications associated with the transfer of ownership of Betty Boop to Fleischer becoming exclusive and final in 1997. While the issue of the suit was over an unauthorized use of the title "Betty Boop" as a trademark, the case focused on the copyright aspect, citing Fleischer's failure to provide proof of copyright. The copyright matter was not the issue, but one of trademark, which was argued in appeal, finally ruled in Fleischer's favor in 2014. Accordingly, "they couldn't take Fleischer's Boop-Oop-A-Doop" away.

Conclusion

Understanding the full impact of the Max Fleischer story made approaching survivors seem a sensitive issue. Surprisingly, family members were very open and generous with their time and recollections, harboring no animosity largely because they had been shielded from the turmoil associated with studio business, living their own lives and becoming well-balanced adults grounded in reality. Lou's son, Bernie, offered this considerate summary:

> Looking back on it now, I don't think they gave themselves enough credit for what they did. I think the beginnings were extremely wondrous and magical. And I think that the more it got toward the end of its cycle the less value it had. Collectively, the brothers worked together like the fingers of the hand that dipped the pen into the famous inkwell. Max definitely was the animation genius. He thought of the concepts that the animation was built on. Dave would think of situations for the animation, and they were good situations. And then they would explain to Charlie and Joe what the concept was, and they would say, "No problem" and build whatever equipment was needed to create that animation. They were absolute geniuses in adapting mechanics and the principles of electricity to the animation process. And when sound came in Lou brought technical perfection in synchronization and creativity in music to the cartoons, completing the quintet of brothers.

The art and inventions of Max Fleischer is the story of the magnetic force that attracted raw talent in the building of one of the most vital and influential studios in motion picture history. It is the story of a generation who, equipped with only a public school education, contributed to a documentation of American culture through the advancement of the animation medium. Through their mixture of inventiveness and craftsmanship, outlandish ideas solved problems, transforming sorrow to joy. And animation was the perfect arena where such imaginative concepts could materialize with the added dimensions of action, satire, drama, and supernatural fantasy. These are the elements that made the best of the Fleischer studio so unique because as Max Fleischer said quite simply, "If it can be done in real life, it isn't animation."

Filmography

Any complete list of Fleischer films is nearly impossible since several are considered lost, especially those from 100 years ago.

Rotoscope, 1914–1916

Experiment No. 1—*Boy Scout Semaphore, Rotoscope Patent Demonstration.*
Experiment No. 2—*Chaplin Cartoon* (unreleased).
Experiment No. 3—*Clown Antics*
Theodore Roosevelt and the Chanticleer—first commercial job for Pathé (unreleased).

Bray Period

Army Training Films, 1916–1917

How to Operate a Stokes Mortar
How to Fire the Lewis Machine Gun
How to Read a Contour Map

Out of the Inkwell

The Bray-Goldwyn Pictograph Novelty Reel
Experiment No. 1—06/10/1918
Experiment No. 2—(possibly Clown film) 03/5/1919
Experiment No. 3—(possibly Roosevelt film) 04/2/1919
The Clown's Pup 8/30/1919
The Tantalizing Fly 10/4/1919
The Boxing Kangaroo 2/2/1920
The Chinaman 3/19/1920
Slides 4/12/1920
The Circus 5/6/1920
The Ouija Board 6/4/1920
The Clown's Little Brother 7/6/1920
Poker 10/2/1920
Perpetual Motion 10/2/1920
The Restaurant 11/6/1920
Cartoonland 2/2/1921
The Automobile Ride 6/20/1921

Goldwyn-Bray Popular Science Segments

The Eclipse of the Sun 07/1918
The Electric Bell 04/23/1919
The Elevator 04/23/1919
How the Telephone Talks 1919, reissued 06/12/1924
The Birth of the Earth 09/19/1919
Hello, Mars 01/25/1920
All Aboard for the Moon 02/02/1920
If You Could Shrink 08/31/1920
If We Lived on the Moon 09/26/1920
A Word About Miss Liberty 10/21/1920
Through the Earth 11/8/1920

Inkwell Studio Period

Modeling 10/1921
November 11/01/1921
Fishing 11/21/1921
Invisible Ink 12/03/1921
The Fish 01/07/1922
The Dresden Doll (a.k.a. *The Mechanical Doll*) 02/07/1922
The Mosquito 03/06/1922
Bubbles 04/20/1922
Flies 05/01/1922
Pay Day 07/08/1922
The Hypnotist 07/26/1922
The Challenge 08/29/1922
The Show 09/21/1922

The Reunion 10/27/1922
The Birthday 11/04/1922
Jumping Beans 12/15/1922
Surprise 03/15/1923
The Puzzle 04/15/1923
Trapped 05/15/1923
The Battle 07/01/1923
False Alarm 08/01/1923
Balloons 09/01/1923
The Fortune Teller 10/01/1923
Shadows 11/01/1923
Bed Time 12/01/1923

Red Seal Period

Masquerade 02/01/1924
The Cartoon Factory 02/21/1924
Mother Gooseland 03/21/1924
Trip to Mars (a.k.a. *First Man to the Moon*) 04/01/1924
A Stitch in Time (a.k.a. *Ko-Ko Needles the Boss*) 05/01/1924
Claytown 05/28/1924
The Runaway 06/25/1924
Vacation 07/23/1924
Vaudeville 08/20/1924
League of Nations 09/17/1924
Sparring Partners 10/01/1924
The Cure 12/13/1924
The Laundry 12/30/1924
Thaddeus and Arlene 01/02/1925
Ko-Ko the Barber 02/25/1925
Big Chief Ko-Ko 03/02/1925
The Storm 03/21/1925
Ko-Ko Trains 'Em (a.k.a. *Koko's Pup Talent*) 05/09/1925
Ko-Ko Sees Spooks 06/13/1925
Ko-Ko Celebrates the Fourth 07/04/1925
Ko-Ko Nuts 09/05/1925
Ko-Ko on the Run 09/26/1925
Ko-Ko Packs 'Em 10/17/1925
Ko-Ko Eats 11/1925
Ko-Ko Steps Out 11/21/1925
Ko-Ko's Thanksgiving (a.k.a. *Thanksgiving*) 11/21/1925
Ko-Ko in Toyland 12/12/1925
Ko-Ko the Hot Shot 12/30/1925
Ko-Ko's Paradise 02/27/1926
Ko-Ko Baffles the Bulls 03/06/1926
It's the Cats 05/01/1926
Ko-Ko at the Circus 05/01/1926
Toot-Toot (a.k.a *Koko's Toot-Toot*) 06/05/1926
Ko-Ko Hot After It (a.k.a. *Koko's Treasure Hunt*) 06/12/1926
The Fadeaway 09/01/1926
Ko-Ko Kidnapped 10/01/1926
Ko-Ko's Queen 10/1/1926
Ko-Ko the Convict 11/1/1926
Ko-Ko Gets Egg-Cited 12/01/1926
Koko in 1999 03/10/1927

In the films produced from 1924 to 1927, "Ko-Ko's" name was hyphenated. After the bankruptcy of the Red Seal Pictures Corporation, the hyphen was dropped.

Ko-Ko Song Car-Tunes

Come Take a Trip in My Airship 03/09/1924
Goodbye, My Lady Love 03/09, 1924
Mother Pin a Rose on Me 06/01/1924
Oh, Mabel 05/01/1924
Come Take a Trip in My Airship 01/15/1925 sound version
Old Folks at Home 02/1925
Mother Pin a Rose on Me 03/01/1925 sound version
I Love a Lassie 03/20/1925
Swanee River 04/25/1925
East Side, West Side 05/01/1925
Daisy Bell 05/30/1925
Nutcracker Suite 09/01/1925
My Bonnie Lies Over the Ocean 09/15/1925
Ta-Ra-Ra-Boom-De-A 10/15/1925
Dixie 11/15/1925
Sailing, Sailing 12/15/1925
Miky ??/??/1926
Darling Nellie Gray 02/06/1926 released with sound
Has Anybody Here Seen Kelly? 02/21/1926 released with sound
My Old Kentucky Home 03/13/1926 silent, reissued in sound in 1928
Beautiful Eyes 04/01/1926
Finiculee Fincula 05/01/1926
Sweet Adeline 05/01/1926 released with sound
In My Harem 05/01/1926
Tramp, Tramp, Tramp the Boys Are Marching

05/08, 1926 silent, reissued with sound in 1928

Goodbye, My Lady Love 05/22/1926 sound version

Comin' Thru the Rye 06/01/1926 released with sound

Pack Up Your Troubles 07/17/1926

The Trail of the Lonesome Pine 07/17/1926

By the Light of the Silvery Moon 08/21/1926 released with sound

In the Good Old Summer Time 09/01/1926

Oh, You Beautiful Doll 09/01/1926

The Sheik of Araby 09/15/1926

Annie Laurie 09/30/1926 released with sound

Oh, How I Hate to Get Up in the Morning, 10/01/1926 released with sound

When I Lost You 10/15/1926 released with sound

Old Black Joe 11/01/1926

When the Midnight Choo-Choo Leaves for Alabam 11/01/1926 released with sound

Oh, What a Pal Was Mary 11/15/1926

Everybody's Doing It 11/30/1926

Dear Old Pal 12/01/1926 released with sound

Yak-A-Hula-Hick-A-Doola 12/15/1926 released with sound

Margie 12/22/1926 released with sound

My Wife's Gone to the Country 12/30/1926 released with sound

Oh, Suzanna 01/01/1927 released with sound

Call Me Up Some Rainy Afternoon 01/15/1927

The Rocky Road to Dublin 02/01/1927

Jingle Bells 04/01/1927

Waiting for the Robert E. Lee 04/15/1927

Oh, I Wish I Was in Michigan 02/15/1928

Animated Hair by "Marcus," 1924–1927

Fifty-one shorts.

Inklings

A series of at least 12 entries released between 1924 and 1925.

Marvels of Motion

A series of 2 minute slow motion novelties released in 1925, including:

Just Cows

Just Dogs

Horses in Motion

Fun from the Press, 1922

A series of short films shown before a feature film in the early 1920s.

Backstage Comedies (a.k.a. Carrie of the Chorus)

A series of at least eight to twelve entries, released in 1926, including:

Berth Marks 10/12/1926, with Ray Bolger and Ruth Fleischer

Morning, Judge 09/01/1926

Another Bottle, Doctor 09/30/1926

Chicken Cooped (release date unavailable)

Breaking into Broadway estimated release date, 01/01/1927

Scientific Features

Relativity 02/08/1923

Evolution 02/11/1923

The Paramount-Weiss Period

The Inkwell Imps

Koko Makes 'Em Laugh 07/29/1927

Koko Plays Pool 08/06/1927

Koko's Kane 08/20/1927

Koko the Knight 09/03/1927

Koko Hops Off 09/17/1927

Koko Explores 10/15/1927

Koko Chops Suey 10/29/1927

Koko's Klock 11/26/1927

Koko's Quest 12/10/1927

Koko Back Tracks (a.k.a. *Koko in Reverse*) 12/24/1927

Koko the Kid 12/24/1927

Koko's Kink 01/07/1928

Koko's Kozy Korner 01/21/1928

Koko's Germ Jam 02/04/1928

Koko's Bawth 02/18/1928

Koko Smokes 03/03/1928

Koko's Tattoo 03/17/1928

Koko's Earth Control 03/31/1928

Koko's Hot Dog 04/14/1928

Koko's Haunted House (a.k.a. *Ko-Ko Goes Ghosting*) 04/28/1924

Koko Lamps Aladdin 05/12/1928
Koko Squeals 05/26/1928
Koko's Field Days 06/09/1928
Koko Goes Over 06/23/1928
Koko's Catch 07/07/1928
Koko's War Dogs 07/21/1928
Koko's Chase 08/11/1928
Ko-Ko Heaves Ho 08/25/1928*
Ko-Ko's Big Pull 09/07/1928
Ko-Ko Cleans Up 09/21/1928
Ko-Ko's Parade 10/08/1928
Ko-Ko's Dog Gone 10/22/1928
Ko-Ko in the Rough 11/03/1928
Ko-Ko's Magic 11/16/1928
Ko-Ko on the Track 12/04/1928
Ko-Ko's Act 12/17/1928
Ko-Ko's Courtship 12/28/1928

*Hyphen in "Ko-Ko" is returned periodically and becomes permanent the end of 1928.

No Eyes Today 01/11/1929
Noise Annoys Ko-Ko 1/25/1929
Ko-Ko Beats Time 02/08/1929
Ko-Ko's Reward 02/23/1929
Ko-Ko's Hot Ink 03/08/1929
Ko-Ko's Crib 03/23/1929
Ko-Ko's Saxaphonies 04/05/1929
Ko-Ko's Knock-Down 04/19/1929
Ko-Ko's Signals 04/03/1929
Ko-Ko's Conquest 05/31/1929*

(From this point, Max Fleischer no longer appears due to the conflict with Weiss.)

Ko-Ko's Focus 05/17/1929
Ko-Ko's Harem Scarem 06/14/1929
Ko-Ko's Big Sale 06/28/1929
Ko-Ko's Hypnotism 07/12/1929
Chemical Ko-Ko 07/26/1929

Commercial Films

Keep 'Em Guessing (Magician's Society of America) 09/01/1926
Now You're Talking (AT&T) 1927
That Little Big Fellow (AT&T) 1927

Fleischer Studios/ Paramount Period

Industrial Films

Finding His Voice (Western Electric—E.R.P.I) 06/21/1929
In My Merry Oldsmobile (Olds Motor Division) 03/01/1931
A Jolt for General Jerm (Lysol) 05/21/1931
Step on It (Texaco) 05/21/1931
Tex in 1999 (Texaco) ??/??/1931
Suited to a Tea (India Tea Company) ??/??/1931

Screen Songs

The Sidewalks of New York 02/05/1929
Old Black Joe 04/05/1929
Yankee Doodle Boy 03/01/1929
Daisy Bell 05/31/1929
Goodbye, My Lady Love 08/31/1929
Chinatown, My Chinatown 08/29/1929
My Pony Boy 09/27/1929
Smiles 09/27/1929
Oh, You Beautiful Doll 10/14/1929
I've Got Rings on My Fingers 12/17/1929
Bedelia 01/03/1929
In the Shade of the Old Apple Tree 01/16/1930
I'm Afraid to Come Home in the Dark 01/30/1930
Prisoner's Song 03/01/1930
La Paloma 03/20/1930
I'm Forever Blowing Bubbles 03/30/1930
Yes! We Have No Bananas 04/25/1930
Come Take a Trip in My Airship 05/23/1930
In the Good Old Summertime 06/06/1930
A Hot Time in the Old Town Tonight 08/01/1930
The Glow Worm 08/10/1930
The Stein Song 09/05/1930
Strike Up the Band 09/26/1930
My Gal Sal 10/18/1930
Mariutch 11/15/1930
On a Sunday Afternoon 11/25/1930
Row, Row, Row 12/19/1930
Please Go 'Way and Let Me Sleep 01/09/1931
By the Beautiful Sea 01/23/1930
I Wonder Who's Kissing Her Now 02/13/1931
I'd Climb the Highest Mountain 03/06/1931

Any Little Girl That's a Nice Little Girl 04/16/1931
Alexander's Rag Time Band 05/09/1931
And the Green Grass Grew All Around 06/01/1931
My Wife's Gone to the Country 06/12/1931
That Old Gang of Mine 07/09/1931
Betty Co-Ed 08/01/1931
Gallagher and Sheen 08/29/1931
You're Driving Me Crazy 09/19/1931
Little Annie Rooney 10/10/1931

The series starts using live action celebrity segments.

Kitty from Kansas City 10/31/1931
By the Light of the Silvery Moon 11/14/1931
My Baby Just Cares for Me 12/05/1931
Russian Lullaby 12/26/1931
Sweet Jenny Lee 01/09/1932
Show Me the Way to Go Home 01/30/1932
When the Red, Red Robin Comes Bob, Bob, Bobbin' Along 02/19/1932
Wait 'Til the Sun Shines, Nellie 03/04/1932
Just One More Chance 04/01/1932
Oh, How I Hate to Get Up in the Morning 04/22/1932
Shine on Harvest Moon 05/06/1932
Let Me Call You Sweetheart 05/20/32
I Ain't Got Nobody 06/17/1932
You Try Somebody Else 07/29/1932
Rudy Valley Melodies 08/05/1932
Down Among the Sugar Cane 08/26/1932
Just a Gigolo 09/09/1932
School Days 09/30/1932
Romantic Melodies 10/21/1932
When It's Sleep Time Down South 11/11/1932
Sing a Song 12/02/1932
Time on My Hands 12/23/1932
Dinah 01/13/1933
Ain't She Sweet 02/03/1933
Reaching for the Moon 02/24/1933
Aloha Oe 03/17/1933
Popular Melodies 04/07/1933
The Peanut Vendor 04/28/1933
Song Shopping 05/19/1933
Boilesk 06/09/1933
Sing, Sisters, Sing 06/30/1933
Down by the Old Mill Stream 07/21/1933
Stoopnocracy 08/18/1933
When Yuba Plays the Rumba on the Tuba 09/15/1933
Boo Boo Theme Song 10/03/1933
I Like Mountain Music 11/10/1933
Sing, Babies, Sing 12/15/1933
Keeps Rainin' All the Time 01/12/1934
Let's All Sing Like the Birdies Sing 02/09/1934
Tune Up and Sing 03/09/1934
Lazy Bones 04/13/1934
This Little Piggy Went to Market 05/25/1934
She Reminds Me of You 06/21/1934
Love Thy Neighbor 07/18/1934

(After a one year hiatus, the series was refashioned to showcase the big bands to promote their live appearances at theaters.)

I Wished on the Moon 09/19/1935
It's Easy to Remember 12/02/1935
No Other One 02/03/1936
I Feel Like a Feather in the Breeze 03/27/1936
I Don't Want to Make History 05/22/1936
The Hills of Old Wyomin' 07/31/1936
I Can't Escape from You 09/25/1936
Talking Through My Heart 01/27/1937
Never Should Have Told You (no copyright registration)
Twilight on the Trail 3/26/1937

Held from release during the Strike Boycott

Please Keep Me in Your Dreams 05/28/1937
You Came to My Rescue (no copyright registration) release date: 07/30/1937 (?)
Whispers in the Dark 9/24/1937

Magic on Broadway 11/26/1937
You Took the Words Right Out of My Heart 01/28/1938
Thanks for the Memory 03/25/1938
You Leave Me Breathless 05/27/1938
Beside a Moonlit Stream 07/29/1938

Talkartoons

Noah's Lark 10/25/1929
Marriage Wows 01/08/1930
Radio Riot 02/13/1930
Hot Dog 03/29/1930
Fire Bugs 05/09/1930

Wise Flies 07/18/1930
Dizzy Dishes 08/09/1930
Barnacle Bill 08/31/1930
Swing You Sinner 09/24/1930
Grand Uproar 10/03/1930
Sky Scraping 11/01/1930
Up to Mars 11/20/1930
Accordion Joe 12/12/1930
Mysterious Mose 12/26/1930
The Ace of Spades 01/16/1931
Teacher's Pest 02/07/1931
Tree Saps 02/03/1931
The Cow's Husband 03/31/1931
The Bum Bandit 04/03/1931
The Male Man 04/24/1931
Silly Scandals 05/23/1931
The Herring Murder Case 06/26/1931
Bimbo's Initiation 07/24/1931
Bimbo's Express 08/22/1931
Minding the Baby 09/26/1931
In the Shade of the Old Applesauce 10/16/1931
Mask-A-Raid 11/07/1931
Jack and the Beanstalk 11/21/1931
Dizzy Red Riding Hood 12/12/1931
Any Rags 01/02/1932
Boop-Oop-A-Doop 01/16/1932
The Robot 02/05/1932
Minnie the Moocher 02/26/1932
Swim or Sink (a.k.a. "SOS") 03/11/1932
Crazy Town 03/25/1932
The Dancing Fool 04/08/1932
A Hunting We Will Go 04/29/1932
Chess Nuts 05/13/1932
Hide and Seek 05/26/1932
Admission Free 06/10/1932
The Betty Boop Limited 07/11/1932

Betty Boop Cartoons

Stopping the Show 08/12/1932
Betty Boop's Bizzy Bee 08/19/1932
Betty Boop, M.D. 09/02/1932
Betty Boop's Bamboo Isle 09/23/1932
Betty Boop's Ups and Downs 10/14/1932
Betty Boop for President 11/04/1932
I'll Be Glad When You're Dead, You Rascal, You 11/25/1932
Betty Boop's Museum 12/16/1932
Betty Boop's Ker-Choo 01/06/1933
Betty Boop's Crazy Inventions 01/27/1933
Is My Palm Red 02/17/1933
Betty Boop's Penthouse 03/10/1933
Snow White 03/31/1933
Betty Boop's Birthday Party 04/21/1933
Betty Boop's May Party 05/12/1933
Betty Boop's Big Boss 05/02/1933
Mother Goose Land 06/23/1933
Popeye the Sailor 07/14/1933—pilot episode.
Old Man of the Mountain 08/04/1933
I Heard 09/01/1933
Morning, Noon, and Night 10/06/1933
Betty Boop's Halloween Party 11/03/1933
Parade of the Wooden Soldiers 12/01/1933
She Wronged Him Right 01/05/1934
Red Hot Mama 02/02/1934
Ha! Ha! Ha! 03/02/1934 (Last appearance of Koko.)
Betty in Blunderland 04/06/1934
Betty Boop's Rise to Fame 05/18/1934
Betty Boop's Trial 06/15/1934
Betty Boop's Life Guard 07/13/1934
There's Something About a Soldier 08/17/1934
Betty Boop's Little Pal 09/21/1934
Betty Boop's Prize Show 10/19/1933
Keep in Style 11/16/1934
When My Ship Comes In 12/21/1934
Baby Be Good 01/18/1935
Taking the Blame 02/15/1935
Stop That Noise 03/15/1935
Swat That Fly 04/19/1935
No! No! A Thousand Times, No! 05/24/1935
A Little Soap and Water 06/21/1935
A Language All My Own 07/19/1935
Betty Boop and Grampy 08/16/1935
Judge for a Day 09/20/1935
Making Starts 10/18/1935
Henry, the Funniest Living American 11/22/1935
Little Nobody 12/27/1935
Betty Boop and the Little King 01/31/1936
Not Now 02/28/1936
Betty Boop and Little Jimmy 03/27/1936
We Did It 04/24/1936
A Song a Day 05/22/1936
More Pep 06/19/1936
You're Not Built That Way 07/17/1936
Happy You and Merry Me 08/21/1936
Training Pidgeon 09/18/1936
Grampy's Indoor Outing 10/16/1936

Be Human 11/20/1936
Making Friends 12/18/1936
House Cleaning Blues 01/15/1937
Whoops! I'm a Cowboy 02/12/1937
The Hot Air Salesman 03/12/1937
Pudgy Takes a Bow-Wow 04/09/1937
The Foxy Hunter 11/26/1937

Held from release during the Strike Boycott
Pudgy Picks a Fight 05/14/1937
The Impractical Joker 07/18/1937
Ding Dong Doggie 07/23/1937
The Candid Candidate 08/27/1937
Service with a Smile 09/23/1937
The New Deal Show 10/22/1937

Zula Hula 12/24/1937
Riding the Rails 01/28/1938
Be Up to Date 02/25/1938
Honest Love and True 03/25/1938
Out of the Inkwell 04/22/1938
Swing School 05/27/1938
Pudgy and the Lost Kitten 06/24/1938
Buzzy Boop 07/29/1938
Pudgy the Watchman 08/12/1938
Buzzy Boop at the Concert 08/16/1938
Sally Swing 10/14/1938
On with the New 12/2/1938
Pudgy in Thrills and Chills 12/23/1938
My Friend, the Monkey 01/27/1939
So Does an Automobile 03/31/1939
Musical Mountaineers 05/12/1939
The Scared Crows 06/09/1939
Rhythm on the Reservation 07/07/1939 (last appearance of Betty Boop)
Yip Yip Yippy 08/11/1939

Color Classics

Poor Cinderella (Cinecolor) 08/03/1934

The following releases from 1934 to 1935 appeared in two-color Technicolor.

Little Dutch Mill 10/26/1934
An Elephant Never Forgets 12/28/1934
The Song of the Birds 03/01/1935
The Kids in the Shoe 05/19/1935
Dancing on the Moon 07/12/1935
Time for Love 09/06/1935
Musical Memories 11/08/1935

The following releases appeared in three-color Technicolor.

Somewhere in Dreamland 01/17/1936
The Little Stranger 03/13/1936
The Cobweb Hotel 05/15/1936
Greedy Humpty Dumpty 07/10/1936
Hawaiian Birds 08/28/1936
Play Safe 10/16/1936
Christmas Comes but Once a Year 12/04/1936
Bunny Mooning 02/12/1937

Held from release during the Strike Boycott
Chicken A La King 04/16/1937
A Car-tune Portrait 06/26/1937
Peeping Penguins 08/26/37

Educated Fish 10/29/1937
Little Lamby 12/31/1937
The Tears of an Onion 02/26/1938
Hold It 04/29/1938
Hunky and Spunky 6/24/1938
All's Fair at the Fair 08/26/1938
The Playful Polar Bears 10/28/1938
Always Kickin' 01/26/1939
Small Fry 04/21/1939
The Barnyard Brat 06/30/1939
The Fresh Vegetable Mystery 09/29/1939
Little Lamkin 02/02/1940
Ants in the Plants 03/15/1940
A Kick in Time 05/17/1940
Snubbed by a Snob 07/19/1940
You Can't Shoe a Horse Fly 08/23/1940
Vitamin Hay 08/22/1941

Popeye Cartoons

I Yam What I Yam 09/29/1933
Blow Me Down 10/27/1933
I Eats My Spinach 11/17/1933
Season's Greetinks 11/17/1933
Wild Elephinks 12/29/1933
Sock-A-Bye Baby 01/19/1934
Let's You and Him Fight 02/16/1934
Man on the Flying Trapeze 03/16/1934
Can You Take It? 04/27/1934
Shoein' Hosses 06/01/1934
Strong to the Finich 06/29/1934
Shiver Me Timbers 07/27/1934
Ax Me Another 09/38/1934

A Dream Walking 09/26/1934
The Two Alarm Fire 10/26/1934
The Dance Contest 11/23/1934
We Aim to Please 12/28/1934
Beware of Barnacle 01/25/1935
Be Kind to Animals 02/22/1935
Pleased to Meet Cha 03/22/1935
The Hyp-Nut-Tist 04/26/1935
Choose Yer Weppins 05/31/1935
For Better or Worser 06/28/1935
Dizzy Divers 07/26/1935
You Gotta Be a Football Hero 08/31/1935
King of the Mardi Gras 09/27/1935
Adventures of Popeye 10/25/1935
The Spinach Overture 12/07/1935
Vim, Vigor, and Vitaliky 01/03/1936
A Clean Shaven Man 02/07/1936
Brotherly Love 03/06/1936
What, No Spinach? 02/07/1936
I Wanna Be a Lifeguard 06/26/1936
Let's Get Movin' 07/24/1936
Never Kick a Woman 08/30/1936
Little Swee' Pea 09/25/1936
Hold the Wire 10/26/1936
The Spinach Roadster 10/26/1936
I'm in the Army Now 11/25/1936
Popeye the Sailor Meets Sindbad the Sailor (Technicolor two-reel featurette) 11/27/1936
The Paneless Window Washer 01/22/1937
Organ Grinder's Swing 02/19/1937
My Artistical Temperature 03/19/1937
Hospitaliky 04/16/1937

Held from release during the Strike Boycott

The Twisker Pitcher 05/21/1937
Morning, Noon, and Nightclub 06/18/1937
Lost and Foundry 06/16/1937
I Never Changes My Altitude 08/20/1937
I Like Babies and Infinks 09/18/1937
The Football Toucher Downer 10/15/1937

Proteck the Weakerest 11/19/1937
Popeye the Sailor Meets Ali Baba's Forty Thieves (Technicolor two-reel featurette) 11/26/1937
Fowl Play 12/17/1937
Let's Celebrake 01/21/1938
Learn Polikeness 02/18/1938
The House Builder Upper 03/18/1938
Big Chief Ugh-A-Mugh-Ugh 04/25/38
I Am Love Sick 05/29/1938
Plumbin' Is a Pipe 06/17/1938
The Jeep 07/15/1938
Bulldozing the Bull 08/19/1938
Mutiny Ain't Nice 09/23/1938
Goonland 10/21/38
A Date to Skate 11/18/1938
Cops Is Always Right 12/30/1938
Customers Wanted 01/27/1939
Popeye the Sailor Meets Aladdin's Wonderful Lamp (Technicolor two-reel featurette 04/07/1939)
Leave Well Enough Alone 04/28/1939
Wotta Nitemare 05/19/39
Ghosks Is the Bunk 06/14/1939
Hello-How Am I? 07/14/1939
It's the Natural Thing to Do 07/30/1939
Never Sock a Baby 11/03/1939

Feature Release

Gulliver's Travels (Technicolor) 12/22/1939

Popeye Cartoons continued

Shakespearean Spinach 01/19/1940
Females Is Fickle 03/08/1940
Stealin' Ain't Honest 03/22/1940

Two-Reel Featurettes

The Raven (Technicolor) 04/03/1940
Raggedy Ann and Andy (Technicolor) 04/11/1941

Popeye Cartoons continued

Me Feelins Is Hurt 04/12/1940
Onion Pacific 05/24/1940
Wimmen Is a Mystery 06/07/1940
Nurse Mates 06/20/1940
Fightin' Pals 07/12/1940
Doing Impossikible Stunts 08/02/1940
Wimmen Hadn't Oughtta Drive 08/16/1940
Puttin' on the Act 08/30/1940
Popeye Meets William Tell 09/20/1940
My Pop, My Pop 10/18/1940
With Poopdeck Pappy 1015/1940
Popeye Presents Eugene the Jeep 12/13/1940
Problem Pappy 01/10/1941
Quiet Pleeze 02/07/1941

Olive's Sweepstakes Ticket 03/07/1941
Flies Ain't Human 04/04/1941
Popeye Meets Rip Van Winkle 05/09/1941
Olive's Boithday Presink 06/13/1941
Child Psykology 07/11/1941
Pest Pilot 08/08/1941
I'll Never Crow Again 09/19/1941
The Mighty Navy 10/14/1941 (First placement in contemporary Navy.)
Nix on Hynotricks 12/19/1941 (Last appearance in black shirt and skipper's cap.)
Kickin' the Congo Around 01/17/1942
Blunder Below 02/13/1942
Fleets of Stren'th 03/13/1942
Pip-eye, Pup-eye, Poop-eye, and Peep-eye 04/10/1942
Olive Oyl and Water Don't Mix 05/08/1942
Many Tanks 06/16/1942
Baby Wants a Bottleship 07/03/1942

Stone Age

Way Back When the Triangle Had Its Points 02/09/1940
Way Back When a Nag Was Only a Horse 03/08/1940
Granite Hotel 04/26/1940
Way Back When a Night Club Was a Stick 05/10/1940
The Foul Ball Player 05/24/1940
The Ugly Dino 06/14/1940
Wedding Belts 07/05/1940
Way Back When a Razzberry Was a Fruit 07/26/1940
The Fulla Bluff Man 08/09/1940
Springtime in the Rockage 08/30/1940
Pedagogical Institution (College to You) 09/13/1940
Way Back When Women Had Their Weigh 09/26/1940

Gabby

King for a Day 10/18/1940
The Constable 11/15/1940
All's Well 01/17/1941
Two for the Zoo 02/14/1941
Swing Cleaning 04/11/1941
Fire Cheese 06/20/1941
Gabby Goes Fishing 07/11/1941
It's a Hap-Hap-Happy Day 08/15/1941

Animated Antics

The Dandy Lion 09/20/1940
Sneak, Snoop, and Snitch 10/25/1940
Mommy Loves Puppy 11/29/1940
Bring Himself Back Alive 12/20/1940
Pop and Mom in Wild Oysters (Charles Bowers stop motion) 02/14/1941
Twinkletoes Gets the Bird 03/14/1941
Down on the Farm—Speaking of Animals (pilot)—Academy Award winner 04/18/1941
Sneak, Snoop, and Snitch in Triple Trouble 05/09/1941
Zero the Hound 05/30/1941
Twinkletoes—Where He Goes—Nobody Knows 06/27/1941
Copy Cat 07/18/1941
The Wizard of Arts 08/08/1941
Twinkletoes in Hat Stuff 08/29/1941

Feature Film

Mr. Bug Goes to Town (Technicolor) 12/05/1941

Superman

Superman 09/26/1941
Mechanical Monsters 11/21/1941
The Billion Dollar Limited 01/09/1942
The Arctic Giant 02/26/1942
The Bulleteers 03/26/1942
The Magnetic Telescope 04/24/1942
The Electrical Earthquake 06/05/1942
Volcano 07/10/1942
Terror on the Midway 08/30/1942 (Last Fleischer release)

List of Animators

Because the studio records were allegedly destroyed during the transition to Famous Studios, it is difficult to offer a complete list of every animator employed by Fleischer Studios. The only documentation that survives are screen credits, photographs, or rare notations on scripts and artwork designating assignments on certain cartoons. Every effort has been made to recognize the many talented animators who helped make Fleischer animation so distinctive.

Tom Baron
Raoul Barré
Bruce Blezard
Tom Bonfiglio
Willard Bowsky
Eli Brucker
Orestes Calpini
George Cannata
Frank Carino
Herman Cohen
Roland Crandall
James Culhane
Art Davis
James Davis
Mannie Davis
Nelson Demorest
Tony Di Paolo
Irv Dressler
Rudy Eggeman
Frank Endres
Alfred Eugster
Paul Fennell
Otto Feuer
Don Figlozzi
Lillian Freidman
George Germanetti
Arnold Gillespie
Burt Gillett
Tom Golden
Rube Grossman
Charles Hastings
William Henning
Dave Hoffman
Winfield Hoskins
Dick Huemer
Tom Johnson
Frank Kelling
Saul Kessler
Isidore Klein
Abner Mathew Kneitel (a.k.a. Abner Matthews)
Seymour Kneitel
Robert Leffingwell
Hicks Lokey
Dick Marion (a.k.a. Dick Hall)
Joe Miller
Tom Moore
Steve Muffati
Grim Natwick
Ed Nolan
Joe Oriolo
Jack Ozark
Tom Palmer
William Pattengill
Sidney Pillet
Graham Place
Stan Quackenbush
Lod Rossner
George Ruffle
Hal Seegar
Ben Sharpsteen
Gordon Sheehan
Ben Solomon
Sam Stimson
William Sturm
Ralph Summerville
Nicholas Tafuri
Dave Tendlar
Edith Vernick
Ted Vosk
Myron Waldman
Harold Walker
Berny Wolf
Rudy Zamora
Lou Zukor

Chapter Notes

Chapter 1

1. George B. Bridgman, *Bridgman's Complete Guide to Drawing from Life: With Drawings and Text by George B. Bridgman*. New York: Sterling, 1952, p. 216.
2. Lou Fleischer interview, June 10, 1980.

Chapter 2

1. Joe Fleischer, lecture on Fleischer Studios, 1976.
2. Joe Adamson, "Where Can I Get a Good Corned Beef Sandwich?": An Oral History of David Fleischer, 1968.
3. Max Fleischer, unpublished autobiography, 1939.
4. *Ibid.*
5. Adamson, "Where Can I Get a Good Corned Beef Sandwich?"
6. *Ibid.*
7. *Ibid.*
8. *Ibid.*

Chapter 3

1. Berny Wolf interview, 1996.
2. *Ibid.*
3. Shamus Culhane, *Talking Animals and Other People*, p. 35.
4. Letter to the author from Frank Goldman, May 11, 1972.
5. Michael Barrier, *Hollywood Cartoons*, p. 25.
6. Adamson, "Where Can I Get a Good Corned Beef Sandwich?"
7. Bernard Fleischer interview, 2001.
8. Richard Fleischer, *Betty Boop's 70th Birthday Celebration*, AMC, August, 2000.
9. Bernard Fleischer interview.
10. Richard Fleischer, *Out of the Inkwell: Max Fleischer and the Animation Revolution*, p. 46.
11. *Ibid.*
12. Ward Kimball, *Mindrot*, May 1977.
13. John Canemaker, *Winsor McCay: His Life and Art*, p. 159
14. Adamson, "Where Can I Get a Good Corned Beef Sandwich?"
15. Barrier, *Hollywood Cartoons*, p. 579.
16. Richard Fleischer, *Out of the Inkwell*, p. 47.

Chapter 4

1. Fleischer, *Out of the Inkwell*, p. 48.
2. Barrier, *Cartoons*, pp. 56–57.
3. *Ibid.*
4. *Ibid.*
5. *Ibid.*
6. *New York Times*, Jan. 17, 1930, p. 48.
7. Lou Fleischer interview, June 10, 1980.
8. Adamson, "Where Can I Get a Good Corned Beef Sandwich?"
9. *Ibid.*
10. Richard Fleischer, *Out of the Inkwell*, p. 157.
11. *Ibid.*, p. 160.
12. Culhane, *Talking Animals and Other People*, pp. 34–35.

Chapter 5

1. Culhane, *Talking Animals and Other People*, p. 52.
2. *The Lewiston Daily Sun*, Apr. 20, 1934.
3. *Ibid.*

Chapter 6

1. Culhane, *Talking Animals and Other People*, p. 52.
2. *Ibid.*, p. 54.

Chapter 7

1. Richard Fleischer, *Out of the Inkwell*, pp. 72–73.
2. Barrier, *Cartoons*, p. 177.
3. Culhane, *Talking Animals and Other People*, p. 61.
4. *Ibid.*, p. 62.
5. Berny Wolf interview, 1996.

Chapter 8

1. Michael Sporn interview with Jack Mercer, 1977.
2. *Ibid.*
3. "Disney's Rival by "Close-up," *The Argus*, Melbourne, Australia, October 3, 1934.
4. Culhane, *Talking Animals and Other People*, p. 60.
5. Barrier, *Cartoons*, pp. 294–295.
6. Alden Getz Interview, Aug. 14, 1979, AMMI Oral History Program.
7. Harvey Deneroff, *Graffiti*, December 1984, p. 7.
8. Bill Littlejohn interview, July 12, 1980, Deneroff dissertation.
9. I. Klein interview, July 22, 1979, Deneroff dissertation.
10. National Labor Relations Board, Van Beuren hearing, p. 18.
11. *Ibid.*
12. Marty Taras interview, July 7, 1979, Deneroff dissertation.
13. Lou Appet Interview, Sept. 5, 1981, Deneroff dissertation.

Chapter 9

1. Bernard Fleischer, interview.
2. *Ibid.*
3. Edith Vernick interview, Aug. 15, 1980, Deneroff dissertation.
4. Berny Wolf interview, 1996.

5. Joseph Barbera, *My Life in Toons*, p. 40.
6. *Ibid.*, p. 41.
7. Lenard Kester interview, Dec. 27, 1981, Deneroff dissertation.
8. Culhane, *Talking Animals and Other People*, p. 200.
9. Marty Taras interview, July 7, 1979, Deneroff dissertation.
10. Dave Tendlar interview, Apr. 24, 1981, Deneroff dissertation.
11. Frank Paiker interview, Dec. 16, 1981, Deneroff dissertation.
12. Bernard Fleischer interview.
13. Paiker interview.
14. Tom Sito, *Drawing the Line*, pp. 99–100.

Chapter 10

1. Bernard Fleischer interview.
2. An internal memo from A.M. Botsford to Russell Holman dated Jan. 19, 1938.
3. An internal memo dated Mar. 1, 1938.
4. Letter to the author from Frank Goldman, May 11, 1972.
5. Berny Wolf interview, Aug. 5, 1995.

Chapter 11

1. Deneroff, *Popeye the Union Man*, pp. 290–291.
2. Bob Thomas, *Walt Disney: An American Original*, p. 113.
3. Schickel, *The Disney Version*, pp. 150–151.
4. *Ibid.*, p. 215.
5. Max Fleischer unpublished autobiography, 1939.
6. Culhane, *Talking Animals and Other People*, p. 207.
7. *The Miami News*, Dec. 25, 1936.
8. *Good Housekeeping*, February 1940.
9. Adamson, "Where Can I Get a Good Corned Beef Sandwich?"
10. *Ibid.*

Chapter 12

1. Richard Fleischer, *Out of the Inkwell*, pp. 79–80.
2. *Ibid.*
3. Bernard Fleischer, interview.
4. Fleischer, *Out of the Inkwell*, p. 111.
5. *Ibid.*

Chapter 13

1. Culhane, *Talking Animals and Other People*, p. 218.
2. Dave Fleischer, interview.
3. Richard Fleischer, *Out of the Inkwell*, pp. 110–111.
4. *Ibid.*, p.114.
5. *Ibid.*, p. 159.
6. *Ibid.*, p. 121.

Chapter 14

1. Leonard Maltin, *Of Mice and Magic*, p. 306.
2. Stephanie McCrummen, "Jackson Beck, 92; His Voice Became Staple of Radio Shows," Obituary, *The Boston Globe*, July 30, 2004.
3. Maltin, *Of Mice and Magic*, *Ibid.*, p. 307.

Chapter 15

1. Fleischer, *Out of the Inkwell*, p. 127.
2. *Ibid.*, p. 129.
3. *Ibid.*, p. 131.

Chapter 16

1. Richard Fleischer, *Just Tell Me When to Cry*, p. 103.
2. Fleischer, *Out of the Inkwell*, p. 146.
3. Dick Murray testimony, court transcript, *U.S. District Court Southern District of New York, Dave Fleischer v. A.A.P. Inc.*, et al., Dec. 6, 1957.
4. Fleischer, *Out of the Inkwell*, p. 148.
5. Rebuttal U.S. District Court Southern District of New York, *Dave Fleischer v. A.A.P. Inc., et al.*, Nov. 25, 1957.
6. Murray testimony.
7. *Ibid.*

Chapter 17

1. Jerry Beck, *Mindrot*, Issue 19, Nov. 30, 1980, p. 24.
2. *Ibid.*
3. Culhane, *Talking Animals and Other People*, p. 385.
4. Beck, *Mindrot*, p. 27.
5. Fleischer, *Out of the Inkwell*, pp. 156–157.
6. *Ibid.*, pp. 164–166.

Bibliography

Adamson, Joe. *Tex Avery: King of Cartoons.* New York: Popular Library, 1975.

_____. "Where Can I Get a Good Corned-Beef Sandwich?": An Oral History of David Fleischer, Los Angeles: American Film Institute–University of California at Los Angeles Oral History Project, 1968–1969.

Barbera, Joseph. *My Life in Toons.* Atlanta: Turner, 1994.

Barrier, Michael. *Hollywood Cartoons.* New York: Oxford University Press, 1999.

Bridgman, George B. *Bridgman's Complete Guide to Drawing from Life: With Drawings and Text by George B. Bridgman.* New York: Sterling, 1952.

Canemaker, John. *Winsor McCay: His Life and Art.* New York: Abbeville, 1987.

Culhane, Shamus. *Talking Animals and Other People.* New York: St. Martin's, 1986.

Deitch, Gene. "How to Succeed in Animation." November 18, 2013. Animation World Network.com. http://www.awn.com/genedeitch

Deneroff, Harvey. *Popeye the Union Man: A Historical Study of the Fleischer Strike.* Dissertation, University of Southern California, 1985.

Fleischer, Max. Unpublished autobiography, 1939.

Fleischer, Richard. *Just Tell Me When to Cry.* New York: Carroll & Graf, 1993.

_____. *Out of the Inkwell: Max Fleischer and the Animation Revolution.* Lexington: University Press of Kentucky, 2005.

Maltin, Leonard. *Of Mice and Magic.* New York: McGraw-Hill, 1980.

McCrummen, Stephanie. "Jackson Beck, 92; His Voice Became Staple of Radio Shows," Obituary, *The Boston Globe*, July 30, 2004.

Merritt, Russell, and J. B. Kaufman. *Walt in Wonderland.* Baltimore: Johns Hopkins University Press, 1993.

Schickel, Richard. *The Disney Version.* New York: Simon & Schuster, 1968.

Sito, Tom. *Drawing the Line.* Lexington: University Press of Kentucky, 2006.

Thomas, Bob. *Walt Disney: An American Original.* New York: Hyperion Press, 1994.

Index